POGIEBAIT'S WAR

A Son's Quest for His Father's Wartime Life

BY JACK H. McCALL, JR.

Library of Congress Number:		00-193451
ISBN #:	Hardcover	0-7388-5764-5
	Softcover	0-7388-5765-3

This book was printed in the United States of America.

To order additional copies of this book, contact:
Xlibris Corporation
1-888-7-XLIBRIS
www.Xlibris.com
Orders@Xlibris.com

Portrait of Jack McCall, taken in spring 1945 while serving as a corporal in the III Amphibious Corps. (Author's collection)

CONTENTS

DEDICATION

For Margaret

They will live a long time, these men of the South Pacific. They had an American quality. They, like their victories, will be remembered as long as our generation lives. After that, like the men of the Confederacy, they will become strangers. Longer and longer shadows will obscure them, until the name Guadalcanal sounds distant on the ear like Shiloh and Valley Forge.

James Michener
Tales of the South Pacific

[In] the end, of course, a true war story is never about war. . . . It's about love and memory. It's about sorrow.

Tim O'Brien
The Things They Carried

INTRODUCTION

Definition of "Pogey Bait": Candy. Old naval term.

Henry Berry
Semper Fi, Mac

My father, Jack McCall, Sr., was a lifelong resident of Franklin, Tennessee, a small town nestled in the rolling hills just south of Nashville. Apart from spending part of his childhood years in various cities around the Southeast, Jack called Franklin home during almost all of his 75 years. After moving back to Franklin with his family, more or less permanently, around 1928, he seldom spent more than a few weeks or months away from Franklin for the rest of his life—with one notable exception. That exception was four years of service in the United States Marines in World War II.

As his son, I thought I knew how much the time he spent in service during the war years affected my father. A favorite Friday-night childhood pastime of ours was for my sister Holly and me to ask him to tell us a story. He was a natural-born story-teller and raconteur, but of all the stories he told, we would most often prompt him with a recurring request: "Tell us what you did in the war, please, Dad?" This prompted him to regale us with his favorite "war stories."

The litany of geographical names routinely cropping up in these tales were mysterious, yet alliterative and lyrical things, like some destinations out of a boy's adventure book: *Guantanamo*; *Noumea*; *Guadalcanal*; *Nalimbiu*; *Tenaru*; *Gavutu*; *Rendova*; *Munda*; *Vella Lavella*; *Roviana*; *Banika*; *Eniwetok; Bangi Point; Agana; Pago Bay*; *the Golden Gate*. Sometimes after thirty minutes or so of his story-telling, the family would troop upstairs to a big cedar chest to unload his war souvenirs: his dress green uniform, a tattered Japanese flag, an Imperial Navy sailor's cap and pocketknife, a tin case full of crumbling Japanese cigarettes, and other artifacts he'd salvaged from some Pacific battlefield 20 or 25 years before.

Some of my earliest memories of my sister often feature Holly wearing her favorite headgear: our dad's battered campaign hat (which we dubbed the "Sergeant Carter hat" after Gomer Pyle's much-harassed drill sergeant), perched precariously on her as she tricycled around the backyard or snacked in the kitchen. Occasionally, one of my Cub Scout buddies would gape at a finger-sized hole in the crown of that same hat and, awestruck, ask as he fingered it: "Wow! I'll bet you were you shot at by a Jap sniper, weren't you, Mr. McCall?" "Aw, no, that's not how I got that hole!" my father would chuckle. Inevitably to my friends' disappointment that something more bloody had not occurred, he would explain that a large rat had once nibbled on the hat while he was stationed at Guantanamo Bay, Cuba—that is, until my dad caught the rat in the act.

On every Fourth of July, there would be two or three phone calls along these lines: "Hey, little Jack. Where's *Pogiebait*? You know, kid; your old man? Can I speak to him?" Within a few minutes, I would hear my father chortling into the phone: "That was the best Fourth of July I ever had! I love you like a brother!" It was a mystery to me what he was talking about so jovially and to whom, except that when I asked him who was on the phone, he'd simply respond with a name seldom heard during the rest of the year and say: "He's an old Leatherneck buddy of mine." As much as my father laughed with these strangers—and as much as I heard him occasionally argue and bicker heatedly with my uncles over every topic imaginable—I began to suspect that he maybe loved these mysterious callers *more* than his real brothers.

As for his wartime pals' favorite nickname, frequently used to his family's wonderment whenever these buddies called or wrote him, he confessed to having earned the moniker "Pogiebait" while a young recruit at Boot Camp in an escapade involving his lifelong and incorrigible sweet tooth. When I was a teenager, he would tell me that the men of his unit never got any real leave once sent overseas and that, for its one "R&R" break, his battalion was stationed in a "swamp." When I challenged him on that, cynical and dubious teen that I was—*Come on, Dad, don't pull my leg; they wouldn't put you in a swamp while you were on R&R!*—he testily responded as he peered irritably at me over his glasses: "Son, don't you think I know what a *swamp* is?"

My father's war stories themselves were exciting and usually humorous (often recounted at his own expense), but on the whole, they suggested that he'd never been really *that* much in danger. That is, except, maybe, from an attack or two of food poisoning or tropical disease and, most definitely, in self-inflicted danger from the Japanese hand grenades he tried to deactivate during his months on New Georgia and Guam by soaking them, in a helmet under his cot, which was full of kerosene. ("Don't let me ever catch *you* trying to do something that dumb, son!" he'd sternly lecture me.) From hearing these tales, no one would ever have mistaken my father for Audie Murphy, Chesty Puller or George S. Patton. Still, they were enough to set me on a lifelong interest in history, and they partly contributed to my own decision late in high school to try the military as a career.

Yet, for many years, there was also a certain distance to

my father. He always seemed to be at work on something very important: his slide rule in hand, calculating weekly or monthly sales figures; checking through his ledgers to see what was left in his inventory and what needed to be reordered; either going to or returning from the Chicago or Dallas clothing marts, sample case of his wares in hand. He was at times oddly overprotective of my sister and me, too, in ways that were strikingly different from so many of our peers' parents whose average ages were five to twenty years younger than his. *No BB guns for the boy . . . no bunk beds for the kids, they might roll out and break their necks in the middle of the night . . .no football or baseball; he might break a bone. . . did we really give our son a chemistry set for Christmas? My God, Pat, what were we thinking? Your son might blow himself up*. . . and on, and on. What was he protecting us from? And, moreover, why was he going to such extremes?

By the time I entered high school, this overprotectiveness did not seem to be merely a personal quirk; to me, it seemed positively neurotic. Despite my best efforts to be a good son, he and I fought pitched battles over almost everything: over the times I stayed out late (even if it were only for a track or cross-country meet), over driving lessons, over the first time I dented the car, over my first date. Yet, despite his lectures and our verbal grappling and arguments, I did not feel any closer to understanding what made him tick. I began to get a better inkling after I entered the military myself. It wasn't, however, until very close to the end of his life, after I had completed my military service and become a father myself, that I truly began to "get" the insights I lacked for so long. Sadly, the greatest insights would only come after his death, when it was too late for me to say: *Now, at last, I see. I think I finally understand, Dad, what you were about.*

Some thirty years passed from the times during which I first recall hearing my dad's war stories to a day in late May 1997 when he lay in a hospital room in Franklin. My father was propped up in his bed at a 45-degree angle to ease his breathing, which was shallow and fast. He was covered only by a thin hospital smock and sheet. He was dying, and we—and he—knew it. In fact, he had been dying in front of our eyes for eight years. Years of heavy cigarette smoking had taken its toll, and in spring 1990, he was diagnosed with emphysema. On the day my father learned it in March 1990, before he underwent what should have been minor nasal surgery, his physician pushed open the door and tossed a batch of x-rays on his chest. "Mr. McCall, do you have any idea what these are?"the physician curtly asked. As I could feel my anger rising at the doctor's harshness—*the jerk, just who the hell does he think he is to do that to my dad!*—but before anyone could utter a word, the doctor delivered his follow-up, in a deliberate and icy cold tone: "Mr. McCall, these are the worst lungs of any *living* man I've ever seen. *You have emphysema.* Do you understand me?" This blunt but effective pronouncement finally succeeded in doing what Jack's family had strived for years to do—he stopped smoking, cold turkey, immediately thereafter—but the worst damage had already been done, and it was far too late to reverse its course. A living death sentence had effectively been pronounced on my father, albeit one with a seven-year stay of execution. In spring 1990, his doctors had expected him to last less than five.

By Memorial Day 1997, however, my father's stay of execution was lifted, and his life was ebbing quickly as pneumonia set in. Watching someone die of any disease can be, in its own way, as emotionally and spiritually debilitating to the family and loved ones as it is physically to the sufferer. Emphysema has its own hideous etiology. The convulsive and shuddering coughs would often be followed by his hacking, as he expectorated fluid from the weakened lungs, and by a gentle, sad wheezing as he gulped in air. The onset of sudden losses of breath made him claustrophobic and panicky, and every breath was painful. His debilitated condition sometimes left him embarrassed and, most unlike the energetic man of my youth, tired to the core of his soul. He lacked the energy to walk further than a few paces without becoming desperately short of breath. It was somewhat like watching someone drown in slow motion on dry land. I could not help but sometimes think of the doughboy gas victims of World War I that Jack had seen as a young boy not long after that war ended, as I watched my own father suffer what must have been a similar fate, at least physiologically speaking.

By six months before he died, Jack's world, his very field of vision, had narrowed to only three rooms. He would pace from the bedroom, to the easy chair in the den, then to the bathroom—all the time tethered to life, like a deep-sea diver, by a plastic tube and an oxygen-generating machine. His body had become its own prison, but the tortures it imposed extended far beyond what he felt. Jack's family watched this once robust man dwindle to a specter of his former self, yet his humor remained largely intact to the end. This fight was for his life: it took all his available energy to wage it, and he did not dare let down his guard until the very end. Little held his interest anymore, yet every day seemed like such a fight for him—which it was: he was fighting for air and with it, for mere survival.

As he lay in his bed in the intensive care unit late that May, my father gripped my hand with both of his, with an amazing strength for one so weakened. He had a lifelong love of history and genealogy, but the passion of his request still surprised me. "Son, when the county historical association . . . wanted to interview me . . . oh, I wished I had done it . . . but I just never felt up to it." "Don't worry, Dad," I responded, partly out of despair and partly hoping against hope to give him something to perk him up. "Between what you've told me and Holly and what I can find out from your friends, Uncle Al and Mom, I'll do a biographical sketch for you. Okay?" "I'd appreciate that, son," he gently replied, and he closed his eyes and laid his head down on his pillow for a fitful nap.

Then, a few hours later, the bitter realization was admitted: "Son, tell me the truth. *I'm not coming out of this, am I?*" It was there; it was out in the open; and nothing would work but the truth, although I failed immediately to grasp his full meaning. "Yeah, sure, Dad. You'll probably be here for a few weeks or so, but you'll be out of the hospital soon enough if you keep trying." He saw through my temporizing immediately. "You're one hell of an actor, kid; you ought to be on the stage," he muttered bitterly, looking me straight in the eyes, when I vainly tried to reassure him that he'd be alright. Then, bluntly, a few minutes later: "You're a lawyer. Can't you tell me what a person has to do to get out of *here*?" The truth dawned on me: the "here" to which he was referring wasn't the hospital, it was *life*, and he was both resigned to death and maybe welcomed it as a release. My father had long said that he would not want to face an existence in a nursing home or as a burden on his family, and he saw that these were about the only certainties for him if he survived this round of pneumonia.

He began to shrug off my mother's and Holly's and the nurses' efforts to cheer him up as well. Five days earlier, Jack had already told his wife that he felt the closeness of death; he could *sense* it, and it was closer now than at any time since the war. He had told his family in the past that death could be felt, could be perceived, like a tangible sensation—but, cynics and disbelievers that we were, we did not wholly believe him. We could not grasp it, we could not let ourselves believe it, and so we refused to believe.

Within two more days, my father was dead, and his request became more than a mere wish, but a son's last duty to his father and his father's memory. It also became a tribute to other men like my father, who themselves are fast becoming fewer in number as the bloody 20th century nears its end, and it is my attempt to preserve a portion of their memories as well.

I realized even better what my father had really gone through with these wartime buddies when I picked up his address book the day after his death and began making calls to tell his friends, business associates and other family members the news. Jack McCall's relatives and business cronies were saddened, sure, but their responses were often more in the way of persons used to accepting bad news, espcially since he had been ill for so long. Yet, as I called his Marine Corps friends, not merely the words, but the tenor of their responses, were utterly different than I had expected from these crusty old warriors: to my amazement, many of them *cried*, more so than amongst his other family and friends. One of them, a pal since Boot Camp, Al Downs, told me how much my father had meant to him in these words: "You don't go through what we all went through without becoming close. He and I shared our last cola together just before I left the Ninth Defense and came back Stateside in '44. I knew he'd be left out there, and I worried for a long time that he'd be killed." Another, Frank Chadwick, also cried as he took the news, but then he said, "Your father was such a good man, Nick. You know, I think we talked every July 4th for the last twenty years. I guess he must have told you about the time he was nearly blown up on Guam. We all thought we'd lost him that time, for sure."

I was flabbergasted. Of all the stories my father had told me, this one was news to me. "No, Frank. He never told me about that."

Likewise, Bill Galloway, another Marine buddy, told me on that same day: "Well, I'm sure your dad must have told you about how he was almost killed when my crew's Long Tom"—a heavy artillery piece, of which my father had often spoken—"exploded." Again, I was stupefied. *My father, nearly blown up by an exploding cannon?* "No, sir. That's all news to me." "Well, Nick," Bill continued, "I still carry around a hunk of metal inside me today from that gun. Your dad was damn lucky that day. He was a good man."

And the trickle of information I received on that June day on what my father had *really* experienced in World War II—far, far beyond the usually humorous tales of my childhood—became a torrent over the next few months, as more of his friends and wartime buddies contacted me, and as I reached out to them to learn more of my father's life in those grim years.

This work is my obligation to the man who, more than anyone I have ever encountered, has taught me what life—and death—ultimately means. I have come to suspect that what my father had faced fifty years before, as a mere teenaged boy in the jungles of the Pacific, somehow helped give him the courage and dignity he needed to face death one last time; to grasp that death, too, is a part of life; and to die with enormous dignity—to "die well." It was a hard death, but he did die well, and he tried to make as much of his life as he could while there was yet time. His buddies would have been proud of the man they once called "Pogiebait."

It has only been after his death that I now truly appreciate how much his wartime experience irrevocably altered Jack McCall's life and my family's lives as well. I have better learned how how truly hazardous service in the Pacific was, even to those not in direct combat, and how indebted today's Americans are to the sacrifices of those like him—both those who came home and those who did not. One thing that becomes readily apparent from Jack's account—something forgotten or, at best, half understood by modern Americans—is, however, remembered by almost all the surviving veterans of the Pacific war. That is the fact that the Pacific fighting was very much, in the Duke of Wellington's trenchant summary of the Battle of Waterloo, a "close-run thing." The final Allied victory was, by no means, inevitable for much of the war. In 1941-42, the Allies' situation looked grim. This was certainly true for much of the Guadalcanal campaign and, in many respects, as late as 1944, the prospect of final victory was still debatable, at least to those at the front. Several circumstances, both fortunate and unfortunate, marked the conduct of the Central Solomons campaign in mid-1943 in which my father participated. Instances of "friendly fire" casualties abounded, including the sinking of the command ship for the New Georgia campaign. Likewise, the presence of a large undetected reef off the invasion beaches jeopardized the American initial landings on Guam and, more personally, nearly led to Jack's death.

Jack's physical condition in his last few months of life severely limited his ability to follow through on his wish to provide a personal history of his war years. This narrative is partly a payment of my debt to my father, and it is also my way to help him honor his desire to preserve a small, highly individual part of the history of World War II. Obviously, while this narrative may not necessarily reflect what he would have said were he still alive today, I hope that this account will accurately record many of his recollections. These reminiscences were provided to me by him (some of which, in the form of his war stories, are some of my earliest childhood memories) and also by relatives, friends and Marine buddies. It is also my hope that this will help give the reader an idea of "what it was all about" and "what it was like," at least as viewed through the eyes of one young and low-ranking participant, over fifty years later.

My father did, however, take some steps to record at least a fraction of his wartime history in his own words. He began a short, typewritten manuscript, which he never finished but which gives some of this history as he saw it. I will, therefore, begin each chapter of this narrative with his words, put in italics, as an introduction.

I have tried to use Jack's own words to the greatest degree possible, although much of these words, I admit, I have reconstructed from memory. I have, however, sought to corroborate every significant event or incident he recounted to me, either by the historical record or by the testimony of other veterans of his battalion. In many respects, this story is not just a retelling of Jack McCall's wartime life but also the lives of his buddies, the men of the Marines' 9th Defense Battalion with whom he served. This is, however, not intended purely as a history book, strictly speaking, although some history lessons may inevitably be part of this story.

Some 9th Defense veterans may feel slighted in that this account centers around one part of this unique and heterogeneous battalion, the 155mm Group, the portion of the Battalion to which Jack belonged. While there are tales yet to be told about the Ninth's antiaircraft gunners and tank and radar crews, each of whom pioneered new methods of warfare in the South Pacific's jungles, those must be told in detail elsewhere. Still, as will be seen, the stories of these other key elements of the Ninth will overlap with Jack's experiences.

While comic moments are described throughout this tale, this is certainly not always a happy story. The memories of sacrifices made by a generation are being lost to time. There are some frank admissions of feelings shared by my father and fellow veterans of the Pacific Theater towards their old adversary, Japan and her people. As a consequence, certain wartime events are recounted which, to the present-day reader, may be despicable or horrifying. For the sake of presenting as complete a picture as possible of the life and times of a fairly average Marine enlisted man in the Pacific War from his worm's-eye point of view—why and how he fought; why he fought in the manner he did; what his fears and hopes were; how he survived and kept his sanity intact—I find it necessary to be as candid as possible and include unpleasant reminders of the ancient hatreds of fifty years ago. Those sentiments were often an integral factor in the reasons he and others enlisted in the Marines. They were very much a factor in the ways that the fighting developed and were an adjunct to the greater geopolitical events that shaped the larger war. The saga of the average Marine in the South and Central Pacific was also, as shall be seen, mostly a white man's war.

For those readers who may find this insensitive, I ask your indulgence. I also ask you to remember: for better or worse, those times *were* different, and such things did occur, much as they still occur today. We can look back and marvel, or be disturbed (sometimes simultaneously) at what transpired on the islands and waters of the Pacific over fifty years ago. The average Marine, Seaman, Seabee or Army "dogface"—or, for that matter, their respective Japanese counterparts—seldom had the luxury of time to contemplate an often brutish existence that encompassed both the heights and depths of the human experience. Again, my goal has been to capture the events and attitudes of those times—most importantly, Jack McCall's and his friends' recollections— as authentically as possible. To be true to this goal, this narrative will occasionally adhere to General Sherman's admonition: "War is cruelty, and you cannot refine it."

There were, however, good times, too, mainly arising from the camaraderie of men thrown together for three years in a sometimes ridiculous, *Catch 22*-like situation. As several of Jack's Marine buddies have noted, too, the Pacific war's veterans have to talk among themselves and at their reunions about their good times in the last "good war," to use Studs

Terkel's expression. "Otherwise, it just wouldn't be worth talking about," as more than one of them have commented to me.

While a son can never truly know and understand all aspects of his father's life, it is clear to me that his service in World War II was a defining period in the life of my father. This book is, above all, one son's recollections and attempts to reconstruct this defining moment in his father's life.

Jack H. (Nick) McCall, Jr.

PROLOGUE

To one young Marine, all hell broke loose at about 1:35 p.m.—1335 hours, in military time—on Rendova, a stiflingly muggy island 200 miles north of Guadalcanal in the South Pacific on Friday, July 2, 1943.

Rendova is a semi-volcanic outcropping, barely ten miles long and at its narrowest point, less than one mile away from the much larger island of New Georgia. Hundreds of land crabs and ravenous ants scuttered through its untended coconut groves, abandoned by its British and Australian plantation masters over a year earlier when the islands were seized by the Japanese. Those Japanese forces were now in the second day of opposing a new invasion, this time by hosts of U.S. Marines and Army troops massing on Rendova to bombard and seize New Georgia's prize: a large Japanese airfield on that island's rocky southwestern tip, Munda Point. These Americans were predominantly young and, except for a handful of Japanese-American *nisei* interpreters, all were white—it was, after all, still a segregated military at this point in the nation's history.

That Friday morning, it rained heavily, much as it had periodically for the last two days, and the area around Rendova Harbor emitted an ether of steam and other, more pungent, miasmas: of jungle decay and rot, of sweat, of death. The reek of putrefaction was noticeable, as several of the dead Japanese defenders, killed the previous day, still lay unburied and hidden in the dense foliage. Piles of boxes, supplies and equipment were stacked up around a group of open-sided, corrugated metal sheds, formerly the property of Lever Brothers. Large landing craft disgorged heavy artillery pieces, towed by Caterpillar tractors and accompanied by the cursing and shouting of sergeants and troops. During the unloading process, others manning the gun positions and conning towers aboard the landing craft or awaiting orders noted a large group of planes passing over the dormant peak of Mount Rendova, and they nonchalantly debated their make, model and mission. "Must be our guys," several of the observers speculated, "heading back to The Canal"—Guadalcanal. Others were not so sure.

Nearby, a lanky, young Marine, just under six feet tall and looking vaguely like a clean-shaven and younger version of Clark Gable, looked up, too, as he widened his small foxhole. His faded green shirt opened wide to fight the heat and cigarette draped from his lips, the "PFC"—Private, First Class—rested on his shovel, took a brief puff, and leaned back into the shovel and his work. He glanced over at a mass of hoses and boxes, collapsible canvas tubs and a pump, and sighed. The young Marine was a "gizmo"—a technical specialist, the bane of all Marine sergeants, and in this case, a water purification man—and then he cursed to himself as he imagined having to set up his equipment laboriously after having finished his small foxhole. His back was so wet with perspiration that one could barely make out the name "J.H. MCCALL," stenciled in faded black ink on the back of his green herringbone-twill jacket. His platoon sergeant was nowhere to be found—no surprise there, he was probably nursing that ever present "sick headache" of his—and so the odds of getting a couple of helping hands to set this gear up quickly were fading fast.

As the young Marine glumly pondered how to set up all this gear by himself before nightfall, he heard the roar of multiple aircraft engines, straining in a dive, and a belated chorus of screams: "Take cover, now! *They're Japs!*" Having already had his "bells rung" by a marauding squadron of Japanese planes earlier that day while offloading a landing craft, he had quickly learned to recognize the sound of Zero fighters' engines, and he leapt into his shallow hole.

As the Japanese planes soared overhead, their Rising Sun "meatball" insignia now easily visible, many of the men cluttering the narrow beachhead were caught in the open without warning. The more experienced Marines and sailors yelled "*Condition Red*! *Take cover*! Hit the deck!," long before the keening sirens, ships' bells and blasts of air horns erupted from the landing craft and ships bobbing in Blanche Channel. Clusters of Marines and Seabees near the beach either ran for the nearest cover or gun positions, but there were also lines of heavily-laden troops from the Army's 43rd Infantry Division struggling off a line of beached LCI infantry landing craft. While wading through the surf to the beach, these troops were caught squarely in the open and suffered terribly. "Now the earth began to vibrate with blasts," Lieutenant Christopher Donner, a young Marine officer, recalled, of his huddling in a foxhole with eleven others. "Above the sound of the firing came the high scream of planes diving, and bullets smacked into the palms over our heads." Drums of gasoline and diesel, boxes of ammunition and the 43rd Division's casualty clearing station were all hit, and five tons of Navy construction engineer ("Seabee") demolition materials exploded in brilliant flames. Jack McCall, the young Marine "gizmo," later recalled that it was "absolute pandemonium."

Caught in the open without foxholes, on the hard coral of the small peninsula, the 24th Seabee Battalion took the brunt of the attack, surrounded by drums and crates of fuel and ammo. The colossal explosion of the Seabees' demolitions dump on a peninsula jutting into Rendova Harbor arguably "[caused] more damage than the bombs themselves," as noted by the Australian coastwatcher D.C. Horton who also witnessed the scene. The colossal blasts erupting from the dynamite dump, only a few hundred feet from young Jack McCall's location, disintegrated a bulldozer and a group of nearby Seabees. The sounds were deafening and, although the air raid only lasted a few minutes, it felt like hours were passing by. The elements of the 43rd Infantry Division, caught wading through the surf as they left their landing craft, were mercilessly strafed by the marauding fighters.

McCall grabbed his rifle and looked up again through the shredded treetops to see these Japanese fighters—the dreaded Mitsubishi "Zero"—roaring by, "on the deck," fifty to sixty feet above the harbor. He was close enough to them to see the pilots' grimacing faces, intent on their mission as they strafed the beach, mounds of supplies and the 43rd's hapless troops. The noise was defeaning, the humidity was suffocating, and the heat generated by the explosions incredible: more fireballs and columns of acrid and oily black smoke billowed over the battered treeline. Men rushed or staggered about—some in fear, some blackened or bleeding or missing limbs, some in shock, some dying—and pieces of debris, human and otherwise, rained down from the explosions. Over the sounds of gunfire and exploding munitions, McCall and his buddies heard another, more disturbing sound over the roar of engines, gunfire, sirens and ships' horns and detonations: the keening wails of men in pain, the yells of medics and stretcher bearers frantically seeking out those who can be saved, and the obscenities, curses and prayers of others watching their buddies dying. And, during the entire raid, nowhere was the much-expected Allied airpower in evidence. Unknown to those on the beach, rain squalls over Guadalcanal and the Russell Island air bases had grounded the American and New Zealand fighters intended to provide cover to the troops on Rendova.

Over 200 Americans lay dead, wounded or, quite simply, missing—disintegrated either by exploding Japanese bombs or the demolition materials in the Seabees' supply dump, their grisly remains hanging from the battered trees and littering the beach and lagoon. The "All Clear" order was yelled out over the stacatto popping of clips of rifle bullets exploding in burning vehicles and the screams of the seriously injured. As one of his own officers yelped out to a group of machine gunners still firing at the retreating Zeroes, "*Cease fire, now, goddammit, or I'll shoot you myself!*", McCall gazed around at the debris littering the area, took off his helmet and ran his fingers through his sweat-plastered hair, and wondered how he had arrived at this condition and how in the hell he would ever survive it. As he caught the smells of burning rubber, wood and fabric, scorched metal and flesh, he realized how utterly scared and alone he felt. He was as "terrified as a 21-year-old Marine could be," he remarked later.

But, as he heard a sergeant yell, "Hey, Pogiebait! We need a hand over here!", he brushed the sand off himself and grabbed his helmet, ammo belt and rifle and leaped out of his foxhole. It was time to get back to work.

As an old man today reflecting on the past—and my days as a young boy growing up in Franklin—I remember:

The fun of hunting arrowheads along the riverbanks, minnie balls in the fields and the sheer joy of finding a couple a day.

The hikes to Roper's Knob and a lunch of pork and beans, our own reenactment of the Civil War at the "Old Fort" and then a skinny dip in the muddy Harpeth by the trestle.

My day etching my name deeply in a large flat rock on the Fort, overhanging the river, with a hammer and railroad spike—it stayed for at least 40 or 50 more years, before a local historian removed it, and had it sent to a museum somewhere to preserve the name of a "long gone" Federal soldier!

And I remember when "damn" was a dirty word and only acceptable when used with "Yankee."

I remember not more than fifteen or twenty cars would even be parked around the High School, and school never closed because of snow.

Jack H. McCall, Sr.
April 3, 1996

The waters of the Harpeth River meander circuitously through the green hills of Middle Tennessee, some twenty miles south of Nashville. The often muddy valley of the Harpeth has given sustenance for years to numerous peoples. Early native American tribes found it to be a excellent hunting ground and left traces of their presence by the large number of flint arrowheads, pottery shards and burial mounds found throughout the valley of the Harpeth River. Around a small valley in the rolling Middle Tennessee hills, the Harpeth makes a number of snakelike turns. This part of the Harpeth River's basin was later found by itinerant European trappers, who bartered pottery and other goods with the local Chickasaw tribe. The valley was discovered anew by early American settlers from Virginia and the Carolinas who settled in the area shortly after the 1779 founding of nearby Fort Nashborough. They, too, found the valley of the Harpeth to be an agreeable spot for hunting, fishing and the cultivation of crops. Duly appreciative of their connections, these settlers christened their settlement after Benjamin Franklin and their county after Hugh Williamson, a Continental general from North Carolina who had been many of the settlers' wartime commander. In time, many of these Indian arrowheads, pottery shards and other artifacts would be found by a young boy, born in Birmingham on May 1, 1922 but soon transplanted at a tender age to his own father's old homeplace in Franklin, a few hundred yards from the banks of the muddy Harpeth. His name was Jack McCall.

In many respects, his hometown was a town marked by history. More to the point, it was very much a town made by war and haunted by its aftermath. Andrew Jackson ended a long-running conflict with the Cherokee and Chickasaw tribes by a peace treaty signed in Franklin's Masonic Lodge in 1830, a treaty which, regrettably, helped pave the way for the "Trail of Tears" deportation a few years later of the Cherokees. President Jackson's Secretary of War, John Henry Eaton, was from Franklin, as were Senator Thomas Hart Benton and Matthew Fontaine Maury, the "Pathfinder of the Seas," an early pioneer of oceanography, an explorer of the Gulf Stream and, in the service of the Confederate Navy, an inventor of the naval mine.

One of the bloodiest battles of the Civil War occurred within a few miles of the McCall house. In about five hours on the late afternoon of November 30, 1864, more than 8,000 Confederate and Union soldiers were killed or wounded. Among the casualties were five dead and two mortally wounded Confederate generals, several of whose bodies were laid side by side on the broad porch of Carnton, a local plantation. In the words of one Rebel veteran, Sam Watkins, the Battle of Franklin was "the grand coronation of death": "My flesh trembles, and creeps, and crawls when I think of it today. Would to God that I had never witnessed such a scene!" Although the Union forces holding the town withdrew to

Nashville, the Confederates' victory at Franklin was a Pyrrhic one. The battle decimated the South's Army of Tennessee, which was annihilated as a fighting entity three weeks later at the Battle of Nashville. Following its defeat at Nashville, the shattered Southern army retreated through Franklin, depositing even more wounded and dying men on its wretched inhabitants. For months thereafter, the casualties of both sides were cared for in Franklin's churches and private homes, transforming the town into a vast infirmary, morgue and graveyard. The largest Confederate cemetery of the war was created on the grounds of the Carnton plantation, the final resting place for almost 1,500 dead Southerners.

While the battle crippled the Confederacy's last chance for victory in the west, the battle and its aftermath permeated much of the life of the town for years to come. Not surprisingly, as in many Southern towns, chapters of the United Daughters of the Confederacy and the Sons of the Confederate Veterans flourished. The local high school adopted the "Rebel," a grizzled Confederate soldier, as its school mascot. Franklin High's hometown rival, the all-male Battle Ground Academy, erected its campus in 1889 on a portion of the Union breastworks near the Carter House; the entrenchments were still readily traceable many years after the battle.

About two thousand yards behind the McCall home, the squat, overgrown earthwork hump of the Union's Fort Granger provided the finest castle that a young boy, his brothers and friends could ever have. Later, while he was in high school, Jack and several of his buddies chiseled their names into a flat limestone rock near the old Louisville & Nashville Railroad trestle spanning the Harpeth under the massive carapace of the fort that was, after all, partly built to dominate the Civil War era rail line that had passed through at that spot. In the fields around Franklin, limestone-encrusted "minnie ball" musket bullets, buttons, belt buckles and an occasional rusted bayonet or musket pieces could be turned up by a farm plow or hoe. Once, behind the old McCall homestead, Jack was lucky enough to find the rusted, but relatively intact, remains of a Civil War revolver. And, over it all, surveying the town square and second in prominence only to the hills surrounding Franklin and the town's mighty grain elevator on the banks of the Harpeth, the town's silent sentinel stood, a granite Confederate soldier overlooking the antebellum courthouse. Its dour stone features were marred by a nick in his hat—caused, it was long rumored, by a gun-toting drunk who had proved to be a menace only to the local statuary but in fact created by an accident at the statue's erection.

Franklin was also proud of its latest war heroes, the veterans of the Great War. These included a local businessman, Captain Tom Henderson, who, it was reputed, was involved in a plot to kidnap and bring to justice Kaiser Wilhelm II after his abdication and flight from Germany to the Netherlands. "Cap'n Tom" kept mum about the affair for many years, with good reason. He and the other participants, a group of Tennessee National Guard officers led by their commander, Colonel Luke Lea, the publisher of the Nashville *Tennessean*, came within a hair's-breadth of being court-martialed by General Pershing. They had entered into the endeavor with the best of intentions. Sickened by the slaughter they had seen on the Western Front and disgusted by the Allies' apparent reluctance to seize and prosecute the Kaiser for war crimes, the group requested leave for purposes of sightseeing in Holland, where Wilhelm was temporarily residing after his abdication. The intrepid band of Tennesseans actually infiltrated the Dutch castle where the Kaiser was temporarily lodged, before being apprehended by the nobleman owning the castle and a squad of Dutch policemen and soldiers. But the Great War had not been fun and games. While over a hundred Williamson Countians had served in the military during the Great War, 32 of them died. Many others came home wounded, maimed, gassed or mentally crippled. And the

"Great Influenza" epidemic of late 1918 had claimed many other victims, both in the service and on the homefront.

Franklinites were extremely proud of their town's heritage and their identity. In late 1941, another war was about to change the lives of its residents again. One of those whose lives would be ineradicably altered was Jack McCall, recent graduate of the Franklin High School Class of 1941.

Jack was the youngest of the three McCall boys, whose family could trace their unbroken lineage in the county back to its founding. His oldest brother, Albert, Jr., was the quieter, intellectual part of the triumvirate. Robert, the middle brother, was the classic redhead: boisterous, feisty and fiery-tempered at times, and from an early age, unafraid to challenge his parents' authority in very direct ways. Because of his yellowish complexion after birth, his dark hair and his slightly Oriental eyes, his mother and father nicknamed baby Jack "Jappy," to the hoots of his older brothers. He was definitely the baby of the family, but he was by no means a runt. While he was not afraid to fight when he had to, from an early age, he always preferred to turn aside another's wrath with a smile or a wisecrack.

Jack loved practical jokes, but as much as he perpetrated them on others, he almost as often had the tables turned on him and his brothers. One of his first recollections of a practical joke was one played on big brother Al by his own grandfather, Robert Lycurgus McCall, who recalled hearing the sounds of the fighting at Franklin as a teenager from his home ten miles east of town. While visiting a gas station down the street from the McCall house one day, crusty old "R.L." offered his grandsons what appeared to be vanilla wafers made into an Oreo or Hydrox-like sandwich cookie, only to laugh hysterically as little Al, the first to try the "cookies," tearfully spit his out: liberally sandwiched in between the two cookies was a coating of axle grease. It was a favorite trick of the old man, and R.L. and his "cracker barrel" buddies guffawed every time the joke succeeded.

By the time he reached junior high school, certain practical jokes became old standbys for Jack and his partners-in-crime. A particular favorite, guaranteed to make some of the leading citizens of Franklin turn red, was to tie a billfold on a string, with a crisp dollar bill peeking temptingly out of its folds. Hidden behind bushes near the County Courthouse or a local bank, Jack would throw the billfold out and see how many "bites" he could get. When a lawyer or banker reached down to pick up the billfold—*poof!*—it would mysteriously run away. That gag was always good for a few laughs at the expense of a few highfalutin' "muckety-mucks."

While in certain respects Jack's childhood and teenage life was idyllic, it was hardly tranquil. The family suffered, though not as badly as many families of the period suffered, from the Great Depression and its effects, but Jack and his brothers recalled days when the family went hungry. In a time when the average Southern family remained more or less in one vicinity, A.G. McCall's family moved a considerable number of times—to Birmingham (where Jack was born); to Atlanta; to Lynchburg, Virginia (where the McCall boys befriended a neighborhood kid, Jackie Cooper, soon to be an actor and one of the child stars of the "Our Gang" comedies); and to Murray, Kentucky. Part of this was due to the Depression's effects on A.G.'s jobs; part, however, may have been due to a darker side of his character. Although generally a congenial man, A.G. was subject to spells of depression and drinking, and his temper could be moody, and his methods of discipline of his sons were fierce.

Fortunately for his boys, A.G. was well-balanced by his wife. Originally a professional milliner, Ruth was also a talented seamstress and somewhat artistically inclined but, in a day when few married women, Southern or otherwise, had independent jobs after their wedding days, regardless of the family situation, she was left to devote herself to homemaking and her boys. Ruth immersed herself completely in these tasks, much as she did later with her work for the local Methodist Church.

The McCall boys were imbued very early in their lives with a sense of the family's history, including its military history. One of the progenitors of the McCall line was a Revolutionary War veteran who had acquired his acreage in the county by land grant in recognition of his wartime service. Ruth McCall's father and uncle both served in sister Kentucky regiments in the Confederate Army: her family's first links to her future home of Franklin occurred when her father, a regimental surgeon, found himself there in 1864 in the wake of the Battle of Franklin. A.G. McCall had been called up for service in the Spanish-America War but never made it overseas; a cousin, owner of Franklin's leading electric store, served on the battleship *Tennessee* in World War I; and a distant cousin was an early Army Air Corps aviator and U.S. Mail Service pilot who was killed in a flying accident in the early 1920s. Draft or no draft and the horrors of the Great War aside, this was not a family that shirked in its military obligations.

As a boy, besides the fun of watching ten-cent serial Westerns and the "Our Gang" and "Little Rascals" comedies at Saturday matinees at the movie theater, the farmland around Franklin offered various treats. These were both of the vegetable and mineral varieties, particularly in springtime and fall as crops were planted and harvested and as the soil was plowed up to reveal the artifacts left by the area's prior occupants. Besides the debris of the Civil War, the tilled fields yielded arrowheads, flintstone hatchet heads and other Indian relics. Jack and his brothers would occasionally go hunting for these relics with the able help of their next-door neighbor, the Tennessee state archaeologist and the son of one of Nathan Bedford Forrest's officers, Dr. P.E. Cox, an expert on early native American archaeology who had amassed a sizeable collection of such artifacts.

Despite the eminent Dr. Cox's erudite lectures on Native American life and the Civil War, Jack's mother was concerned that her youngest boy was a little "uncivilized." Like many parents who wanted their sons to have a modicum of culture, Ruth McCall signed him up for piano lessons from Miss Lahatte, the elderly spinster boarding in Dr. Cox's house. Although she could be an unholy terror—Jack recalled getting his knuckles rapped on occasion by her—Miss Lahatte rewarded good lessons with ginger snaps. These were a big incentive for a kid with a sweet tooth in the days of the Great Depression like Jack, when candy and sweets were very often a scarce thing. Unfortunately, he soon found that the ginger snap rewards were few and far between, as musical skills were just not his forte.

Physical activities, on the other hand, were much more to Jack's liking and talents. By the time he reached high school, football had become a passion. He was soon playing football on Franklin High's team under the discipline and tutelage of Coach Overbey and picking up spending money after school with his buddy David Gentry by doing chores at the Coach's farm or at the small general store down the road that the Coach's brother ran. High school brought new illicit pleasures: "playin' hooky"; rolling and smoking Bull Durham handmade cigarettes behind the football bleachers and trying hard to avoid the wrath of the principal when he smelled the smoke; and joining several boys in trying to hijack an old Spanish-American War cannon in front of the high school but, in the process, giving it a good push downhill. The cannon rolled some distance until its ancient wooden-spoke wheels cracked. In another game effort, he decided to run away from home to hitchhike to Florida. Even though the cost of living in the late 1930s was far less than it is today, Jack soon learned that a person could only travel so far on less than 50 cents.

He made it as far as the Alabama-Tennessee border before hitchhiking back to Franklin and getting a sound whipping and chewing-out from his royally irate but worried father.

High school also brought out a creative side to Jack. He took up drawing, co-wrote a fight song for Franklin High, and became the "publisher and editor in chief" of a daily underground newspaper that satirized about every teacher, student and coach imaginable. Dating and flirting with the girls at Franklin High was another new experience to him, and soon, Jack was popular enough (and cute enough, as far as the girls were concerned) to be elected Senior Class President of the Class of 1941. Like his father, whose best talents had always been in haberdashery, Jack was known to his family and friends as a natty dresser: a real "jellybean," complete with slicked-back hair and a rakish fedora on special occasions, a fancy stickpin in his tie, and a nicely pressed pocket square always in his jacket pocket.

Oh, the Class of '41. For teenagers in Franklin, life was fun and fairly innocent. Unlike the depth of the Depression, jobs were less scarce, and yet war in Europe was a worry to many Americans. After all, hadn't FDR reinstituted the draft just a year before? Hadn't Bob McCall and four of Jack's Class of 1940 buddies joined the Marines? Hadn't a Southern Presbyterian missionary from Franklin and friend of Ruth McCall's been captured and held on a Nazi prison ship for several weeks in April 1941 when a German "Q-ship" raider, the *Kormorant*, sank the Egyptian civilian steamship she was aboard, the *Zamzam*, off Africa? Yet, despite these harbingers, the storm clouds still seemed far enough off in the summer of 1941. It was, in the words of the Gershwin song, "summertime, and the livin' was easy" in Franklin. For a treat, a teenager could cadge a ride to Nashville and see the sights of the "big city," the Athens of the South, or cool off locally with a swim. For dates and family events, there was the beautiful Willow Plunge swimming pool, later described in Peter

Taylor's novel of those times, *A Summons to Memphis*, on the Kinnard estate off Lewisburg Pike. Almost as good a sumertime treat for the local boys was skinny-dipping with your buddies—definitely no girls allowed—at the old swimming holes or in the waters of the Harpeth just behind the McCall house.

As summer 1941 turned into fall, there were crops—mainly, corn and tobacco—to be harvested, and the extra help was always appreciated by the local farmers. Jack's father, A.G. McCall, the manager of National Stores in downtown Franklin, was debating whether or not to enter one of his prized pedigree hogs in time for the Tennessee State Fair. Jack accepted a job as a sales clerk at a dry goods store in Nashville, and he picked up some extra spending money on the side with weekend odd jobs to help Coach Overbey on his farm. Someday, he thought, he might even become the first McCall to go to college. He had been a high school athlete, earning letters in several varsity sports, so the University of Tennessee seemed to him to be a good place to earn a college degree. Its academics were good enough, which pleased his parents, but its athletic teams and vaunted fraternity night life were even more of a draw to Jack and his Franklin High buddies. Not this fall, but maybe in the fall of '42, there would be a new, cocky "Tennessee Volunteer" walking the streets of Knoxville. A.G. McCall only shook his head and grumbled to himself about his youngest son going off to become a "college boy."

But, in late 1941, fate, in the guise of global events, was about to stop Jack McCall's dating life, his school plans and his orderly, laid-back, small-town life dead in its tracks for many years—and, quite possibly, forever.

1

The Making of a Young Marine: Pearl Harbor to Cuba

I volunteered for the Marines about a week after Pearl Harbor, with the agreement that I would not leave until after Christmas. This being okay, I had my physical exam then. I reported back and was sworn in New Year's Eve, the last marine to be sworn in [during] 1941 in the Nashville office.

I spent the night in the Tulane Hotel, and enjoyed my last night as a civilian in the festivities of the evening. Early the next morning, Jan. 1st, we boarded at the Union Station a train loaded with other volunteers from the east, and bound for Parris Island, South Carolina.

Our introduction and reception in the Marines was anything but cordial—and our Drill Instructor went to extra efforts to convince us of our crude backgrounds and stupidity. This being the on-going procedure along with the hustling, shoving and cussings, we finished "Boot Camp" in less than half the time usually taken.

On February the 12th, we were railed to Norfolk, Virginia, and boarded the William Biddle, *shipping out on Friday the 13th for Guantanamo Bay, Cuba. En route we had three U-boat attacks, and our destroyer escorts destroyed two.*

It may be of interest that this was only 68 days from the "Pearl" attack, and of the eight hundred men in our first formed Marine unit since war was declared, 80% of them had no military experience. We formed the 9th Defense Battalion.

Jack H. McCall, Sr.

"*Yesterday, December 7, 1941—a date that will live in infamy—the United States was suddenly and deliberately attacked by naval and air forces of the Empire of Japan.*" Like so many of his friends, for the rest of his life Jack McCall could recall exactly where he was and what he was doing the day that Pearl Harbor, Hawaii was attacked and when President Franklin Delano Roosevelt grimly asked Congress to declare war on Japan the next day. He was 19 years old and had graduated seven months before from Franklin High. His older brothers Al and Bob had long since moved away from Franklin. Al was working in Baltimore as a draftsman and designer for the Glenn Martin Aircraft Company. Things between Bob and A.G. had gotten so tense and the atmosphere at home so oppressive that, after high school graduation, Bob's mother secretly arranged for him to go to California to work at his uncle's store. After a few years there, Bob enlisted in the Marine Corps in 1939 and hinted to his little brother that someday, he might consider doing the same.

On Sunday afternoon, December 7, 1941, Jack was at home. His mother Ruth had just returned from church, and he was getting ready to do some chores for his dad. Like most Americans (and Franklinites), neither Jack nor his parents had any idea where Pearl Harbor was, so they rummaged around the house to find a map to spot it. Also, like most Americans, they had figured the country would have to fight the Nazis long before it had to fight the Japanese. Jack remembered that, back then, not much respect was given to things that came from Japan: they were considered to be cheaply made and not well put together, like toys. Thus, the fact that *Japanese*-made planes and *Japanese*-made aircraft carriers, flown not by the stereotypically nearsighted and inept pilots but by well-trained and determined aviators, were good enough to attack the battleships of the Pacific Fleet and escape unmolested helped make the surprise attack even more bitter. Following FDR's address to a stunned nation and his request to Congress for a formal declaration of war against the Japanese empire, the headlines of the next day's *Nashville Banner* screamed the news: "*CONGRESS DECLARES WAR: 3,000 CASUALTIES AT HAWAII.*" A smaller caption reported "*Tennesseans Rush to Enlist in Services*" and noted: "The ringing traditions of the old Volunteer State struck a new note this morning as Tennesseans of all ages thronged Nashville recruiting stations seeking enlistment in the military services of their country. Before noon more than sixty men had applied for enlistment in the Army, Navy or Marines and men were still coming in." After reading the paper and talking with several of his buddies—*Ain't you gonna enlist now, Jack? It's the thing to do, man!*—Jack thought the matter over and figured that he knew what he had to do.

With brother Bob in the service, Jack knew that his joining up would greatly displease his parents, but with Bob also being a Marine, he took little time in making his decision. He was certain that he would be drafted, as he was classified "1-A," the prime draft classification. A lot of his buddies had already been drafted into the Army, and others had volunteered for the Navy and Marines. Still, he thought, why not go ahead and join a crack outfit like the Marines when he still had a choice in the matter? Bob seemed to like it well enough, and in the two or so years he had already been a Marine, it had been good for him; he was already a corporal and probably would be promoted to sergeant soon. Jack thought about it and concluded he was "all for the Marines." After talking it over with some of his pals for a few days, he hopped a lift to Nashville and went to the Customs House on Broadway, where the Marine Corps Recruiting Station was located.

The recruiting sergeant, clad in his dress blue uniform, promised Jack that his departure for basic training would be postponed for a few weeks, during which time he would need to get a physical examination from his doctor. The recruiter knew his man: *Look at it this way, pal; you'll get to spend some time with your family, maybe with your gal, get to say your goodbyes to your mother, and stick around for the holidays. You won't need to shove off until New Year's Day. That's the best deal I can give you, Mac; after all, there's a war on, you know. Now, how about it?* "Alright," Jack enthusiastically said, and he signed the enlistment application with his most grown-up signature. He pledged to the recruiting sergeant to return after Christmas to complete the enlistment process, with the report of his physical in hand. Back home he went, to break the news to his parents.

Soon after Bob enlisted in the Marines in 1939, Jack also had mulled over joining the Marines, and he had broken the idea to his parents at that time. They did not take it well. His father called him a "damn fool" for wanting to enlist in the Marines when it certainly wasn't his time to go yet—couldn't he just get out of high school first and wait it out to see when he'd get his draft notice? Wasn't it enough for Jack that his big brother Bob had already gone out and done the same dumb thing? With Pearl Harbor, though, everything changed, and when he mentioned to his father that he was thinking again about joining up, A.G. took it more in stride.

It did not dawn on Jack precisely what he had done, however, until some days later when Jack returned home from work one afternoon. As Jack entered the living room, A.G. looked up from his evening newspaper and said: "There's a letter for you on the mantel, son. It's from the Government." The Marines had accepted Jack's application, and the letter instructed him to return on the 31st of December for his oath of enlistment and, thereafter, departure for basic training. His mother cried. Jack said that despite all the hard times the family had endured through the Depression and their moves from city to city, this was one time he knew he'd done something to break his mother's heart, and it made him feel sad—but not yet regretful that he had made this decision.

The holidays were filled with farewells to family and friends, and he quit his job at the store on Christmas Eve to celebrate a somber Christmas with his mother and father in Franklin. Bob had sent word that his unit was moving out, but he didn't know where; Al, working in war production, reported that his factory was being camouflaged and that rumors were rampant in Baltimore of Nazi subs and commando parties cruising off Chesapeake Bay. Ruth cried a lot; A.G. was tense and irritable with Jack but did not tell his son off; he knew that these days might be the last he might see of his youngest child. Instead, he barked, "Go do your chores, boy," and Jack sullenly collected his tools to clean the barn and feed his father's prize pigs, now questioning why he had delayed his departure as long as he had.

Late in the afternoon of December 31, 1941, after a difficult goodbye with his parents and in accordance with his instructions, Jack returned to the recruiting station to complete his enlistment. He would be sworn in before departing for Parris Island, South Carolina, the soon-to-be fabled home of the Marines' Recruit Depot. Although many other Middle Tennessee-area volunteers were waiting with him, several had already taken their oaths of enlistment, and Jack was sworn in individually, making him one of the last local Marine inductees of 1941. He was enlisted in the U.S. Marine Corps Reserve, in service "for the duration of the war" as opposed to a "regular" Marine recruit who signed up for a fixed four-year enlistment term. As they filed out of the Customs House after having sworn their oaths and signed the last papers, Jack and his fellow enlistees began to harbor some doubts as to the wisdom of their actions as the once jovial Marine recruiting sergeant, still resplendent in his dress blues, grinned broadly and croaked: "Welcome to the Marine Corps, *boys*. Just you wait: *you'll be sorrrr-ree!*" For effect, the sergeant drew out the syllables with evident glee.

Early on New Year's Day, after catching a few hours of sleep in the old Tulane Hotel after a night of farewell revelry, Jack boarded a train waiting under a metal-roofed shed at Union Station in downtown Nashville, a few blocks south of the Customs House. The train soon was full of a raucous (if slightly hungover) crowd of other Marine recruits, all headed for Parris Island. As the train pulled away from Union Station, Jack wondered when he would see it again Because they had enlisted during the holidays, the fresh Marine recruits arriving in this period were becoming known throughout the Marine Corps as the "Pearl Harbor Avengers" and the "Christmas Tree Marines." Despite Jack's own mental preparations, including his earlier talks with his brother Bob, as to what he could expect, his initiation into the Marines would still be a rude awakening.

As they set forth for their military training, Jack and many of his peers had high expectations to match their high spirits as to the likely length of the war. "I think most of us figured it would last a year at most and that we'd be home by the following Christmas" was Jack's answer when questioned as to how long he thought it would take to beat the Japanese. In the end, it would be four years—and many close calls later—before he made it home to his beleoved Franklin.

What Jack also did not fully appreciate at the time was that he would soon be transformed from a young and brash teenager, with the world at his feet, into the world's most unexalted specimen of humanity: the lowly Marine Corps trainee—the "boot."

Boot Camp Days

At Yemassee Junction, South Carolina the next morning, a miniature but grim-visaged Marine corporal boarded Jack's train. Jack recalled somewhat ruefully years later: "I knew I'd played hell at Yemassee when that little cocky corporal came aboard—he explained how it was going to be." The diminutive NCO loudly and abruptly began the new recruits' initiation into the Corps by bellowing out: "*Now hear this!* You *will* remain on this train car until you are told to dismount. You will not *get out* of this car until I give you the word. You *will* remain in your seats at all times. You *will* keep order. Is *that* understood?" The mob of roughhousing enlistees quickly fell silent and scrambled for their seats under the withering glare of the corporal. Another group of stone-silent recruits—all from the Eastern Seaboard (enlistees from west of the Mississippi River were trained at the Corps's other recruit depot at San Diego)—emerged from a spartan-looking rail-side building to line up in single file. Laden with all their suitcases and bags, this somber group now boarded a nearby Parris Island-bound train waiting on a separate siding at Yemassee Junction. Soon thereafter, Jack and the men in his train followed suit.

A few hours later, the train was greeted at Port Royal, the debarkation point for "Boot Camp," by a line of crisply dressed—and very hostile—Marine noncoms, with clipboards tucked under their arms, who began bawling orders the moment the train stopped. On arrival at Parris Island itself and after hustling from one clerk's office to another for in-processing, Jack was assigned to the 9th Platoon of the Marine Training Barracks. As the new recruits ran and plodded from one station to another, they were greeted by platoons of only slightly less green boots, who yelled out the same chilling threat that the recruiting sergeant had made to Jack following his oath-taking ceremony, the words drawn out in the same manner: "*You'll be sorrrr-ree*!" Jack and his peers were double-timed from place to place: to draw uniforms; to draw sundry issue items, known as a "bucket issue" because they were placed in a metal bucket—all other non-combat gear and personal clothing, underwear ("skivvies" in the Marines' argot), toiletries, brushes and other cleaning gear; and to undergo a quick battery of medical and psychological tests. The "psycho" test was brief in the extreme, consisting of three simple questions:

"Are you happy?"

"Do you like girls?"

"Do you play with yourself?"

Finally, after all was complete (and assuming all three questions were answered to the examiner's satisfaction), the dazed, weary and fully-laden boots were double-timed to the platoon's barracks area by the menacing figures of the two people they would come to hate more than anyone they had ever hated before and (quite possibly) since: their drill instructor and assistant drill instructor.

The members of the 9th Platoon were lucky in one sense, as their quarters were two-story wooden and brick barracks; these facilities were hardly comfortable, but they were better than the alternatives. The term "barracks," for many other enlistees in other platoons, was an entirely inapt name: in the freezing dead of January and February, several platoons were billeted outdoors in old, ragged tents, while others were billeted in more substantial (but scarcely less chilly) all-metal Quonset huts. For those quartered in the two-man tents, the sleeping arrangements were spartan in the extreme: each man had a cot, mattress, pillow, one sheet, pillow case, footlocker and only one blanket. In South Carolina, which in early 1942 was experiencing sub-freezing wintertime temperatures, the boots fought off discomfort by sleeping in their clothes and wadding newspapers under their mattresses for insulation. The barracks and huts were thoughtfully equipped with small potbellied stoves—not that it mattered much, though. As the drill instructors or "DIs" said, in time-honored military tradition: "You won't be here to use 'em in the daytime; you can't light 'em up at night because we don't have enough fuel for 'em; you'll just have to polish 'em. Make 'em shine!" As a result, the boots likely had some of the least used—but shiniest—potbellied stoves in the U.S. military by the time they graduated from the rigors of "P.I."

Parris Island's other facilities for the care and treatment of the boots were equally suitable for production-line-type efficiency, so that even the simplest and most basic tasks often seemed to be a refinement in cruelty. The recruits' toilet facilities provide one graphic example. While several platoons had latrines in their Quonset huts or permanent barracks buildings, for ten other platoons, the latrine area, or "head," was an unheated, corrugated-metal building. These were equipped with shower heads at one end. Along one wall, a long sheet-metal trough served as a urinal; instead of providing enclosed individual toilets for defecation, the opposite wall featured an identical trough covered with simple wooden slats for seats. Another trough was centrally located for washing-up and was supplied with small single-faucet, cold-water-only stations and a polished piece of aluminum over each faucet to serve as a mirror. The entire latrine was large enough to handle an entire platoon of boots, roughly 60 to 70 men, at one time; however, because it was also the only latrine for the accommodation of ten platoons' hygienic needs, each platoon had a fixed schedule for use of the head. In the freezing South Carolina winter, with cracks in the sheet metal siding and no heat, with no hot water for shaving or showering, and with the ever-present DIs relentlessly monitoring their platoon's time in the head between shifts, latrine time was a Spartan experience.

Forget today's advertising images of dress-blue uniforms with razor-sharp creases and immaculate white-topped caps, or even John Wayne's *Sands of Iwo Jima* version of World War II: these new Marine recruits of 1942 were a shabby looking crew. The Corps's overall supply system rated low in the Navy Department's logistical priorities at this stage of World War II, and with Pacific garrisons under siege or falling, the sartorial splendor of new recruits was not high on the list of the Marines' priority items of supply. Some were outfitted in cotton dungarees; some wore wool; others were in khaki; and even a few were clad in World War I-vintage high-collared tunics and campaign hats, which today would be called "Smokey the Bear" hats. Under these circumstances, the term "uniform" took on a completely different meaning. The only things about their apparel that made the recruit platoons uniform were that they were no longer in civilian garb, and their rag-tag clothing were, at least, government issue. Before leaving P.I., the uniform situation improved, as attested to by the 9th Platoon's graduation picture: the new Marines and their DIs resplendent in freshly issued (but temporarily loaned) dress greens, khaki shirts and "field scarves" and overseas caps. For their first few weeks, however, they were a motley-looking bunch, much to the self-serving horror of the DIs.

Jack's two drill instructors, Corporal Stallings and PFC Story, were "the meanest little SOBs I ever ran into in all my born days." At this stage in the development of Boot Camp, almost all of the DIs were corporals, often sarcastically referred to as "little colonels," who, practically speaking, possessed as much authority over their charges' daily lives as would any true colonel. The assistant DIs were privates first class, often scarcely out of Boot Camp themselves. The boots addressed all DIs—and, for that matter, any other uniformed Marine—as "sir," regardless of their rank. Out of a desire to win the coveted two stripes of a corporal (which would make them officially non-commissioned officers, with the privileges that NCO status conveyed) and to prove their own toughness, the assistant DIs often vied with the lead DIs as to who could be the worst martinets. One of their two DIs was truly despised by all of the boots in 9th Platoon (they were not yet Marine privates: that esteemed rank could only be earned by surviving Boot Camp). One of Jack's platoon mates, Jim Kruse, remembered this particular DI as being "of small stature" and being one who liked to "take advantage of the situation to curse and browbeat men of larger size, ripping the shirt off one of them." About the nicest things the boots were ever called by the DIs were "maggot," "shitbird" and "eightball," with the categories of insults only going downhill from there. Depending on each DI's whim, sometimes, the sobriquets were all mixed together in a melange of insults. Thus, a boot could be called a "maggoty shitbird," a "shitbird boot," a "frigging eightball" or a "slimy maggot." The more adjectives and expletives that were strung together and thrown in the face of a cringing boot, the greater was the DI's wrath. These combinations were often punctuated at the very end by that hated word, spit out like the worst possible curse to be bestowed on mankind, and capped off with a sneering rictus to match: "*boot*!"

Several examples of the mental harassment inflicted by the DIs on the boots suffice to give an impression of the environment and its goals of breaking down the personal pride and individualism of each boot so that he could be remolded into a Marine. Reveille was at 0400 hours—4:00 a.m.—with police call, cleanup of the platoon area, beginning at 0430. In the pitch-black morning, the boots would line up, ten abreast, on hands and knees and would crawl up the company street running through each platoon's area (itself little better than a sandy path), searching for cigarette butts, twigs, pieces of paper and other debris. After roll call, morning inspection and chow, the DIs would inspect the company street. Inevitably, the DI would find something and would mete out some kind of collective punishment to the group.

One favorite form of mass humiliation was saved for immediately before "Taps" and lights-out. A fellow boot at the time who would later become one of Jack's fast friends, Frank Chadwick, vividly recalled the typical scene:

> Another favorite, almost nightly ritual, was in the evening. The boots who had screwed up that day had to run through the tent area, yelling, "I'm a shitbird from Yemassee, the biggest shitbird you'll ever see, then flap his arms (attempting to fly) and shouting "Yak, yak" (like a bird). All platoons would have to stand at attention, with the DI checking over his platoon. If he thought you smiled or your eyes moved, you joined the single file when they came through your tent area. Very shortly, you had 640 boots running through the Company area. This usually lasted 1 1/2 to 2 hours, depending on how long it took the DIs to get the boots in formation.

Each boot was trained to refer to his assigned firearm as a "rifle," never as a "gun." Anyone making that mistake was forced by the DI to step out in front of the platoon, chanting as loudly as possible while clutching his rifle with one hand and grabbing his genitals with the other: "This is my rifle; this is my gun; this [here, the boot would gesture with his rifle] is for shooting, and this [now, grabbing his crotch] is for fun." To help drive the point home further, a DI would occasionally order any offending boot who persisted in calling his rifle a "gun" to sleep with his rifle in his cot. If a young, beardless kid neglected to shave or if a boot had a hint of beard stubble, the DI would condemn him to being dry-shaved with a dull razor by a comrade—or, for the worst offenders, having to wear a bucket over his head while another boot dry-shaved him by touch alone.

The peculiar jargon of the Marine Corps also took some mental adjustments to master, as the boots had to quickly learn there was a new name for everything else besides their "guns." Many terms had nautical origins, derived from the Corps's historic role as the Navy's sea soldiers. Left was *port*, right was *starboard*, floors were *decks*, duffle bags were *sea bags*, and the correct answer in the affirmative to a senior Marine was not a mere "Yes, sir" but a smartly rendered "*Aye, aye, sir*!" A jail or prison was the *brig* and the man holding the power to send one to the brig, the unit's commanding officer, was the *skipper*. The origins of other slang terms were more esoteric. A Marine unit's buglers and musicians were its *field musics*, who also doubled as medical orderlies and stretcher-bearers in combat. A Marine did not attend chapel, he went to the *God Box*, and he drank beer not in a bar but in a *slop chute*. Slackers, goof-offs and other disreputable characters were *goldbricks* and *yardbirds*. Candy was *pogy bait* (also spelled "*pogey bait*," of which more, in Jack's case, later). A Marine's khaki necktie was a *field scarf*, and his underwear was his *skivvies*. Marines did not make their camps in the field or jungle: instead, they pitched their tents in the *boondocks*, and the rough leather boots worn on such occasions were *boondockers*, accompanied by khaki spats called *leggings*, and not a cap but a *cover* garnished the head of a Marine. Few of the Marines" names for food were appetizing: coffee was *Joe*, ketchup was *redlead*, pancakes were *collision mats*, and mustard was *babyshit*. Horseplay was *grabass*; rumors and gossip were pieces of *scuttlebutt*, as distinguished from real information and news, which was *poop*. Hence, any newspaper or bulletin was the *poop sheet* because it provided the reader with the latest "poop."

Instead of being an opportunity to provide some relief from the tension, mail call also soon became dreaded. Anyone receiving a parcel from home had to open it in front of the DI, who would first search it for contraband. Assuming it passed muster, the DI would then pass the parcel through the platoon formation, and each boot had to sample the contents. If the contents were food, the parcel would usually be empty by the time it was returned to the recipient. Another favorite ploy of the DIs was to throw the pieces of mail to the boots: if anyone dared move to pick up his mail, he (and depending on the DI's whim, possibly the entire platoon) would be punished for breaking ranks without authorization. Sometimes, the letters remained where they fell on the parade ground for the rest of the morning.

Letters from a sweetheart brought similar abuse and, from the DI's perspective, were excellent fodder for personalizing the harassment, all of which was part and parcel of one of Boot Camp's goals: to reduce each boot to a lowest common denominator and, from there, to remodel the boots from a bunch of rugged individualists into a team of Marines. If a letter was clearly from a girlfriend—if perfumed or sealed with lipstick, for example—the DI would force the recipient to stand at attention in front of the entire platoon and read the letter while the DI checked to make sure absolutely nothing was left out. As if this was not embarrassing enough, the DI would begin to question the boot, lewdly and graphically, about his sex life: did he and his girlfriend have sex? (Put more bluntly: "Well, *maggot*, did you screw her?") If they had never had sex, what was the boot's problem: was his girlfriend ugly, or, maybe, was the boot "queer?" How, exactly, did the boot and his girlfriend "do it?" Nose-to-nose with a cringing boot, a DI would often leeringly grunt: "So, you little *shitbird*, did you '69' her?" The next sound frequently heard thereafter was the nervous gulp of an utterly confused young boot, who had no idea that arithmetic was a part of sexual relations and who was desperately groping for *any* answer that might save him from humiliation before the DI and his peers.

The scatological and sexual slang used by the DI during these interrogations—amounting to a grotesque *Kama Sutra*, provided in a weird kind of Southern accent often favored by the DIs—was often entirely new to many teenaged boots. This included Jack, who later freely confessed: "I heard more dirty words used in Boot Camp than I ever knew existed—and, you know, I still don't know what some of them mean!" He definitely was not alone. Certainly, in a more circumspect time when Clark Gable's utterance as Rhett Butler of "Frankly, my dear, I don't give a damn!" was enough to get *Gone With the Wind* banned from public viewing in various cities, profanities and vulgarities were generally more out of place than today, and it was possible for young men to leave high school without having a vocabulary as salty as those of today's Americans. As the then 16-year-old New Yorker Frank Chadwick recounted of his DI's blunt and caustic descriptions of certain lovemaking techniques to a platoon of clueless boots:

> Most of us had no idea what the hell [the DI] was talking about, and his explanation for us stupid Yankees was hilarious in itself. It was shortly after the first mail calls that no packages arrived; no lipstick or perfume was found on any letters, as everyone wrote home, begging them to just send plain envelopes.

While not immune to female charms, Jack had a bit of a puritanical streak to him, possibly inherited from his good-hearted and God-fearing mother. While well used to "cussing," the DIs' highly creative use of obscenities and blasphemies dumbfounded Jack at first; although he adapted to this, and could soon swear with the best of them, he never quite forgot this initial shock. Although he had been around farm animals and farm kids all of his life and thus knew something about sex and the facts of life—after all, he was a country boy himself—Jack began to suspect that he had maybe a more sheltered life than he had thought possible.

Likewise, the first payday brought little joy to the boots. When enlisting, each boot received a monthly pay of $21, minus $5 for mandatory life insurance. The boots were shaved bald by the post barber shortly after arrival at P.I. and later during training for the going rate of 25 cents; as the ditty went: "Shave and a haircut; two bits!" The Corps also required the boots to pay for their bucket-issued goods issued on their first day at Boot Camp. After all these expenses were tallied up, the recruits would be "in the hole" on their pay for the next three months.

The first payday only heightened the sense of unreality. Each platoon's boots marched in alphabetical order to a large hall, where each man reported to a very surly paymaster. The paymaster grouchily informed the boot that, although his entire month's pay had been docked to defray costs, it was illegal to work for the government without any pay. Therefore, the paymaster concluded, he had the duty to "pay a bunch of maggot boots" 25 cents each. On leaving the paymaster's desk, the boot was next greeted by his DI, lurking near the exit. The DI helpfully suggested that, since he would have no use for his quarter anyway, a contribution to the Navy-Marine Corps Relief Agency bucket conveniently placed nearby would be a good use for it. The DI then menacingly hinted to the boot that he wouldn't have the guts to pocket the change: "He was right again," one former boot sadly recalled.

Nor, as Jim Kruse's account suggests, was the petty harassment of the DIs limited to verbal abuse: the DIs had *carte blanche* to grab, punch and kick the recruits, if and when they deemed it appropriate. Because no officers were generally found, by custom if not by rule, in the recruit training areas, any physical abuse that occurred would not be meted out by the DIs in sight of any commissioned officers. While those born in the last decades of the 20th century may be horrified to read this, times were very different in 1942. Corporal punishment was still frequently used in school, from first grade to the senior year of high school, and "spare the rod and spoil the child" was still widely followed by A.G. McCall and others as a tool of both parental and educational discipline. Jack and many others had grown up in such an environment, and if mere schoolboys were expected to take their licks without crying, young men who had volunteered to become Marines would be expected by their peers and superiors to do likewise—indeed, they themselves expected to do so. A full night's sleep was rare, and a full stomach was even rarer. On the other hand, freezing weather, seemingly endless training and work details, and the perpetual harassment of the DIs were too common. In the space of the four weeks he spent in Boot Camp, Jack lost almost 30 pounds.

Apart from the mental and physical testing, Boot Camp was devoted to learning the School of the Marine (marching and drilling, military courtesy, use and care of the rifle, etc.). The boots were also soon being taught by the DIs the Marines' Hymn, bawling it out in something less than perfect harmony but with admirable volume and spirit:

From the Halls of Montezuma
To the shores of Tripoli,
We will fight our country's battles
On the land and on the sea.
First to fight for right and freedom
And to keep our honor clean,
We will proudly claim the title

Of United States Marines.

Each DI also relentlessly grilled his boots on their knowledge of their General Orders (as David Slater reminisced: "If a DI came and stuck his nose in your face and yelled, 'What's General Order Number 3?' and you didn't know it, brother, you were in deep doo-doo") and the Marines' chain of command, beginning with the commandant of the Corps. "The Commandant of the United States Marine Corps is General *Holcomb*! That's Thomas A. *Holcomb*, you bunch of slimy maggots. Now, if *anyone* asks *you* who the *hell* the Commandant is, *what* will you tell them?," Corporal Stallings roared. "Holcomb, sir!," Jack, Downs, Kruse and their nervous buddies tentatively responded. "*What* did you say?" "*Holcomb, sir*!," the platoon yelled back loudly. "Like hell, you will, you shitbirds; you'll forget!" the DI cynically growled back.

A primary aspect of their training, perhaps the most critical in terms of combat survival, was basic rifle marksmanship. Regardless of what military specialty one would receive or which unit he would be assigned after Boot Camp, at this stage of the war each Marine was expected to qualify as a marksman with the rifle and to be capable of serving as an infantryman. The boots drilled for hours with their bolt-action Springfield rifles, exercising and practicing firing positions ("snapping-in") with them, spending more hours on the rifle ranges and even more hours afterward, disassembling, cleaning and oiling their rifles. The only thing possibly more humiliating than dropping a rifle (which earned the immediate and *very* personal attention of the DI) was to miss not only the bullseye but the whole target completely during qualification shooting. This failing was called "pulling a Maggie's Drawers" because a bright red flag (vaguely suggestive of women's panties and with the racy, if implicit, meaning that "Maggie's" suitor had "fired blanks" in making love to her—hence, the red color) was raised by the crew manning the targets to pinpoint any boot who had failed so miserably to hit the target. Those not firing or cleaning their rifles—the latter of which, even with the easy-to-disassemble Springfield, was still time-consuming—were put to work policing up the area or were on the firing range themselves, manning the pits under the targets, or "butts."

These targets were large paper bull's-eyes tacked to wooden frames that were manually raised and lowered from the safety of the butts, and each boot had 50 bullets—fired in increments, at various distances and shooting positions—with which to qualify. The shooters' scores were recorded by the men in the butts, who used pointers to point out the holes made in the targets or, in the case of someone who missed the target completely, the hated "Maggie's Drawers" flag was raised accordingly. Moreover, to lessen the dangers posed by so many untrained men with loaded firearms, range discipline was especially harsh, even by P.I.'s rigorous standards. Yet, despite the discipline and though theoretically dangerous duty, since a bullet could easily ricochet off the support frames into the butts, for Jack, range duty was the highlight of his stay at P.I. It was one of the very few times he and his buddies could escape the ever-present scrutiny of the DIs and could "skylark" among themselves in the pits, telling jokes to liven things up or (despite the DIs' order "No smoking in the butts!") occasionally sneaking an illicit smoke.

Moreover, qualification day on the rifle range was the last big test as to whether a boot could hack it in the Corps before graduation from Boot Camp, and it was not only a mark of honor to qualify at the highest grades but also a source of additional monetary incentives. Jack ultimately won a marksman badge for his rifle skills, although he'd never fired anything bigger than a BB gun before he joined the Marines. Regrettably, he did not qualify as a "sharpshooter" or "expert," which, besides providing the prestige that such titles brought, also brought an extra $5 and $10 per month, respectively.

Back to the paucity of food. Besides drilling and training, Marine recruits at Parris Island were also "in quarantine" during their four-odd weeks of training. "Quarantine" meant neither talking to *anyone*—not even a bunkmate or tentmate—in public nor any letter-writing home unless authorized to do so by the DIs (and very definitely, in those days, there were no telephone calls home). Smoking was prohibited except during strictly limited times; each boot was rationed to one cigarette per day and once it was smoked, that was it. No departures from post or liberty passes were authorized. After the first couple of weeks, the boots were assigned frequent stretches of guard duty, in addition to the grueling training days and hours spent cleaning one's barracks, rifle and gear. Above all else, there was *absolutely* no unauthorized "pogy bait"—that is, candy.

One evening, while the platoon was undergoing rifle training and billeted at the rifle range in drafty metal Quonset huts, Jack was assigned to guard a small and strictly off-limits PX-type area, not a place usually frequented by the likes of the flat-broke, starving and dog-tired boots. He patrolled his "beat" listlessly, when, what to his wondering eyes should appear but—wonder of wonders, holy of holies—an intact, unopened box of Baby Ruth candy bars. Manna from heaven! Furtively looking around to make sure he remained unseen, he immediately set to consuming the whole box with relish.

Very early the next morning, the 9th Platoon was engaged in physical training drills on the rifle range. The boots were put through "snapping-in" exercises, grueling calisthenics in platoon formation involving lifting, stretching and holding their rifles at arm's length for prolonged periods of time as well as moving rapidly on command into simulated standing, seated and prone firing positions. In the midst of these exertions, Boot McCall collapsed in the ranks, apparently from over-exertion or "cat fever" (catarrhal fever, endemic to the masses of shivering boots). Unknown to Al Downs and several others who, on the DI's orders, broke formation to aid him, the shock to Jack's famished system from the candy bars had raised his blood sugar level massively, making him sick to high heaven. In a dazed state, he was carried off to the Recruit Depot's sick bay, where the diagnosis was made and his confession recorded: McCall had overdosed on Baby Ruth bars. Despite his embarrassment (and Corporal Stallings's fury that an entire box of candy had been gobbled down by one who was supposed to be guarding them, not wolfing them down wholesale), word of Jack's fainting spell and its cause spread quickly through the platoon. Hence, Jack earned—the hard way—what would be his lifelong nickname among his Marine buddies: "Pogy Bait" (or, as Jack typically spelled it, "Pogiebait") McCall.

The 9th Platoon went through P.I. on what might charitably be called an accelerated program, graduating from Boot Camp in four weeks, much more quickly than any prewar predecessors who faced a twelve-week training cycle. The haste of this training cycle, however, was undoubtedly due to the exigent circumstances as much as the platoon's zeal. After a valiant defense, Wake Island and its 1st Defense Battalion garrison had fallen, as had Guam, the first American territory to be captured in the war. The Philippines had been invaded, and U.S. and Filipino forces, including the 4th Marines, were retreating to the Bataan peninsula and the Manila Bay fortress of Corregidor. The British colonies in Hong Kong and Singapore had fallen as well. The Soviets were fending off Nazi assaults on Moscow and Leningrad, throwing its manpower into a costly winter counteroffensive against the invaders, and Erwin Rommel's panzers were on the move again in Libya against Britain's beleaguered "Desert Rats." The situation was grim; the time was coming for new Marines to face their baptism of fire.

Sixty-three Marine privates, including Jack McCall, graduated from the 9th Platoon in early February 1942. His graduation picture shows him, "grinning like a possum," standing third from the left in the third row from the bottom, clutching his Springfield at port arms, with his buddies Jim Kruse and Al Downs to his right and left. Following graduation, the new privates were told that despite the aptitude tests they had taken, all their requests for different military specialties were rejected and that all were assigned—immediately—to the combat units of the Fleet Marine Force. Each platoon's DIs could not help but add a parting shot: "If you thought Boot Camp was tough, you idiots, just you wait and see." As Frank Chadwick, at 16 years old the youngest Marine in one of the 9th Platoon's sister platoons, recalled: "How right he was, but after Boot Camp we all were new Marines, and nothing could not be done, and we could whip the world." They were no longer boots; even if they were still woefully inexperienced, they were, at least, now Marines.

Graduation photograph of Platoon 9, Marine Recruit Barracks, February 1942. Jack McCall is in the third row, third from the left, flanked by Jim Kruse (on Jack's right) and Al Downs (on Jack's left). The DIs, PFC Story and Corporal Stallings, are seated without rifles in the first row, front and center. (Author's collection)

After Boot Camp graduation, Chadwick's DI had one last insult in mind for the "chick" Chadwick, to teach him a final lesson and to "put the fear of God" in him of Marine NCOs:

> I had just turned 16 when I joined the Corps and did not receive any mail from home. [Chadwick had joined without his family's permission and ran away from home to enlist. To prove he was old enough, Chadwick visited a bookie, who forged the necessary certificates for five dollars.] The D.I. called me to his tent and questioned my age. I kept stating, "17, with parents' consent." He put his face into mine and informed me, in no uncertain terms, that if I received

> no mail by the next week, I had better give my soul to God as my ass belonged to him. He chewed me out in such a manner I could feel my body shaking. You can bet I very shortly had mail! After Boot Camp, I met him in the slop chute. He bought me a beer, called me a liar and kicked my ass out of the slop chute.

The majority of the 9th Platoon, U.S Marine Training Barracks, and the members of several other newly-graduated platoons of the Christmas Tree Marines were about to join the newly-formed 9th Defense Battalion for overseas deployment. At this point, a few words about the 9th Defense and its kind are in order.

Welcome to the 9th Defense, Private McCall!

The 9th Defense Battalion was an example of a type of unit peculiar to the Marines during a relatively short period of time, with such battalions' active life encompassing almost the entire span of World War II: never before, and not after, would such a unit be part of the organization of the Fleet Marine Force. The Defense Battalion concept partly originated from Marine and Navy studies during the 1920s and 1930s concerning the defense of coaling stations, forward bases, harbors and naval anchorages and air stations. In order to better protect such critical but isolated sites, the Marine Corps staff developed the idea of using relatively large, self-contained forces, which could defend islands like Midway, Guam and Wake and which would have enough artillery and antiaircraft firepower that, if attacked, could drive off the enemy or at least hold their own until reinforcements arrived. Another practical consideration was funding. In the isolationist environment of the 1930s, military spending was rigorously scrutinized, and military force projections were anathema. Hence, the likelihood that Congress would support the formation and funding of any military units intended for *offensive* action was slim. Thus, to a large degree, the Navy Department's formation of Marine units officially labeled "defense battalions" would help elicit at least minimal funding for their creation and support. That such battalions might also be strong enough to undertake limited offensive activities was, of course, an additional benefit.

A lack of consensus existed in the Corps, however, as to the potential value of the new Defense Battalions. One of the strongest critics of the concept was the influential Marine Brigadier General A.A. Vandegrift, soon to command of the 1st Marine Division. Vandegrift detested the idea as a drain on manpower and scarce logistics assets and as a sideshow that would detract from the formation of all-arms Marine divisions, which he viewed as being the most desirable structure for a wartime Corps. Against his strenuous objections, the formation of the Defense Battalions went ahead. When finally implemented in the 1940-41 period, the nearest Army equivalent to the Marine Defense Battalions may have been its Coast Artillery and Field Artillery battalions and regiments, but even this was an unsatisfactory comparison: there was really nothing else quite like these weird and heterogeneous units in the rest of the U.S. military.

For starters, the size of the 9th Defense Battalion was much larger than that of the average Marine or Army battalion, with its number of assigned personnel—15 officers and 800 enlisted men, when fully activated in February 1942, but growing within a few months to over 1,250 Marines—being closer in size to a small regiment or brigade. The battalion initially was comprised of a Seacoast Artillery Group, a Heavy Antiaircraft ("AA") Group, a Machine Gun Group (later called the "Special Weapons Group"), and a Headquarters and Service ("H&S") Battery. The idea was to create a unit with fully-integrated and substantial defensive capabilities: the Seacoast Group to counter enemy seaborne threats;

the AA Group to take on high-altitude aircraft; the automatic weapons of the Machine Gun Group to challenge low-altitude airplanes and numerous smaller threats, whether landborne, seaborne and airborne; and the H&S Battery to provide command and control and logistics (and, in time, tank support)—but also capable of undertaking limited offensive missions as well, on an as-needed. As a result, the structure and armament of each Defense Battalion varied widely, and no common table of organization and equipment existed between any of the twenty Defense Battalions in being by mid-1944. The first eight Defense Battalions were intended primarily for static defense and had precious little offensive capabilities or mobility. The Ninth would be the first of its kind to receive enhanced mobility and offensive capabilities and would be—if not the largest—one of the largest Defense Battalions.

On February 1, 1942, the headquarters and training detachment of the Ninth was formed at Parris Island under Major Wallace Thompson. Of the 15 officers and 800 enlisted men forming the Ninth, a trained cadre of over 150 senior officers and NCOs were veterans of World War I and the Chinese, Philippine and Central American campaigns of the 1920s and early 1930s . Most of the enlisted were fresh out of Boot Camp, and most of the lieutenants were "90-day wonders" (more often referred to, sometimes less than affectionately, as "shavetails" by their dubious charges). Ironically, many of these new officers felt little better trained than the men they were to command. One of the new battery "skippers," then-Second Lieutenant Henry Reichner, remembered his own introduction to his new battery as a very perfunctory matter: "Sometime during those first hectic few days at Parris Island, I was taken to part of the Boot Camp and shown a row of tents occupied by newly graduated recruits. 'This row is "A" Battery. Take charge,' were my orders." Likewise, Jack, Al Downs and Jim Kruse soon found themselves meeting their new CO of H&S Battery of the Ninth's 155mm Group, Second Lieutenant William T. Box, and their new sergeants. Eleven days later, Jack and his "compadres" from his training platoon were loaded on trains and shipped off to Norfolk Navy Yard in Virginia, where the new battalion was forming up *en masse*.

This departure from P.I. was hardly comfortable or speedy, although it was furtive. The Marines were trucked from P.I. to Yemassee Junction around midnight to shroud their departure, and not even the officers accompanying Jack and his buddies seemed to have a clear idea of their final destination. Once in Yemassee Junction, they formed up by platoons and marched in files from the trucks to a waiting troop train made up of wooden passenger cars. Each man had somehow to squeeze his seabag, rifle and equipment into a narrow seating area. Heating in the drafty cars was provided by a pot-bellied stove, making for an uncomfortable ride for officers, sergeants and enlisted men alike. "The train coaches were Civil War relics, or so they seemed," Lieutenant Hank Reichner remembered. After a near-sleepless, nightlong trip with all shades drawn, the occupants of the train found themselves in the morning at a newly-constructed Marine encampment at New River, North Carolina (later to be named Camp Lejeune). Trucks carrying hot chow were waiting, and each Marine was then handed a box lunch of liverwurst sausage and an apple to sustain him for the rest of the day. After waiting at a siding all day, the train again pulled onto the main rail line at dark and resumed its northbound journey under the cover of night.

The next morning—Friday, February 13th, 1942—the Marines awoke groggily to find the troop train drawn up alongside a mile-long pier at Norfolk Naval Base in tidewater Virginia. The occupants of the train were marched single-file to the rearmost car and, from there, straight off the back and up the gangway of a waiting transport, the U.S.S. *William Biddle*, to sail through U-boat infested waters to the U.S. Naval Operating Base at Guantanamo Bay, Cuba. Upon their arrival at the gangway, the new Marines learned that they were officially a part of the 9th Defense Battalion, Fleet Marine Force. At Guantanamo Bay, the Ninth was to be "trained as a defense battalion, utilizing such weapons at the Naval Operating Base as may be made available." Its secondary mission would be to assist in the defense of the base from German U-boats, since Guantanamo Bay served as a way station and convoying point for U.S.-bound oil tankers en route from Venezuela and freighters plying the Caribbean. Except for newly issued rifles and personal equipment, the Ninth lacked all of the basic field equipment and heavy equipment—and the advanced training—it needed to be turned into an effective fighting force. The platoons full of newly graduated boots (and second lieutenants) would be joined in Cuba by a large detachment from the 5th Defense Battalion, the "Polar Bears" (so-called because of their shoulder patches, the insignia of the British Army division they were sent to assist) who were sent to Iceland in fall 1941 to help the British defend that island from German attack.

On "Black Friday," the night of the *Biddle*'s departure, as they left Norfolk, Jack and most of his pals were much more worried about whether they would ever make it again to dry land than whether they would see combat soon. With all personnel on board and manifests checked off, the *Biddle* lifted anchor and moved to the outer Chesapeake Bay to sail after dark. As the ship steamed out of the bay, the sound of gunfire and depth charges were clearly audible: an escorting destroyer thought it had detected a German U-boat. Locked down below deck, with all hatches shut and all portholes blacked out, the first "sub attack" induced a real sense of fear in many of the new Marines. The winter seas were choppy, and most of the Marines on board the *Biddle* (by one estimate, at least 70% of the Leathernecks) were seasick—a condition which was not improved by the decision, while the *Biddle* was in especially choppy seas off Cape Hatteras, to move a number of the Marines and their gear from one hold to another for organizational reasons. Three U-boat alerts were called during the six-day trip. Escorting Navy destroyers continued to drop depth charges sporadically, claiming two U-boats "kills," although no German subs were sunk by these efforts. Several of the more seasoned members of the Ninth were already trained in basic artillery tactics. Those men soon found themselves helping to man the *Biddle*'s 5-inch gun crews. When relieved from their shift on deck, several of these breathlessly reported spotting the prow of a sunken tanker just off the Virginia coast, sent to the bottom less than a fortnight before the *Biddle*'s departure. After this report and as the depth charging continued, nerves began to fray, and several poker games turned into fistfights among the Marines cooped up in the holds and bunks down below. Others, feeling violently seasick from the late winter swells, stayed in their bunks as much as possible and closed their eyes to quell their nausea pangs. Unaware until now of the true menace posed by roving U-boat packs offshore, Jack and many other queasy Leathernecks thought to themselves as the blasts of the depth charges reverberated through the holds: "*Damn! Will we be next*?"

After hugging the U.S. coastline, the lights of Havana were spotted on the evening of Feburary 16, and the *Biddle* and her escorts followed along the Cuban coast. In the early morning hours three days later, another landfall was sighted—the rocky promontories surrounding Guantanamo Bay—and Jack and the Ninth's sea-weary "landlubbers" disembarked for what would be an eight-month stay.

2

"Where're You Going, Marine?" The Road From Cuba to the South Pacific

Our time in Cuba was spent in advanced training, much with World War I equipment. U-boats roved the area's seas, and one was rammed by our destroyer just out of our bay, its occupants being brought and "brigged" ashore.

Our outfit consisted of 155MM artillery guns, 90MM anti-aircraft [guns], search lights, radar units, and special weapons—of 40 & 20MM guns.

We soon learned that we would be shipping out, and found that we would be joining the 1st Marine Division in the first U.S. offensive of World War II in the Solomon Islands, specifically Guadalcanal.

Jack H. McCall, Sr.

"Where're you going, Marine?"
"I'm off to Sumatra, son:
Killing Christians there, a godless mob,
And it may or may not be my job,
But it will before we're done!"

Popular Marine Corps rhyme, author unknown

Before entering Guantanamo Bay, the *Biddle* passed through a large anti-submarine net. Despite its bright, crystalline blue waters and the exotic trees and blooming shrubs, "Gitmo" Bay displayed a military sense of purpose to it: barges, small craft and sub chasers plied the azure waters of the bay, and barracks, camouflaged gun installations and searchlight positions studded the coast. The Marines' excitement (coupled with their relief to get the hell off the *Biddle*) was palpable. As he gathered up his gear and prepared to leave the *Biddle*, Jack thought to himself: "So, *this* is war!"

On disembarking, the Ninth formed up by batteries and platoons and moved out—mainly on foot—to Defense Point, a craggy promontory overlooking Guantanamo Bay. The Point projected well into the Bay, and the Ninth's guard posts on the leeward and windward sides of the bay's entrance provided an excellent vantage point for watching the incoming shipping and searching for U-boats. Unlike the Army elsewhere, which often hired laborers or contractors to build their barracks and facilities, the first order of business for Jack and his buddies was to help complete their own partially constructed camp. Although some brick and wooden barracks were complete and available, the Ninth's Marines had the chore of finishing some half-finished wooden facilities started by the recently departed 4th Defense Battalion and 5th Marines. This work, which began soon after they landed, included setting up latrines, mess halls, guard posts and huts. No heavy equipment for the unit was yet available, and the task essentially was all labor by hand—moving lumber, breaking rock, digging holes for fenceposts and latrines.

Added to these labors was continued training in infantry tactics, since the Battalion would not receive its artillery and heavy equipment for at least three more months. While Boot Camp training had been grueling, the new privates soon learned that there was also much that it had not taught them. Parris Island had provided them the emotional armor and toughening-up they needed to survive as Marines, but little else in the way of serious combat skills. That was about to be remedied by the Ninth's senior NCOs. One hard-bitten Gunnery Sergeant, a grizzled veteran of World War I and the Corps's 1920s Central American campaigns, held high his copy of the Marines' field manual on basic infantry training, only to throw it over his shoulder, pointedly telling his men that he would teach them everything they needed to know for survival. The Ninth's men also soon learned how to dig—one and two-man foxholes; trenches; bunkers; radio and "commo" positions; gun pits—as if their life depended on it. Those assigned as artillerymen began receiving their first training in seacoast-defense and antiaircraft work, training in shifts on obsolete 6-inch naval guns and 3-inch AA guns. Despite the long days, full military discipline continued—drills; inspections; periodic forced marches with full packs (some across the Naval Operating Base's golf course, leading the more sarcastic of the Leathernecks to suggest to flustered Navy officers that they were "just playing through"); personal equipment layouts; etc. One major test for the entire unit was the completion of a fifty-mile forced march with rifle, full pack and field equipment. The course took Jack and his buddies over salt flats, high ridges and through a semitropical rain forest. The Battalion completed the grueling march within 24 hours, although not without its share of blisters, sprained ankles and bruised and bloodied feet. As Battery A skipper Henry Reichner recalled, it was not only the distance that made this march with full gear so exhausting: "We made well over four miles an hour with packs in intense heat—not enjoyable to those with an overdose of rum or beer."

Among the field exercises, the new hands had their first experience of bayonet and judo training. This was taught by Captain Walter Wells, a tall, cocky and imposing young officer. He was a former collegiate wrestler at Columbia University and a muscular expert in self-defense, who prided himself in his mastery of bayonet drill and hand-to-hand fighting. Jack and his peers had to endure Wells's rigorous and occasionally terrifying classes on these tactics. Nevertheless, his awestruck students could surprise "Waldo" Wells at times and could fight back with vigor. Frank Marshall, another veteran of the Ninth, recalled one of Captain Wells's early bayonet-training classes:

> Captain Wells was a man of supreme self-confidence in his ability to defend himself. This was demonstrated often when he found that the men were reluctant to charge him with bare bayonets as directed. He finally convinced one class by getting a big fellow irritated with taunts. . .irritated enough to lose his temper and charge the Captain full bore with M-1 and naked blade out-thrust. Wells neatly sidestepped, popped one hand on the muzzle and the other up under the butt and flipped the hapless attacker buns over brains to the ground. The man wasn't hurt—just scuffed up a little—and more than amazed at his put-down. Wells gazed at the prostrate Marine for a second and remarked to himself, *sotto voce*, "Goddam . . . gonna have to watch that."

Captain Wells' bayonet training was intended to instill fighting spirit in his men, but at this time, the Ninth's primary adversary was certainly not yet the Japanese. Instead, with German submarines cruising the waters of the Caribbean and Atlantic virtually unmolested, the likely menaces were U-boats, surface raiders or German naval parties. As torpedoed freighters and tankers periodically limped into Guantanamo Bay, Jack and the other Marines soon began training in operation of the Naval Base's 6-inch coast defense guns, practiced anti-landing drills, and manned lookout posts to watch for enemy submarines. Lookout duty generally meant sharing one's sun-baked post with the local scorpions and large Cuban iguanas, at least one of which fell prey to a trigger-happy lieutenant's pistol. It sometimes meant patrols on horseback around the barbed wire fences separating the base from the Cuban interior; these were installed to help protect the base from sabotage by local Falangists (a Cuban offshoot of Francisco Franco's pro-fascist Spanish party) or from sub-landed German commandos. Jack found himself on several horse patrols led by Lieutenant Box. A self-admitted "city boy," Box found the "horse Marine" patrols a bit absurd: "All we had were a couple of guys walking around and a horse, and that was supposed to be good enough! We had three horses to patrol the fence and about 40 or 50 guys, I guess."

Still, these efforts were no mere make-work tasks: since early 1942, Nazi submarines plied the Caribbean waters, and the survivors of various sinkings would be routinely brought to Guantanamo for medical care and debriefing by the Navy. At least one of these prowling German subs was within close range of Guantanamo Bay and Allied subchasers, and in August 1942, *U-94* became the quarry instead of the hunter. After being depth-charged and brought to the surface by a Navy seaplane on August 28, 1942, the U-boat was rammed at full speed by the *Oakville*, a Canadian corvette, and its surviving crewmen were captured after they scuttled out of the hatches of their sinking boat. According to the "poop" making the rounds of the Battalion at the time of *U-94*'s destruction, after the *Oakville* rammed *U-94*, the German crew first tried to shoot it out on the surface with the corvette. A machine-gun battle broke out and only the timely arrival of an American destroyer kept the infuriated Canadians from killing the sub's remaining crewmen. These 26 survivors, in due course, were hauled back to Guantanamo Bay, as it was the closest Allied facility. Several members of Jack's battery were detailed to escort the *U-94*'s sodden crewmen to the Naval Operating Base's brig near Caravetta Point and *Oberleutnant zur See* Ites (the sub's wounded and highly decorated skipper) and a wounded machinist for medical treatment.

The fact that they were now prisoners seemed to do little to quash the cocky Nazis' superiority complexes. Despite their arrogance and the close proximity of the POWs' brig to the Ninth's obstacle course (which ensured the jeering of the Germans anytime a clumsy leatherneck took a fall during a workout), the Ninth's Marines were able to put them in their place, at least verbally. One officer, Captain Norm Pozinsky, the skipper of the 90mm Group's Battery D, spoke fluent German. Accordingly, Captain Pozinsky was able to serve back at least as many taunts and insults as any bitter *U-bootmann* would send Pozinsky's way. Accompanied by Captain Pozinsky and Gunnery Sergeant Smith (*nee* Schmidt, a World War One veteran—some said, of the Kaiser's army), the Ninth's guard detachment was lucky enough to escort their prisoners all the way to Miami. Since this was the closest the 9th Defense had yet come to hostile action at the time, it instilled a new air of excitement and realism to the otherwise drab monotony of drilling, cleaning, standing inspections, policing the area and guarding the coastline. After 3 1/2 months of this tedium, more excitement came as the heavy equipment began arriving in earnest towards the end of May. The Battalion's training then began to take a more coherent and focused form.

The heavy artillery core of the Ninth would be comprised of the 155mm Group: two batteries (A and B), each now armed with four 1918-vintage 155mm "GPF" long-range guns, which made up the seacoast defense portion of the unit. Another large portion of the 9th Defense was comprised of Batteries C, D, E and F, making up the 90mm Antiaircraft ("AA") Group. Each of these four batteries now had four 90mm AA guns, networked together with searchlights and sound detection teams. Most importantly, the Ninth was issued six radar sets—five SCR-268 fire control sets and a SCR-270 long-range detection set. Light AA support was provided by Batteries G, H and I forming the Special Weapons Group. Its batteries were armed principally with 20mm Oerlikon and 40mm Bofors light automatic guns and water-cooled .50 caliber heavy machine guns. The infantry support firepower of all of these batteries combined was substantial, as the Special Weapons Group's guns potentially could be used (and, as will be seen, on one occasion would be so used) to stop a ground attack. Coupled with this already powerful force was the shock impact of a full platoon of eight M-3 light tanks, assigned as part of the Headquarters and Service ("H&S") Group.

Some fifty years later, Joe Pratl stands next to a 155mm M1918 "GPF" heavy artillery piece as originally issued to Batteries A and B of the Ninth. (Courtesy of Joseph Pratl)

Let it not be believed, however, that much of the Ninth's equipment was well and truly new; it was "new" only in the sense that the unit had just been issued it. Old World War I 155s; old Springfield rifles for many (although quite a few Marines, including most of Battery B, trained in Cuba with the new M-1 Garand semi-automatic rifles); out-of-date equipment and field gear; and, apart from their personal weapons, none of the heavy weapons' crews had fired a shot yet to calibrate their guns.

Part of the reason for the obsolescence and shortage of first-rate equipment may have been due to military-wide supply shortfalls, but part also was directly related to pre-war funding issues. As a branch of the Department of the Navy, the Marine Corps was utterly dependent on the Navy for its funding allocations and equipment procurement needs. Before the war, the Corps nominally received about 20% of the Navy's manpower and funding allocations, but the Navy earmarked a large proportion of these funds to maintain its own internal programs. Fundamentally, apart from payrolls, uniforms and subsistence-related budgets, the Corps received little to no funding for major projects or new equipment until after Pearl Harbor, making it very much the the navy's poor stepsister.

Each Marine, true to his Boot Camp basic training, was also prepared to serve not just as an artilleryman, ammo handler, radar crewman, radioman or tank gunner, but also as an infantryman. These basic training skills would be put to the test in due time. However, the selection of crews for these weapons were made using the most rudimentary vocational testing standards. No special aptitude testing was necessary for a 9th Defense Marine to end up as an AA gunner, a sound detection expert, a tank driver or (as did Jack) a water purification expert. The selection process was much more random and sporadic: *We need gunners and ammo handlers for the 155s; you look like you've lifted a few weights in your time; you'll do; get in line! We need radiomen; anybody here know Morse code? Good enough; now, get going.* To form the Tank Platoon, the platoon's sergeants asked which of the Marines assigned to the motor pool had been farm kids who had driven tractors: that was all the job experience needed. Jack was selected and trained to become a "gizmo," in his case, a water purification specialist, as well as serving as a basic Marine artilleryman. In Jack's case, when asked if he had studied anything special in high school, his admission that he had taken chemistry classes was probably all his leaders needed to hear: *Good; he'll be able to handle chemicals without blowing us all up.*

By early July, the 9th was training seven days a week, fifteen to twenty hours a day—though, still, without "ammo" or without test-firing their artillery pieces and tank guns. By this time, though, some additional experience was infused into the Battalion by the arrival of a large contingent of veterans of the 5th Defense Battalion, the Iceland-based "Polar

Bears," who were reassigned to flesh out the Ninth and arrived in Guantanamo Bay in June 1942. Despite the rigorous training and tedious moments, life in Cuba had its own vices and, for some, its tawdry rewards.

Caimanera, a town across Gitmo Bay located on Cuban soil, was the local booze and bordello area. Together with another nearby hamlet, the "Brooks Island Resort," Caimanera's red-light district became so infamous and such a source of venereal disease that, in early September 1942, both it and Brooks Island were declared off-limits by order of the base commander. Beer and rum were cheap and plentiful, and the Marines took full advantage of it. The Ninth had three slop chutes around Defense Point—one for officers, one for NCOs and one for all the enlisted men ("EMs")—where beer could be bought by the case, and nightly brawls were a common occurrence, at least at the EMs' slop chute. The enlisted Marines would also smuggle in banana cases full of the local brands of beer ("*cerveza*"), Hatuey and Cristal, 44 bottles to the case, three cents a bottle. Twenty-five cents were good for a quart of Bacardi rum. A private's pay was low, even by 1940s standards. At $21 per month, with only five dollars left after all the required deductions, each platoon's members would form tight-knit circles of pals to pool their meager funds for beer, rum, cigarettes, shaving supplies and other sundries. When time permitted, they might take whatever leftover money they had and go for high-stakes poker games, or frequent Caimanera's seedy establishments. Such pastimes provided an off-duty chance for young men from highly diverse backgrounds to get to learn more about their fellow Americans.

Downtown Caimanera, Cuba, circa 1942. (Author's collection)

Privates McCall and Downs threw in their lot at the EMs' slop chute with a good-natured Polish-American private from Erie, Pennsylvania, John Dobkowski. After a few drinks, Dobkowski taught his newfound buddies Polish drinking songs. Another source of pratfalls was an on-post Chinese restaurant, where Pogiebait, Dobkowski and "Rosie" Downs would occasionally go to get a break from mess hall fare. While the food was cheap, the main source of amusement was provided by the fact that this Chinese restaurant featured fruit pies as dessert. Without fail, someone would buy a pie and with a good-natured shout of "*Take that, you bastard!*", heave it across a table at a buddy with whom he had a temporary grudge. Inevitably, this triggered a pie fight and general free-for-all that lasted until the harried restaurant manager threatened to call in the Shore Patrol, the Navy's police squad, and the pie-encrusted Marines would help clean up the joint in repayment for the damage they had caused.

Quite a few of the Ninth's Marines took advantage of cheap alcohol to unwind from the rigorous training and work schedule. Likewise, so did Jack—once, so much so that, after one particularly wild night in "Caimanooch," he consumed one too many *"Cuba Libre"* rum-and-cola drinks, passed out, and missed the liberty boat returning the Marines to camp. The result was inevitable. Jack was charged by his platoon sergeant with committing an "unauthorized absence"—the Marines' equivalent of being absent without leave—a serious breach of military discipline, which carried with it a possible court martial and potential jail time in a Navy brig. Jack was now in very hot water with Colonel David Nimmer, the Ninth's new battalion commander, who had already cultivated a reputation as being a tough disciplinarian by chewing out the entire Battalion *en masse* on his first day in command. The Colonel was ready to throw the book at him and told him so at a "masthead" proceeding convened for the imposition of non-judicial (*i.e.*, non-court martial) punishment. Jack's battery commander, 1st Lieutenant Box, spoke up on Jack's behalf, and told the Colonel that, until then, Private McCall had been a model Marine. Lieutenant Box was already well respected among his subordinates; his willingness to stick his neck out for Jack clinched his reputation as being something other than the average hard-nosed Marine officer. Because Jack got off with only a stern reprimand and a smirk from the "Old Man" and some additional guard and KP duty instead of brig time or a court-martial, he counted himself lucky, indeed.

As befitting its seamy reputation, Caimanera was known for its "senoritas" of the night, of various ages and reputations, and their unromantic solicitations for business could be heard amidst the traffic on its streets. Frank Marshall remembered their cries for business: "Hey, Ma-leen, peese up a rope!" "*Una peso*, Chico!" These off-limits transactions nevertheless indirectly provided Jack, Al Downs and some of their buddies with an opportunity for revenge on an obnoxious junior NCO.

This corporal had been the bane of Jack's platoon and, in particular, Jack's squad. He tended to take his two stripes very seriously and lorded it over the privates as if he were the battalion commander himself. This hard-bitten corporal was notorious for keeping a pint of gin in his footlocker. As part of his morning ritual, he would break out the pint, take a swig, and gargle with it, a stunt that never ceased to amaze his squad members. After one weekend liberty in Caimanera, as they passed by one of the now off-limits bordellos, Jack and his pals thought of the perfect plan to get the pesky "boy corporal" off their backs, permanently.

A rumor circulated after one weekend's liberty that Jack, Al and company had passed by a Caimanera bordello, where—clearly visible from an open window—one of the Ninth's Marines was spotted *in flagrante delicto* with a local prostitute. The only trouble was that his face could not be seen; his only distinguishing characteristic was that he was wearing bright-red skivvies while in this compromising position. A really good and juicy piece of "scuttlebutt" like this one tended to make the rounds very quickly, and from Taps that Sunday to Reveille the next morning, it was the talk of the battery. The question of the day was: "Who was that masked man?" The over-zealous corporal heard the rumors and swore he'd find the culprit and hand him over to Lieutenant Box for disciplinary action, for "conduct unbecoming a Marine." The corporal changed his harsh tune somewhat after the next morning's inspection. Asking "What is *this*?," a clearly bewildered officer pulled nothing less than a pair of bright-red skivvies out of the corporal's footlocker, in front of a crowd of at-attention, but bemused, Marine privates.

Another Marine, Gene Duffy, enjoyed himself enormously in Cuba; so much so one night that, to the concern of his friends one Monday morning, he had not made it back to post from liberty. Duffy was not in evidence after Reveille was trumpeted and the order to fall in for inspection was given. Duffy's battery was led by a Marine Gunner, a former sergeant who was now the U.S.M.C.'s equivalent of a warrant officer—neither NCO nor commissioned officer—and a man who neither gave slack nor took any. Duly noting Duffy's absence from his formation, the Gunner also quietly observed a group of Cuban day laborers passing nearby, carrying lumber and various implements. One of these workers was oddly taller than the average Cuban and was wearing heavy Marine "boondockers" and a huge sombrero-like hat, pulled down low over his face. The Gunner sauntered over to the unorthodox-looking Cuban laborer and, according to Battery B's Frank Chadwick, initiated the following conversation:

"*Buenos dias. Que paso, amigo*?"

"*Que paso, Marino*?"

"I'll tell you what: if you can sing me the Cuban national anthem, I'll let you keep going. But if not, *Duffy*," the Gunner muttered, "your ass is in the brig!"

The "*amigo*" peeped out from under his sombrero and pensively blew out a mouthful of air. A brief silence followed, and then the miscreant mournfully blurted out, "Let's go!"

The End of the Ninth's Cuban Sojourn: The Voyage to "Destination Unknown"

By September 1942, the scuttlebutt was that the Ninth would not be living out the rest of its wartime days in the balmy Cuban climate. Since August, the 1st Marine Division, reinforced by the 3rd Defense Battalion and Marine and Army air units, had been engaged in the fight of its life in a Solomon Islands jungle hellhole called Guadalcanal. Orders were soon cut by Marine Corps headquarters, transferring the 9th Defense to the Fleet Marine Force-Pacific.

On October 4, Jack and the Ninth were on the move again—this time, in preparation for actual combat. The Battalion was loaded on three transports, the U.S.S. *Kenmore* (a twenty-year-old Presidential Lines civilian liner now under Navy auspices), the S.S. *Robin Wentley* and the S.S. *Fairisle* (the latter two being civilian-crewed Merchant Marine vessels). The three ships sailed around noontime, accompanied by a fourth cargo ship and a destroyer, en route to "Destination Unknown." Jack had boarded the *Kenmore*, headed for the Pacific Ocean via the Panama Canal. Despite the intended secrecy of their departure, many of the Ninth's Marines were more than a little startled to see large parties of Cubans cheerfully lined up on shore, serenading the ships with songs and bidding them adieu. To add to the suspense, as the small convoy sailed through the submarine nets and booms securing the mouth of Guantanamo Bay, an escorting Navy destroyer detected what seemed to be a German submarine and dropped a defensive pattern of depth charges for good measure. *Wham!* The troops below decks were highly perturbed when the series of concussions reverberated loudly off the *Kenmore*'s hull. Sounding much like a giant sledgehammer being slammed against a steel drum, the blasts pitched men out of their bunks and vibrated through the old ship's decks and bulkheads. Having gone through this before on the *Biddle*'s voyage to Cuba was not any more reassuring, and choruses of obscenities, curses and yells of "Jesus Christ!" echoed through the *Kenmore*'s decks until the senior NCOs moved in to reassure and otherwise shut up their clamoring troops.

The heavily defended Panama Canal Zone provided further evidence, if any was necessary, that the unit was en route to a war zone. Roving patrols of Army MPs and the Shore Patrol, the Navy's MP equivalent, were not enough to deter a few Marines from making impromptu shore leaves. While the *Kenmore* was temporarily tied up in Balboa, on the western side of the Panama Canal, one enterprising soul wrapped up his uniform in a waterproof poncho and dropped the bundle over the *Kenmore*'s side. Stark naked, he went down one of the mooring ropes and slipped into the water. Groping around frantically in the dark and smelly brew, he found that his bundle of clothes was rapidly being washed out to sea. Realizing that the jig was up, the Marine decided to surrender himself. After swimming back to the ship, he hoisted himself up onto the accommodation ladder. Still nude and dripping wet, he briskly marched up to the officer of the deck and, undaunted, gave the befuddled "OD" a snappy salute: "Request permission to come aboard, sir!" With the officer's permission not being immediately forthcoming, the Marine bolted past the OD up the ladder and ran for his compartment. Being easily identified, he was caught fairly quickly by the ship's guards, amid the cheers and hoots of his buddies. Several other AWOL Marines were seized on shore by the SPs. It was an easy matter to apprehend them because the official duty uniform in the Canal Zone was khakis, while the Marines aboard the *Kenmore* were in green field dungarees. When the Navy area commander informed Colonel Nimmer that his SPs had apprehended his absent men and planned to escort them back to the *Kenmore*, the Colonel briskly responded that, as far as he was concerned, the Navy could keep them all in the brig; he did not want or need that kind of Marine in his outfit. The *Kenmore* resumed sail without this handful.

After passing through the canal, surrounded by the green jungle and the steel and concrete locks, big guns and fortifications of the Canal Zone, the little flotilla entered the Pacific. It was a sobering thought to most, if not all, of the Ninth's personnel that they still had not test-fired most of their major weapons. They were due to meet up with their ammunition supplies later, and the heavy guns were stowed deep in the ships' holds. The convoy's naval escort dwindled to one ancient, four-stacker destroyer, itself likely a veteran of World War I. Despite this destroyer's presence, long-range Japanese submarines were a possible threat. As Captain Hank Reichner recalled: "The *Kenmore* was no speedster. The maximum speed of the convoy was about six knots, and at times, when things broke down, we were almost dead in the water." Even so, the small convoy was steaming well out of the range of friendly air cover. The *Kenmore* had some armament onboard—one 5-inch and five 3-inch deck guns, plus various .50 caliber machine guns—hardly enough to deter the determined skipper of a Japanese submarine.

The U.S.S. *Kenmore*, circa 1942. (Author's collection)

The *Kenmore* was cramped and grimy, and it stank as a result of being host to so many passengers with limited chances to bathe. Jack and the Ninth's Marines and their Navy traveling companions were rationed to limited periods for showering, during which the showers dispensed only salt water. Some men learned the hard way the means of making the best of a proper salt-water shower. As Frank Marshall recounted, the first lesson was to use the right kind of soap:

> One young Marine, desperate for a good, soapy shower, believed the rumor that Lava soap was a good salt water type. He climbed into the shower, tried to lather up his close-cropped hair and wound up with a skull cap of black slime that was insoluble in the sea water. He was nearly reduced to tears in his frustration, and woe betide the man who tried to make a joke of it.

Likewise, fresh water for drinking was strictly rationed

by compartments, each compartment having a limit of only one hour of fresh water or until the "fresh" water (which was yellowish and reeked of chlorination) ran out. With each Marines having two canteens to fill, the drinking water usually ran out before the time limit was up. Seasickness again plagued many of the Marines, and with nighttime blackout conditions being in effect, they were often denied a favorite addiction, cigarettes on deck, for fear of the glow being spotted by enemy subs. The Special Weapons Group's .50 caliber machine guns were lined up on the boat deck, four per side, further constricting what little open-air space was available.

The *Kenmore* had been reconfigured to accommodate 2,000 persons, but with approximately 1,500 Navy personnel also being aboard (including two battalions of Seabees and the crews of eight PT boats, which boats were lashed to the decks of the *Fairisle* and *Wentley*), the Ninth's 1,200-odd Marines had to share extremely cramped quarters. Many Leathernecks were billeted in the most peculiar spots imaginable. Several groups slept in the open air on the boat decks or tried to rig hammocks underneath the barrels of the ship's heavy guns. Many others, however (Jack included), were assigned bunks in the *Kenmore*'s hold, which, as Bob Landon of Battery B recalled, could only be described as a "tragedy." The holds reeked of vomit, sweat, grease and bilge water. The bunks in the holds were narrow, cramped and stacked four bunks high. Somehow, each Marine was expected to stow all of his gear in this assigned space except when he went to sleep, at which time, all the seabags were piled up in a cluster in the narrow passageways. The heat and humidity in the troop areas was stifling, and anyone who got the chance to get some fresh air "topside" on watch duty relished the opportunity. Those assigned to the topmost bunks felt these effects the worst; the only saving grace being that, if someone got seasick, at least those in the higher bunks were spared.

Those left without bunks were issued hammocks, which were airier and were slung in the ship's mess area and in the gangways. All hammocks had to be stowed by 4:00 a.m., in time for the cooks to reconfigure the room for mess and to prepare the morning's chow. Chow was served in shifts, the men in each shift having a different color-coded card. Each Marine could expect one warm meal per day and a box lunch for dinner; mess commenced at 10:00 a.m. and lasted until 4:00 p.m. Even with the serving-by-shifts arrangements, chow lines on board the *Kenmore* were lengthy, and after waits of several hours, the Marines at the end of the lines could usually expect little food. It was little wonder that the tired old ship was sarcastically renamed the "Killmore" by many of her disgusted passengers, officers and men alike.

With several thousand young men from rival services onboard, the officers were forced to devise ways to keep their troops and sailors busy. The *Kenmore*'s decks and portions of her hull would be sanded, chipped, scraped, painted and repainted. For the most part, however, the Marines' idle hours onboard were spent in endless games of cards, cleaning clothes (ingeniously washed by suspending pants or shirts on lines, casting the lines off the ship's side, allowing the articles to bounce along in the bow waves!), tending to gear and weapons, and writing letters. After an outbreak of body lice and impetigo, delousing inspections, mandatory applications of merthiolate and salves kept the shipboard medical officers busy. When the salves and ointments seemed to fail, the medical officers decreed that all afflicted personnel must shave their pubic areas and then resume the merthiolate-and-salve treatments. With the outbreak of body lice having been attributed to one of the Marines who had gone AWOL in Balboa and returned unapprehended, venereal disease ("short-arm") inspections, another ample source of humiliation and embarrassment, were conducted by a jaded Navy doctor, who dispensed suitable doses of sarcasm along with the inspection. Whenever a Marine got too close to him during the VD inspection, the old doctor would growl, "Back up, son; I just want to look at it, not marry you!" The officers and NCOs threatened a summary court martial to anyone found to have contracted a social disease. Fortunately, no cases were detected.

Still, it was not all work, nausea, claustrophobia and boredom. As the *Kenmore* and her accompanying ships crossed the Equator, Jack and his buddies—"pollywogs" who had never crossed the Equator—had to be indoctrinated into the mysteries of the briny deep. Equator-crossing ceremonies were traditional rituals on Navy ships for generations and, war or no war, naval tradition had to be obeyed. According to Jack's certificate from the "Ancient Order of the Deep," signed by Davey Jones and "Neptunus Rex" (also known as M. Richardson, Commander, USN, the captain of the *Kenmore*), Private Jack H. McCall, U.S.M.C.R.,

> Has been gathered into our Fold as a TRUSTY SHELLBACK having crossed the equator on board the U.S.S. KENMORE bound from Panama to a unknown destination Longitude—"not given"—Latitude 00 00' 00." Date—"Certified in 1942."

Jack's family asked him many times what was involved in this ceremony, but always without luck. Time and again, Jack's only response would be to roll his eyes around behind his glasses and say, "You're just a pollywog! Shellbacks are sworn to secrecy never to tell a pollywog what happens." Suffice it to say, however, from various descriptions available, the *Kenmore*'s ceremony combined medieval pageantry and semireligious trappings (the grand appearance of King Neptune and his court and Davey Jones before the unworthy pollywogs) with all the worst aspects of fraternity Hell Week (getting stripped down to "skivvy" shorts and being liberally greased with motor oil, being blasted with a fire hose full of cold sea water, etc.), all in the space of one day and on the high seas, at that. Given the rivalries between sailors and Marines, this Equator-crossing ceremony—with the Leathernecks on the *Kenmore* outnumbering the "swabbies," but having to take their abuse in stride and with swallowed pride—must have been especially rigorous.

Several weeks before reaching port, the *Kenmore* ran out of fresh food, and her passengers had to begin using boxed rations intended for combat. These rations were nothing to write home about: several Marines later swore they (like so much else, it seemed) were of World War I vintage, with each box consisting mainly of cans of hash, corned beef ("bully beef") or stew, a can of beans, a pack of hardtack crackers, a tin of powdered coffee and a piece of hard candy. The *Kenmore*'s escorting destroyer, however, was in even worse shape in the way of provisions: it not only ran out of its food rations but also had to maintain continuous watches, which required it to run additional hours for chow calls for its tired and hungry sailors. Believing the *Kenmore* to be better supplied than it actually was, the destroyer's captain requested extra fresh food from the *Kenmore*'s master, only to be advised of the sad state of the *Kenmore*'s own provisions. It took some convincing for the destroyer's captain to accept that the *Kenmore*'s occupants were themselves now living on ancient rations, but, faced with the reality, the destroyer's crew gratefully accepted whatever could be spared. To add to the stress, the benighted *Kenmore* broke down about one week before reaching New Caledonia. The *Fairisle* and *Wentley* and an additional cargo ship made for New Caledonia, leaving the one destroyer to guard the *Kenmore* until she got underway again. The false sighting of a "Japanese sub" by a lookout on the *Kenmore*, resulting in the firing of the *Kenmore*'s stern-mounted 5-inch gun—a tooth-rattling and bone-jarring experience that shook the old ship's fantail—added to everyone's worries as the old liner plied its way towards New Caledonia.

Time: Early November 1942

Place: Aboard U.S.S. Kenmore in mid-Pacific. Officers' meeting in wardroom.

Speaker: Col. David Nimmer

"I have this day received orders for this unit to land in a rear area. I immediately sent a message in reply, stating that this unit was combat ready and demanded assignment to a combat area."

(You could have heard a pin drop.)

Captain Walter Wells

After 39 days at sea, which Jack recalled as being, on the whole, a "nightmare," on November 11, 1942, the little convoy anchored in the outer harbor of Dunbea Bay, the anchorage of Noumea, New Caledonia. The inner harbor was crammed full of the ships of a task force that steamed out of New Caledonia for Guadalcanal, while small craft bobbed and weaved on the bay's waters, trying to clear the larger ships. In the case of one 30-foot sloop, however, these frantic maneuvers were all for naught. As Frank Marshall recounted:

> It was making its way through the navigational maze with a very dignified Army officer as passenger cargo. He was sitting on deck aft of the main mast on a coil of hemp. The three-man crew attempted to jibe the boat about 100 yards off the starboard beam of the

> *Kenmore.* There was a large contingent of Marines and SeaBees at the rail idly watching this maneuver when suddenly things went haywire. The skipper, who was at the helm, started to jibe and the main sheet went loose. All hands on the sailboat panicked, since by this time, they were only about 60 yards from the *Kenmore*'s midship and coming down out of control like gangbusters. By this time, the Army officer lost his cool and began to discuss things with the skipper, who was shouting orders to his crew in frantic Vietnamese—all this to the delight of the spectators on board the *Kenmore.* They began to cheer everyone out of sheer enthusiasm for the welcome comedy relief. Shortly the inevitable happened, and the sloop collided head-on with the unyielding (surprise?) steel hull of the *Kenmore*, lost its bowsprit and headsails and driven by the steady afternoon breeze, began bumping forward along the hull of the *Kenmore*... The applause was thunderous.

A pall would soon be cast on the "comedic relief," however, by somber sights and sounds. As the large task force embarked and the Ninth's far-smaller convoy resumed steam into Noumea's inner harbor, the Marines craned their necks to identify the departing cruisers: the *Juneau*, the *Northampton*, the *Helena*—two of which, the *Juneau* and *Northampton*, would lie at the bottom of Guadalcanal's waters before November had ended. The battleships *Washington* and *South Dakota*—the latter temporarily undergoing repairs—and the damaged aircraft carrier *Enterprise* were also nearby, such ships having been extensively damaged off Guadalcanal. Years later, Frank Yemma, then a private in Lieutenant (soon, Captain) Box's Battery B, recalled a startling incident taking place onboard one of the two battleships:

> I seem to think it was the *South Dakota* because she seemed to be shot up the worst. The order was given to drop anchor, and they literally did drop the anchor and chain and all—-I mean *the whole thing.* These links alone were the size of a couch, and the whole anchor and the whole chain-—the whole team—-went right into the water. It must have got shot away or something.

"Sweet Jesus, will ya look at that?," Yemma muttered to his equally dumbfounded buddies lining the *Kenmore*'s deck. Another sobering touch was added moments later when several Marines on one of the Ninth's transports, peeking through a telescopic gunsight on the ship's stern gun, witnessed a burial-at-sea ceremony in progress. Among others, Yemma clearly heard "Taps" being played from the stern of one of the warships. These manifestations provided more reminders that the Ninth was now on the cusp of the combat zone.

New Caledonia was a French colony—originally under Vichy French control but ultimately falling under the Free French influence of General DeGaulle and his allies—that served as a major staging area for U.S. troops and supplies bound throughout the South Pacific. Contrary to any notions they may have had of New Caledonia being a tropical paradise of dusky, exotic Franco-Tahitian beauties, Dunbea Bay was a large, rear-area military anchorage and encampment populated mainly by Navy and Army personnel with a general hostility to "Gyrenes."

Another new arrival to New Caledonia, 2nd Lieutenant Christopher S. Donner, a former history teacher and Stanford graduate student who later joined the Ninth in June 1943, noted not long after war's end his first impressions of Noumea:

> We loaded into trucks and wound through the wildly colored town, dominated by a large Catholic

> church and the old French barracks. We looked in amazement at the blacks with their hair bleached to a bright orange. Young, attractive French girls moved through the streets, and everywhere were small statured Malays, the women resembling little dolls. [However, the] French were almost hostile, the stores charged outrageous prices, wine was $15 a bottle, whiskey $20. . . .Hard liquor was scarce.

While the French colonists' homes were attractive, the port area was a muddy quagmire, the colonists (particularly supporters of the Vichy government) largely despised the Americans and, with combat approaching, there was no time to waste ashore anyway. The Ninth was now assigned to the I Marine Amphibious Corps—"I MAC"—whose blue shoulder insignia included the Southern Cross, the famed Southern Hemisphere constellation now readily visible to all after crossing the Equator.

It was also common knowledge to Jack and his pals by now that the *Kenmore*'s "Destination Unknown" had a name—Guadalcanal. It was not as if, however, their operational security efforts had been as tight as the Ninth's officers may have desired. To his consternation, Battery A commander Hank Reichner was greeted on arriving in Noumea by his best friend from civilian days, now stationed in the Navy at Noumea, as soon as Reichner disembarked from the *Kenmore*. While Reichner had no idea of his friend's whereabouts, the same could not be said for his old pal, who exclaimed joyfully, "There you are, old man! I knew you were coming!" "How did you know that?," Reichner asked suspiciously. "Uh, I'd heard all about it," was his friend's less-than-reassuring response. So much for operational security.

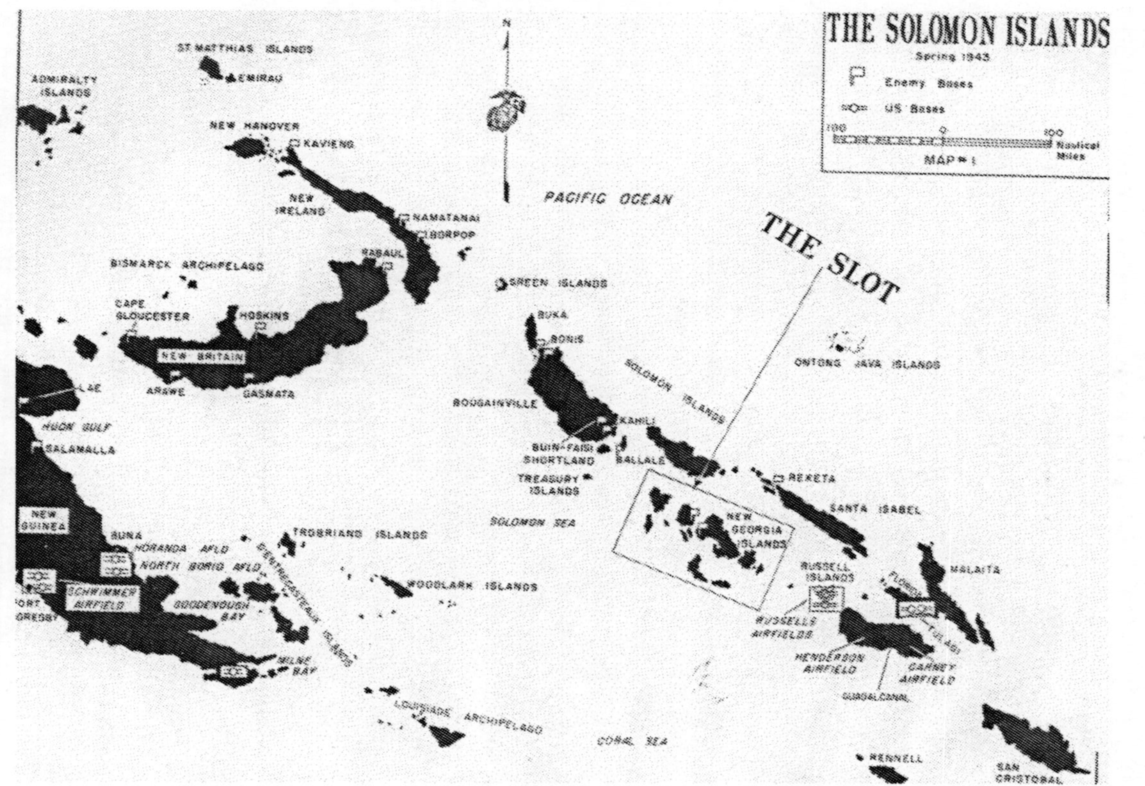
THE SOLOMON ISLANDS
Spring 1943
Enemy Bases
US Bases
100
0
100
Nautical Miles
MAP # 1
N
ST. MATTHIAS ISLANDS
EMIRAU
ADMIRALTY ISLANDS
NEW HANOVER
KAVIENG
NEW IRELAND
NAMATANAI
BORPOP
RABAUL
BISMARCK ARCHIPELAGO
CAPE GLOUCESTER
HOSKINS
NEW BRITAIN
ARAWE
GASMATA
LAE
HUON GULF
SALAMAUA
NEW GUINEA
BUNA
DOBODURA AFLD
NORTH BORIO AFLD
SCHWIMMER AIRFIELD
PORT MORESBY
GOODENOUGH BAY
D'ENTRECASTEAUX ISLANDS
MILNE BAY
TROBRIAND ISLANDS
WOODLARK ISLANDS
LOUISIADE ARCHIPELAGO
CORAL SEA
SOLOMON SEA
PACIFIC OCEAN
GREEN ISLANDS
BUKA
BONIS
BOUGAINVILLE
KAHILI
BUIN-FAISI
SHORTLAND
BALLALE
TREASURY ISLANDS
SOLOMON ISLANDS
THE SLOT
ONTONG JAVA ISLANDS
REKETA
SANTA ISABEL
NEW GEORGIA ISLANDS
RUSSELL ISLANDS
RUSSELLS AIRFIELDS
FLORIDA
TULAGI
MALAITA
HENDERSON AIRFIELD
CARNEY AIRFIELD
GUADALCANAL
RENNELL
SAN CRISTOBAL

At Noumea, the Ninth's materiel on board the *Fairisle* and *Robin Wentley* were off-loaded to other ships because, as merchant ships, they were prohibited at this stage of the war from entering a forward combat area, and—more to the point—their Merchant Marine crews refused to enter the combat area without hazardous duty pay, which was not forthcoming. Also, because it had been "administratively" loaded in Cuba, the *Kenmore* had to be reloaded for combat operations, a task that would require maximum speed and efficiency in disembarking non-essential supplies and cargo and in readying the ship for combat. The working parties followed a grueling four hours-on, eight-hours off work routine; all cargo movement was by hand, cargo nets, block and tackle. Anything deemed to be merely a comfort item was regarded as unessential and was unloaded at Noumea for storage.

For Jack, this process entailed at least one nerve-wracking incident while he, Frank Chadwick, and a group of others were detailed to help unload ammunition in the ship's forward hold. The ammunition had been loaded in no apparent order: 155mm shells were intermixed with other calibers of shells and small arms ammunition, and in the course of sailing, some of the unevenly-distributed cargo had tilted and fallen. Worse, the wooden pallets to which the larger shells (the 90s and 155s) were strapped were poorly banded, so that, as their pallets were hoisted out of the hold by the ship's crane, the shells *very* perceptibly moved around on the pallets.

Worse was yet to come. As one pallet of 155mm shells was being hauled out of the hot, dingy and dirty hold, twelve shells per pallet, several of the 95-pound shells *did* work loose and they fell back into the hold. These hit several other pallets of shells, which then broke loose, and shells began careening off the walls and bulkheads. In the dark, the only thing Jack and his buddies could see were the sparks being struck as steel scraped against steel. The little group threw themselves against the bulkheads, convinced they were to go up in a fireball; fortunately, because none of the shells were fitted with fuses (which themselves were present in the hold, although stored separately, as were bags and cardboard tubes of gunpowder for the unit's big guns), nothing exploded.

As soon as it was apparent that no real damage had been done, the hold erupted in jeers, curses and obscenities. These were aimed chiefly at the idiot ordnance personnel who had supposedly secured the pallets and shells together in the first place. After venting their frustrations, the ammo detail decided it had earned itself a short break. At this moment, a belligerent second lieutenant appeared at the hold's hatchway, looking down into the dark. He immediately began shouting, "Knock it off down there, dammit! Do you want me to come down there? Get back to work!" The group wasted no time with its response, and rank be damned. One of the work party yelled back: "Come down here and say that to our faces, *sir*, if you have the guts to, and we'll throw your ass overboard!" Rank or no rank, the "shavetail" beat a hasty retreat, wisely letting the ammo team continue to catch its collective breath and regroup a little longer, and the unloading process eventually resumed without further incident. Still amazed at their luck years later, Jack said, "It was just a wonder we didn't all get blown up;" as Chadwick recalled, "God was with us this day." The same officer was later encountered by a slightly more senior Hank Reichner, who recalled: "[While] loading the 155 projectiles, tempers ran short. There was one particularly obnoxious officer running things in the #1 hold. I was on deck when one of the winch operators looked at me and said, 'Say the word, Lieutenant, and I'll drop this next pallet on the son-of-a-bitch.' Fortunately, cool heads prevailed."

While the ship-to-ship loading was backbreaking work for all involved, some found the laborious process had its own rewards. While David ("Biggie") Slater and a team of Battalion H&S Battery communications men were unloading one of the transports, they found a crate marked "Medical Supplies." They asked one of the Battalion's assigned medical corpsman who had personally helped pack and load all the Ninth's medical supplies, what it was, but he did not recognize the crate. "Beats me, fellas," the medic muttered; "go ahead and take a look if you like." On breaking open the crate, Slater and his pals were overjoyed to find the crate was a case of scotch, which—needless to say—Biggie and company "liberated" after destroying the crate to hide the evidence. Fortunately for the Ninth's cadre of officers, this same group did not happen to inspect the stack of coffins accompanying the Battalion's medical supplies since leaving Cuba. As Hank Reichner recalled: "Among other items that arrived in preparation for our voyage to God-knows- where were several coffins assigned as part of the Battalion's Table of Equipment. Colonel Nimmer solved the problem of maximizing their use by authorizing the packing of a liquor supply in each one for future use!"

Had Biggie Slater and his buddies only known what a treat barely escaped their grasp . . .

After 16 days of frenetic activities, the *Kenmore* and another Navy transport, the *Hunter Liggett*, set sail on November 27, this time filled with a much more somber-minded group of young Marines. Battery B, led by Captains Stafford and Box, remained aboard the *Kenmore*. Jack boarded the *Liggett* with the contingent from the 155mm Group's H&S Battery. An advance party from Battery A had already departed for Guadalcanal six days earlier on the transport U.S.S. *Neville*, while Colonel Nimmer and his flew from New Caledonia to Guadalcanal for an advance reconnaissance. Exactly where they all were going, and the grim situation they would face there, was no longer secret, and they were going there, a more or less brand-new outfit, with old and often untested equipment.

Apart from some firing of the Special Weapons Group's .50 calibers and a few 20mms at a airplane-towed target at low altitude, performed a few hours after the convoy set sail from Noumea (as to which test, several veterans gratefully noted, they were overjoyed that the tow plane was unscathed!), practice gunnery conducted on Guantanamo of the 90mm guns, and (for the 155mm Group) firing drills conducted with obsolete ex-naval pieces now used as coast-defense guns, several of the Ninth's major weapons remained relatively untried. Despite their training in Cuba, the knowledge that the 155mm Group had still never had the opportunity to test-fire its big guns gnawed on the minds of its officers, NCOs and enlisted men alike.

The Battalion was bound for what the Japanese rank-and-file were beginning to call to one another in whispers, out of earshot of their officers and sergeants, "Starvation Island" or *Gadarukanaru*, the "Island of Death:" a place from which, once sent, no one returned, and an island hellhole that, three months into the battle, was a tropical Verdun, sucking into its maw thousands of both Japan's and America's young soldiers, sailors and airmen. It was not for nothing that "The Slot," the narrow waterway separating between Guadalcanal and the various outlying islands in the Solomons chain, was called Ironbottom Sound: the sea floor was already covered with scores of Allied and Japanese ships and aircraft, and many more victims were yet to come.

Before landing on Guadalcanal, Jack recalled some unexpected consternation late one night aboard the *Liggett*. He was wakened from a groggy sleep by wild yelling. As Pogiebait mumbled "What the hell . . .," a nearby Marine muttered, "They just caught a pair of perverts onboard." To a chorus of curses and jeers, the two suspects were roughly seized from the bunk where they were found and were hauled topside by a pair of NCOs, where Jack recalled them being kept, "penned up like animals in the open," as an object for general spite and contempt for several days until the troopship reached its destination.

As the Ninth's convoy steamed into view of Guadalcanal in the twilight of December 3, 1942, Jack and his fellow Marines and Seabees scrambled out of the ships' innards to line the rails and catch a glimpse of the island's darkened silhouette. Over fifty years later, another of the Ninth's leathernecks, Willie Dufour, would remember some "wise guy's" decision to pick this moment to play a then-popular record, *Blues In the Night*, with its sinister minor-key opening notes filtering onto the deck. "Blues in the night," indeed! The sight of the blood-soaked island was enough to give even the most hardened warrior a case of the blues.

Guantanamo Bay had not been war, after all. The real war was finally here for Jack and the 9th Defense.

3

Guadalcanal: The Fighting Ninth Meets the Island of Death

Our mission [on Guadalcanal], besides sea coast defense, was to defend the construction of an additional air field to Henderson. Air raids, both day and night, were frequent, one of which reached the size of one hundred Japanese planes. Mosquitoes, malaria, and monsoons all took their toll, and several men were lost to malaria.

Jack H. McCall, Sr.

For us who were there, or whose friends were there, Guadalcanal is not a name but an emotion, recalling desperate fights in the air, furious night naval battles, frantic work at supply or construction, savage fighting in the sodden jungle, nights broken by screaming bombs and deafening explosions of naval shells.

Samuel Eliot Morison

And when he gets to Heaven,
To St. Peter he will tell:
Another Marine reporting, Sir;
I've served my time in Hell!

Inscribed on a Marine's tombstone on Guadalcanal

If nothing to date had served as a wake-up call to the horrors of warfare, Jack's arrival on board the *Hunter Liggett* to Guadalcanal's waters provided him with a quick and grim reality check. Several major naval engagements had just been fought shortly before the Ninth's arrival. In mid-November's Naval Battle of Guadalcanal, while a U.S. naval squadron had crippled the Japanese battleship *Kirishima* (scuttled by her own fleet) and sunk a heavy cruiser, three destroyers and eleven transports, the U.S. Navy had still suffered a mauling. The new battleship *South Dakota* had taken over forty hits. Days before the Ninth's arrival, the Navy had lost the cruiser *Northampton* (which Jack and his pals had just seen leaving Noumea a few weeks earlier) and had three other cruisers crippled in the Battle of Tassafaronga on November 30. This vicious naval engagement had delayed Battery A, on board the *Neville*, from coming ashore; that ship and several others bearing reinforcements were forced to wait at anchor for several days off the island of Espiritu Santo, some 600 miles southeast of Guadalcanal, until the Japanese naval threat cooled down.

The oily detritus of Tassafaronga and the other recent sea battles still floated upon the water as the *Neville*, then later the *Kenmore* and the *Hunter Liggett*, sailed into Ironbottom Sound on December 3, 1942 and weighed anchor off Koli Point, near the beaches on which the 1st Marine Division had stormed ashore in early August and where major fighting had occurred early in November. In Noumea's inner harbor, after the reinforcing task force had departed for Guadalcanal, the Ninth's transports had again passed the length of the *South Dakota*. This was not long after her battle with the *Kirishima*, and the U.S. battleship rested at anchor with, as Jack remembered, "a hole in her side as big as a school bus." He recalled that he and his buddies stared at the massive hole in the ship's lower forward 16-inch gun turret. Jack wondered that if the Japanese could wreak damage like that to a steel-plated monster like the *South Dakota*, what else could they do? He had one answer shortly: near the *South Dakota*, the carrier *Enterprise* was also anchored in Noumea's inner harbor, similarly undergoing repairs, her forward elevator crumpled and canted upwards from a Japanese bomb. These were sobering sights for a bunch of young Marines shipping out to the war zone.

Soon after arriving off Koli Point on November 30, the *Neville* briefly ran aground in an area of uncharted sandbanks, and the wake of a Japanese submarine was detected nearby. Only days later, with the *Hunter Liggett* anchored nearby, the *Kenmore* also ran aground on an uncharted sandbar in shallow water when the ship retired for the night towards the nearby harbor of Tulagi, to the temporary amusement of many of its Marine passengers:

> We got to laughing so hard [Frank Chadwick recalled], the [*Kenmore*'s] captain became embarrassed and finally asked a destroyer to pass a line to get the ship off the bar. During the rescue operation, while the destroyer was occupied with the task at hand and the second destroyer [was] patrolling out in the channel (at a distance of about 10-plus miles), a Jap sub surfaced and fired one or two torpedoes (depending on who you talk to), passing the bow of the ship and ending up on the beach. The sub submerged before the destroyers could get on station and slipped away.

> That Jap sub commander had a lot of courage to carry out this operation. We quickly returned to the grim reality of war and started unloading and securing the beachhead with renewed vigor, as we realized very quickly we were facing a clever and courageous enemy.

Organized by their NCOs into a close-order drill group, several hundred of the Ninth's Marines were able, in a synchronized way, to rock the ship somewhat, but not enough to release it from the sandbar's grasp. At high tide, a tug slipped a line onto the *Kenmore* and finally freed it from the sandbar.

Several aircraft were dispatched from Henderson Field on Guadalcanal to search for the escaping submarine. Still onboard the *Hunter Liggett*, Jack watched in horror as a U.S. Navy SBD Dauntless dive bomber arced down out of the blue, cloudless sky, in a near-vertical dive, to bomb the apparent wake of the Japanese submarine as it submerged—only to fail to pull out of the dive and to be caught up in the massive water plume from its depth charge, into Ironbottom Sound. The two-man dive bomber crew did not escape from their airplane's watery grave. "What a welcome to Guadalcanal," Jack later recalled thinking.

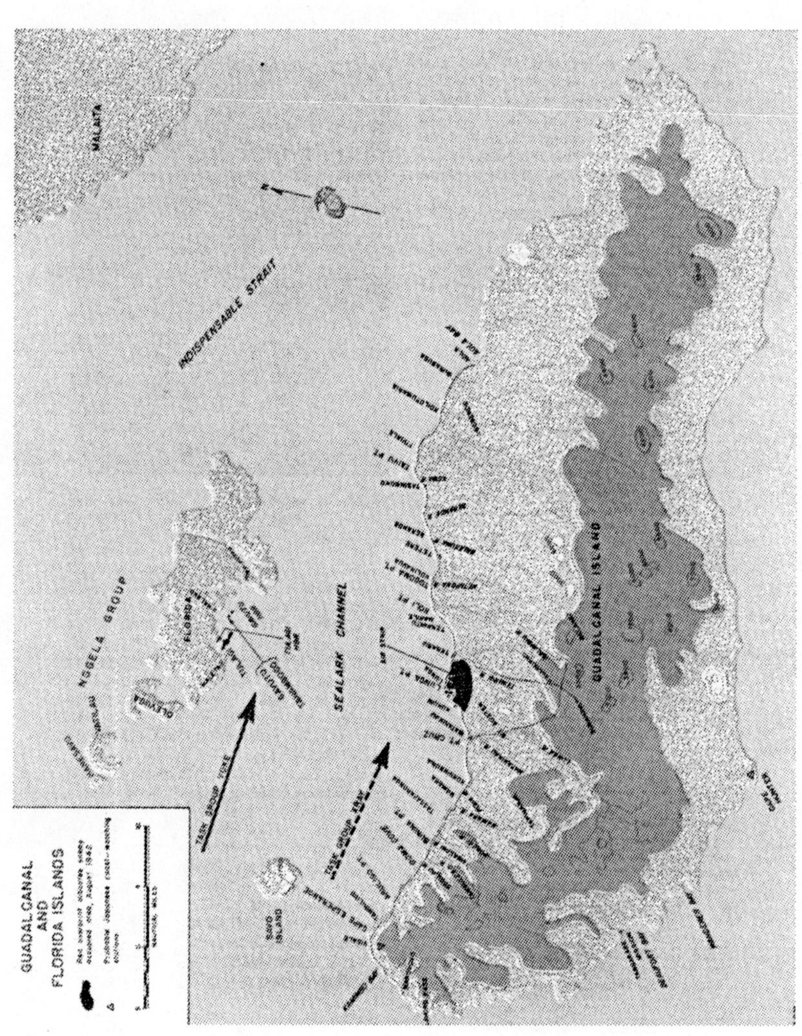
GUADALCANAL
AND
FLORIDA ISLANDS
MALAITA
INDISPENSABLE STRAIT
NGGELA GROUP
FLORIDA
SEALARK CHANNEL
GUADALCANAL ISLAND
SAVO ISLAND

-MCCA

The Battalion's landings near Koli Point were unopposed. The scene of a battle in early November, a welter of discarded Japanese equipment still littered Koli Point, and members of the working parties began collecting souvenirs shortly after landing. With the arrival of the *Hunter Liggett* and *Kenmore*, the Ninth, minus 150 Marines in a rear echelon detachment left behind at New Caledonia, was reunited and officially attached to the 1st Marine Division. The unit began to set up gun positions and unload guns, ammo, and equipment. It was back-breaking work: many of the supplies had to be moved by hand across the beach. The unloading was accomplished partly by small LCP landing craft—none of which had landing ramps, which would have aided in their unloading immensely—and by 20-foot prefabricated barges made of steel boxes fastened together and propelled by outboard motors. The 9th Defense was not organically equipped with the trucks, jeeps and prime movers needed to haul heavy guns from place to place. Therefore, the lighter automatic guns generally were manhandled into place, and even the larger 90mm and 155mm guns had to be dragged by manpower into their positions. The whole process took almost ten days before it was completed.

The terrain in which the Ninth was treacherous and would present its own major difficulties to be surmounted; as Frank Marshall recounted:

> The Battalion was charged with occupying and defending the area between the Nalimbiu River on the west and the Metapona River on the east and inland for a depth of several miles. The terrain was flat in the designated area. The rivers were bordered by jungle so thick that, in some areas, it was not possible to walk erect; pigs and other small animals had made paths, but other than that there were no passages. There was a variety of native thorn that grew up through the

> branches of the various trees and bushes with a recurved thorn that tore the clothing and flesh unmercifully. To make one's way through this dense and threatening foliage was a slow job of hacking with machete and axe. Between the two rivers was a flat, grassy plain covered with a variety of high weed called kunai grass. The stuff grew to a height of about six feet and was quite dense. The soil structure was similar to adobe, being a heavy, rich black soil deposited to a depth of three to four feet. The fact was that this grassy plain three miles wide by ten miles deep was the drainage basin of the two bounding rivers . . . a fact that would become only too apparent in the coming months.

The first night on the Canal was a nerve-wracking one for all parties concerned. Frequent but false cries of "Condition Red"—the alarm for an imminent air raid—set the tone of nervousness that worsened as the men got their first taste of the jet-blackness of a tropical nightfall. Despite the officers' best efforts, fear got the better of some Marines, and their overreactions to the sounds of the jungle would, in Jack's words, "scare the hell out of me." Captain Hank Reichner of Battery A sets the scene:

> To prepare ourselves for Japanese infiltration during the night, we were given the password "SMASH" and the response "AND DRIVE." We bivouacked slightly inshore and set up a rather poor perimeter defense. Many other elements of the battalion were located in the vicinity under similar circumstances. We really did not expect any Japanese attack but everyone's nerves were on edge. Naturally, it took only one blast from one blasted Reising gun [a type of submachine gun used by the Marines] to start things

> off. For at least an hour the night was punctuated with "SMASHES" and "AND DRIVES" accompanied by incessant bursts of fire and curses. I shouted a few "Knock it offs" as did the Sergeants, but to wander around to seek out any perpetrators of this mess would have been suicide. Embarrassment and calmness settled in and the rest of the night went by peaceably and sleeplessly enough. I understand that this happened to others in the early days of the assault. It was almost an initiation but it did show a certain lack of experience on our part.

The results of these boy-crying-wolf incidents would, in a few weeks, help jeopardize Jack's own life when the "Japanese infiltrators" he would see proved to be very real.

Many of the Battalion's AA guns were situated about six miles from Henderson Field. This airfield was the home of the "Cactus Air Force" that had been defending the " Canal" against Japanese aerial onslaughts for the past 2 1/2 months. Battery A and half of Battery B were set up around the Koli Point area, their World War I-vintage GPFs emplaced as coast defense guns against the "Tokyo Express." The Tokyo Express comprised near-fortnightly raids and resupply runs made by a Japanese destroyer and cruiser squadron led by its resourceful commander, Admiral Raizo Tanaka. Up until the Ninth's arrival, the Marines' prime defense against the Tokyo Express had been almost solely naval in nature, with only a handful of land-based airplanes stationed at Henderson Field capable of launching bombing or torpedo attacks as well. The Ninth's 155s would add a punch that might deter any close-in bombardments or at least make their outcome more painful to the Japanese. They also would provide some much-needed heavy firepower for the beleaguered 1st Division and the fresh Army divisions (the Americal and the 25th Infantry) that were beginning to arrive on Guadalcanal.

Due to the 15-mile range of the 155mm Group's aged GPFs and the need to site the guns to as to best maximize their effectiveness within this limited range, Colonel Nimmer decided to place all of Battery A in the Koli Point beachhead area. He split Battery B in half, and H&S Battery—to which Jack now belonged, an outfit less than affectionately called the "Ham and Shitheads" by the rest of the Group—would oversee the Group's operations and logistics. While he was still part of H&S, Jack remained with Battery A and Captain Stafford's half of Battery B at Koli Point. The other half of Battery B was shipped on the *Hunter Liggett* across the Sound to the small island of Gavutu. Here, the Japanese had built an observation point and gun position atop the imposing Hill 181. This promontory had a commanding view of much of the Sound, the large harbor of Tulagi on nearby Florida Island and a sweeping vista of the northern coast of Guadalcanal. Gavutu was linked by a narrow 300-foot causeway to a smaller islet, Tanambogo, and both islands had been taken only by a very bloody assault by Marine paratroopers ("Paramarines") during the August 1942 landings.

As Battery B's detachment arrived there, three crippled heavy cruisers, the U.S.S. *Minneapolis*, the *Pensacola* and *New Orleans*—all survivors of the wild sea fight off Tassafaronga—lay anchored under heavy camouflage netting off Tulagi and Gavutu. The *Minneapolis*'s bow had been blasted away, and the *Pensacola*'s fantail had been smashed by a Japanese torpedo. Their crews were busily sealing up all inner compartments to make the ships seaworthy for towing to New Caledonia for repairs. The camouflage job festooning the battered cruisers was impressive; Frank Yemma of Battery B's Gavutu section remarked:

> There were a bunch of sailors on Gavutu when we landed, and I couldn't figure out what the hell they were doing there or why they were there, until I saw this cruiser with its bow blown off [*i.e.*, the *Minneapolis*], and there was camouflage over it, and it was very well done because I couldn't see it; just as the light was coming up, I still couldn't see it. They did a hell of a job camouflaging what was left of that cruiser.

Box's Marines gaped at the damage inflicted to these ships. Viewed so soon after the Ninth's Marines had witnessed the *South Dakota*'s and *Enterprise*'s injuries, the battered cruisers again reinforced the true gravity of the Anerican situation.

The 40 men or so on Gavutu, including Al Downs, Frank Chadwick and Frank Yemma, faced immediately a huge technical challenge: how to manhandle one of the colossal GPFs, plus ammunition and firing equipment, to the top of Hill 181, a rugged, nearly 200-foot outcropping covered in jungle trees and vines, without heavy lifting or construction equipment? Shortly after landing, the men broke out all the axes, saws and shovels available and began hacking a trail up the slope of Hill 181 through the jungle. The men used the felled logs to corduroy the trail. Everyone—gunners, ammo section handlers, etc.—pitched in, and working day and night, after seven days, the corduroyed trail was complete. Using little more than hand tools, some thirty Marines pushed the first massive gun up the hill; using ropes, block and tackle, the second gun was slowly winched into place near the water's edge. Fifty years later, Box and Chadwick returned to Gavutu and marveled that they were able to achieve this feat, their first assigned mission in the Guadalcanal sector. In retrospect, however, Bill Box also realized how ineffectual his little detachment from Battery B would have been if the Japanese had ever attempted to retake Gavutu in earnest:

> It was pretty stupid, really, [especially] since our two guns had only 30 or 40 rounds of ammo [apiece]. They put these bodies on an island, so if the Japanese ever came on it, they would have to fight us or they'd kill us—one or the other. We were kind of like human guns, when you think of it, left on this island like this.

To help improve their ability to traverse quickly onto potential targets, A and B Batteries' 155s on Koli Point and Gavutu were positioned on "Panama mounts"—concrete pads with turntables, on which each GPF's carriage was mounted and on which the entire gun could be turned through 360 degrees. Part of the gunners went to work mixing concrete, setting up wooden molds, the turntable and the circular metal tracks for each Panama mount, and pouring the concrete, while others filled and stacked sandbags in the sweltering heat and humidity. Each gun was soon protected by a high wall of sandbags (and occasionally 55-gallon steel fuel drums packed with whatever filler—earth, rocks, cement—was readily at hand). Camouflage netting was draped overhead to screen the guns from enemy observation planes, including the despised "Washing Machine Charlie" (also called "Trashcan Charlie" or "Louie the Louse," of which, more, later). To help protect the Marines from bombing and naval raids, large foxholes were dug—around tents, around gun positions, and even in the hospital area next to patients' stretchers and cots, so that each sick or wounded man merely needed to roll off the edge into his hole—and were further walled in by sandbags where possible. Although intended to provide better safety, ironically, these foxholes and trenches dotting the Ninth's position generated another peril, as an inattentive person could easily break a leg or sprain an ankle (and more than a few Marines did) by tripping into one in the dark.

Men of Captain Box's Battery B detachment on Gavutu. Note the "Panama mount" for the GPF and Hill 181, with its Japanese-built observation post, in the background. (Photo by Leo McDonald, courtesy of David Slater)

Besides adding defensive firepower to protect Henderson Field and the logistical areas from naval and air attack, another of the Ninth's missions was the defense of Carney Field, a new Army Air Corps field under construction near Koli Point, some twenty miles from Henderson Field. That the fighting had shifted from the Tenaru and Matanikau River areas along the coast to the western and central parts of the island provided little comfort to the battalion: Japanese troops had just finished combat near Koli Point the previous month, and their patrols still meandered far across the area. The tropical rain forest and terrain provided these intruders with ample opportunities to work their way through Marine and Army front-line positions and infiltrate into the rear areas: the dense vegetation masked movements, particularly at nighttime, when the leafy canopy blocked out all moonlight. The Ninth had guards patrolling in watch shifts all night long, with all guards being advised to be especially vigilant between 10:00 p.m. and 2:00 a.m. and in the early morning hours just before daybreak.

As one of the Battalion's water purification technicians or "gizmos," Jack was in possibly the most isolated position of the Ninth. This was a small area off the Nalimbiu River, not far from Battery A's guns and campsite and a SCR-268 fire control radar of Battery F, but far enough away that Jack seldom saw his buddies except at chow time or when delivering supplies of purified water. Here on the Nalimbiu, he set up his equipment and made a small shack for himself and his gear out of a tent and whatever materials he could scrounge. His water purification gear was comprised of various hoses and large pumps, sets of filtration units, a large portable canvas tub, and boxes for storing his chemical testing kit. The purified water ("Putrefied was more like it," Bob Landon joked) was dispensed from canvas-and-rubber Lister bags. As Battery A's skipper, Hank Reichner, recalled, these bags "can best be described as looking like a huge cow's udder with push-button spigots for teats," jutting symmetrically out of each bag's bottom.

Jack had the reputation for being quite a successful scrounger, which is a useful thing to be in any military unit, but maybe particularly so in a unit like the 9th Defense. He was already looking pretty rangy in his faded and ripped herringbone-twill utility uniform and well-broken-in "boondockers," which tended to make the wearer's feet resemble those of the cartoon character Li'l Abner. To complete the look of an "old salt" Marine, he added a World War I-model trench knife, complete with evil-looking brass knuckles on the handle, and an old Marine campaign hat with a hole the size of his thumb in the crown, nibbled out back in Cuba one evening by a hungry rat. (As one of Jack's high school monikers had been "Rathead" because of a stubborn cowlick that refused to be combed down, Jack appreciated the irony of now wearing a rat-eaten hat.) Jack was hardly alone in his unorthodox appearance. The herringbone-twill fatigues of almost all the Marines on Guadalcanal were sweaty, ripped and faded from a pristine olive drab to a bleached-out tint of green. Surviving photos of the Ninth's gunners show a motley array of headgear being worn, with everything from World War I-pattern helmets, pith helmets and campaign hats to something that vaguely resembled a Greek fisherman's hat. Later, a few of the Marines would receive camouflaged overalls, which they called "zoot suits" after the baggily-cut civilian men's suits that were a popular style of the late 1930s and 1941. As the chorus of one of their favorite marching and drinking songs concluded: "*The raggedy-assed Marines are on the way*!"

Jack's Nalimbiu riverbank was, however, another prime area for Japanese infiltrators who followed the river down to the beachhead, either to rendezvous with submarines trying to smuggle supplies or reinforcements ashore or to try to steal from or sabotage the Marines' beachside supply dumps. Shortly after setting up the water purification point, he was given a field telephone with which he could stay in contact with H&S Battery headquarters. Soon thereafter, shortly after dawn, the battery's switchboard operator received a whispered call: "This is Private McCall. Can the Skipper send a patrol down here? There are Japs all over the place down here!" "Calm down, Pogiebait; you're just seeing things!" was the response. The line was disconnected on Jack's end with a less than reassuring "*click*." A few mornings later, a similar exchange occurred.

Jack, however, needed no convincing from anybody else as to what he was or was not seeing: there definitely *were* Japanese out there, ten to fifteen-man patrols of them, meandering through the steamy mist and vegetation near the riverbank. This activity continued for several mornings, until at last a patrol of the Ninth came down to draw some water from Jack just as a Japanese patrol emerged from the kunai brush beside the Nalimbiu. A firefight ensued, more or less over Jack's head, with him squeezing off a few shots with his rifle into the bushes. "Now, will you believe me next time?" he recalled saying to his "saviors." As additional proof of what he had seen, the patrol found several trails of blood leading back into the jungle and salvaged some pieces of Japanese equipment, including a small, bloodstained Japanese "Rising Sun" flag, which Jack split in two with a buddy as a souvenir of his close call. From that time on, he saw no more Japanese as close to him on Guadalcanal as he had on that day and previous days.

Infantry attacks, though, were not the only peril Jack and his pals faced. Despite the American air buildup and the Navy's efforts to keep substantial forces in the area, "Torpedo" Tanaka and the Tokyo Express would still periodically appear to shell Henderson Field. While Tanaka's guns sometimes delivered fire in close proximity to the Ninth's positions and the airfield construction at Carney Field, his ships outranged the 155s. Even when Tanaka's shells fell far from the Battalion's positions, the blasts from his ships' guns could be seen in the distance. The naval bombardments and battles at sea reminded Jack of heat lightning, and the distant roar of naval gunnery sounded not unlike thunder on a humid Tennessee summer's night.

Also, despite the AAA buildup, Japanese air raids remained a common occurrence. In early January, several large raids occurred, made up primarily of Mitsubishi G3M2 "Nell" medium bombers, which enabled one of the Ninth's AA batteries to make its first kill on January 14. Air raids were frequent and persistent: the 90mm Group alone was in action 117 times from December to June 1943. Thirty-seven of these raids occurred in January 1943 in connection with Operation KE, a final and massive Japanese drive to reinforce their troops and make a last-ditch effort to drive the Americans off the island. In one raid, over 100 Japanese planes—mainly Nells and Mitsubishi G4M2 "Betty" bombers—came over at nighttime, and the skies around Henderson Field were lit up with heavy AA bursts and tracers. Because the 1st Division's hospital was nearby Henderson Field, unless they were in truly desperate shape, the wounded and sick there often felt safer by returning to duty rather than being passive "sitting ducks" adjacent to a prime target. As if the Ninth's AA guns were not enough to defend Carney Field, one of the 90mm Group's battery commanders, Captain Bill Tracy, enlisted the help of some "Seabees" of the 18th Naval Construction Battalion, engaged in the construction of Carney Field, to construct a complete but bogus 90mm position. This was "armed" with realistic-looking dummy guns to further confuse and distract the Japanese. Despite the presence of several squadrons of fighters on the island, the Allies hardly had total air supremacy.

During one massive, nighttime bomber raid in early December, Jack was near the headquarters of Maj. General Alexander Archer Vandegrift, the 1st Marine Division's commanding general and, at the time, still the overall U.S. commander on the Canal. Hand-cranked air raid sirens screeched, the fingers of searchlights began probing the skies, bombs exploded nearby, AA fire became increasingly heavy, and Jack and others without AA positions to man ran to the nearest shelters. What he found was little better than a slit trench, he recalled, with a bottom half-full of water and muck—only to see a glowing cigarette coming from another trench close by. Jack's immediate thought was of his earlier training to the effect that a well-trained airman could see a cigar glowing on the ground from even several thousand feet. He knew *he* didn't want to be hiding next to some moron who had the functional equivalent of a bull's eye painted on his back.

"Hey, you damn idiot, knock off the smoking! Do you want to get us killed?" he yelled at the knucklehead with the cigarette.

"Shut up, Mac; that's the General's trench you're talking about!" a voice roared from another hole.

"*Screw the General*!" Jack yelled back without thinking; then, immediately realizing the court-martial offense he felt certain he had just committed, he felt *very* glad that the night was a dark one and his trench was deep!

On December 4, just the second day the entire Battalion was on the Canal—the radar operators on one of the Battalion's five SCR-268 radars set in motion what many of the 9th Defense's veterans would recall as the Battalion's only real "night of panic." The early radars, of which the SCR-268 was one, relied on vacuum tubes and the recently invented cavity magnetron, the first electronics "black box," and the glitches had not yet been fully worked out of this equipment. It was, after all, suspicion as to the effectiveness of the early radar sets that partly contributed to the success of the surprise attack on Pearl Harbor. In the year since December 7, 1941, the technology had advanced greatly, but errors were still far from uncommon, and the early radar equipment was particularly prone to atmospheric changes providing false echoes and altering the quality of reception. In fact, similar problems resulting from the inability of early U.S. Navy radars to factor out false echoes resulting from landmasses limited its maximum effectiveness in several crucial naval actions off Guadalcanal, and the new technology's teething pains led some Navy commanders to discount its potential advantages, with tragic results as at the battle of Tassafaronga.

Unlike the Ninth's largest radar, the SCR-270—a collapsible tripod-latticework mast set on a trailer-mounted, 14-foot, slowly rotating turntable, which was used exclusively for long-range surface surveillance and required a twelve-man crew—the five SCR-268s were used for searchlight and AA fire control. Each "268" set required three operators—each manning an oscilloscope and equipped with several hand cranks to adjust the range and altitude readings—for a 14 to 15-man crew. These early radars had a usual effective range of 22 miles, but this particular 268's chief, Martin Jones, had performed his own unauthorized yet effective "field modifications" to increase its effective range to some 44 miles. As a practical result, the Ninth now had two long-range search systems, but it would soon become clear that "Jonesy" still had some electronic gremlins left to work out in his modified set.

Late on that December evening, as this SCR-268's huge latticework antenna scanned across the skies and over the waters of Ironbottom Sound, its three operators gaped at their oscilloscopes with amazement: there appeared to be at least forty ships approaching. A quick call to headquarters established that no U.S. convoy was anticipated, so there must be only one explanation—a massive "visit" from the Tokyo Express was underway. Confirming what Jonesy and the operators saw, the watch officer in the "filter room," where all radar data was collected and analyzed, spread the word: "*Condition Black*!" All hands to battle stations! All hell broke loose throughout the battalion area, as alert sirens cranked and field telephones rattled. Jack grabbed his Springfield and gear out of his lean-to near the Nalimbiu and scooted for the nearest foxhole. With many clad in little more than their skivvies and boots, A and B Batteries' gunners raced to their guns, pulling on their helmets, priming shells, removing muzzle covers and generally getting into readiness for the massive bombardment that was sure to come—but nothing happened. Ironbottom Sound was tranquil, and no flares or gunfire lit the sky. The Battalion HQ's signalmen broke out their blinker light to semaphore messages across the Sound to Tulagi and Gavutu, inquiring if anything unusual had been sighted, but all responses were negative.

The next morning, apart from the usual oily film drifting up from the hulls of the smashed ships littering its bottom, no trace whatsoever of a Tokyo Express convoy could be detected on the Sound. What had happened? It had been a false alarm, and Jonesy's modified radar had apparently misidentified surface trash or gotten false atmospheric readings, but the sleepless night only worsened everyone's jitters. As it was, Colonel Nimmer decided that his headquarters was too exposed and too close to the Koli Point beach. As a precaution, he had the Battalion's command post moved further inland. For his part, Jack desperately wanted to drop back into his riverside shanty and sleep, but he found himself lugging tables, tents and equipment to help the CO make his transition.

In addition to periodic naval bombardments and large nighttime bomber raids, the Japanese provided a less dangerous, but more persistent, nightly irritant over Guadalcanal. On evenings, even when Japanese air activity was not heavy, either a bimotored bomber or single-engined seaplane would fly over, drop flares and a few bombs and generally serve as a nuisance. Because its engines grumbled noisily like a washing machine, this airborne pest was variously nicknamed "Washing Machine Charlie," "Maytag Charley," "Trashcan Charlie" or "Louie the Louse." Charlie was the bane of the existence of all Marines and Army troops on Guadalcanal because, if nothing else, Charlie succeeded in ensuring that absolutely nobody got a good night's sleep during his midnight and early morning flights. While Charlie was roundly disliked, the raider was quite possibly even more hated by the Ninth's AA crews. Try as they might, and despite their other successes in downing, diverting or crippling Japanese planes, Charlie appeared untouchable, mainly because the pilot wisely kept just out of range of AA fire and flew like a madman possessed. As one official historian noted: "Charley was a difficult target for the antiaircraft guns since he usually flew high and maneuvered violently when searchlights and guns went into action." Since no radar-equipped U.S. night fighter planes were found on the Canal until late February 1943, Washing Machine Charlie usually escaped unmolested.

The 90mm Group's ack-ack gunners must have taken an incredible ribbing for their lack of success in downing this highly irritating nocturnal marauder. Night after night, despite a dense screen of 90mm anti-aircraft fire and searchlights and the occasional scrambling of fighters from Henderson Field to intercept him, Charlie just kept on coming. This situation continued until spring 1943 when the Army Air Forces finally began deploying radar-equipped night fighters on the Canal. For the rest of his life, Jack could imitate the sound of Washing Machine Charlie's obnoxiously unsynchronized engines. The sound was, as his impersonation of Charlie can best be recalled, a deep "rum-rum-rum" rumbling sound.

Mother Nature added her own challenges to the dangers and discomforts provided by the Japanese, which, for many Marines proved at least as deadly as enemy action. The climate itself was a challenge, even to Southerners like Jack used to 90-degree summer heat and humidity. The jungle was extremely dense in places, the forest floor a gnarled tangle of slippery roots and vines. As noted earlier, deep under the jungle canopy, nighttime was pitch black, with almost no breaks in the treetop canopy to let moonlight or starlight shine through. The weather was unremittingly hot and humid; when rain fell (which was almost a daily occurrence), the result was a tropical steambath as the raindrops rapidly turned to mist upon contact with the overheated soil, plants and rotted vegetation. The smell of the rotting plant life could be overwhelming (particularly when combined with the putrid stink of the decomposing dead). In the sodden soil, water pooled rapidly in foxholes and trenches, and the soil liquified rapidly to create an extremely thick and viscous mud, making it almost impossible for a person to stay dry. The Battalion's positions near Koli Point were on a grassy floodplain between two rivers, the Metapona and Nalimbiu, which were ideal locations to become swampland in the event of heavy rains or floods. Monsoon-like rains from typhoons in May flooded the Ninth's entire area. As Frank Marshall recalled: "On May 9th the heavens opened and stayed so through the 10th. In the Solomons, the rain drops must weight 2 pounds each. This was a biblical rain. This was the rain of Genesis."

Despite the unit's best efforts to build dikes and levees with some Seabees' help provided in gratitude to Captain Tracy's help in building the fake AA battery at Carney Field, the floodwaters drowned one of the Ninth's Marines, wrecked several Panama mounts and saturated the gun positions. The monsoon floods also washed Jack out of his area on the Nalimbiu and forced him to higher (but only slightly drier) ground: "I was visiting the guys in Searchlights and my tent was washed away into the bay in a matter of a few hours. I managed to salvage my seabag and rifle in water [that was] waist deep." Combined with a plethora of types of fungus, jungle rot and an especially virulent kind of athlete's foot plagued the already miserable Marines, giving some of them "souvenirs" of their jungle stay that lasted the rest of their lives.

Wild hogs and boars roamed Guadalcanal's jungles, sometimes charging the Marines or rooting through encampments and battle sites for anything edible. During the spring's heaviest monsoons, one of Jack's pals, Bill Galloway, and another Marine had found and killed one of these wild hogs. To help stave off flooding from the onrushing seas, the Marines piled up a levee of sandbags to keep the water out, however, but their positions were open to the flood waters of the Nalimbiu. Few of the Ninth's Marines were country boys experienced in slaughtering hogs. The Kentucky-bred Galloway had learned how to dress a hog, and once this specimen was cleaned and dressed, he and his pals hung it up from a tree near their position, about 250 to 300 yards from Jack's water purification point. The water, however, continued to rise, and the flood soon immersed the hog's head. To prevent contamination, Galloway cut it off. As the water crept up, soon the muddy flood was up to the hog's shoulders. Galloway cut away the shoulders and again rehung the hog. The water continued to rise, and it was obvious that it would cover what was left of the hog. In disgust, Galloway and his buddies cut the carcass adrift and watched it float away in the flood. Imagine Jack's surprise when, after the floodwaters cleared, he went to clean up and reopen his water purification site for business—only to find half of a slaughtered pig in the middle of his gear, clogging up his pumps!

Dead pigs weren't the only animals floating in the waters of the Nalimbiu. Large snakes could be found from time to time; although they were non-poisonous, Jack was deathly afraid of them. Crocodiles also dwelled in the rivers of Guadalcanal, and several lurked near Jack's water point. His buddy Jim Kruse, a clerk for H&S Battery of the 155mm Group, reminded Jack after the war: "I saw many crocodiles in [the Nalimbiu]. Upstream I saw some that were in excess of eight feet in length. In the underbrush near you I saw a lizard that was in the vicinity of five feet in length. I didn't know what it was until I got back to the States and looked it up." The presence of so many large reptiles kept Jack always a little on edge. Jack recalled watching a bored Army machine gun crew across the Nalimbiu that, after spotting and shooting some crocodiles, unsuccessfully "tried to skin one and tan his hide—quite a mess, really."

In one branch of the Nalimbiu, Jack and the Ninth's sentries often were on the lookout for a particularly large crocodile. After several near-misses, Bill Galloway recalled, Paxton and Prejean, two Louisiana leathernecks, finally shot and killed the crocodile, which sank to the bottom of the creek. The pair's efforts to retrieve the dead animal with a 20-foot boat hook borrowed from the Navy failed: the hook did not reach far enough. After several days, however, the crocodile's body floated to the surface. Soon after, it was hauled out by the Cajuns and staked out to several posts. Desperate for anything resembling fresh meat, the two were considering whether to dress the dead "croc" and cook it or just skin it when Lt. Commander Miles Krepela, the Ninth's Navy doctor, happened upon the scene. To their chagrin, instead of doing any cooking or skinning, the pair ended up digging a deep grave to bury their stinking "prize" on Doc Krepela's orders. While an ample supply of wooden coffins was stacked near the Battalion's sick bay, none were required for the crocodile or for its two frustrated chefs.

The local insect life was plentiful: mosquitoes and flies were constant companions, carrying a host of tropical diseases. Local bodies of water were infested with leeches. Giant centipedes and millipedes, often reddish-orange in color and up to several inches long, lurked in the rotten plant life littering the jungle floor and in the dark recesses of tents, holes and personal gear. Their stings were highly painful and poisonous but what could cause almost as much pain were the infections resulting from the tracks of their paths across bare skin, left by their myriad prickly legs. To Captain Reichner, between a centipede's bite and his own attack of malaria, "it was [the] centipede that put me out of action. As I remember, the critter was in one of my boots and resented my attempt to put it on. The bite hurt like hell, my leg swelled rapidly, and ultimately I spent a night or two in the battalion sick bay, which was just one more tent."

And, because of the clouds of mosquitoes, there were malaria, dengue fever and other jungle diseases to cope with. In many respects, these diseases were as great a hazard for the troops on Guadalcanal as enemy contact: of the 1st Marine Division, out of 10,635 casualties on the Canal from August to December 10, 1942, only 1,472 were gunshot victims; malaria, on the other hand, claimed 5,749 men. This fact is scarcely unsurprising considering that, even to this day, the Solomon Islands have the world's highest per capita incidence of malaria. In the case of the 9th Defense, this was absolutely true: malaria struck almost 90% of the Battalion's personnel—some suffering from multiple relapses-at one time or another, including Jack. Despite the introduction of Atabrine artificial quinine tablets, Jack had recurring bouts of malaria throughout his stay in the South Pacific. Beginning on Guadalcanal, he suffered more than once the raging fevers, sweats and sudden, deep chills. Dengue fever, which made a man feel like he had acquired arthritis overnight, with aching joints and bones, also plagued the Ninth's personnel. Jack fared better, though, than many victims of these diseases, some of whom were so severely sickened or crippled that they had to be shipped stateside. One victim was Colonel Nimmer, who was temporarily relieved as the Battalion's CO by Lt. Colonel William Scheyer, the Battalion Exec, in February 1943 and again, permanently, in March. Two of the Ninth's leathernecks, both members of Battery A, actually died on Guadalcanal from malignant tertian malaria. This was also called "blackwater fever" from the passing of black urine, a condition caused by a massive breakdown of red blood cells. It was frequently fatal unless properly and aggressively treated, and it inflicted more casualties on the Ninth than fell prey to the enemy on Guadalcanal. Malaria was no disease to take lightly, nor was yellow jaundice, a severe case of which resulted in Captain Box being relieved of command of Battery B and being "surveyed out"—*i.e.*, evacuated—to a hospital in the New Hebrides for a month. His colleague, Captain Reichner, remembered that one of the two victims of blackwater fever

> happened to have a brother on board that we were unable to send home. Because we really had no doc-

> tor, I spent most of my time administering morphine and other drugs designed to alleviate the fever. In short, no Corpsman, I was Battery Doctor and Corpsman as well. I remember that we had a rule that nobody went to Battalion Sickbay unless his temperature was at least 103!

Unless a malaria sufferer had a fever greater than 101 degrees, he would try to perform his regular duties, at least, and thus avoid being sent to the Ninth's sick bay. The onset of malaria usually brought about a high (103 to 106-degree) fever and collapse, so a severe case of malaria could hardly be concealed from one's buddies, NCOs and officers. A 9th Defense malaria victim was first sent to the Battalion's medical station on the Metapona River, about 1 1/2 miles from the Koli Point beach, which consisted of several tents and was supplied with a highly visible stack of coffins—a sight likely to deter most but the truly sick from visiting. Anyone who failed to recover quickly at the battalion level, however, was fated for a trip to XIV Corps's main hospital near Henderson Field and, if his situation deteriorated or failed to improve, evacuation to Australia, Espiritu Santo, New Zealand or Hawaii.

Thinking of the wretched physical condition of so many of his men due to the rampant disease on the Canal, Reichner later mused, "At one point, I don't think 'A' Battery could have fought its way out of a paper bag." Despite official hectoring to take their Atabrine, for many—Jack included—it was too little, too late, and Pogiebait himself contracted a case of malaria on the Canal that would resurface periodically in relapses, usually in the form of chills and fever attacks leaving him with torrents of sweat, over the next several years.

The raging fevers caused by the more serious forms of malaria frequently induced nightmarish visions and altered all sense of time and space. Biggie Slater provides this account, written in the third person, of his own experience with malaria on the Canal:

> Biggie sank to the ground, barely conscious, fever blasting across his shoulder blades. Later, a litter-filled jeep jounced him to battalion sickbay—four large storage tents, cunningly squeezed in among the columns of a few close-gathered trees in a low bog. Biggie was carried to a cot and tucked in the mosquito netting. He gasped and quivered, gulping the thick hot air as though it were a shimmering soup flecked through with muted sounds and jagged motions.
>
> Time altered for Biggie. There was a roaring in his ears, icy chills, scalding washes of pain from skull to tailbone. The corpsman took a blood sample and temperature. The man in the next cot raged and scrabbled at his net, and groaned and tossed. Someone lifted Biggie's head and teased pills into his gorge. His neighbor cried out again. Night came suddenly—was it the second or the third?
>
> In the tent, the calls became clearer to Biggie. "Corpsman, water." "Corpsman, duck." "Corpsman." "Corpsman." Bedpans seemed not to exist in field hospitals; perhaps marines scorned such appliances. A slit trench was just outside his tent. Biggie eased brittlely from under the net and stumbled his way to the makeshift head, striking cots and tentpoles as he went. Suddenly, a nightmare: rushing figures tore at the air; one howled, in delirium. Biggie felt the struggle in the dark; four or five vague forms swirled weirdly, just touching him.

> Back on his cot, breathing hard, Biggie saw the group bent over his quieted neighbor. "What's the scoop; what's up?"
>
> "Stay in your sack—this guy just died."
>
> Biggie's feverish brain flared. "*Will that happen to me*?"
>
> It didn't.

Likewise, on Gavutu, after having escaped these tropical illnesses longer than most of his buddies, Frank Yemma of Captain Box's Battery B detachment fell prey during the construction work on the trail up Hill 181:

> As we built that roadway going up the hill to mount our guns, we all came down with fever. One by one, we were just dropping like flies, and there was a tent and the guys were in there, just laying there. . . . What they were doing, those corpsmen that were in there, was putting quinine into toilet paper. You had to swallow that. Try that sometime! But that's all they had at the time. They had powdered quinine, and you put it in this toilet paper and swallowed it. . . .
>
> I don't know, I think there [were] only five of us left walking down the road, and we're all bragging you know, being very macho about the whole thing. All the other guys had hit the deck—pooped out on us. I got my come-uppance because all of a sudden I didn't feel good; I had a headache. And they all [began saying to me]: "What's the matter, Frankie?" "You don't feel good?" "You're crapping out on us, huh?"

> Well, of course, I dropped my shuttle and right down to the tent I went, and I didn't come out of there for five days. But that's the way it goes.

The average Marine had precious little in the way of medical supplies to combat wounds, fevers and disease. Few effective treatments were available once one had contracted malaria or dengue, and medical support was in such short supply that as a postwar historian noted, "attacks of malaria in the Pacific 'were given little more nursing care or rest than the average common cold at home.' "

The anti-infection "wonder drug" invented shortly before the war was sulfanilamide powder. Small packets of sulfa drugs were carried in every man's first aid pouch and in every medical corpsman's bag, together with "APC" (aspirin with caffeine) tablets, red and blue merthiolate (similar to mercurochrome) and a "field dressing," or bandage. The key anti-malarial drugs were quinine and Atabrine, the latter artificially produced substitute for quinine. When supplies were available and before Atabrine was readily available, quinine was provided not as tablets but in powdered form. It was often taken by being shaken onto a tiny piece of toilet paper, rolled into a small, tight ball, and swallowed down with huge gulps of water (the latter, of course, courtesy of Pogiebait and his water purification plant), preferably before the toilet paper disintegrated and one got a long-lasting mouthful of the bitter stuff.

Like many Marines, Jack admitted that he had serious doubts as to the effectiveness of Atabrine, which, combined in addition to turning the taker's skin slightly yellow ("Hey, buddy, do ya wanna look like a Jap?" was a jeer frequently made to anyone seen taking his Atabrine), was rumored to leave men impotent. Hence, close scrutiny was required by each battery's officers and NCOs to ensure it was taken by their reluctant troops. Sometimes, the sergeants lurked with a supply of these tablets at the end of the chow line, actually waiting to pop an Atabrine tablet into each leatherneck's mouth. With almost all of the Battalion's personnel contracting malaria during their stay on the Canal, what Atabrine was available had too little effect or—despite the leaders' and corpsmen's entreaties and best efforts—was either just not taken by the suspicious Leathernecks or spit out by them the moment their leaders were no longer looking.

Besides the difficult medical situation, sanitation in the Ninth's campsites was fairly crude. Captain Hank Reichner vividly recalled the rough sanitary arrangements, including one toilet feature that provided certain members of the Navy with a convenient way to harass their rivals, the "Gyrenes" of the Ninth:

> Thanks to our helmets we had a ready basin for shaving and washing. Thanks to the SeaBees, we had a 55-gallon drum on a short tower to provide us with showers. We urinated into old powder tubes located around the battery area. These gave the place a somewhat distinctive odor and we moved them from time to time. We had two kinds of head (latrine)—the standard four-by-four hole in the ground, and the sea-going head built out over the water [and] flushed by the sea. These last were favorite targets for our destroyers, which would pass close by under forced draft and flush the heads and their occupants into the sea. One skipper's motto was "Run Like Hell, Here Comes Simpson." Instead of airplanes [as so often stenciled on a Navy warship to indicate its anti-aircraft victories], he had latrines painted on the sides of the bridge to indicate the ship's conquests!

Personal hygiene was even worse on Gavutu, where equipment like Pogiebait's was lacking and where the only potable water was rain collected in an open-air metal tank. As Frank Yemma recalled, this tank provided more than just the detachment's drinking water: it was also an excellent breeding ground for mosquitoes that spread malaria:

> [Y]ou could look and see the mosquitoes, the larvae coming up out of the water.... And, so somebody got the idea—said it wouldn't hurt the water—to put a little film of oil on top of the water so [the] larvae couldn't breathe. Let them die instead of breeding to become mosquitoes. And that's what they did. Of course, it tasted lousy.

The personal gear and arms of the Ninth's personnel were a varied assortment. At this stage of the war, many of the 9th Defense's Marines, including Jack, were still armed with Great War-vintage Springfield rifles with long bayonets. Others had already received semi-automatic M-1 Garands. For Marines like those in the Ninth, the bayonet would have been the worst kind of last-ditch weapon—they figured that, if they needed bayonets to defend themselves, then the U.S. position on the Canal was in even worse shape then they had been told—but the bayonets proved more useful for mundane tasks like opening crates and cutting down the stiff and sharp-leafed blades of kunai grass. Officers generally carried .45 caliber Colt pistols.

Several hundred of the Ninth's Marines had been issued Reising .45 caliber submachine guns. More frequently used by Marine Raiders and Marine paratroops, the Reising generally resembled a sawed-off Thompson submachine gun (the "Tommy gun") but was used exclusively by the Marine Corps. Despite their automatic firepower, many Leathernecks found the Reising to be prone to jamming and rusting, and it was tricky to maintain. It was also a poorly balanced weapon—it tended to nose upwards when firing ("We often said that's why they were called " 'Risings,' " David Slater lamented; "you'd fire ten rounds, and it'd be pointed at the sky"). As the Corps eventually acknowledged the Reising guns' defects, many owners of Reisings were gratified to exchange them in due course for more reliable firearms. Some Marines (including several of the tankers and the 155mm Group's Exec and, later, the Battalion Exec, Major Robert C. Hiatt) sported the drum-fed, Chicago-gangster-style Tommy gun. These were also difficult to maintain, but they were far more efficient than Reisings. Many Marines tried to acquire other personal weapons—one old-timer Marine Gunner carried a shotgun, while Jonesy, the radar chief, sported an old Colt six-shooter—and knives of all kinds and sizes were exceedingly common. Jack's favorite knife (probably because of the true ugliness of its looks, if not due to its practicality) was a World War I-style trench knife, complete with a built-in brass "knuckle-duster" with metal points protruding from the knuckles. Many other Marines preferred the more compact and versatile Marine-issue Ka-Bar knife.

The Ninth's experiences on Guadalcanal suggested to its leaders that it lacked sufficient firepower in light automatic weapons; the Reisings helped a little but could not overcome the Battalion's lack of good light machine guns. By the end of that campaign and before its future battles in the Central Solomons, the unit negotiated with the Army's XIV Corps, to which the Ninth was later attached, to acquire more light automatic weapons, including the Browning Automatic Rifle. Firing the same cartridge as Springfields and Garands but from a large magazine, the BAR was more a type of light machine gun than a rifle. It was heavy and cumbersome; nevertheless, due to its firepower, reliability and portable nature, the BAR was a useful weapon to have.

That the Ninth was dependent at this stage on the kindness of the Army for many of these vitally needed weapons was due to shortfalls throughout I MAC for such types of guns and other critical supplies. Those BARs and .30 caliber light machine guns as were available were allocated by the corps to its primary combat forces, the 1st and 2nd Marine Divisions. Many of these logistical difficulties would still plague the 9th Defense's effectiveness well into 1943, as will be seen.

H&S Battery, 155mm Group, on Guadalcanal in spring 1943. Jack is on the top row, far left; Jim Kruse is in the front row, fourth from right. Major Stafford and Group CO Lt. Col. Wright Taylor are seated (with open collars) in the center. (Author's collection).

In early February 1943, U.S. forces linked up in the Cape Esperance area in the island's far northwest, and pushed towards Mount Austen in the island's center. By February 9, 1943, the fighting on Guadalcanal wound down, as the Japanese withdrew what was left of their battered forces from Cape Esperance and other pockets of resistance along the west coast. Batteries A and B had not had a chance to engage enemy ships, and, because of the high altitude of most Japanese air attacks, Special Weapons' lighter AA guns had not claimed any enemy planes killed. Still, the 90mm Group's batteries had downed twelve Japanese planes between January and the end of the campaign, and the Ninth was beginning to earn its sobriquet, "The Fighting Ninth."

The Ninth's flak gunners got a massive workout on April 7, 1943, as Admiral Yamamoto launched his last major air operation before his death eleven days later, amassing 350 warplanes to strike out at American airbases throughout the Solomons and New Guinea. On April 7, the Ninth's gunners scrambled to the cry of "Condition *very* Red!," as 67 Aichi D3A1 "Val" dive bombers and 110 Zeroes hit the Canal. The raiders sank several Allied ships, including a U.S. destroyer, but lost heavily in the process. Despite their mounting losses of aircraft, the Japanese persisted, launching a last major daytime air raid of 120 planes on June 16; only thirteen of these escaped.

With unbridled pleasure, Jack and his friends watched and cheered as their AA guns and Navy, Army and Marine fighters chopped up the attackers. Some U.S. planes were always easily recognizable, even in the wildest dogfight: the Army Air Forces' P-38 Lightning with its twin-boomed tail, the Navy's and Marines' tubby little F4F Wildcat, and after February 1943, the Marines' new F4U-1 Corsair with its seagull-like wings, all of which were being stationed in increasing numbers at Henderson Field. Beginning in March 1943, several squadrons of B-25 Mitchell medium bombers and B-24 Liberator heavy bombers of the 13th Air Force joined the growing air presence on Guadalcanal and were based next to the Ninth at Carney Field. Brought in to help in the bombing of Rabaul, the Japanese headquarters and logistics center located some 565 miles northwest of the Canal, the twin-engined Mitchells and the hulking, four-engined Liberators provided an illicit opportunity for several Special Weapons machine gunners to hone their skills, as aerial gunners, as they secretly "joined" the Army Air Force crews on several bombing missions in the Solomons area. Had they been caught doing so by their officers, they would hardly have been heroes—their participation was strictly unauthorized—but several succeeded in making some flights on board the bombers.

A V-Mail Letter Home from Guadalcanal

PFC Jack H. McCall
Batt. B, 155mm GP.
9th Def. Bn., F.M.F.
c/o Fleet P.O.
San Francisco, Cal.

Mr. & Mrs. A.G. McCall
Rt. #1
Franklin, Tenn.
May 9, '43

Dearest Family,

Have been awfully busy lately and have neglected my writing some. Raining to beat the band here and I've been trying to keep my tent intact.[1] *I hope all of you are well. I'm fine, still fighting the darned mosquitoes though. I suppose by now Al has already been home? Have you been hearing from Bob alright lately? I hope he's well. They might even hit the States soon, the "lucky stiff." Has Reams*[2] *ever left Cal.? I wish I could see some of the fellows. Without a doubt some are around here close.*

So, Dad's in 4B.[3] *Ha. Do you think you could fix a small box with some candy bars and stationery? Gives a guy something to look forward to. Looks like I've just run out of space so will close.*

Much love,
Jack

Once again, "Pogiebait's" lifetime love of sweets has manifested itself in this V-mail[4/] letter home. Packages from home were highly treasured by all, but were often shared by the recipients. Woe betide the unfortunate Marine who had gotten a package from home, only to squirrel it away from his buddies and have them learn of the fact! Even if moldy or stale when it arrived (which was often the case, as it may have been three to four months in transit), food from home was treasured, precisely because it was from home and it was a reminder that another, safer world existed "across the water." In short, food parcels from home served as much as a kind of sentimental "reality check" for the recipients as it did as sustenance and as a reminder of all the things they missed—clean sheets, a solid roof over one's head, "civvie" clothes, women, etc.—about home. Besides the emotional pull, this partly alleviated both the scarcity and the blandness of combat food when field kitchens were not available, as was often the case on the Canal.

Due to supply shortages, the 1st Marine Division's and I MAC's hungry Leathernecks resorted to eating captured Japanese supplies, particularly rice, during much of their five-month ordeal before the Ninth's arrival in early December. By December, the Marines were no longer surviving on the sometimes weevilly rice (there were bitter jokes about the wormy rice having more protein than other available foodstuffs) and Spam, but after the initial joy of receiving new U.S.-made fare, the novelty of the new rations wore off. Fresh food of any sort was a rarity, as the shipping and refrigerator space for these items was scarce.

Most frequently found in the Pacific were K rations, containing ham-and-eggs (which often acquired a disagreeable olive-greenish hue after being canned for a length of time), canned cheese—the usual lunch selection—or Spam or hash, crackers, instant coffee, candy, cigarettes, toilet paper and chewing gum. Another variety, less available in the Pacific until later in the war, was "Ration C," consisting of a cardboard box holding two cans. One can was filled with crackers, powdered coffee or tea, candy, toilet paper, various condiments, and four cigarettes (preferably Lucky Strikes or Camels, but often of the widely-deemed unsmokable Chelsea brand), and the other was filled with canned food like hash, stew and the ubiquitous Spam.

Another semi-edible innovation, different from the small chocolate bars found in K rations or C rations, was the Ration D bar. Originally intended as emergency fare, D rations appeared at first blush to be large and thick chocolate bars. Because these had been specially hardened to keep from melting—some claimed this was done with paraffin—and vitamin-reinforced, D rations tasted far differently from any Hershey bar Jack had ever eaten, yet it still did the trick for his sweet tooth. Rounding out the bill of fare were the bulky "10-in-1" rations, similar to the rations used onboard the *Kenmore*. These may have been the pick of the litter in terms of quantity as well as quality, since (depending on the need) this ration was ostensibly intended to feed either one man for ten days or ten men for one day, and contained a wider selection of foodstuffs.

Because K and D rations and Spam were often the only food available—and on the Canal, even that was always a questionable proposition—the Ninth's Marines actively scrounged anything edible. While Jack may have been largely out of luck on the Canal itself until the Ninth's mess tents could be safely emplaced, Captain Box's section on Gavutu had one rare treat—fresh seafood—at least once. Frank Yemma recalled:

> I happened to be in the tent one afternoon, and I heard all of this firing of weapons going off, hand grenades and rifle shots and pistol shots, and I thought to myself, "What the hell's going on?" Ran out and what it was, some of the fellows there—-there were only 26 or 30 of us on Gavutu—-some of the guys had built a raft. And this big blue marlin was chasing bait coming in, and it was on the shoals, and the guys out on the raft happened to see this big blue marlin, so they threw hand grenades at it and fired all their weapons that they could at it and, sure enough, they got the fish, and I ran down there and helped them. They got it on a pole, and we brought it over to our makeshift galley, and we talked to the chef about it. And, of course, they had to get the corpsman, and I don't know where in the hell he got the book, but he looked in the book and he says, "Yeah, you can eat it. It's safe. It's a blue marlin, and it's safe to eat," so needless to say, we had fish for a few days.

Food, or the lack thereof, was a chronic difficulty on the Canal for Americans and Japanese alike, and it was with good reason that the Japanese would refer to it as "Starvation Island." Of course, if it was bad enough for the Americans, it was much worse for the Japanese, whose logistics and supply lifelines to the outside world had been effectively severed by early 1943. One Japanese officer noted: "It is said if you lose your appetite it is the end." Another chronicled the final life expectancies of his starving and disease-riddled troops with grimly calibrated precision on the following scale:

Those who can stand: Thirty days;
Those who can sit up: Three weeks;
Those who cannot sit up: One week;
Those who can only urinate lying down: Three days;
Those who have stopped speaking: Two days;
Those who have stopped blinking: Tomorrow.

Years after the war, Jack read *Into the Valley*, John Hersey's report of his combat patrol with a 1st Marine Division infantry company on the Canal. While he thought much of Hersey's saga was "pretty tame stuff" in comparison with the reality—most notably the relative softness of language the author attributed to the Marines—Jack noted Hersey's account of a group of Marines talking longingly—not about women, alcohol, politics or sports—but *food*, and what would be the first thing they would eat when they got home. "Jesus, what I'd give for a piece of blueberry pie!" "Personally I prefer mince," the dialogue begins.

Jack testified that there was more than a shade of truth to that discussion, particularly given the direness of the supply system on Guadalcanal. "It was all you thought about, for weeks on end," he once recalled. In his few leisure moments, Jack would dream of food and going home. He would develop his own schemes of what would be the first food *he* would eat when he got home—and, as much as it was his favorite dessert, it would not be pie, but something decidedly as unmilitary as could be.

In addition to the seemingly endless search for food, another pastime—what could charitably be called "scrounging"—very quickly assumed its role in the life of Jack and his fellow enlisted men on Guadalcanal, even though it was most definitely frowned upon by Colonel Nimmer and his staff. Part of this arose from necessity, particularly as the supply system on the Canal seemed at best to be in shambles. With major shortages of even basic field equipment, and—when such equipment was available—finding that it was often World War I-era gear, the Ninth's Marines were desperate for anything. Partly, too, this arose from competitiveness and from the average Leatherneck's quest to do something, anything, to discomfit his "swabby" and "dogface" rivals. Faced with the arrival later in the campaign of fresh Army and Navy units supplied with the latest equipment, Jack and many of his buddies often took to making midnight forays to obtain from their non-Marine neighbors whatever could be "liberated." As expected, some of these raids brought out the entrepreneurial spirit in the Leathernecks, as Frank Chadwick recounted.

When confronted with one well-stocked, but also well-guarded, beachside Army supply dump, several 155mm Group Marines found a nearby bell. Guessing (as it turned out, correctly) that it was probably set up as an impromptu air raid alert device, they began ringing the bell loudly and, with loud screams of "*Condition Red!*," convinced all onlookers that an air raid was imminent. As the soldiers ran into the jungle to seek cover, the Marines grabbed as many crates as they could carry. Once back in camp, they were disappointed to find that these contained only Army-issue rubberized boots, worthless for tropical climates because of their tendency to cause feet to sweat and thus to worsen athlete's foot, tropical sores and jungle rot. At least the crates were themselves put to good use to make floor boards for tents.

A similar foraging treat was provided by the arrival *en masse* of another Army unit on the Canal. As David Slater relates:

> One day in March '43 when we spotted a convoy approaching Koli Point, our scouts learned it was an Army unit . . . coming ashore right in our area. We all

> went down to the beach in force, trucks, jeeps and even ambulances. We looked with incredulity as they landed and immediately started to string barbed wire *behind us* within the plantation. They also put ashore large stocks of all sorts of gear which our people immediately dipped into, usually, if challenged, claiming they had been *ordered* to transport the stuff to Army depots! I wandered about until I spotted a marvelous inner-spring mattress which I appropriated and began to lug back to the 90 H&S [Battery's] ambulance (I intended to endear myself to Captain Tracy by presenting him with this treasure). Unfortunately, I was almost immediately challenged by an Army officer who asked this raggedy-ass Marine what the hell he was doing with the General's mattress. My explanation, proving unsatisfactory, brought about the immediate command, "Drop it!" However, the battalion [still] did quite well.

Besides scrounging, buying and trading Japanese equipment and supplies provided cottage industries in and of themselves, beginning almost from the day the Battalion landed on Koli Point in the midst of piles of abandoned Japanese field equipment from the earlier battles waged there in November. So did the clandestine manufacture of "Japanese flags" on Guadalcanal. Until curbed (by personal directive of Army Maj. General Alexander Patch, Vandegrift's successor as the island-wide commanding general on the Canal), this hobby involved taking squares of white silk from abandoned parachutes and using a tincture of red merthiolate to dye Rising Sun "meatballs" onto the silk. The resulting "Jap flags" were then sold by the Ninth's budding entrepreneurs to gullible Army and Navy personnel or were traded in exchange for "hooch" or other scarce goodies. Chadwick recalled derisively, "By the end of February or early March, there were more Jap battle flags on the Canal than there were Japs."

Incensed, General Patch's headquarters announced that any Marine caught in this activity would receive a general court martial from him, personally. Suspecting that, as he was an Army commander, General Patch's threat might not get the attention it deserved, Colonel Nimmer simply said that he, too, expected the trade would stop and added his own promise of a court martial to any violators. This more or less brought the fake-flag business to a close. As will be seen, though, all the entrepreneurial skills learned on Guadalcanal would stick with Jack and his buddies through the Ninth's successive campaigns.

The Ninth's Next Destination?

> *Total and complete defeat of Japanese forces on Guadalcanal effected . . . Am happy to report this kind of compliance with your orders . . .because Tokyo Express no longer has terminus on Guadalcanal.*
>
> General Patch reporting to Admiral Halsey,
> February 9, 1943

As the Guadalcanal campaign wound down, the food, pogy bait and cigarette situation improved greatly. For many months, the Ninth's Marines had counted themselves lucky when they had two cold meals a day, which—when available—usually was canned Spam, rice or K rations, or quantities of orange marmalade (the latter with such frequency that Jack "swore off of orange marmalade for life"). By one estimate, during the campaign, the Ninth's leathernecks ate twice a day about 20% of the time and once daily about 70% of the time; hence, no food was available for perhaps a tenth of the time. This nutritional regimen was hardly enough to support an active 20-year old male in normal times, and much less so for one suffering from several tropical diseases and sometimes working 15 to 20-hour days in a humid jungle climate. The only readily available drink was water, usually the iodine-flavored brew Jack himself distilled from his water purification shop on the Nalimbiu. This water was warm when poured in and only got warmer in the heat of an aluminum canteen. On this sparse and bland diet, coupled with his malaria, Jack lost substantial weight during his stay and was down to 120 pounds (he had weighed about 170 when he had enlisted). By campaign's end, the food situation was moderately better, with fewer meals of powdered eggs or canned spinach and kraut and more fresh meat. "We had graduated into frozen mutton from New Zealand, Spam and occasional fresh food," Captain Reichner recollected; "I lost a lot of weight, as did most of my Battery. It was years before I could eat mutton or Spam again."

By mid-June, Army units were taking over the burden of the Ninth's AA and coast defense positions. The Army artillerymen's transition was accompanied by the frequent jeers of the Leathernecks, who made cracks—not intended humorously—about "Dugout Doug of the Philippines." While Marines generally took a patronizing attitude towards the Army's "dogfaces" anyway, many (if not all) Guadalcanal Marines—those of the Ninth included—had developed an abiding dislike of General MacArthur, believing him personally responsible for abandoning them on the island for so many months without resupply or Army relief. Whenever he was engaged long after the war in an argument over MacArthur's relative merits as a commander, Jack often quoted a rhyme that was a special Marine favorite: "*With the help of God and a few Marines/MacArthur retook the Philippines.*"

The replacement of the 9th Defense by fresh Army units, however, could mean one thing: the Battalion would be on the move again. The next set of islands in the Solomons chain was the Central Solomon group, where intelligence since November 1942 had shown the Japanese building a large air base at Munda Point on the island of New Georgia, and various support positions on nearby islands. When completed, this airfield was expected to support several hundred aircraft. Only 170 miles west-northwest of Guadalcanal, the Munda airfield would help the Japanese recapture local air superiority lost when Henderson Field was taken and provide a checkmate to the Allies' possible moves further into the Solomons. As part of Operation CARTWHEEL, a series of Allied offensives designed to eliminate Rabaul, the massive Japanese air, naval and logistics bastion on New Britain, the South Pacific Area commander, Rear Admiral William Halsey, won approval to assault New Georgia and seize Munda Field, not only before it became a real menace to Guadalcanal but also to provide a springboard to encircle Rabaul.

The Battalion officially stood down from its defensive mission on June 17, 1943 and began preparations for its next mission. An upgrade in all of the Battalion's equipment before the next operation was underway, as the Ninth's higher command was shifted from the 1st Marine Division and to I MAC, and then again from I MAC to the Army's XIV Corps. Batteries A and B exchanged the old GPFs for new model M-1 155mm rifles, known ubiquitously throughout the U.S. military as the "Long Tom." These had greater accuracy and mobility than provided by the old, tired GPFs. In keeping with the Marines' penchant for nicknaming everything, these too acquired nicknames. Suspecting the imminent start of a new campaign with the arrival of the new equipment, one Battery A member asked: "Where do you think we'll be taking these guns?" He was answered by someone who blurted out: "Who knows?" Translated into Spanish by PFC Gustavo ("Chili Bean") Cervantes, Battery A's sole Hispanic member, this was emblazoned on the barrel of the battery's Gun 3, *Quien Sabe*, and the TD-9 tractor assigned to move it was named in turn, as if in answer, *Quien Cuida*—"Who Cares?" Captain Reichner, sensing that his boys were on to something good for their morale, encouraged them to name the other new guns. These were dubbed *Sudden Death* (later renamed *Oscar*, in memory of Oscar King, one of the two malaria victims); *Pistol Pete*, after a Walt Disney character; and *Semper Fidelis*.

***Quien Sabe*, a Battery A 155mm M-1 or "Long Tom," is heaved into position by its gun crew on Rendova, June 30, 1943. (Official U.S. Marine Corps photo, courtesy of Col. William T. Box)**

With the delivery of the Long Toms and with the New Georgia operation requiring a major change in the 155mm Group's primary mission from seacoast defense to heavy field artillery work, the gun crews received accelerated training in field artillery tactics and gunnery. After completing this difficult training in near-record time—just 22 days—the new CO of the 155mm Group, Lt. Colonel Archie O'Neil, received a personal commendation from Admiral Halsey. Described by Lieutenant Chris Donner as a "slight, dapper individual with flat gray hair parted at the side, a small moustache and a very yellow caste to his skin" (perhaps from too much Atabrine) and with a slight accent betraying his West Virginia roots, O'Neil looked considerably older than his 38 years.

The Tank Platoon had joined up with the rest of the Ninth on Guadalcanal some months earlier, and its training was accelerated. Many of the Ninth's men finally traded in their old Springfields for new semiautomatic M1 Garands (which the "old salts"—Jack included—never quite got used to, preferring the Springfield's ease of maintenance and reliability in all conditions, even if the Springfield was slower to fire) or the smaller, less powerful, M1 carbines (with which, as a non-infantry unit, the Ninth would, by 1944, be largely armed). The 90mm and Special Weapons Groups even traded in their well-used ordnance to an Army battalion in exchange for brand-new guns with power-operated rammers, remote-control features and better mobility. Manually-operated 20mm guns were remounted in pairs on power-operated carriages, making their ability to traverse and elevate on targets much faster and more efficient. Additional machine guns were issued liberally; three LVT-1 "Alligator" tracked amphibious cargo vehicles, named "*Gladys*," "*Frances*" and "*Tootsie*," were issued to the Battalion, and another nine LVTs were lent by the 3rd Marine Division.

Such improvements, however, did not come cheaply; in exchange for a supply of additional weapons and parts, the new Battalion CO, Lt. Colonel Scheyer, traded to the Army all the battalion's movies, P.X. supplies and other creature comforts not deemed absolutely essential for combat. Although technically assigned under the command of Army XIV Corps for the upcoming operation, "Wild Bill" Scheyer also shrewdly took advantage of doctrinal differences in Army and

Marine Corps logistics to procure additional ammunition. His canniness was recognized by an Army official historian:

> Loading orders specified three units of fire were to be carried. Since an Army unit of fire for the 90mm guns was 125 rounds and a Marine unit of fire [was] 300 rounds, the 9th interpreted the orders to mean Marine Corps units of fire and carried the extra ammunition.

With increases in personnel, 53 officers, 8 warrant officers, 1371 enlisted Marines, three navy officers and 24 navy enlisted (the Navy personnel serving as "corpsmen," or medics of the Marines) comprised the Ninth by the end of June 1943. To the horror of Jack and the "old salts," an overload of Army draftees and temporary shortages in volunteers at home required the Marines to begin taking conscripts seconded to the Corps, and more than a few of these new bodies joining the Battalion were draftees. In addition, several of the 10th Defense Battalion members—frustrated by that sister unit's lack of action and its officers' and NCOs' pettifogging spit-and-polish discipline, even in a war zone—applied for and received transfers to the Ninth, and several, among them Joe Pratl and Jack Sorensen, joined Battery A just in time for the next offensive. Pratl recalled his welcome to the Ninth:

> The transition for us didn't seem to be a big deal. We were moving so much and working so hard, this change didn't seem so big. The men of the 9th also didn't seem too disturbed as they now put out the welcome mat. Seemed like the 9th had the same chow [as the 10th Defense] but their drinks were better, like 190 and grapefruit juice.

When Private Pratl asked where he could find Battery A's CO so he could report in, he was told, "Oh, he's over there." Seeing only a young man clad in shorts, Pratl asked again, "Over where?" "Like I said, he's *over there*!" came the insistent response and gesturing finger. Pratl and several other new arrivals rushed over to meet the skipper, and they passed a tent where a Battery A Marine appeared to be drinking a bottle of hooch. Pratl flinched, knowing the blistering response that would have been forthcoming from any officer in the 10th Defense. To his amazement, when the drinker said, "Care for a drink, sir?" and held out the bottle, Captain Reichner simply looked at the proffering arm and nonchalantly said, "No, thanks." "He was a no-nonsense and very down-to-earth skipper," Pratl remembered, and Captain Reichner's serious yet nonchalant style immediately won over him and his fellow 10th Defense transferees.

Group photo of Battery A, spring 1943. (Courtesy of Dr. Christopher S. Donner)

Wherever the 9th Defense was going next, it would need all its new weapons, supplies and men, and more. Although not heavily bloodied by its campaign on Guadalcanal, the experience of the hardships it endured there would serve its personnel well in the months to come, and the latter days of the campaign had provided a first hard dose of the realities of combat. The old veterans of the Ninth could not recall any comparable American unit, either Army or Marine, that had begun such a critical campaign without at least test-firing *some*, if not all, of its artillery pieces. At last, the Battalion had finally gotten to test its guns in anger and to train its artillery crews by live-firing in combat—truly a trial by fire, if ever one existed—and they had survived and grown in experience with this first test. More challenges were soon to follow.

The next campaign for Jack, although less well known than the battle for Guadalcanal, would place him and the Fighting Ninth in much more direct danger than he and his buddies had been in for the past.

4

A Forgotten Victory: The Rendova/New Georgia Campaign

June 30, 1943 brought us to another move, the invasion of Rendova and Munda islands in the New Georgia group and attached to the Army's XIV Corps and 43rd Army Division. July 2nd, our landing docks, gasoline, and ammunition dumps went up in smoke as a large Japanese air strike took us by surprise. We lost several men, and had quite a few weapons destroyed. Apparently this raid was so successful for them, they planned another for the 4th, which was not to be. Our 90MMs destroyed twelve bombers and one fighter in less than three minutes with only 88 rounds. Wa-hoos, fist shakings and screams of delight were heard up and down the coast.

Our 155's shelled both day and night the Munda air field and surrounding Jap forces, doing great destruction. I may mention also that the island of Rendova was the haven for a group of PT boats, one commander of which became a U.S. President, John Kennedy.

After Munda, we secured our 90's, set up positions around the field and on a couple of smaller islands. Our 155's were located in the Piru plantation and shelled the island of Kolombangara. One of the Japanese artillery pieces we dubbed "Pistol Pete," for he would open fire on us every afternoon about dusk, and our "chow time;" as soon as we returned the fire he would be quiet until the next afternoon, and we would have cold chow. Soon afterward, a aerial spotter sighted him and we made short order of him. No more cold chow!

Jack H. McCall, Sr.

No one joked; no one yacked; no one bitched. They just hacked it.

Marine combat correspondent
Samuel E. Stavisky, accompanying
the Ninth on Rendova

Operation TOENAILS, the New Georgia campaign, was already in the planning stages well before the end of the battle for Guadalcanal. It would be an all-arms effort, combining Navy, Marine and Army units in a multi-stage operation to seize New Georgia and its neighboring islands. While one pre-invasion estimate pegged the number of defenders of Munda as being 4,000 troops, in reality, twice that number defended the area. With approximately 15,000 Japanese Army and Special Naval Landing Force (in Japanese, *rikusentai*) troops in the entire New Georgia island group, not counting air units beginning to move in to the Munda airfield—the Japanese had some 400 aircraft based at Rabaul, within striking range of New Georgia—the U.S. planners decided that several landings would be made on and around New Georgia nearly simultaneously.

A key part of the operation involved seizing Rendova Island, just south of New Georgia, and several other small adjacent islands for artillery and AA emplacements and PT boat anchorages. Being only eight miles southeast from Munda Point, Rendova's capture would put most of New Georgia—especially the Munda airfield—within range of the Ninth's 155s. With some of the most powerful and mobile heavy artillery assets in the South Pacific area, the men of the 9th Defense learned their unit was selected to play a primary role in the campaign.

The Ninth's orders for the initial phase of the upcoming operation, in recognition of the Battalion's wide range of capabilities, combined both the original defensive roles of a Defense Battalion with some novel offensive tasks for such a unit. Each of these capabilities would soon be put to the test. The Ninth was ordered to assist in the capture and occupation of Rendova Island; to provide all-around AA defense to U.S. troops on the island; to bombard Japanese installations and defenses on New Georgia, particularly the Munda Point area and its airfield; to defend Rendova against attack by hostile vessels; and to support infantry operations on New Georgia with its Tank Platoon.The 155mm Group, in particular, had a critical mission in Operation TOENAILS because of the ranges of the Army divisions' 75mm guns and 105mm howitzers. These guns' shorter ranges required them to be landed on Bau, Kokorana and Roviana, tiny islets within a few miles of Munda Field, to give them any chance of striking Japanese targets. Once landed, however, it became apparent that the firing tables for these guns had been miscalculated and that few, if any, were emplaced in positions from which they could fire on the Japanese. The Battalion's Long Toms would be expected to bear the brunt of the heavy artillery support in the upcoming campaign.

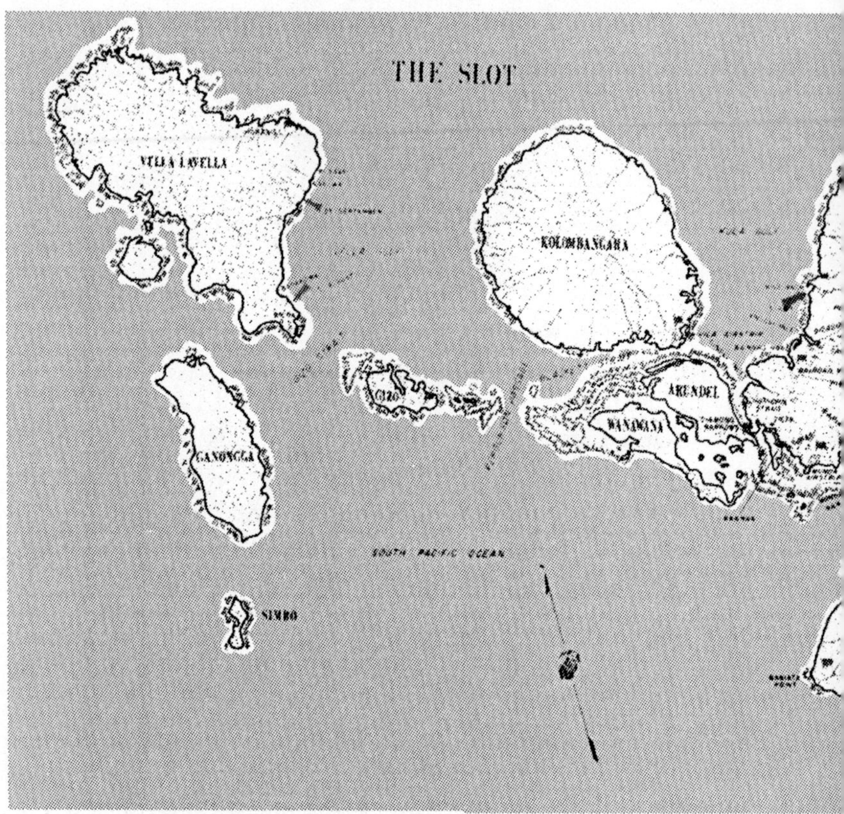

Shortly before leaving Guadalcanal, Colonel Scheyer issued his orders of the day on the conduct of the upcoming campaign, concluding with some pumped-up motivational rhetoric: "If any of you have the idea that the Japs are supermen, get it out of your heads. They are fifth raters who have a mistaken notion that they must die for their Emperor and our job is to help them do just that as fast as we possibly can." Joe Pratl, however, remembered a different form of motivation coming from the 155mm Group's new CO, Lt.

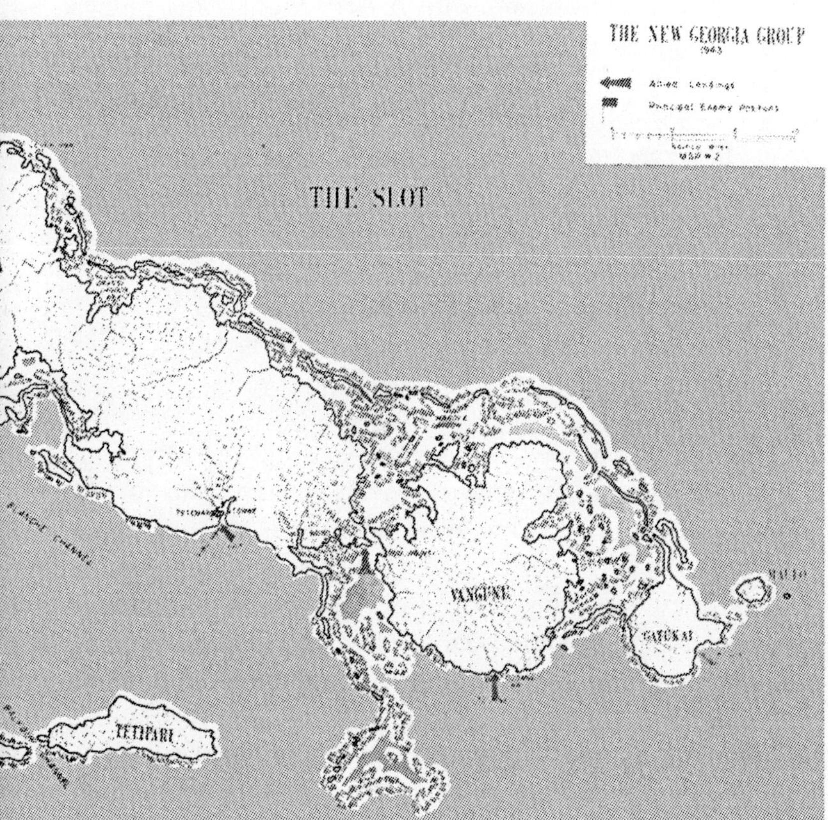

Colonel Archie O'Neil, whose "Godspeed address was, in fact, a reaming-out because, like all boys, if you don't keep 'em busy, somebody's going to plan a party"—which, in fact, Battery A did: a true all-out, rip-snorting party, featuring ample quantities of 190-proof alcohol. Not surprisingly, Colonel O'Neil was furious: "We caught hell," Pratl recalled sheepishly. To top things off, a batch of cans of medical alcohol disappeared and, for some reason, the 155mm Group immediately fell under suspicion, with Battery A being the prime suspect. Hank Reichner picks up the story:

> I issued a strong warning to the effect that I did not expect to have any of the missing cans found in our battery area. Apparently one was found at B Battery, which then bore the brunt of anger and suspicion by our superiors although they, along with Waldo "The Beast" Wells, B Battery commander, expressed strong doubts about A Battery. Waldo bore the brunt of the recriminations, I am sorry to report.

Despite all inquiries, the missing cans did not resurface before the Battalion's departure, leaving Reichner, his junior officers and senior sergeants to wonder when and how they would resurface.

Before embarkation, there was still time for skylarking and some brief comic relief. Jack's boot camp pal, Jim Kruse, serving as a clerk on the Headquarters staff of the 155mm Group, recalled daring one of their buddies, George Confer, an H&S Battery Field Music (*i.e.*, a bugler), to play "Reveille" while Colonel Scheyer conducted a final battalion-wide formation on Guadalcanal. After much cajoling, Confer agreed to take the bet. As the Battalion formed, rank after rank, the bugler stepped out of formation unheralded and began playing a jazzed-up and syncopated version of "Reveille" with all of his might. The Field Music soon froze, however, as Colonel Scheyer and his staff stared him down, and he trembled nervously as the CO asked him to step forward. As the terrified bugler saluted the Colonel in front of the entire formation, Colonel Scheyer announced, eyeball-to-eyeball, that he had only one thing to say to Confer: "Don't *ever* do that again!" Enough said; the intrepid Field Music got the point.

At about the same time that a group of crack Marine Raiders made their first, stealthy landings on New Georgia, the Battalion boarded the heavily camouflaged attack cargo ships U.S.S. *Libra* and U.S.S. *Algorab* off Guadalcanal late in the afternoon of June 29, 1943. The unit's guns, radar and rangefinders, vehicles and other heavy equipment were loaded separately aboard four green-camouflaged Landing Ships, Tank ("LSTs"). After laboring to stow the battery's heavy gear on the LSTs, Jack and a few others in H&S Battery and the Battalion's staff, boarded another transport, the *U.S.S. McCawley*, known far and wide as the "Wacky Mac." It was also the radar-equipped flagship of the Navy task force commander, Rear Admiral Richmond Kelly Turner. Soon to be familiar to a generation of American soldiers, Marines and sailors in both the European and Pacific theaters, the LSTs would receive their combat baptism in the Rendova landings; their bulky shapes and slow speed inspired some wags to claim that "LST" actually stood for "*L*ong *S*low *T*arget."

The unit was to land in three echelons, the idea being to get most of the personnel together with light AA weapons and .50 caliber machine guns ashore as quickly as possible to set up a defensive perimeter. Next, half of the 90mm and 155mm guns would arrive in the second echelon, and the remaining men, vehicles and guns would follow soon thereafter on the "Green Dragons" after positions had been established for them. Many of the Special Weapons Group's Oerlikon and Bofors guns were set up on the LSTs' decks to augment the little ships' own defensive firepower. It was only about 175 miles for the invasion convoy's voyage from Guadalcanal to Rendova, but the transport fleet sailed in complete blackout, escorted by destroyers and several cruisers, while lookouts were posted to keep watch for Japanese aircraft, submarines and warships.

After their experiences on Guadalcanal and in the embarcation lead-up, tensions were running high among the men. Reports that Japanese air attacks were expected at any minute heightened the expectant atmosphere. Still, there were many who looked forward to some "action." As Hank Reichner noted: "Our biggest morale problem on Guadalcanal had nothing to do with meager and lousy food, the weather or lack of mail. Simply stated, we were anxious for a real fight with the enemy. Many of 'A' Battery's Marines pled with me [on Guadalcanal] for a transfer to a Marine infantry unit." With some of its men sarcastically dubbing themselves the "lost battalion" due to their lack of action on the Canal, the thrill-seekers among the Ninth's leathernecks were about to get their wish. As Colonel Scheyer noted: "[T]he prospect of closing with the enemy was all that was needed to supply morale."

The voyage to New Georgia created different sensations than the men felt during the *Kenmore*'s approach off Guadalcanal because most of the men thought that they now had a clearer degree of awareness of what they would face on landing. Thus, the inklings of what was to come either heightened or lessened one's doubts and fears, depending on each man's makeup. For many, one worry was that of letting one's buddies down, and personal fear was suppressed as best as possible and kept to oneself. Battery B's Frank Yemma recalled having something of a panic attack as he heard depth charges going off around his LST during a sub alert en route to Rendova:

> I was on an LST; I have no idea which one it was; I don't know. I know we packed a lot of stuff in those ships—an awful lot of stuff on those ships. And, away we went. We got underway and, I think we were on the other side of the Russell Islands going off to Rendova. I was down below deck and, all of a sudden,

> these depth charges started going off, and it just shook the hell out of that LST. Well, I tell you, I went up the gangway, and there was some sailor who was just ready to batten down the door as I was going up, and I tell you, I laid my foot, I just pushed my foot, right against that door because he was ready to close it. And I hit him with the door, and I knocked him out, cold as a cucumber, but I said "They're not going to lock me down below." I was going to get out on deck in case we got hit! But anyway, he survived the hit; his forehead was hit a bit; he just was stunned.

For others, pre-invasion fear was much worse than a mere case of the jitters, with one Marine's fear apparently leading to him becoming the Ninth's first casualty well before the *Libra*, *Algorab* and the accompanying LSTs reached Rendova. As Frank Chadwick later recalled:

> We were on a ship going to Rendova. . . . There was a guy sitting on gun watch. We'd been through some air raids. It was nighttime. He stood up and said, "I've had enough of this," and he dove overboard and was gone. We didn't even stop.

In a memoir written only a few months after war's end, Lieutenant Chris Donner vividly recalled the same incident (which occurred aboard his LST) and the grim hubbub that followed:

> It rained that night, June 30th. I slept fitfully until near 2:00 a.m., when I dressed and reported to the bridge for watch. There was some excitement among the personnel topside. Ten minutes before my arrival, one of our radar operators for the 9th Defense, a boy who had been in my Replacement Company, had jumped overboard. He was one of those sleeping on

> deck. . . . Suddenly the boy jumped up from his cot and fell on the wet deck. He rose again and vanished over the guard wire into the dark ocean. The Skipper, who had been summoned to the bridge, figured that the unfortunate lad must have been caught by the screw, for on an L.S.T. there is a propeller near each side of the blunt stern.

For most Marines, suicide or self-inflicted wounds were simply not serious options. No matter how truly scared one might be, each man's ability to "hang in and take it" was regarded as being a matter of pride and self-respect. The highest contempt of Marines were reserved for cowards and "goldbricks," and no Marine wanted his buddies to contemplate, even if only for a minute, that he might fall into one of those despised categories. When one's own personal survival—not to mention the survival of one's squad or platoon mates, or the company, battalion or regiment as a whole—was at stake, teamwork and trust were critical commodities. Practically speaking, too, there was nowhere to run if one was scared or sought to avoid duty—no rear areas, no civilian homes or farms in which to hide, unlike the European environment—and the result would mean ostracism, or worse, from a host of pissed-off young Marines.

In the case of the Ninth's officers, they, too, had ample reasons to feel tense in addition to the concerns of combat. As one of only two Marine units participating in the initial phase of Operation TOENAILS—the other being the crack 1st Marine Raider Regiment—the 9th Defense was very much under the scrutiny of I MAC's and the Fleet Marine Force-Pacific's leadership. One of I MAC's senior artillery officers, Lt. Colonel Edward H. Forney, was accompanying the Ninth, serving both as a field artillery adviser to Colonel Scheyer and as General Vandegrift's official observer of the

Battalion's performance. Another senior observer was Colonel John W. Thomason, a famous Marine veteran of World War I who was best known for his illustrations of trench life in that war, representing the FMF-Pacific headquarters. Accompanying the Army's 43rd Infantry Division and slated to land beside the Ninth on Rendova was the 2nd Marine Division's senior observer for the operation, Lt. Colonel David M. Shoup. Though little known to many outside the Battalion's senior leadership, Colonel Shoup would become very well known throughout the Corps in only five months, and he would enter the pantheon of American military heroes as the intrepid CO of the 2nd Marines on Tarawa. Much was at stake in this operation, besides the taking of Munda Field; Operation TOENAILS would be a test both of interservice cooperation and, as well, for Marine amphibious planners and for those who were backing the Defense Battalion concept as to how well these "defensive warfare" units could be turned to offensive tasks.

Rain squalls and fog shrouded the hulk of Rendova Mountain as a group of Navy cruisers and destroyers began a brief but savage bombardment of Rendova very early on the morning of Wednesday, June 30, 1943. As the phosphorescent red and green flares and tracer shells of the bombardment faded away, the landing parties prepared to board the landing craft for the assault. The previous night's traditional "send-off" dinner aboard the LSTs—pork chops, with plenty enough for seconds—had long been digested, and the waiting men nervously munched on whatever rations they had available as they waited to board their landing craft. Already sweating profusely in the humid early morning air (a rainstorm had recently drenched the area, and low clouds obscured Rendova Mountain, the extinct volcano that dominated Rendova Island) and with some fighting nausea—each battery's officers and NCOs went up and down the ranks, checking the serviceability of their platoon members' equipment and, in particular, asking them whether or not they had contraband. Diaries and personal journals were strictly forbidden (although some Marines kept them in secret) for fear that, if captured, the diary entries might provided Japanese intelligence with useful information—not necessarily from a purely military basis, but enough to get an idea of morale in the unit and on the home front, and possibly enough to give the detested "Tokyo Rose" extra fodder for her radio shows.[5/]

Also, each battery's cadre shook down the enlisted Marines for Japanese souvenirs carried along from the Canal. Scuttlebutt had made the rounds as to what the Japanese did to Marines and G.I.s who were captured with Japanese letters, photos, flags or souvenirs on their persons, and it didn't take much more hectoring by the officers or NCOs to make the point. When Jack's turn came on the deck of the *McCawley*, out on the transport's deck went most of the artifacts he had scrounged or traded on the Canal: parts of a Japanese officer's Nambu pistol, some items of Japanese insignia and—worst of all—his prized trench knife with the built-in brass knuckles. "What the hell do you think the Japs will do to you if they catch you with that thing, Pogiebait?" Not much imagination was required for Jack to get a pretty good mental picture of the consequences, and he did not like it. Over the side of the "Wacky Mac," it all went, with one exception—the half Japanese flag Jack had won on Guadalcanal. That artifact stayed hidden in the lining of his helmet. Then, at about 6:35 a.m., over the rails went Jack and all his buddies.

Jack recalled that the Rendova landing was the first time he'd had to go down a cargo net into a pitching and yawing landing craft. This task was itself a difficult and risky process: the mass of 60-70 pounds of rifle, ammo and equipment weighted down the wearer, while the landing craft bobbed unevenly beside their transports. A real sense of timing was necessary to negotiate the process with any measure of safety. First, each man had to let go of the net at the exact moment that the swells lifted the landing craft up and beside the ship. If one's timing was off, he would either drop a considerable distance and crash onto the steel floor of the landing craft or onto his angry (and often seasick) buddies below. Otherwise, he might fall between the landing craft and the ship, to be drowned or pinioned between the sides of the ship and the landing craft. Fortunately, Jack timed it just right and let go, so that his feet felt nothing but the hard, bobbing floor of the landing craft—not that he had too much choice in timing his jump, since he could feel the boot of the Marine hanging on above him beginning to step on his helmeted head!

Laden with vehicles and equipment, one of the LSTs transporting the 9th Defense approaches Rendova Harbor early on June 30, 1943. (Official U.S. Marine Corps photograph, courtesy of Col. (Ret'd) William T. Box)

With several dozen nauseated Marines and their equipment now packed tightly into the landing craft's well, the Navy coxswain pulled the landing craft ahead and then away from the *McCawley*. It was a relatively brief trip from the ship to shore, but it felt like an eternity. Smoke and flames were coming up from the edge of the Lever Brothers plantation besides the narrow stretch of beach; the tops of many coconut trees[6/] had been shredded in places by the naval shelling, and the surrounding ground was littered with coconuts. The sound of small arms fire was audible and coming from the near distance. The beach at Rendova was narrow and the treeline near the water. Rifles, pistols and submachine guns at the ready, the Marines at first clustered among the roots of mangrove and coconut trees and swamp grass along the edge of the beach, before getting up and moving a few yards inland, after prompting by a chorus of yells and curses from their NCOs. Sodden from head to toe from storming ashore onto the beachhead, and hunkered down near the foot of a large beachside palm tree to get his bearings, Jack was now entering a world of utter chaos and pandemonium unlike anything he had ever encountered before.

The 9th Defense was not supposed to be leading the charge on Rendova, yet it was. Specially trained assault units of the Army's 43rd Infantry Division, called the "Barracudas," had been assigned to take the beach before the Ninth landed. The sequence of landings of the Army and Marine troops had somehow gotten seriously off-schedule, however, and it was now the Ninth's leatherneck gunners who were landing well ahead of the infantrymen of the Barracudas. Instead of coming ashore at Rendova harbor, most of the Barracudas had come ashore eight miles north, leaving the harbor still occupied by Japanese *rikusentai* naval troops. The main Rendova landing force, including Colonel Scheyer and his leathernecks, was ignorant of this gross mistake and expected to make an unopposed landing, until confronted moments before disembarking by urgent orders from the irascible Admiral Richmond Kelly Turner: "*You are the first to land! You are the first to land! Expect opposition*!"

D.C. Horton, a coastwatcher who witnessed the Rendova landings, wrote:

> The coxswains of the Army landing craft, thinking that the beaches were clear, vied with each other to get their troops ashore first. This happy state of affairs soon ceased and all became confusion tinged with not a little dismay as the first troops were met with machine gun fire from the Japanese. It was realised, somewhat belatedly, that the Barracudas had not cleared the beachhead and that the incoming troops would have to fight for it.... The already bad situation was not improved by a mounting hysteria as coxswains on incoming landing craft sprayed the beaches and coconuts indiscriminately with machine gun fire which only ceased when an officer on the beach threatened to shoot back.

Out of sequence or not, the Ninth was already approaching the beach and was going to have to take it by itself. So, the Battalion's artillerymen had to revert quickly to their infantry skills first learned in Boot Camp and on Cuba. Several firefights broke out between the first parties from the 155mm Group and the misplaced Barracudas and the Japanese defenders of Rendova, with several Japanese *rikusentai* troops being killed. The 9th Defense had drawn first blood in the New Georgia campaign.

Once he was certain that the beachhead was secure and

after his recon parties had driven off or killed Rendova's 200-odd Japanese defenders, Major Robert Hiatt, the 155mm Group's Exec, decided it was time to unload the heavy equipment. Although an Army combat engineer battalion had been slated to land behind the Ninth and help it set up, the engineer unit's commander refused to land until he was certain that Rendova's beachhead was secure. In frustration, aware that the tiny harbor was clogged with landing craft awaiting the chance to unload and depart, and watching supplies, guns and equipment stack up on the beach, Lt. Colonel Scheyer requested that a Navy construction engineer unit land ahead of schedule to assist in beach clearance. As a line of Marines held the edge of the beachhead and fanned out, all other available hands began unloading the various craft and helping the Special Weapons Group build hasty AA gun positions up and down Rendova beach. The 90mm Group's personnel began staking out sites for their guns and radar sets; and recon patrols from A and B Batteries began to move inland to look for good positions to emplace their "Long Toms." Working parties cut and blasted down trees to clear positions and provide unobstructed fields of fire for the big guns. To add to the confusion and urgency, Japanese air raids were again reported as being expected at any minute: radar on nearby ship radars were detecting incoming Japanese aircraft, probably coming from Rabaul, the massive Japanese air and naval base located some 400 miles away on New Britain Island off New Guinea's northeast coast. Colonel Scheyer and Major Hiatt were furious with the Army engineers. Time was running out: ships and landing craft were backing up in Blanche Channel and equipment and supplies waited to be unloaded. As requested by Lt. Colonel Scheyer, members of the Navy's 24th Construction Battalion—"Seabees"—soon began coming ashore, and they pitched in and helped with the unloading and digging-in process.

An LST disgorges troops and Long Toms of the 155mm Group at a former Lever Brothers pier at Rendova harbor. (Official U.S. Marine Corps photo, courtesy of Col. (Ret'd) William T. Box)

Still, as Marines and Seabees poured ashore, clogging Rendova's beachline, it was a scene of chaos and near-bedlam. "Since we had been expected to saunter ashore, all the first echelon gear had also come along—seabags, tents, etc.—and was dumped in a huge mound off to the left of the initial landing zone on Rendova. That became my vantage point to survey the hectic scene of wild activity of boats coming in with people and gear, destroyers rushing back and forth, dive bombers whacking New Georgia, dogfights in the sky, and an occasional Zero roaring by. I thought I was in a movie," Dave Slater recollected. Some of the Seabees' bulldozer crews found themselves under sporadic rifle fire from a few remaining Japanese defenders, while other Seabees hacked down coconut trees to improvise corduroyed roads to fight the mud that was already beginning to slow down the deployments. The Seabees' game efforts met with mixed results at best:

> This expedient was fine for the tracked vehicles [like the LVT-1 Alligators], but the spinning wheels of ordinary trucks and jeeps were soon throwing the logs in all directions as the trucks and jeeps sank into the mud. The Seabee bulldozers than had to be used to pull out the imbedded vehicles: the bulldozers were lashed to large coconut palms for traction before painstakingly winching each truck or jeep onto the semisolid ground beside the putative road.

Captains Hank Reichner and Walter Wells, the respective COs of Batteries A and B and competitors at almost everything, were themselves equally peeved at the situation. Despite their and their NCOs' incessant hustling, cursing and urgings, the two batteries faced struggles similar to those of the Seabees in getting their eight Long Toms off the beach. Despite Major Hiatt's personal reconnaissance and the best intelligence "poop" available as to the condition and location of Rendova's trails, these were little better than wide footpaths. To improve the trails enough to enable Long Toms and vehicles to move down them, Batteries A and B and the Seabees had to cut, hack and blast with dynamite some 600 coconut trees. To add to the two battery commanders' woes, it began raining again, and the slimy muck created by the incessant downpours were bogging the guns up to the hubs of their wheels. Every spare body in the 155mm Group (Jack included), every Caterpillar TD-9 prime mover (similar to the Seabees' bulldozers, but without the blades) and every Alligator were set to work heaving the guns out of the mud and trundling them to their designated positions, but at an agonizingly slow pace. Battery E, one of the 90mm Group's batteries, somehow managed to get its own large AA guns in position and in operation on nearby Kokorana Island at Rendova's northern tip (but without its vital fire control equipment, which had been unceremoniously dumped on Rendova) by 4:45 p.m. During the initial recon of Kokorana by a detachment from the 90mm Group that morning, an errant group of Barracudas materialized: since neither party knew there were other Americans on that island, it was only by the narrowest margin that the two groups avoided shooting each other.

In the afternoon, despite the failure of several early-morning Japanese air attacks and during a break in the rains, one Zero fighter made it through to Rendova, flying the length of the beach at near tree-top level. "Will you look at that? What guts!," one Marine turned to Jack and exclaimed, half in awe. Every Special Weapons light AA gun available began firing at the Zero, accompanied by every Marine or Seabee who could lay his hands on a weapon. Somehow the plane escaped unscathed. The Zero pilot's lucky escape did not seem to be a good omen. At 2:00, two .50-caliber gun teams downed the Ninth's first Japanese plane of the campaign, another Zero, to the cheers of onlookers. However, in doing so, the Ninth suffered its first true combat fatality, as one of the gunners was killed in the Zero's strafing run.

Later that evening, the monsoon-like rains resumed, and the rain came down for hours. The water table on Rendova lay naturally close to the surface, and drainage ditches were carved throughout the old Lever Brothers copra plantations. Despite these drainage ditches, it took little time before the area became a quagmire. Marines slipped and fell in the mud, as deep as four feet in some places and aptly described by one of the official Marine histories as a "slimy gumbo." The LVTs *Frances*, *Tootsie* and *Gladys* were put to good use, since the caterpillar-tracked amphibians were about the only vehicles that could negotiate the mud. Even using Caterpillar

TD-9 tractors and the sturdy Alligators, it still took teams of thirty or forty mud-smeared men and two tractors to lug each big 90mm and 155mm into position. Several of the Battalion's trucks and jeeps had to be written off; their engines and drive trains, already well overdue for an overhaul after Guadalcanal, burned out in the fight with the slime, and the TD-9 "bull-dozers" at times sank deeply into the glutinous mess. Still, Battery A was in position by 1800 hours (6:00 p.m.) that evening and began firing registration shots onto Munda Field soon thereafter. Colonel O'Neil, the 155mm Group's new CO, was then able to report all guns ashore, and the Group was officially placed under the control of Brigadier General Harold Barker, the 43rd Division's artillery commander and the senior artillery officer present.

Captain Wells' Battery B gunners face a tough pull with this Long Tom and its TD-9 tractor mired in glutinous mud. (Official U.S. Marine Corps photo, courtesy of Col. (Ret'd) William T. Box)

As Battery A set up its four 155s for firing, a peculiar thing happened. As one gun team cleaned its Long Tom in preparation for firing its first shot, a rammer staff inserted from the gun's muzzle clinked against something metallic. The rest of the crew froze, as the ramrod squarely tapped the metallic item again. The crewmen gingerly pressed home the ramrod once again. With the gun's breechblock open, a row of large tin cans fell to the ground. It was the missing medical alcohol, in pristine condition and in plain view both of battery skipper Hank Reichner—who, only days before, had fervently sworn to Colonels O'Neil and Scheyer that *his* boys hadn't filched the stolen medical alcohol—and Colonel Forney, one of the official observers from I MAC. "Colonel Forney observed with a wry smile and said: 'Von Reichner, I knew you bastards had that alcohol!' Fortunately we had other things to do, and I never heard about the matter again," Reichner thankfully noted.

The first night ashore on Rendova was a fearful one for many, even for Jack and those who had already experienced the pitch blackness and noises of tropic nights on the Canal. Colonel Scheyer's pre-invasion orders and each battery commander's own instructions to his men stressed the importance of not resorting to unwarranted gunfire but of challenging intruders with the correct password and then using bayonets, knives and rifle butts in night combat. Nevertheless, there were still frequent outbreaks of random gunfire, with some startling results the next day. "Cattle could be heard rustling about," Joe Pratl remembered, "and a group of farm lads said cattle don't move unless they are prompted by Jap infantry trying to find their way in the dark."

Those rumors, coupled with the sounds of movement in front of their hastily dug foxholes, were all that was needed to prompt an outburst of wild shooting in the 155mm Group's sector. Frank Yemma of Battery B picks up the tale:

> There was a lot of firing that night—BARs, machine guns, rifles, the whole thing. The next morning, they found steers—*cattle.* It seems that the British or the Australians, I guess they were, that were there, they let the cattle go when the Japanese got there, and I don't know, about four steers came down through the jungle, and everybody opened up because they didn't know what the hell it was, hearing all this commotion! So we found four steers, and needless to say, we had some meat to eat at that particular time.

Unfortunately, one of Battery A's platoon sergeants in charge of guard duty, who had left his foxhole to check the perimeter's security, wandered out in front of his platoon's positions around the same time that the cattle stampeded through the area. He was shot during the random fusillade, and his body was found the next day by men from Lieutenant Donner's platoon, "his face swollen to an unrecognizable shape, a bullet having pierced his windpipe." Ironically, after having repeatedly told his sentries to fire only if their challenge went unanswered, the sergeant failed to reply with the password and was shot as he tried to run away. His death was a sobering and unforgettable reminder as to the reasons behind Colonel Scheyer's and Captains Reichner's and Wells's orders. However, this accident would not be the only "friendly-fire" incident during Operation TOENAILS.

Black Friday: The Japanese Strike Back

The next day, July 1, Jack, Jim Kruse and all available hands began unloading the second echelon of the Ninth off two Green Dragons as quickly as possible. While the 155mm and 90mm Groups' members unloaded the two LSTs, other members of the Special Weapons and 90mm Groups improved their firing positions. To Jack's and Jim Kruse's frustration, their platoon sergeant who frequently suffered from migraine headaches, with perfect timing, came down with one such massive headache during the unloading of the LSTs. In the midst of activity, he disappeared. "Where the hell's your goddammed Platoon Sergeant?" a more senior NCO yelped at Pogiebait and Kruse, who could only unhelpfully stammer back, "Uh, Gunny, we haven't seen him lately." Much to their disgust, their absent sergeant was soon found lurking onboard a Green Dragon from which, despite all entreaties and curses, he would not move until his sick headache had abated.

In a matter of days, the Platoon Sergeant was evacuated from the island. "What a hell of a way for that bum to get out of this place, Pogiebait!" Kruse commented to Jack. "Well, look at it this way, buddy," Jack rejoined: "at least, he's out of our hair now."

Because of the high water table and muck, the Leathernecks had to build up their positions rather than digging in to the rain-sodden soil. They created high protective berms and revetments made of sandbags, coconut logs, coral-filled 55-gallon steel fuel drums and mud-filled wooden ammo crates. In this way, the 90mm Group began to set up its radar, searchlights and aerial target acquisition equipment. Adding to the hubbub, Japanese air raids were continually expected, radar on the nearby Navy ships having detected Japanese aircraft en route from Rabaul.

Jack was helping to manhandle one of the 155mm guns out of a Green Dragon when one of its bow doors dropped with a sudden jolt and caught his uniform. The LST had not landed directly on the beach but rather where the water was deep, and Jack was pulled under the clamshell door. In the haste and confusion of unloading, he feared nobody would see him; and he was being dragged down by the weight of the steel door. He began to panic, and the time he was underwater seemed like minutes. Jack seldom discussed this incident, although he admitted later it was one of the most frightening experiences he ever had in his life; "I thought I was going to die." At last, he broke free and rose to the surface, his lungs near to bursting, pulled out by some fellows who noticed his thrashing underwater. One of his sergeants said, "Why don't you go onboard and take a break, McCall?" Jack gratefully accepted the sergeant's offer, and he meandered onboard the LST where he saw his pal Chadwick, helping to man a 40mm gun on deck.

As Jack's pals continued to unload the two Green Dragons, the first of several major Japanese air raids began. Without warning, a low-flying flight of Zeroes skimmed over the treetops and dropped several small bombs at the Green Dragons, including the one Jack had just boarded. One bomb landed on the ship's left side, across from Jack's position on the right-hand side. The blast lifted the LST out of the water, throwing Jack and others to the deck. The second bomb landed at its fantail, and its explosion lifted the LST's stern high and slewed the ship around. The two successive blasts "rang the bells" of those nearby who were otherwise uninjured by metal fragments from the bombs and shards of debris from the injured LST. As the first wave of Zeroes departed, Jack muttered to himself, "*Damn*, that was close!" But it wasn't over yet.

Frank Chadwick, who was helping on the 40mm AA gun on deck, ran to get additional clips of shells from the LST's ammo locker near the bow. He reached the locker precisely at the time the bombs fell, and the concussion knocked him to the deck. As a second wave of Zeroes came over Rendova, Jack and the slightly stunned Chadwick had ringside seats, and they watched the Zeroes strafe the beach and blast a nearby Special Weapons' 40mm position. They watched as the gunners cleared their dead and wounded from the smashed site, uprighted the 40mm gun and resumed fire at the second wave of attackers. It was not until the attack had passed that Chadwick also realized his dungaree jacket had been peppered with holes from tiny bits of shrapnel from one of the bombs. Two Special Weapons .50 caliber gunners, however, shot down the Battalion's first confirmed AA victim of the new campaign, a fighter strafing the beach around 1400 hours that afternoon. The unloading drill was to be continued the next day, July 2, with two remaining Green Dragons being scheduled to disgorge their cargoes.

On Friday, July 2, Jack joined the 155mm Group's gunners in unpacking powder and shell fuses to set up an ammo supply point. In the midst of intermittent showers, a group of newsreel cameramen and combat correspondents set up their equipment to film the beginning of the bombardment of Munda Field. Chris Donner noted that "a small group of Army officers had gathered near [Battery A's] Number Four gun to give the opening of fire the atmosphere of a spectacle," while "a large number of Seabees" labored around the coral peninsula to build a more durable access road. Nearby, the 155mm Group's headquarters staff set up a observation post for their fires in a 150-foot casuarina tree. By mid-day, Batteries A and B began that day's mission, firing registration shots at Kokengolo Hill, a large hill overlooking Munda Field: "The first rounds from 155 Long Toms in the Pacific began to crack out of the muzzles," Lieutenant Donner proudly remembered.

During these first few days on Rendova, Japanese air raids were frequent, vicious and deadly. Jack vividly recalled the most severe air raid of the Rendova landings on July 2, in which, besides having to suffer raids by Japanese bombers, the beachhead was again strafed with near-impunity by Zeroes. The Japanese airmen concentrated on hitting the ammo and supply dumps sited on a small peninsula jutting into the harbor.

Around 1:30 p.m.—not long after another extremely intense line of rainstorms had drenched Rendova but had cleared—a formation of 24 medium bombers and 44 fighters flew over Rendova Harbor in perfect formation from the direction of Rendova Mountain, the extinct volcano that formed the highest point on the island. From their appearance and the direction of their approach, many onlookers quickly concluded that these were Allied planes, with several identifying them to the benefit of their friends as being friendly B-25 Mitchell medium bombers. Biggie Slater of the 90mm Group recalled watching "a Sea Bee working party of a hundred or so led by a young lieutenant unloading and maintaining road capabilities. He saw the planes and reassured his men that they were our B-25s, these being two-engined, twin-tailed (as were the planes [overhead])." Unknown to the men on Rendova, however, all Allied aircraft on Guadalcanal and the Russells were grounded that day because of the heavy periodic rainstorms.

Captain Bill Box and Lieutenant Donner, down at the beachside ammo point to procure more shells for Reichner's guns, stopped a idle truck driver. Just as Donner asked the driver to pitch in and help them, "a 40mm began to set the air throbbing with its fire, and I heard the guns of a plane open up. I caught sight of the truck driver, now out of the cab, diving into the ground; others followed, and I instinctively went along." Nearby, while the crews of *Frances*, *Gladys* and *Tootsie*, the Ninth's three permanently assigned LVT-1s, still argued over the identity of the aircraft, a bomb landed near *Gladys*, wrecking the valuable Alligator and killing one of her three crewmen while wounding the other two. Two other bombs simultaneously fell near *Frances* and *Tootsie*, damaging one of the vehicles and scattering their crews. The "Black Friday" attack was on.

Private Frank Yemma was caught in the open as he was helping unload another of Battery B's Long Toms from one of the two Green Dragons:

> When we got to Rendova and we pulled up onto the shore, on this LST, they had these big doors that opened up in the front, and I was up topside; I was up on a 20 millimeter. And Bookie Bentley—he was my

corporal—says "Yemma!" I say "Yeah, Bookie?" He says, "Look, I need somebody to go down and guide the tractor driver, haul the gun out. Would you go down and guide him out?" I said, "Jesus, Bookie, I got it made here!" He said, "Go on. I got to have somebody." Okay. So I went down, and I straddled the gun. And I told the driver, "Line up, pull it on up," so he kicked that tractor over, and out we went.

And just as we got out on the shore, on the beach, I heard these planes, and I looked up and there was no camouflage on them. None. They were silver. I remember that very well. They looked like commercial aircraft. I said, "What the hell?" I kept looking. Then I could see the Rising Sun on [them]. I said, "Oh, my God," and here they come, the bombs . . .50 gallon drums of 100 octane gasoline [were] going up into the air like fireworks. I never saw anything like it. I dove up under the gun, [under] the trails of the gun.... Because [the driver] pulled it in under the palm trees, thank God, I [was able to dive] under the gun, and there was debris flying all over the place. And it didn't last very long. [There were] quite a few killed, and especially the Seabees; the Navy really caught hell. We lost, I think, four or five men, and one of the guns of A Battery got hit. But, anyway, I wasn't five minutes ashore, and the Japanese welcomed me that way.

Packed on a narrow stretch of Rendova beachline "less than a mile long and 500 yards deep," the conditions were ripe for a slaughter.

Drums of gasoline and diesel, boxes of ammunition and the 43rd Division's casualty clearing station were all hit, and five tons of Seabee demolition materials exploded in brilliant flames. Jack recalled that it was absolute pandemonium. Caught in the open without foxholes, on the hard coral of the small peninsula, the Seabees took the brunt of the attack, surrounded by drums and crates of fuel and ammo. The colossal explosion of the 24th Seabees' gelignite dump on a peninsula jutting into Rendova Harbor may have caused more damage than the Japanese bombs themselves. In this explosion, only a few hundred yards from Jack's location, a bulldozer and several Seabees disintegrated as they, too, were blasted skyhigh. The sounds were deafening and, although the air raid only lasted a few minutes, the helpless men lost all sense of accurate time.

Not long before being pressed into stevedore duties, Jack had set up his water purification gear on a stream near the beachhead, and he remembered crouching low in a shallow foxhole, shooting away (like almost everyone else around him, it seemed) with his rifle at the Japanese planes flying low over the beachhead. He recalled his amazement that no U.S. planes were in evidence anywhere, and he cursed to himself, "Where in the hell is our air force?" His rifle kept jamming, but at least shooting it gave him the feeling of doing something useful. Besides, because the Zero pilots flew their machines extremely low to the ground during this attack, the 40mm and 90mm guns were practically useless: the Japanese fighters came in at tree-top level, anywhere from 50 to 90 feet above the beach or lower. "One got so low, I could see the face of the pilot. He was grinning away under his helmet and goggles, and I could see his machine guns blazing. If I had a rock, I probably could have hit him; he was that low." Jack also recalled that this pilot's antics—and his incredible lowness to the ground—so stupefied him that he stopped firing and gaped in amazement as the plane machine-gunned its way along the length of Rendova harbor. Of this air raid, Frank Chadwick recalled similar details: the Zeroes were painted in a brownish camouflage, and the canopy hoods were opened back so that the pilots' helmeted and goggled faces could be easily seen. But, within ten minutes, the air raid was over: not a single attacker had been harmed.

Suicide Point ablaze on July 2, 1943 after the Japanese air raid. (Official U.S. Marine Corps photo, courtesy of Col. (Ret'd) William T. Box)

The Japanese aviators' attentions to this area of Rendova harbor near Battery A's gun positions earned from its occupants the nickname "Suicide Point." Between them, all three branches of service took well over 200 casualties during the "Black Friday" air raid. Four of the Ninth's Marines were killed, one was declared missing in action, and 22 (including Chadwick) were wounded. The wounded also included one of Australian coastwatcher D.C. Horton's native scouts, hit by bomb fragments as he and two others tried to frantically paddle a native canoe out of harm's way. The fear caused by the Japanese air raid was not confined, of course, merely to the enlisted men or the Solomonese and Fijian scouts. One of the Marines' casualties was the redoubtable Colonel Shoup, the 2nd Division's observer assigned to cover the 43rd Division to learn first-hand about amphibious operations. Although lightly injured, Shoup wrote vividly in his diary of the pandemonium and terror of that raid:

> Air raid at 1335—*terrible*! No warning. Right in bull's eye. Estimate 300 casualties. All HQ hit badly. Gross sights—arms and legs moving all directions... Nearly crapped out myself.

The fact that a man as tough, trained and disciplined as Dave Shoup—later to be the only surviving recipient among the five Medals of Honor issued for the bloody fighting on Tarawa—"nearly crapped out" as a result of the July 2 raid is testimony as to the savagery and carnage of that air strike.

Four 9th Defense leathernecks died when three bombs hit Captain Reichner's Battery A. An unexploded bomb wedged itself between the gun trails of one of Battery A's 155s, which included in its crew Jack's buddy Bill Galloway, and dented one of its nitrogen-filled recoil cylinders in the process. The "dud" bomb put Galloway's Long Tom out of action for 72 hours, both to allow bomb-disposal personnel to remove and defuse the dud and to make repairs to the damaged gun. Adding to an already bad situation for Battery A, its gunpowder reserves had been set ablaze in the attack; so was a vehicle loaded with small arms ammo, the heat of the flames "cooking off" rifle bullets that spewed in all directions. Several of the Battalion's motor vehicles, including a couple of the precious Alligators and a massive Caterpillar TD-18 prime mover, were smashed beyond repair. The Battalion's surgeon and assistant surgeon, Navy Lt. Commander Miles Krepela and Lt. Nathan Gershon, had their work cut out for them and their Navy corpsmen. Even Navy Lt. Jake Goodwin, the Battalion's dentist, provided first aid on the beach.

The medical help, however, came too late for some men.

Emerging from a water-filled ditch full of red ants not far from Suicide Point, David "Biggie" Slater of the Battalion H&S Battery observed first-hand some of the human costs of the raid:

> Out of the smoke and dust tottered two men. One, his left arm shredded, leaned heavily on the other. A corpsman leaped up and relieved the second man of his burden. He walked on toward Biggie, who saw he was covered with blood.
>
> Biggie pointed. "Hey, Mac, is that your buddy's blood, or yours?"
>
> "I don't know, his, I guess."
>
> As the man passed, Biggie saw the pencil-sized splinter projecting from the man's chest, and he called out, "Corpsman, corpsman."
> "Mac, you're hit."
>
> The man looked at Biggie and then down at himself. He breathed pink bubbles.
>
> "Gee, gee. Oh!"
>
> His eyes rolled. He fell. He died.

The July 2 air raid was the first and bloodiest of over 150 air raids the Japanese were to make during the course of the Rendova/New Georgia campaign. The Japanese surface fleet added to the chaos by shelling Rendova later that evening. Led by a cruiser and nine destroyers, this flotilla fired several volleys of shells at the beachhead, but without much material success. The Japanese ships escaped, challenged only briefly by a small group of PT boats that failed to inflict significant damage on the retreating enemy flotilla.

Even after the dead and wounded had been evacuated, the area around Suicide Point after the July 2 air raid remained a gruesome scene for several days thereafter and was described by the Ninth's assigned combat correspondent, Staff Sergeant Sam Stavisky, as looking "like the face of the moon." "Down at the point the holocaust had taken a heavy loss of life and created a mess of burned supplies, wrecked small boats and water-filled coral craters," Lieutenant Donner recounted. His skipper, Captain Reichner, also recalled:

> While we were hard hit on July 2, the Army infantry landing from the LCIs and SeaBees were hit much harder. Bodies, body parts and body remnants were all over the place, on the ground, amidst fallen trees and floating in bomb craters. Many of the survivors were totally demoralized and appeared mentally deranged. The stench after a day or so was pretty bad, and body after body began to float to the surface of the water-filled bomb craters. Pathetic piles of soldiers' gear were everywhere, sad memorials to those who gave their lives on Suicide Point.

"Air raid at 1335—terrible!" **Dr. Krepela's navy corpsmen assist a casualty of the Suicide Point air raid. (Official U.S. Marine Corps photo, courtesy of Col. (Ret'd) William T. Box)**

Nevertheless, despite July 2's turmoil and its grisly remnants, all of the Long Toms soon were back in position and were lobbing their 95-pound shells across the narrow stretch of water separating Rendova from New Georgia. The eight Long Toms began administering a severe pummeling to enemy forces, both in support of the Army's July 2 main landings on New Georgia at Zanana Beach and on Munda Field itself and adjacent Kokengolo Hill. As one postwar historian noted, "Munda's fate was sealed in an instant" when the Ninth's Long Toms began their bombardment of the field: "Had any aircraft been there [which, in fact, was the case], they would have been blown to oblivion in a moment".

Frank Yemma recounted the spectacular effects of some of Battery B's first shots on Munda Field itself:

> Through all these firing missions they were getting, [Battery B had] four guns—1, 2, 3, 4—and they'd have one gun zero in on a particular target and fire, maybe, five rounds, and once they were on target, then . . .all four guns would fire on that particular target. And I guess we did a pretty good job, we found out later on, through diaries and the devastation when we went over there and saw what we did. I guess we killed a lot of them with our 155s.
>
> The only thing we actually saw—-because with field artillery, you never see your target, what you're hitting, but we were told when we saw all this black smoke going up—that we had hit an ammunition dump. That's what we were shooting for, and we hit our target . . . and we could see that from Rendova, we could see the smoke going up on Munda so, for once, we knew that we hit it.

The obvious success of their July 2 air raid, and the clear dangers presented by the 155mm Group's efforts to the continued occupation of Munda Field, inspired the Japanese high command in Rabaul to launch an even heavier air raid with the goal of putting the Ninth and the other American units on Rendova and the Army's Zanana beachhead on New Georgia out of action. Whether Vice Admiral Jinichi Kusaka, the commander of the Southeast Area Fleet in charge of the Rabaul and Solomons areas, had a sense of historical irony in terms of planning this next raid is unclear, but the date his staff selected for it was July 4, 1943.

The Fourth of July Raid

One of Jack's peers in the 90mm Group, Edmund Hadley, would later recall, "I will always think of July 4, 1943, as the day the planes fell." On that day, the Japanese 11th Air Fleet at Rabaul dispatched another raiding party of 100 medium bombers and numerous Zero fighters to finish off the work of July 2. As before, the primary target of the raid was Rendova's beaches and supply dumps and the Ninth's heavy artillery positions. This time, though, they would be in for a major surprise. Contrasted with the glitches that had plagued the Ninth's air-defense network in the earlier days, Frank Marshall wrote gleefully of the "glorious 4th" that "[t]his was one day that Murphy wasn't working."

Besides the rainstorms that had thwarted Allied air cover and the fatal airplane misidentifications, another reason for the major Japanese success on July 2 was that the Ninth's radar screen was off-line, partly due to a terrible error: its newest SCR-602 radar had broken down, and its largest radar, the gasoline-powered SCR-270 in Battery E used for long-range target acquisition, was out of commission from a true "snafu." The precious set had been foolishly refueled with diesel fuel from a drum mislabeled as gasoline, and a mechanic, attempting to clear the fuel stoppage during the midst of the July 2 raid, was electrocuted. The bombers' flight path compounded the problem, as the incoming raiders' approach from around Rendova Mountain helped shroud them from radar detection by the five smaller and shorter-range SCR-268s.

July 4 dawned bright and sunny on Rendova. By noontime, all the defects in the Ninth's radars had been remedied, and shortly after 1300 hours (1:35 p.m.), huddled over the big radar's oscilloscope, the SCR-270's crew reported: "Incoming bogies, at about 15,000 feet!" Around 1335 hours (1:35 p.m.), "Condition Red" was again sounded across the island as the fully operable radars detected and tracked a massed group of over 80 Japanese aircraft on a course heading for Rendova. "*Aw, hell, here we go again!*" the Leathernecks fumed and griped as they hastened about.

First in were the fighters, arriving over Rendova at about 1430 hours. As they did on July 2, a wave of 66 Zeroes dived down to roar in at treetop heights. This time, however, Special Weapons' light AA guns and .50 caliber machine guns were ready, and the rapid fire of these light guns downed one Zero and dissuaded the rest from completing their low-level strafing. Thinking back on July 2's fiascoes, Frank Marshall of the Special Weapons Group noted: "It was refreshing to be able to get in a punch now and then." Still, it was not an unmitigated American success. A Special Weapons officer, Lieutenant Joe La Cesa, was killed from the concussion of a bomb near a 40mm position at Suicide Point, as well as another group of 43rd Division dogfaces. In addition, three more Marines were wounded and much equipment shot up again, including a pair of LCI landing craft, before the Zeroes left. Pogiebait sought out the nearest foxhole and spent the raid firing (more or less) fitfully and futilely at the attacking Zeroes with his rifle.

Of the 100-odd Japanese bombers dispatched from Rabaul, only sixteen penetrated the Allied fighter screen. Because they flew from a westerly direction, that is, apparently coming in from New Georgia and over Rendova Mountain, many of the Americans again made the same initial mistake they had on July 2 and once more assumed these were Allied B-25s coming back from a raid. The presence of so many nearby Zeroes, who obviously were making no efforts to attack the "friendly" bombers, rapidly convinced them otherwise. The bombers came in at a much higher altitude than the Zeroes and were in perfect formation at about a 12,500-foot altitude, "just like they were a bunch of migrating geese," Jack remembered. This height was well within the effective range of the 90mm Group's guns. With all the Group's radars and AA fire control equipment again fully operational, the 90mm guns' aiming would be dead-on the targets.

A 90mm AA gun and its crew in position after the July 2 and 4 air raids. Note the coconut-log and sandbag revetment. (Official U.S. Marine Corps photo, courtesy of Col. (Ret'd) William T. Box)

At 1410, a Special Weapons 40mm gun led off: "Within a few seconds the enemy planes became the target for every antiaircraft weapon on the island, joined in happy futility by a number of weapons with insufficient range or destructive power for such employment." Never mind the ineffectual fire of the peashooters: the powerful 90mm guns of the Ninth had the range and capabilities to finish the job. While only one of the 90mm Group's batteries, Battery E, was fully operational, as it turned out, its four guns were enough. In the words of Captain Bill Tracy, Battery E's commander on neighboring Kokorana Island, "Opening bursts were right on target. . . . the flight entered a large cloud. Pieces of plane were noted falling out of the cloud." Despite the lead bomber's rapid destruction with Captain Tracy's first burst of 90mm fire, "the formation flew straight ahead, closing its ranks and remaining a beautiful target." With each gun averaging five to six shells per minute, Tracy's four 90mm guns put up a withering volume of fire.

Like an aerial Charge of the Light Brigade and with little (if any) time to respond to the devastation being wrought on the formation, not a single Japanese bomber broke ranks to take evasive action, and all flew straight and level into the 90mm flak bursts. One bomber after another literally disintegrated in the bursts or fell earthward in flaming pieces. "Even as bits and pieces of aircraft came plummeting and fluttering down, the formation continued to close up, presenting a marvelous target," as David Slater recalled. Of the 16 bombers in the formation, only four escaped, all to be finished off by American and New Zealand fighters just scrambled from the Russells, a small island chain 35 miles northwest of Guadalcanal. With only 88 shells and in two to three minutes of firing time, Captain Tracy's battery had destroyed twelve bombers, and Special Weapons' gunners had claimed one Zero, setting a world record for the largest number of aircraft destroyed by antiaircraft fire with the least ammunition expended. The victory was immediate and total and was readily observed by many of the Americans on Rendova and the neighboring islands.

The CO of an Army field artillery battalion supporting the 37th Infantry Division was one of these witnesses. Based on a small island off New Georgia, Lt. Colonel Henry Shafer had a rare vantage point from which to watch the entire spectacle from start to finish:

> [He] saw sixteen bombers fly out of the west and proceed right over his head in a superb stepped-up vee-of-vees formation. . . . Shafer could not yet identify the insignae *[sic]*, but since the bombers paid his battalion no attention, he swallowed in pride and comfort, convinced they were Americans. The bombers continued in a gentle curve from Segi [on New Georgia] and made straight for Rendova . . . . Then Lieutenant Colonel Shafer and his gunners had a ringside seat to an incredible spectacle. Antiaircraft shells from Rendova and Kokorana [where Battery E was stationed] blossomed blackly within the bomber formation, and Betty after Betty fell away in flames. None of the remaining warplanes veered from its initial heading until only two *[sic]* were left. The antiaircraft fire ceased as the last two bombers flew out of range—right into the guns of waiting fighters, which destroyed them.

As the Ninth's official history records: "That day cheers were heard all over Rendova 'like a "Babe" homer in Yankee stadium,'" or, as Jack recalled fifty years later: "Wa-hoos, fist shakings and screams of delight were heard up and down the coast." Lt. Colonel Scheyer celebrated the occasion by helping to stencil a fresh line of miniature "Rising Sun" flags down the barrels of Battery E's 90mm guns, thirteen red flags for thirteen kills. It was a textbook example of precision antiaircraft gunnery. It was perhaps also a textbook example of how *not* to conduct a bombing run under AA fire.

Lt. Colonel Bill Scheyer (squatting on box) and Battery E's Captain Bill Tracy (stooping, far right) help stencil "victory marks" on one of Battery E's 90mm guns after the July 4 victory. (Official U.S. Marine Corps photo)

After the air battle, some of the Marines were puzzled by the Japanese bomber pilots' behavior. Granted, the entire action had lasted only a few minutes, but despite the brief elapsed time, it seemed clear that the bomber flight could have used a more spread-out formation and still have inflicted significant damage to Rendova. As David Slater recalled, "The flight of bombers was flying in a diamond formation: four bombers in small diamonds—each group of four being corners of the squadron diamond." From his wartime notes, Biggie Slater depicted the bomber formation as looking much like this when it entered Rendova's airspace:

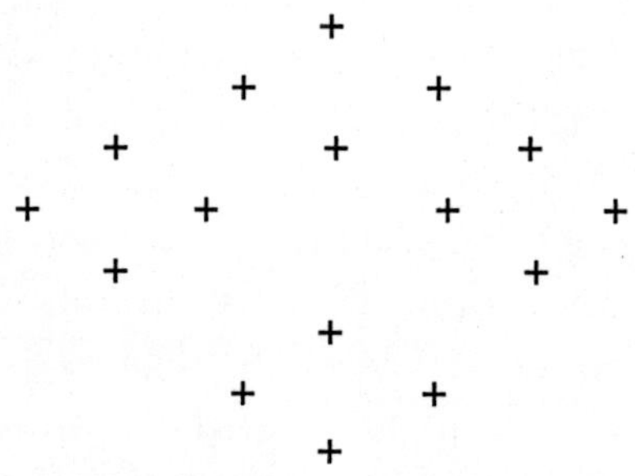

A more open bombing formation may have reduced the effectiveness of the bombing run somewhat, but why was such a formation not adopted? After all, it was ultimately fatal for the flight of bombers to have remained in its boxy formation. What prompted the Japanese pilots to maintain this spectacular, but highly ineffectual, flight plan? Was it fanaticism or blind obedience to orders? Was it out of some sense of professionalism? Was it fear, or some kind of death wish?

In truth, it may have been just simple lack of training and combat experience, which by mid-1943, because of increasing losses of skilled pilots and airmen, was becoming a major problem for Japan's naval and army air forces. In a formation like that used at Rendova, the better trained aircrews could lead and direct the rest of the formation with greater ease, in a sort of aerial "follow-the-leader." This simplified command of a bomber squadron but with fatal consequences: once enemy AA gunners pegged the precise range and height, the entire formation was also that much easier to bracket and hit. To Jack and most of his buddies, though, no lengthy or technical explanation was necessary: "They were crazy. It was just suicide to fly like that!" If the Japanese pilots' behavior seemed foolhardy, the existence of the Ninth's secret weapon indeed made this kind of formation flying suicidal. That "secret weapon" was, of course, radar.

While still fairly primitive in 1943, and while searchlights and optical telescopes would continue to be used for the rest of the war, the Battalion's radar sets helped make the 4th of July victory complete. Once the enemy's altitude, approximate speed and distance were fixed by the radar operators, this data was provided to the 90mm Group's fire control station. It, in turn, relayed the data to each 90mm battery's CO or fire control officer and, at nighttime, to Battery F's huge searchlights. The fire control officer translated this information into the correct elevation and deflection for the 90mms. Once radar had initially gotten the guns on target, however, and so long as the weather was good or distances to the targets were favorable, the rest of the target tracking was all done visually; hence, AA fire was not yet purely an automated, "hands-off" system that removed human effort and skill from the equation. The shells' fuses would be set to explode at the correct altitude, and each 22-pound shell, with its brass cartridge case, would be hefted into a cradle connected to the gun platform. Next, the shell was pushed by a mechanical ramming arm into the breech, and the sliding breechblock closed for firing. Within seconds after the battery began firing, the black puffs of flak bursts would be seen around the target.

One of Battery F's six searchlights. (Official U.S. Marine Corps photo, courtesy of Col. (Ret'd) William T. Box)

The various models of radar, coupled with the automated loading and aiming features of the new model 90mm guns the Ninth had acquired as it left Guadalcanal, undoubtedly helped Battery E rack up this world record. While these improvements in technology cannot detract from the AA gunners' skill and courage, they did give the gun crews an edge in speed and accuracy that was better than with optical, searchlight or sound-ranging equipment. Naturally, while it was optimal to destroy as many enemy bombers as possible, simply forcing the enemy away from choice targets like the ammo and supply dumps of Suicide Point was also a goal of AA gunnery. Hence, the Ninth's AA crews could claim a two-fold victory: the destruction of as many aircraft as they downed on that 4th of July, and the successful defense of a critical area. That fewer than 90 shells were needed to accomplish this feat was, in a sense, a bonus.

The Ninth's AA gunners of the 90mm and Special Weapons Groups claimed 46 Japanese aircraft kills during the entire New Georgia campaign, and at least 80 Japanese air attacks were recorded in the first twenty days of the fighting on Rendova and New Georgia. To many observers, however, the Battalion's performance during the 4th of July raid was its finest hour, and it partly redeemed the frustrations of the July 2 raid. Witnessed as it was by so many onlookers (sailors and Army "dogfaces" as well as Marines), it was an enormous tonic for the hard-pressed U.S. forces and helped bolster the confidence of many. In the years to come, Jack, Frank Chadwick, Al Downs, Jim Kruse, Bill Galloway and other veterans of the 9th Defense would celebrate each Independence Day by calling each other on the telephone to reminding themselves of what they had lived through on that one notable July 4th of 1943, when the "bombs bursting in air" were very real indeed, and the "red glare" was more than the plumes of skyrockets.

One last, puzzling note exists as to the identity of the Japanese medium bombers used in the July 2 and 4 attacks. Various records, including the Marines' own history of the campaign, have identified the bombers as being of the Mitsubishi G4M1 "Betty" model. These sources also note that when the Japanese bombers were first spotted on both days, they were misidentified not by one, but by many individuals and groups, as U.S. B-25 Mitchells. Frank Yemma even recalled the Japanese raiders as looking at first glance like civilian-style transports due to their uncamouflaged, bare aluminum bodies. The same official Marine history reported: "Inexperienced ground troops, lacking sufficient training in aircraft identification, stood in open-mouthed admiration of the 'friendly B-25s.' " Unseasoned troops were not, however, the only American personnel to think these hostile bombers were B-25s. Even several comparably better-trained AA gunners and officers made the same mistake.

Both the Betty and Mitchell were twin-engined, low-wing-position medium bombers, of roughly the same size and bomb capacity, with a partly glassed-in "greenhouse" nose for their bombardiers. Apart from such similarities, there was one critical, and relatively easily identifiable difference, even in the haste and stress of combat: the Mitchell had a twin-rudder tail assembly, readily visible from almost all angles, while the stubbier Betty had a single rudder at its tail. Given that this makes for a strikingly dissimilar feature between the two types of aircraft, how could such an error have occurred, with—at least on July 2—the devastating consequences that followed?

The likeliest answer may be that the Japanese Navy often used another bomber that, at a quick glance, closely resembled the B-25. This bomber, the Mitsubishi G3M2 "Nell," was developed several years before the Betty and was instrumental in the sinking of the British warships *Prince of Wales* and *Repulse* off Singapore in December 1941. Like the Betty, the Nell had the range to enable it to fly the 770-mile circuit from New Britain's airfields to Rendova and back. Like the Betty, it had already encountered the Ninth's AA gunners in several missions over Guadalcanal. And, like the B-25, the Nell had a highly distinctive twin-rudder tail assembly. In terms of *ex post facto* record-keeping after the July 2 and July 4 raids, it may have been easier simply to call all the Japanese bombers "Bettys" than to break them down by type.

At least one veteran of the Ninth is adamant that the bombers were Nells, not Bettys. According to David Slater, who witnessed both air raids:

> The planes that attacked us on July 2 and 4, 1943 were definitely NELLs. I watched the entire affair on the 4th from start to finish, and I was good at aircraft identification (plus eagle eyes). An aside is the memory that it was reported at the time that a Lt. (j.g.) in command of a Sea Bee work detail on the 2nd had seen the planes and kept his crew working because he remarked about them being B-25s. His bunch was heavily hit and constituted the major number of casualties that day.

This Seabee officer was certainly not alone in making what, in his unit's case, was a fatal error. Other witnesses, including Captain Reichner and the Army's Lt. Colonel Shafer, fell prey to this initial misidentification as well. A comparison of silhouettes and photographs of the two kinds of Japanese bombers against a B-25, however, show that, even in combat, it would be difficult to confuse a Betty with a B-25, or *vice versa*. Hence, two errors of aircraft I.D. occurred: the mistaking of Japanese bombers for "friendly" Mitchells, and the mistaking of Nells for Bettys.

Friend or foe? Comparative aircraft recognition sillhouettes, from left to right: a Mitsubishi "Nell"; a B-25 Mitchell; and a Mitsubishi "Betty." (Author's collection)

Errors of aircraft identification cut both ways, however. During one of the early Japanese air raids on Rendova, Jack vividly recalled watching two planes zooming low across the beach near Suicide Point, engines screaming loudly. Recognizing the lead plane as a Zero, several Battery B gunners, including Jack's friend "Zombie" Jones, decided that they would not let this one get away. The gunners furiously peppered the airspace in front of them with automatic weapons fire. Unfortunately, Zombie and his cohorts failed to "lead" the Zero, that is, firing far enough in front of the enemy plane for the bullets to hit it in a timely manner—and the bullets riddled not the first plane but the second, which turned out to be a U.S. fighter in hot pursuit of the Zero. Zombie, Jack and their buddies watched dumbstruck as the American pilot barely managed to bail out before his fighter careened into Blanche Channel. Soon thereafter, the American aviator "hit the bay and came out mad as hell," as Jack remembered; he also remembered it took a lot of diplomacy (and the presence of several Marines, who were more heavily armed than the pistol-packing aviator) to keep the battered, half-drowned and thoroughly pissed-off pilot from making his own "friendly fire" casualties out of Zombie and several other Marines!

After that incident and several other near-misses on other members of the notoriously profane VMF-214, the "Black Sheep" (which several Leathernecks remembered brought forth purple torrents of obscenities from the squadron's pilots and Major Gregory "Pappy" Boyington himself into the Battalion's air-to-ground radio sets), one Battery E vet, Jerry Morris, noticed an American flag stencil in an odd place. It was prominently placed on the barrel of a 9th Defense AA gun, next to a row of similarly-sized red "meatball" flag stencils. "Only in the Marines," Morris laughingly recalled, "could you get away with that." Many friendly-fire incidents, however, were no laughing matter, such as the shooting death of one of Battery A's sergeants on the evening of June 30.

The Ninth's Marines were certainly not the only U.S. branch of service to be cursed by friendly fire casualties during the Rendova-New Georgia operations. Navy PT boats had figured in the most embarrassing Central Solomons mishap. This involved the assault transport U.S.S. *McCawley*—Jack's transport to Rendova, the dreaded "Wacky Mac" herself—which was also Admiral Turner's flagship as CO of Task Force 62, the Navy task force for Operation TOENAILS. Not many hours after Jack disembarked from it, the radar-equipped *McCawley* was the victim of a Japanese bomber strike during the first day's landings. Still smoking from its damage and under tow by a U.S. destroyer, the "Wacky Mac" made for Blanche Channel on the evening of June 30. As she entered the channel, a PT boat, mistaking the *McCawley* and her escort for a Japanese convoy (even though the ships clearly made no efforts to take evasive action), launched a spread of torpedoes, and sank the *McCawley*. It was not until their boat returned home that the jubilant PT crew learned the "Japanese ship" they had sunk was Task Force 62's own flagship. As will be seen, too, the Army would suffer more than its fair share of fratricidal shootouts in the jungles of New Georgia, leading in part to the coinage of a new medical term: *combat neurosis*.

When the Army began landing on New Georgia proper, elements of the 9th Defense—particularly the Tank Platoon and elements of Special Weapons—were detached to support Army operations on New Georgia. In many respects, the Tank Platoon's activities were a pioneering effort, as the Allies had not used tanks in true jungle fighting on such a scale before. The Tank Platoon's eight light tanks (now beefed up by an additional four M-3s on loan from other Marine units) saw vicious and sustained action in support of Army infantry attacks, and the tanks' crews faced attacks by small groups of desperate but determined Japanese troops armed with flamethrowers, magnetic mines and Molotov cocktails.

Jack recalled that one of his friends was a driver in Captain Blake's Tank Platoon and served in a M-3 Stuart that took a hit in the nose, almost directly underneath his seat. The driver's seat was a wooden bench, and the force of the explosion splintered the seat. The blast drove splinters deeply into the tank driver's buttocks but otherwise left him shaken yet more or less intact. For many months afterward, his unfortunate tanker friend "had to go to the medics weekly to get splinters pulled out of his butt," Jack ruefully laughed. Despite his pal's wounded dignity, this was hardly the worst or oddest injury suffered by Blake's platoon, however: that had to have been the M-3 crewman whose leg was crushed by a tree limb hurtling through his open hatch. By the end of the battle for New Georgia, all of the platoon's M-3s were destroyed or "deadlined" for major repairs. The Tank Platoon quite probably saw more sustained, direct combat than any other portion of the Ninth, and Captain Blake himself was nearly roasted alive by a Japanese flamethrower that doused his tank with gasoline but, fortunately, failed to ignite. As Biggie Slater observed, "Blake was the epitome of true heroism."

Captain Blake and a Tank Platoon member with a captured Japanese flamethrower, which doused Blake's M-3 tank but failed to ignite. (Official U.S. Marine Corps photo)

The Special Weapons detachments set up light AA and machine gun points on Zanana and Laiana Beaches, the latter being about 2 1/2 miles from Munda Point, close enough to hear the detonations of the 155mm Group's own shells landing on the nearby Japanese defenders. The 155mm Group's guns on Rendova, lined up within a few yards of each other amidst the coconut groves on the island's northern tip, by this time were somewhat better protected from air attack or shelling by coconut-log and sandbagged revetments and loosely shrouded in camouflage nets. The Group was earning for itself the nickname of "Murderers' Row," and the Long Toms' shelling of Munda Point would continue almost unabated for the rest of July.

Around 5:00 a.m. on July 9, the 155mm Group joined in a massive and extensively coordinated assault on Munda Point, later described as one of the heaviest artillery barrages of the war in the Pacific. Almost 6,000 shells were fired in one hour between the Ninth's Long Toms and the smaller 105mm and 155mm howitzers of three Army artillery battalions. A group of destroyers offshore fired another 2,344 shells, and then 52 TBFs and 36 dive bombers finished off the job. Frank Yemma later recalled this particularly wild bombardment of the Japanese positions around Munda Point, which called forth almost every available element of the American arsenal in the Central Solomons:

> [On the night before the firing mission], we were alerted that our Navy was going to open up on the Japanese on Munda Point where they were entrenched in there. There were destroyers, and there were I think two cruisers . . . that opened up on them, and they pounded the hell out of them. And then [the ships] stopped, and then the Army opened up with their 105s, and we opened up with our 155s—A Battery and B Battery—and we pounded them for about an hour.
>
> Then we were told to cease firing, that our planes were going to come over and continue the dive-bombing on the Japanese positions. Which they did: SBD dive bombers came over and dive-bombed them. And I think somebody related—the number sticks in my mind—that 70 tons were dropped on the Japanese positions then. But it was one hell of a night for them, I'll tell you; it was a wonder that any of them lived through that.

Yemma's closing sentiments were certainly echoed by those on the receiving end of these bombardments. One of the defenders of Munda Point serving in an anti-tank and AA cannon unit, Probationary Officer Toshihiro Oura, wrote grimly on July 10, only weeks before his own death: "The artillery shelling's accuracy has become a real thing. We can never tell when we are to die." But for all this mighty outpouring of explosives and sweat, the 43rd Division advanced only 400 yards and still suffered sizeable casualties in vicious hand-to-hand fighting.

At about the same time, in a desperate bid to reinforce New Georgia's defenders, the Japanese Navy dispatched several major convoys much like the Tokyo Express-style runs of Guadalcanal. One attempt was made by the Japanese on July 6, but, in the ensuing Battle of Kula Gulf, they succeeded in moving only a small number of troops closer to Munda and lost two destroyers in the process while sinking the American cruiser *Helena.* The fireworks at sea were readily visible to the 155mm Group's exhausted guncrews on Rendova, who, far out of their own Long Toms' effective range and bereft of ship-to-shore communications, could only guess helplessly whose side was ahead. "We watched the tracers zip through the darkness over Kula Gulf and saw the bright explosions as ships were hit," Chris Donner observed. "All we could do was hope that our forces were winning."

One week later, on the night of July 12-13, Jack and his fellow Marines were able to watch from their Rendova foxholes what looked from a distance like tropical heat lightning and sounded like very loud thunder. It was, in actuality, ships' gunfire again, as an American task force, in the Battle of Kolombangara, intercepted and broke up the Japanese convoy, with the Japanese losing the cruiser *Jintsu.* It was the closest the Ninth's men had come since Guadalcanal to watching a major naval battle unfold. Several Japanese warships, including the *Jintsu* and several destroyers, broke through the U.S. naval cordon, steamed within range of Rendova and opened fire. Due to poor weather conditions and faulty target-spotting, the shells overshot the beachhead by approximately two miles and fell inland. Still, it was close enough for Jack and his fellow Leathernecks to hear the explosions and be thankful that they had been spared the horrors of an accurate naval bombardment.

Although safe from this threat, the Japanese resorted to using an old ploy from Guadalcanal. Shortly after the Naval Battle of Kula Gulf, those nocturnal pests, "Louie the Louse" and "Washing Machine Charlie," returned to make life miserable for the troops on Rendova. Lieutenant Donner wrote:

> And now began the nightly activity which began to wear us down. The Japs began to harass the beachhead by small, intermittent air raids, six or seven throughout the night, which kept us jumping or rolling into foxholes because no one knew where the next load of bombs would drop in the darkness. Each time the sky above the harbor would light up with fireworks as the unwelcome "bogies" and "washing machine Charlies" were caught in the searchlight beams. We came in the next ten days to expect the first warning just after darkness had claimed the sky. The last cigarettes and pipes of the evening would go out, and we would crawl into our holes as we heard the unsynchronized drone of the Nip motors. Very few of these were shot down, for they had no definite bombing run to carry out. Whenever they felt like letting go, down came the stick. We became proficient at estimating the precise point at which the bombs landed. Almost everyone was reduced to sleeping below the deck level during that period, in order to get more than snatches of sleep.

While the Allies were beginning by mid-July to win daylight air superiority over Rendova and New Georgia, Louie and Charlie owned the night for weeks to come, much to the regret of Pogiebait and his sleep-starved, grimy and malarial buddies.

Wantuck and Rothschild: How the Ninth Saved the Day on New Georgia

About July 15, with the 43rd Infantry Division ashore in force on New Georgia and advancing to Munda Point, more elements of the 9th Defense were redeployed from Rendova onto New Georgia itself and other small islands. Although not widely known to Jack and the Ninth's rank-and-file, its officers now knew from their daily briefings and interactions with headquarters that the campaign was not progressing at all according to plan. "By this time, it was evident that the Army attack at Munda had stalled badly," Lieutenant Chris Donner remembered. "We knew, too, that the Marine Raider Battalions, over at Kula Gulf, were being badly hacked up by overwhelming numbers of Japs because of the delay. Theirs was to have been a swift move to cut off the retreat from Munda, but the 43rd Division couldn't force the Nips to retreat." On top of this, several large Japanese units had disappeared: a counter-attack was in the works.

Since early July, part of the Special Weapons Group had been posted at small-caliber AA positions along New Georgia's coast, with a large detachment under Lieutenant John Wismer posted at Zanana, the Army's beachhead for the July 2 main landings. This location helped provide air defense for a rear area command post of the 43rd Division, an antitank platoon from the division's 172nd Infantry, and rear-echelon logistics units; however, to call this a "rear area" was of a misnomer. Numerous Japanese patrols still infiltrated the area, and one of Lieutenant Wismer's patrols killed four Japanese troops in mid-July.

In fact, by this time, two Japanese infantry regiments were moving rapidly through the coconut groves and marshes towards the Zanana beachhead. An experienced and well-trained unit, the 13th Infantry Regiment had been ordered to move from the island of Kolombangara to Bairoko Harbor on New Georgia and to strike the right flank of the U.S. XIV Corps held by the 43rd Division. The regiment moved its three battalions one at a time under cover of nightfall, in barges and small boats, over the course of several evenings beginning on July 9. Amazingly, despite the presence of a nearby screen of PT boats, these barge convoys were undetected by the Americans, and the entire Japanese 13th Infantry and part of the 229th Infantry Regiments then slogged through jungle trails and swamps to their jumping-off points near Bairoko. From start to finish, although this activity took almost a week, the disappearance and movement of two enemy infantry regiments somehow escaped the attention of XIV Corps's and the 43rd Division's intelligence staffs. The Japanese infantry assault groups were fully reassembled in their jumping-off positions in the marshes of the Barike River, southeast of Munda Field, by July 15. Late on the 17th, several patrols reported spotting a column of several hundred Japanese moving eastward. A reconnaissance element of the 43rd failed to intercept this formation.

As he reported to the 43rd's rear-area command post on July 17, passing by the division's and XIV Corps's rear area elements, Lieutenant Wismer noticed that the Corps's right flank appeared to be undefended. When he questioned a senior Army officer as to why this was the case, the officer assured him that the flank was made up of nothing but impenetrable marshland. The Allies' prior experiences with the Japanese army should have reminded those members of the corps and divisional staffs who relied on harsh terrain to thwart Japanese attacks that this was a false hope: as the Marines had learned on the Canal and as British, Dutch and Australian troops had learned to their cost in Malaya and the East Indies, "impassable" swamps, too, could be negotiated by dedicated troops. Lieutenant Wismer chose not to trust solely to this officer's professional judgment. On the night of July 17, he spread his fifty-odd Marines out and put considerable efforts into setting up and improving the detachment's defensive perimeter and observation points. He cut back his AA gun crews to half strength; the Marines freed up by this restaffing dug foxholes on a small knoll 150 yards off the edge of the beach. Several members of the detachment volunteered to beef up their already considerable defensive armament by scrounging some broken-down .30 machine guns from a nearby Army Ordnance small-arms collection and repair point, and they further scrounged some ammo belts to feed the newly acquired guns.

As night fell, the seasoned troops of the Japanese 13th Infantry began to infiltrate the rear areas of the 43rd Division. Around 9:00 p.m., one battalion attacked the XIV Corps's command post area and, launching a bayonet charge, another battalion attacked Wismer's and the 43rd Division's Zanana Beach positions. The first Japanese onrush on the Zanana defenders was driven back, to the apparent surprise of the attackers who had believed they would strike an essentially undefended position. Loud screams and yells and the explosion of grenades and 50mm "knee mortar" shells signaled the onset of a more determined charge. Several of the soldiers and Marines broke and ran, and the first defensive line began to collapse.

Let Lieutenant Wismer tell the rest of the story:

> At about nine o' clock approximately 100 Japanese came into the draw and started to set up mortars. We held our fire at the last moment before they started firing in order that the greatest concentration of enemy troops would be present. Upon opening fire, we drove back the Japanese into the jungle. They regrouped and made a banzai charge. The forward positions were overrun and individually we made our way back to the gun positions on the beach, where we

> prepared to defend against the next charge. To our surprise, it did not materialize.

The reason a final charge was absent was largely due to the guts of two of Wismer's enlisted men.

As Wismer's force fell back to make its final defensive stand alongside their 20mm and 40mm AA guns and machine guns near the beach, Private John Wantuck and Corporal Maier Rothschild volunteered to the lieutenant to stay up front in one-man foxholes near the center of the collapsing defensive line. They took the brunt of the Japanese attack, with each manning one of the scrounged .30 machine guns. Between Wantuck's and Rothschild's fire and that of the light AA guns on the beachhead firing over their heads, the Japanese attack broke up, but it was not until it was almost dawn that Lieutenant Wismer's party finally found Wantuck and Rothschild.

Wantuck's corpse was bullet-riddled and slashed by bayonets and grenade blasts. Rothschild was found under a bush, alive but wounded and still screaming bloody murder, apparently having been slashed in hand-to-hand grappling with a Japanese officer, whose sword Rothschild bare-handedly deflected before killing the officer. Army and Marine investigators determined that, between them, Wantuck and Rothschild had personally killed almost 20 Japanese, wounded 12 to 15 others, and had eliminated a 90mm mortar and its crew, which was deploying to blast the 43rd Division's nearby rear CP out of existence (and, but for them, would have succeeded). In the entire area of the 13th Regiment's attack, over 100 Japanese bodies were found.

John Wantuck (seated) and Maier Rothschild (standing, with clip of 40mm shells) at Zanana Point before the attack. (Official U.S. Marine Corps photo)

For their bravery, Wantuck and Rothschild were recommended by Maj. General Hester, the commander of the 43rd Division, for the Medal of Honor; however, in order to be eligible for this, the highest U.S. military decoration for bravery in action, there must be two credible, living eyewitnesses to the purported act of courage that was "above and beyond the call of duty." Because Rothschild was the only possible living witness, because no other witnesses were available who could corroborate their actions, and because the Marine Corps preferred to "take care of its own," Wantuck and Rothschild ultimately received Navy Crosses. In late 1944, a Navy destroyer was commissioned in Wantuck's honor, and memorial services were held in his honor in his hometown of Elmira, New York. Lieutenant Wismer, a West Pointer who had opted to become a Marine instead of an Army officer, was recommended by the Army commander for a Distinguished Service Cross for his own heroism and tenacity in holding the beachhead, but the Marine Corps apparently failed to act on the recommendation. Apart from a chewing-out from several Marine staff officers for leaving his forward positions and for trying to "play infantryman" when he should have been focusing on AA tactics, however, he received no official recognition from the Corps for his role in saving the Zanana beachhead.

Jack recalled that Rothschild was already something of a loner long before the events of July 17 and that he had the reputation of being "a man with a past" (he was, in fact, a former Wall Street employee). Moreover, Rothschild was somewhat older than the average enlisted Marine, and in fact was one of the few 9th Defense enlisted Marines who had seen prior service in the Corps before the war. Rothschild had "adopted" Wantuck, who was just 17 years old and was regarded by some as being a little slow. There was a suspicion that Rothschild had put Wantuck up to helping him scrounge the machine guns and setting them up in the first place. Those who knew Wantuck well believed it was not an act that would have naturally occurred to him unless somebody had suggested it, as he was fairly naive and otherwise would not have known any better. It was also a risky act in another manner in that the machine guns they manned were apparently tripod-mounted, water-cooled M1917s. To be effective, this model required at least two men to keep the machine gun served with ammo and the barrel's cooling jacket full of water; when the coolant ran out, the gun quickly overheated and jammed. Both guns, of course, were not in pristine condition anyway, having been "junked" and left at an Ordnance Corps collection point, which is where Wantuck and Rothschild found them. Under the circumstances of the attack, Wantuck's and Rothschild's machine guns must have jammed fairly quickly and frequently in the heat of the frenzied firefight. Jack also admitted that, since Rothschild was one of the relatively few Marines of Jewish extraction in the Ninth, that too tended to set him somewhat apart from the typical gentile Marine. Whether due to his background, the death of Wantuck, or perhaps due to his own personal terrors faced in the Zanana Beach jungle, Rothschild became even more withdrawn and, unlike some other Marine heroes, he seemed reluctant to make much of being a Navy Cross recipient when he could possibly have done so to go back home on War Bond or recruiting tours.

Not long after the war, Rothschild broke contact with his fellow 9th Defense veterans and, after requiring treatment in a VA hospital, disappeared completely. Jack and his friends never heard from him again. Like Wantuck, Rothschild, too, was undoubtedly a casualty of the New Georgia campaign.

The casualties inflicted by Wantuck's and Rothschild's efforts and by their detachment's 40mm guns, their guns firing at maximum depression, had stopped one battalion of the 13th Infantry cold, and the survivors withdrew into the nearby swamps. That regiment's other infiltrations, however, proved to be more successful: its troops caused havoc throughout the 43rd Division's positions. In the inky blackness of the New Georgia night, suspecting that Japanese snipers lurked everywhere, some Americans completely lost their fire discipline, firing or throwing grenades at everything that moved. Many casualties in the 43rd Division resulted from G.I.s shooting one another. The psychological state of many troops of this division was already less than good and had led to similar incidents shortly after landing. The events of July 17-18 only worsened that division's overall morale and combat effectiveness.

Other elements of the Japanese 13th Infantry and 229th Infantry Regiments were also sowing confusion behind American lines. Their patrols had succeeded in cutting communications lines between XIV Corps's forward command post and the 43rd Division's main CP. These served as the nerve centers of the Corps's and Division's key operations, the locus for the signals and logistics staffs, and the divisional CP area was soon under direct attack. Some casualty clearing stations were overrun, and several patients and doctors were massacred. In the words of the Army's official history of the campaign:

> Elsewhere on the night of 17-18 July the Japanese caused alarms and uproar. They launched simultaneous raids against the engineer and medical bivouacs and the 43rd Division command post at Zanana. . . .The attacks against the engineer and medical bivouacs were easily beaten off, but at the command post the raiders' first onslaught carried them through the security detachment's perimeter and into the communications center where they ripped up telephone wires and damaged the switchboard before being chased off.

While all available soldiers in the area, including cooks, signalers and supply troops, were cobbled together to form a hasty defense, the great likelihood existed that one more determined Japanese assault could seize or wipe out Corps and Division headquarters, thus crippling—if not eliminating outright—any chance of an Allied victory on New Georgia. Fortuitously, the force's senior artillery officer and Colonel Scheyer's nominal boss during Operation TOENAILS, General Barker, was visiting the 43rd's forward CP when the CP was cut off and surrounded by the Japanese. Realizing the enormity of the crisis, he began requesting emergency artillery support from all available Army and Marine artillery. Captain James Buhler, a 43rd Division field artillery office stationed in the CP, found one telephone line that was still functioning. An urgent "call for fire" was soon placed over the surviving phone line to Colonel O'Neil and Major Hiatt at the 155mm Group's headquarters control post—a request for Batteries A and B to provide final protective fires for the CP area.

The 155mm Group's CO and his Exec, Colonel O'Neil and Major Hiatt, certainly understood the gravity of the situation, yet if they felt nervous about their new mission, it would have been wholly understandable. Neither of the 155mm batteries had ever practiced nighttime firing as a field artillery unit before. After some hasty experiments, however, the "Old Man" and the Exec were satisfied that by hanging lanterns on the aiming stakes used to align the guns, the Group could provide accurate fire support to the beleaguered CP. Under Captain Wells's prodding, Battery B retrieved two flashlights that were quickly converted into makeshift lanterns and attached as markers to the aiming stakes. Within 15 minutes of the call for fire, all hands were tumbling out of their foxholes, lean-tos and tents, clad in little more than their skivvies and boots, and the big guns went in action.

Colonel Archie O'Neil (with pipe) and Major Hiatt (with telephone talker) plot a fire mission for Batteries A and B. (Official U.S. Marine Corps photo)

When the massive shells began to explode not far from the CP's defensive perimeter, the Army officers in the besieged command post provided excellent forward observer support by directing the Group's fire over the one unsevered telephone line from the CP. For four hours, the Long Toms blanketed the areas outside the CP with shells, breaking up the Japanese attacks. Like their brethren in the 13th Infantry at Zanana Beach, the battered Japanese survivors pulled back into the nearby marshes and rain forests. Depleted by its losses, the 13th Regiment regrouped in the swamps and marshes and moved back to Bairoko Harbor and thence back to Kolombangara from whence it had set forth nine days earlier.

Elsewhere on New Georgia, no longer exulting over the long-anticipated Japanese counterattack, Toshihiro Oura recorded in his diary entry for July 19 how it felt for his platoon to be on the receiving end of one of the Ninth's bombardments that same evening:

> Last night's shelling was terrific. The road that runs to the rear of the east side of the Field Defense HQ is the infantry's route of advance. The enemy appears to have observed this by air and are concentrating their fire in this sector. This concentration of fire is just over our dugout. Since it has only one entrance, the air is stuffy, and the sounds of the explosions cause ringing in our ears. There were explosions of several shells 15cm in diameter and 70cm long. It is really more than I can bear. The men were really scared, and they all ran into my dugout. I had to take them out mercilessly and assign them to other dugouts.

The 155mm Group's nighttime mission of July 17-18, 1943 was an extremely hazardous affair, not only because this was a first-time undertaking. Sometime during the four-hour "shoot," a squadron of Japanese bombers was over Rendova. Spotting the Long Toms' incandescent muzzle flashes, flashing like torches through the dark jungle canopy—as Jack recalled, these seemed bright enough to "turn night into day"—the bombers evidently changed their preplanned bombing runs to attack Batteries A and B. This next brought parts of the Special Weapons and 90mm Groups into action: their flak bursts were dense and heavy enough to thwart the bombers, and the 155mm Group was able to continue its fire mission unmolested. Still, several bombs struck nearby. As Frank Chadwick bragged:

> In "B" Battery, we had bombs drop on our right flank and in our rear, some close enough to shake your eyeteeth but never any direct hits or [enough] to deter the Marines from their firing.... This would not have been possible or successful without the support of the 90mm Group. This ["all-arms" effort] was a Marine defense battalion at its best...

The 9th Defense's actions on two fronts—Lieutenant Wismer's stand at Zanana and the 155mm Group's fierce nighttime bombardment from Rendova—helped to save both the 43rd Division and XIV Corps from destruction, thus salvaging the American foothold on New Georgia.

Had Lieutenant Wismer's detachment not been precisely where it was and not held its ground as fiercely as it did, the Japanese 13th Regiment would likely have overrun the 43rd Division's rear area. Even if it were temporary, such a move would have severed the division's ability to resupply and reinforce its forward elements and would have required its combat troops to have to stop their offensive momentum and double-back to secure the rear area. Had the XIV Corps's and 43rd Division's CPs and their respective staffs been captured, killed or otherwise stymied, the effect—both as a practical matter and from the standpoint of American morale—would have been devastating for the course of the Central

Solomons campaign. Not only would the central planning staff for that campaign have been eliminated in one stroke, but the detailed plans for Operation TOENAILS could well have fallen into Japanese hands. Had that occurred, the effects would have been incalculable. Suffice it to say that it certainly would have made the course of a bitterly fought campaign even more difficult, time-consuming and bloody to all involved. The evening of July 17-18 had been, as Wellington said of Waterloo, a "close-run thing." Through its actions, the "Fighting Ninth" helped save the course and maintain the momentum of the entire Central Solomons campaign, a fact of which Jack and his peers were justifiably proud.

On to Munda Point and Kolombangara; The End of TOENAILS

> *The day is set and we are ready. Be alert, and when the enemy appears, shoot calmly, shoot fast, and shoot straight.*
>
> Lt. Gen. A.A. Vandegrift

> *Japanese imperial headquarters admitted today in a Tokyo broadcast recorded by the Associated Press that the American offensive centering around New Georgia Island in the Solomons was continuing on a scale of considerable magnitude although it insisted all attacks were being repulsed with heavy casualties.*
>
> Associated Press communique, August 5, 1943

Soon after the Japanese counterattack, the redoubtable Admiral Halsey, the South Pacific area commander, issued orders to stabilize and strengthen the American presence on New Georgia. Concerned by the report of Maj. General Oscar W. Griswold, XIV Corps's CO, that the 43rd Division was "about to fold up" and with an especially high number of the division's troops in two regiments suffering from combat fatigue, "Bull" Halsey resolved to dispatch massive U.S. reinforcements. Accordingly, he ordered his senior army commander to "take whatever steps were deemed necessary to capture Munda." The rest of the XIV Corps began arriving to reinforce the battered 43rd Division. The Army's 37th Infantry Division, another National Guard division, was also soon bogged down around Munda. It, in turn, was followed by elements of yet another Army outfit, the 25th Infantry Division under Maj. General J. Lawton ("Lightnin' Joe") Collins. This last division had seen combat in the final months of the fight for Guadalcanal and was a particularly well-led and well-trained unit. They were joined by elements of Admiral Halsey's headquarters and the crusty old admiral himself.

The desolate landscape around Munda Field testified to the grim effectiveness of the 155mm Group's work. (Official U.S. Marine Corps photo, courtesy of Joseph Pratl)

Despite their July 4 repulse, the Japanese army and naval air forces continued to make bombing and strafing runs around Rendova, and the Rendova/New Georgia installment of Washing Machine Charlie's antics soon began anew with nighttime raids both by small seaplanes based at Kolombangara and bombers launched from Rabaul. By one Battalion estimate, approximately 3,000 90mm shells were fired one evening alone, without apparent success. On August 1, a Japanese air raid hit Tombusolo, an islet next to Rendova, where part of the Special Weapons Group had been deployed to protect a Navy PT boat anchorage. PT Squadron 9 was stationed there to intercept Japanese barges, canoes and small coastal convoys shuttling supplies and troops to and from New Georgia and its sister isles. Despite furious ack-ack fire, Japanese "Val" dive bombers destroyed a PT boat, blasting its plywood hull into planking.[7/]

July 23 was the day of the last entry in Probationary Officer Oura's war diary, which reflects the progressive deterioration of his and his troops' spirit. The morning's entry begins:

> *Battle Situation*: Nothing aside from annihilation. No cooperation from the Navy. If I were to compare the complete cooperation of the enemy, it would be like the war of a child and an adult. Our mountain artillery positions were knocked to pieces by enemy tanks. We are encircled, so they say, and about to be overrun. Consequently, all we can do is to guard our present positions.

His final diary entry is brief and full of foreboding: "There are signs that I am contracting malaria again." Like Toshihiro Oura—who name was not listed among the relative handful of prisoners taken in the capture of New Georgia—the Japanese forces' days on New Georgia were numbered.

As Army infantry units and Captain Blake's light tanks began closing in on Munda Point, Batteries A and B shifted their fire missions in early August to other Japanese targets. In mid-July, Battery A moved from Rendova to nearby Tombusolo Island to resume the old seacoast-defense mission over Rendova's western approaches, while Jack remained behind with H&S Battery and Battery B on Rendova itself. On July 29, General Noburo Sasaki, the Japanese area commander, began withdrawing his forces from New Georgia to nearby islands. After five weeks of savage fighting, Munda Field fell in savage fighting on August 5, 1943, with the Tank Platoon's surviving tanks in the thick of the fray. Two days later, the bulk of the Ninth began to be shifted from their stations all around New Georgia and Rendova to concentrate the battalion in the Munda Point area, where the AA components' principal mission would become the defense of the airfield. Battery B was also moved to Kindu Point, near Munda, also to resume its old seacoast defense role.

"*Under new management*": Munda Field, New Georgia's prize, photographed from Bibilo Hill in August 1943. (Official U.S. Marine Corps photo, courtesy of Col. (Ret'd) William T. Box)

The move to Kindu Point involved a certain amount of combat. The hills surrounding Munda Field were studded with log bunkers, caves and revetments and had been used as Japanese command posts, bombproofs and supply areas. Bibilo Hill, a prominent feature overlooking Kindu Point and most of Munda Field, had been the last stop in the savage fighting for Munda and was only finally taken with the support of flamethrowers and Captain Blake's Tank Platoon, plus reinforcements from another Defense Battalion's tank platoon. Still, because stragglers were likely hiding in the caves and numerous coconut-log bunkers still studding Munda Point and Kindu Point, Battery B resorted to sealing up as many of the bunkers, caves and tunnel entrances as possible with TNT blocks. Enough Japanese holdouts remained to make this a risky undertaking for Battery B's ad hoc "powder monkeys" who, lacking bangalore torpedoes or explosive satchel charges, had to improvise their own demolitions for bunker-busting, as Frank Chadwick reported to historian Eric Bergerud:

> When we moved out to Kindu Point after the capture of the airfield, the Japs were beginning to lose their effectiveness. We must have killed sixty or seventy Japs in pillboxes or trenches. We burned them out with [quarter-pound] blocks of TNT. We approached positions like this carefully. We had air-cooled .30-caliber machine guns. We also had a 20mm antiaircraft cannon on a wheeled mount [a "Twin Twenty," loaned from Special Weapons]. You'd just lay down a field of fire into those pillboxes, and someone would crawl up with a . . .block of TNT with a hand grenade fixed to it. You'd arm the grenade and push the TNT into the gun slot. That blew them to pieces.

Amazingly, nobody from Battery B was killed or seriously injured in the process of leveling the last dugouts, tunnels and log-roofed bunkers around Munda and Kindu Points.

Navy Seabee units moved into the Munda Field area shortly thereafter with bulldozers, rock crushers and steam-rollers to pave out the battered surface of the runway. To Jack's amazement and happiness, one of the Seabees he met on New Georgia would turn out to be none other than a familiar face from Franklin. Watching an open-air movie one night, Jack was nudged in the dark by a person who whispered, "Hey, buddy, can you spare a match?" The voice sounded oddly familiar, and by the light of the match, Jack recognized Reams Osborne, his hometown next-door neighbor and pal from Franklin High, whose general whereabouts Jack had kept up with in his correspondence with his own parents. By August 13, the runway was patched well enough for Army Air Force and Marine air units—including VMF-214's "Black Sheep"—to redeploy from the Russells and Guadalcanal to Munda Field.

The wreckage of imperial hopes: a grounded "Zero" fighter in its Munda Field revetment (*left*), and the remains of a Japanese antitank gun and its dead gunner (*right*). Jack recalled that this wrecked AT gun was very near his location on Munda Field. (Official U.S. Marine Corps photos, courtesy of Joseph Pratl)

With the Battalion's elements now more or less together for the first time since Cuba, it was something like a reunion: Al Downs, reassigned from Battery B to H&S Battery, to which Jack and Jim Kruse still belonged, had hardly laid eyes on his Boot Camp pals since they landed on the Canal. They were able to get enough guys together for an occasional poker game and scrounged-up bottle of rum or whiskey. Jack and his buddies enjoyed watching the buildup of American aircraft, particularly the gull-winged Corsairs of the Black Sheep and the other Marine fighter squadrons. The Corsairs were always a welcome sight due to their ruggedness, the ease with which they could be recognized and distinguished from Zeroes, and—as a matter of Marine Corps pride—because they were usually flown by Marine pilots.

Jack opened the New Georgia branch of his water purification plant up for business on a stream running near Munda Point, well-positioned so that he could watch and hear Army and Marine fighters coming and going from Munda Field and,

MCCA

sometimes, see PT boats en route to their harbor off Rendova. The wreckage of a Japanese antitank gun, and (until finally covered with quicklime and buried) the reek of its dead gunner, was near his new site. Not far away were the carcasses of wrecked Zeroes and Betty bombers. Jack resumed his hobby of scrounging-around in the area and, soon, he had found and "liberated" from abandoned Japanese positions near the airfield a complete Imperial Navy sailor's blue uniform (probably abandoned by a *rikusentai* member), a painted and lacquered tin case of Japanese cigarettes, emblazoned with the red stripes of the Rising Sun flag (although, suspecting they were poisoned, he never dared to smoke one), and a Japanese pocket knife. He also made a fine ashtray from the brass cartridge case of a Japanese 70mm howitzer shell. Raiding an abandoned bunker near Munda Field, Jack emerged from the bunker's stygian darkness with a Japanese helmet, only to look inside and find the stinking remains of part of its prior owner's head and brains. Nearly retching, he threw the helmet as far away as he could. Although that gruesome outcome curtailed his souvenir-collecting for awhile, he soon began undertaking a lucrative, if highly dangerous, hobby: deactivating Japanese grenades to sell to newly arrived Seabees, Black Sheep pilots and aircraft mechanics at Munda Field.

At first blush, Japanese grenades looked generally like a smaller version of the standard American "pineapple" grenade, having a serrated but more cylindrical steel body and a handle with a metal cotter pin at the top. Beyond this, the activation procedures for the two grenades were vastly different. Instead of simply pulling the pin, letting go of the safety lever attached to the grenade's top and throwing it like the U.S. version, the Japanese model was ignited by pulling the pin and smacking the stem of the fuse hard and squarely on the user's helmet or boot heel, a rock or tree. One then had to throw it as quickly as possible: the fuse was highly erratic and, even without being booby-trapped to explode more quickly, could go off within two to three seconds after the pin-removal/base-striking procedure took place. Somehow, Jack learned how to unscrew the fuses and soak each grenade in a helmet full of kerosene, to loosen up the explosives packed in the grenade's steel body. Given the inherent instability of the Japanese grenade fuses or the possibility that some "son of the Emperor" may have jury-rigged one to do in a "Yankee dog" like Jack, it was a minor miracle that he did not blow himself up in the process.

Jack had been in place only a few days, however, when he was reminded that this island had not yet reverted to being a tropical paradise: on August 15, Japanese long-range guns sporadically began shelling Munda Point from nearby Baanga Island. These guns were reputedly British-made pieces for naval and coast-defense use, likely seized from the garrisons at Hong Kong or Singapore. They were roughly equal to the Long Toms in range and were collectively nicknamed "Pistol Pete" by the Ninth's Marines. Jack remembered that the most hateful thing about Pistol Pete was its (or, more accurately, their) sense of timing. As far as Jack and his pals could tell, Pistol Pete seldom hit anything militarily significant in the Ninth's area, other than holing a few tents with shrapnel and riddling some 55-gallon fuel drums. However, Pistol Pete usually began to fire around chow time, forcing all hands to drop their food and run for cover for anywhere from 10 to 30 minutes. The shelling usually began in the vicinity of Battery B's positions around Kindu Point, and the shells were "walked," in gradual increments, from there to Munda Field.

Consider for a moment the psychological effect this had on the Marines. The move of the bulk of the 9th Defense to Munda meant that the battalion, as a whole, could regularly get hot food for the first time in months. As will be recalled, the Ninth seldom had hot chow until the end of the

Guadalcanal campaign, and its leathernecks were lucky to eat twice a day on the Canal under the very best of conditions. While they were at least able to eat more frequently on Rendova, the food was usually canned: Spam, D rations and K rations. Because the combat situation after Munda's capture was more stable than either on Guadalcanal and Rendova, mess tents and field stoves were now set up. Pistol Pete's dinnertime shellings were less than a major bombardment but more than a mere inconvenience. They were just enough to get a hungry Marine really steamed up and, therefore, they were far worse for Pogiebait's and his buddies' morale that any of Tokyo Rose's radio ravings.

Once Pistol Pete had finished a bombardment—and since only two of Battery B's guns were positioned to return counterbattery fire at Baanga—the job of destroying Pistol Pete was assigned by General Barker's staff to a battery of Army 105mm howitzers. These smaller fieldpieces would return fire, but their shooting was fruitless because Pete's positions on Baanga were well camouflaged and could not be successfully located, plus the lighter 105mm howitzers lacked the power of the Long Toms. The Army's first bombardment seemed to silence Pete—that is, until the next chow time for the Ninth, when the latest nuisance shelling began, and chow was ruined once more. An Army attempt by elements of the 37th Division to storm Baanga with a lightly armed raiding force was repulsed in plain view of Battery B's positions on Kindu Point, as hidden Japanese machine guns opened up on the assault party's landing craft. The sodden survivors of that raid were rescued by a tough but eerie-looking group of scouts from the 1st Fiji Commando, a British Commonwealth unit comprised wholly of Fijians. Frank Yemma was one of the witnesses to Pistol Pete's shellings, the Army's ill-fated raid on Baanga on August 10 and its sequel:

[Battery B's] Guns 1 and 2 could traverse to the right on up to counter-fire against the Japanese, and we requested permission to do so. Don't ask me why, I don't know: all I heard was from scuttlebutt that they wouldn't allow us to do it, but they said the Army would take over with the 105s. Well, they started firing over our heads, and you could see the shells bursting on Baanga. Anyway, the next day we'd line up for chow, and that Pistol Pete would open up again.

Well, the Army wasn't doing its job with the 105s. We were madder than hell. We knew we could blow the hell out of them, but for some reason or another, they just wouldn't give us permission. However, this went on for a couple of days and then the Higgins boats came in with some Army troops, and they piled into 'em, and over they started. It was—honest to God—it was like watching a John Wayne movie. I sat there and the next thing I know, these Nambu machine guns opened up on it. And holy macaroni, they turned it, and guys dove over the side of the Higgins boats and swam to these little islands in front of Baanga Island. The Higgins boat came back into shore. I ran down there and the sailor, this coxswain, he was shot up bad. He was almost cut in half with machine-gun bullets. . . . Well, needless to say, they didn't try that again.

The next thing I saw were these big black Fiji Islanders, and they all carried these British Bren guns. [The Fijians] got into canoes—two—one in the front and one in the back of the canoe, and over they went right where all these soldiers got shot up. . . . The Fiji Islanders went over, and they picked up one or two guys off the islands. You could see the bullets going around the canoes. Well, that didn't stop these Fiji Islanders! They'd pick up one or two soldiers and

> bring them back. Well, they got them all back, believe it or not.

Pistol Pete carried on for about three days before U.S. spotter airplanes sighted the guns' positions by their muzzle flashes during a bombardment. Having been denied the right to strike out at Pete and ordered to leave the job to the Army, Colonel O'Neil finally got the authorization he needed to blast Baanga with his own Long Toms whenever Pete struck again. Between air strikes and a vigorous bombardment of the island, Pistol Pete was finally silenced for good around August 19. Yemma reminisced:

> Pistol Pete had opened up on us for three days, and the 105s just weren't hitting their target. Anyway, the next thing I know here, they've got the planes coming. All they did was take off right. . .to the left of us, from Munda Point. You could see them take off—the SBDs—and I don't know, 12, 14 of them—and next thing I know, here they come, dive-bombing. It was just like watching a movie. I sat right there and watched it. And they blew the hell out of this dang island because this is where they thought the guns might be. We never heard from them again, so they must have done the job because, for Pistol Pete, it was the end of the hill.

The meaning of Pistol Pete's demise was simple, even if it was a bit macabre, to Jack and his buddies: "No more cold chow!"[8/]

Jack did not have much time to settle down on Munda Point before he was moved again. Due to defective ammunition, General Hester had ordered the 155mm Group to fire only "observed" missions (that is, fire missions whose results could be directly watched by forward observers) for several weeks beginning in early August. With fresh ammunition supplies supposedly eliminating the dangers posed by out-of-date and decrepit stocks, by the end of August, Colonel Scheyer felt confident enough to recommend to XIV Corps that his 155mm Group resume its field artillery work, including indirect-fire missions. The Corps staff agreed, believing that the long range and hard-hitting capabilities of the Ninth's Long Toms made them perfect for blasting Kolombangara from Piru Plantation, a former Lever Brothers copra plantation just north and to the east of the Diamond Narrows and Munda Point. With the Japanese forces in the area now largely bottled up on Kolombangara, its harbor of Viru, and adjacent islets, the die was cast for another move of Jack and his buddies with the 155mm Group.

Hence, on August 29, Battery A began moving (by landing craft for the equipment and by foot for many of the personnel through a very treacherous-looking jungle path) to Piru Plantation, an area temporarily used as a logistics base by the 1st Marine Raiders, now advancing through the island's northern jungles. As Bill Box, now on the Group's staff and helping provide site reconnaissance for Major Hiatt, recalled: "[We] hiked from Munda using a native guide . . . through jungle most of the way. I remember that I was scared. I remember I was glad to see that open area with the supply parachutes left by the [Marine] raiders!" Piru Plantation looked across a seven-mile stretch of water to the craggy heights of Kolombangara Island, where the bulk of the Japanese forces in the area—about 10,000 estimated as being there in early July, just before the invasion—were now positioned. Battery A's Long Toms began the siege of Kolombangara on August 31; two days later, Battery B's 155s joined in the shelling, too, after another eventful arrival. Captain Wells's Long Toms arrived by barge on September 1 at a small coral pier that was approximately one foot above the waterline and about six feet wide. While the battery's officers and top NCOs left to select their gun positions, Japanese artillery began to bombard the pier area. The sailors manning the barges, feeling like sitting ducks, threatened to leave but were coerced into staying, and the bombardment stopped as suddenly as it had begun.

Unfortunately, Battery B had already been hammered before reaching Piru. Because of a shortage of landing craft, Battery A had departed for the plantation first, and while Battery B waited beachside with its guns and gear, a Japanese scout plane flew overhead on the early evening of August 31. It sighted Battery B's guns and equipment, and sporadic air raids began on the beach around 10:00 p.m. and lasted until dawn. While the battery lost some equipment, its men, Long Toms and ammunition were, fortunately, intact. To add to the danger, pieces of shrapnel from 90mm AA shells from the Ninth's own guns rained down on the beachside positions. Hence, Battery B's gunners spent the night in foxholes and bomb craters, hiding from both Japanese bombs and fragments of their battalion's own ack-ack shells. Frank Chadwick and another member of Battery B's Gun # 2, who had been assigned to guard the gun from Japanese infiltrators, were nearly killed by an exploding bomb, its blast fortunately deflected by the trunk of a large coconut tree. Despite these attacks, Battery B was in operation at Piru on September 3, and its four Long Toms soon joined in the siege of Kolombangara.

Jack's water purification point at Piru Plantation was located on a freshwater creek just off the beach. This new site took advantage of a coconut log-lined well that the Japanese had dug. This well provided an ample supply of fresh water requiring less purification. His site was 200 or 300 yards directly in front of the barrels of Murderers' Row, close enough to get the full effect of the noise and vibrations of the 155s as they fired. The sound was deafening, particularly when all eight Long Toms of the 155mm Group were firing "in battery," more or less simultaneously so as to maximize their effectiveness. To make matters worse, Japanese artillery on Kolombangara had now identified the 155mm Group's positions at Piru as the source of much of their discomfiture and would, from time to time, fire counter-battery barrages to try to silence the 155s. "They fired at us, and for every round they threw at us, we threw five back. Nothing spectacular. We'd fire, and they'd fire," Frank Yemma remembered.

155mm Group gunners at Piru Plantation prepare to bombard Kolombangara and chalk a suitable slogan on a 95-lb. shell before firing. (Official U.S. Marine Corps photo, courtesy of Col. (Ret'd) William T. Box)

Either of the effects of being beside a battery of 155mm monsters in action or being in the midst of an enemy bombardment was enough to "ring your bells." Now, Jack had to contend with them *both*, often more or less simultaneously. The Japanese shelling was among the worst of experiences, as Chadwick testified to Eric Bergerud:

> Being shelled by artillery was awful. [Before beginning the bombardment of Kolombangara from Piru Plantation], the Japs started shelling us. You'd be in your hole, look out, and see the flashes and count them; you'd see the smoke, too. And then the artillery would come barreling in like a freight train. I used to peer out and think to myself: there's one, two, three, four: now let's see where they're going to hit. The shelling lasted about half an hour. They never got us, but shells landed to the left, in front, and behind us.

Jack was, therefore, truly between a rock and a hard place, with Japanese shells exploding nearby, and the Long Toms essentially firing over his head. This situation lasted for several days before Jack finally decided, in the middle of a barrage by both Batteries A and B on September 17, 1943, that he had just about enough. His head pounded terribly, and no mere APC caffeine-and-aspirin tablet would stop this headache: his ears rang, he was deafened, and he wondered if he might not be suffering from a brain concussion. Even if it meant abandoning his post without a sergeant's permission, Pogiebait decided to take a break, leave his hole, and head back to the 155mm Group's positions.

The Long Tom was loaded by setting the shell's fuse; next, the hefty shell was placed on a two-man cradle (when time permitted; when it didn't, which was often, one of the gunners simply heaved the shell by hand into the breech himself), manhandled up into the breech of the gun, and rammed hard to set the shell's rifling bands into the rifling grooves inside the gun barrel. Then, depending on the desired range, several silk bags of gunpowder (usually, three bags of basic gunpowder and three bags of "super-charged" powder) were rammed directly behind the shell, without a brass cartridge case being used to hold the powder. The gun's breech was screwed shut, the lanyard was attached to the primer, and the gun was fired with a pull of the lanyard. Once a fire mission was completed, five or six members of the twelve-man gun crew would take a TD-9 or TD-18 tractor and a Athey trailer—a weird looking, caterpillar-tracked caisson used to haul ammunition—and locate the nearest supply point to secure more ammunition. While the ammo team went forth, the rest of the 155's crew cleaned and performed post-firing maintenance on the cannon.

A point left unstressed in the official histories, yet one with a major impact on the Ninth's effectiveness, was the vintage and poor quality of the unit's ammunition, especially the gunpowder and fuses. While the 155mm M1 gun was a great improvement over the World War I-era GPFs, the ammo supply was still unreliable. Some of the shells and fuses reportedly dated from World War I; Captain Box, as ammo officer, reported that others left behind on Guadalcanal as unserviceable were salvaged as ammo stocks began running low. Ever since Guadalcanal, the quality of the ammunition posed the weak link in this chain. Because of defective fuses, some shells would explode prematurely. As a result of several premature muzzle bursts, which occurred on July 10 and was the first indication of the severity of this problem, the 155mm gun crews took to ducking down in the gunpits whenever their guns were fired. Some shells appeared to be leaching their contents from their base plates. Others would be safely fired yet not explode on target: the fuses were "duds," leading to some excitement as the Ninth's gunners occasionally had to remove and discard on New Georgia their own unexploded ordnance fired only days before at the enemy.

Similar problems cropped up with the gunpowder supply. Due to the age and deterioration of the powder (combined with rough handling in transit from stateside arsenals, which cracked open many storage tubes and exposed the gunpowder inside to rain, making it worthless), spontaneous combustion sometimes occurred, and the bags might burst into flame while being loaded into their cartridge cases, with the gunners frantically separating the burning bags from the intact ones to prevent a massive explosion. In fact, before the move from Rendova to New Georgia proper, these defects were so severe that Battery B suspended fire missions on August 3.

Considering that this suspension coincided with XIV Corps's final drive on Munda Point, when all guns available would have been needed to support this offensive, one can surmise that these "ammunition problems" (as described in the Ninth's history) posed more than merely trivial concerns. It was, after all, not until early August, when better ammunition stocks began reaching the unit, that General Barker's suspension of indirect-fire missions was rescinded, effectively putting the 155mm Group back in business. The Special Weapons Group had experienced severe problems with defective Army-supplied 40mm shells, a problem only rectified when that group got its hands on Navy-manufactured batches of Bofors ammo. Likewise, the Ninth's 90mm Group faced similar problems with short fuses, with several AA gunners killed and wounded from metal shards. Of two twin brothers serving in the same 90mm gun crew, one was killed as a fuse exploded prematurely, detonating the shell. With the well-publicized loss of the Navy's five Sullivan brothers (all serving on the U.S.S. *Juneau*, sunk off Guadalcanal in November 1942) clearly being in mind, the surviving brother was quickly transferred home.

Returning to September 17, Sergeant Bill Galloway of Battery A, who had survived the July 2 air raid after his gun, *Semper Fidelis*, had been immobilized with a dud bomb between its trails, watched Jack as he jogged back to the 155s' firing positions. Galloway and the others in his gun crew yelled, "Hey, Pogiebait! Where's the fire?" "Where the hell you're going?" "You're leaving your post!" Jack yelled back in response, "My head hurts too bad! I'm going to lay off for a while. I'll go back out in a little bit," and he kept on going. Galloway just shrugged, and he and his gun crew prepared to load and fire another shell. Like some of the other shells in the ammo supply, this one was oozing a sticky, yellowish substance near its base plate, but Galloway's gunners merely took up rags and wiped off the shell, so as not to lose their grip while lifting it. The hefty projectile was loaded and rammed into place; several bags of powder went in next; the breech was screwed tightly down, and the lanyard was affixed for firing.

When the lanyard was pulled, a roar blasted the position: the defective shell was a "short," and the yellowish liquid seeping from it was its highly explosive filler. It had likely ignited in the gun barrel when the Long Tom was fired, and the shell exploded shortly after leaving its barrel. Fragments of steel—both from the shell and *Semper Fidelis*'s barrel—were strewn in various directions. Sergeant Galloway and several others were wounded by shards of metal, with Galloway still carrying a half-inch piece of steel in his lung to this day,[9/] and the massive gun barrel itself was smashed. Jack's water purification gear, on the other hand, was a total wreck: his pumps and filters were riddled, and water sluiced out of his holding tank as if it were a colander. Jack and his buddies could only shake their heads in wonder: if he had not decided on the spur of the moment to take his impromptu break, he would certainly have died or have been horribly mangled.

Pogiebait McCall was a lucky man, indeed!

Another practical challenge facing the 155mm Group throughout the Central Solomons campaign was that of effective fire direction and observation. The Japanese forces on New Georgia and Kolombangara were often concealed in well-sited and camouflaged log bunkers and revetments. Because many Japanese troop movements were made at nighttime, it was extremely difficult to locate their positions. The 155mm Group's Exec and future Battalion Exec, Major Bob Hiatt, had given the problem considerable thought and came up with some tentative solutions in the hope that they would improve the accuracy and results of the group's fire missions.

For awhile, the Ninth "enlisted" a Marine aviator, Captain Lionel Pool of a Marine dive bomber squadron, to serve as a trained aerial observer for the 155mm Group, but more aerial observers were needed. One of Major Hiatt's answers was to co-opt a Navy torpedo bomber squadron based in the nearby Russell Islands, to which he detached two members of his staff, Sergeants Donald Sandager and Herschel Cooper, to become aerial forward observers. Their first missions were hardly rousing successes. The Navy TBF pilots resented the nerve-wracking, dirty and dangerous work of flying low-level reconnaissance with a pair of half-crazy Marines, who kept telling them, "Fly lower; I can't see anything!" The pilots assigned to fly Sandager and Cooper were usually the lowest men on the totem pole for any particular day's missions. The task of flying the two FOs was also frequently rotated—a different pilot, every day—complicating matters considerably. For instance, because of the daily turnover in pilots, neither Sandager nor Cooper could simply say, "Take me where we went yesterday." Instead, the two observers daily had to brief their new pilots in exacting detail as to what routes to fly and where to look for possible targets to observe or Japanese AA positions to avoid. Due to the fierce

Japanese AA fire over Kolombangara, these missions were no "milk runs" and were hardly welcomed by the resentful pilots.

On his second mission, Sandager found the Avenger torpedo bomber to which he had been assigned to have no parachute for him. When Sandager challenged him, the Avenger's pilot brusquely responded that it wasn't his problem: he had *his* chute, and if Sandager wanted his own chute, well, he'd just have to find one on his own. Sandager responded by drawing his .45 pistol, placing it near the pilot, and slowly telling him that if it were necessary to bail out, he knew who would be wearing the parachute. After that altercation, parachutes were made readily available to the two Marines.

While his aerial FOs experimented with perfecting their duties, Major Hiatt devised another plan that he hoped would improve his fire direction capabilities. "Turret Top" Hiatt seemed to have a mania for using trees as observation platforms, despite the risk that enemy artillerymen often preregistered their guns on tall objects such as trees or towers, for the very reason that they made such excellent observation posts or "OPs". On Rendova, his reconnaissance party found the highest tree on the island and, at the behest of Colonel Forney, converted a 130-foot tree to an OP equipped with a Japanese battery commander's 300-pound telescope with lenses much superior to the standard-issue Marine telescope. On New Georgia, the 155mm Group's penchant for "treehouse" OPs was soon again in the forefront, both near Munda and at Piru Plantation.

On a large hill northwest of Munda Field, Major Hiatt found a colossal banyan tree, wide-based and at least 70 feet tall, which he decided would make an excellent OP, notwithstanding that the tree was in an area that was still largely Japanese-held territory. Only a short distance away, the hill steeply dropped off into a 100-foot cliff overlooking the Diamond Narrows channel. The Major ordered the Group's communications section to cut notches into the massive trunk to support wires for field telephones and to nail wooden slats to its side to form a primitive ladder to its top. (As "water boy" for the Group, when he was not lugging around ammunition or Lister bags full of water, Jack sometimes found himself carrying wooden boards, nails and tools around, although to what purpose he, as yet, had no idea.) At the top of the tree, the unit's carpenters built a small platform, which was then equipped with the captured Japanese telescope, a compass, a map table, a field phone, two rickety seats and simple belts to strap down the observers in case of high winds.

Climbing the tree was itself a major chore. The wooden rungs were often slippery and not well placed, so each observer would take off his boondockers and climb barefoot, locking his toes around the lower rung and pulling himself up to the next one. Under the best of conditions in daylight, while trying to be as inconspicuous a target as possible for an eagle-eyed Japanese sniper, it often took 20 to 25 minutes to climb to the top. With the ever-present fear that a sniper would spot the observers and pick them off as they made their journey to the treetop OP, the climbers had a real incentive to hurry their ascent.

When an observer reached the top, however, he was greeted with an incredible vista: the "treehouse" offered a commanding, 360-degree view of the nearby islands of Kolombangara and Arundel, the Diamond Narrows between New Georgia and Arundel, and much of New Georgia itself. On a clear day, the observers could scan some 60 miles in any direction, viewing cloud-covered peaks on the farthest islands. On most days, the view from the OP tree was magnificent, but the observers quickly remembered that they were there for a more serious purpose and got to work, calling in on the field phone to Major Hiatt at the Fire Direction Center to get his orders for target sightings. The hill surrounding the tree was heavily jungled. A small trail had been hacked out of the foliage to the tree, and a small campsite was made in a clearing at the foot of the tree for a guard party. While the observers took their turn manning the treehouse, the others stayed under cover and guarded the trail.

After several days of manning the OP tree, the observation crew got a case of the jitters when they heard unexpected sounds of movement coming up the trail; those on the ground got their rifles ready to defend the tree. The approaching patrol turned out to be Army infantrymen, several of whom were Guadalcanal veterans. As the patrol drew nearer, the Leathernecks yelled, "Don't shoot! We're Marines!" and the patrol leaders, an Army lieutenant and sergeant, stepped forward to ask the Marines what in the devil they were doing there. After hearing the team's explanation, the Army lieutenant announced that the area was just being secured from the Japanese and that his patrol's assignment was to drive the enemy to the east. "You know, don't you, that you're behind Jap lines?" the lieutenant told the observers. He was amazed to hear the Marines cockily respond, "Yessir, we know that." Frank Chadwick recalled what happened next:

> Then the lieutenant wanted to know if we were scared up here by ourselves. Lying through our teeth, we told him no because we knew where the Japs were; we then showed him our tree, and told him we'd take him up and with the scope he could watch the Japs on Kolombangara. He looked at the tree and said if he had been ordered to climb the tree or face a court-martial and be shot, he'd tell them to shoot him. He told us that he had learned to respect the Marines on the Canal and New Georgia and thought we were a very courageous group, but he had changed his opin-

> ion. He now thought we were all crazy. We took this as a compliment.

When Batteries A and B moved to Piru Plantation, Major Hiatt set up yet another OP post. This one featured another massive tree near the beach and, alternatively, a 15-foot-tall collapsible metal tower, placed within yards of Jack's water purification station. One of the Major's reasons for choosing this particular site could scarcely have made Jack feel any more secure about his water point's location. Hiatt reportedly selected this tree because, besides its being just the right height, he noted that the tree was in an area of the plantation that the Japanese guns on Kolombangara would usually shell first before shifting their fire further inland to the Long Toms' positions. Hence, the OP tree—and Jack's—general location was always somewhat of a "hot spot," although it was somewhat less an object of the Japanese gunners' attention than was the 155s' firing positions further back.

Between the Japanese guns on Kolombangara and nuisance raids from New Georgia's version of Washing Machine Charlie, life for the Long Tom gunners became even more unpleasant. As the Marines' official history of the campaign admitted, things at Piru Plantation rapidly degenerated into a grudge match: each side soon resorted to various ruses to lure their opponents out to take a drubbing by heavy artillery:

> For the men of the 155mm Group, the war soon took on the semblance of a personal fight. Each night the Americans heard the starting sputter and ensuing drone of a Vila-based seaplane that circled overhead to drop a small load of bombs. Several projectiles, fired at irregular intervals by cleverly concealed enemy coast defense guns, usually followed this raid. These nuisance tactics robbed men of sleep but in-

> flicted little damage and no personnel casualties. By day the Japanese had a most annoying habit of shelling the Americans while at mess, resulting in spilled food and ruffled tempers. Whenever boats landed near the Marines' best observation post (the tree near the beach), their opponents would lay in a couple of rounds to make that area untenable.
>
> Naturally a battle of wits ensued. Since the enemy could not hide the gun flashes, the Marines returned the fire to silence the hostile pieces. The foe met this gambit by setting off powder charges at different points every time they discharged their weapons [thus, making it seem that more enemy guns were blasting away at Jack and his buddies than was actually the case]. But cool-headed Americans detected this ruse when they noticed that they were receiving only one shell for every three or four flashes plotted.

Fed up with the interferences to their chow calls and the waste of hot food lost when they had to dive for cover every evening, Colonel O'Neil's and Major Hiatt's boys in the beachside OP tree now spent their mornings looking for signs of cooking fires on Kolombangara. Whenever a wisp of smoke was sighted anywhere on the neighboring island, a salvo or two of 155mm shells followed. When the Japanese responded by concentrating their fire more heavily on the OP tree in Pogiebait's neighborhood, Major Hiatt had his gunners vacate the tree, while he began to rely more heavily on Sandager's and Cooper's aerial spotting reports. Between his two aerial observers in the Avengers and other observers in Higgins boats now plying the waters off Piru, the Long Toms began to saturate large portions of the Kolombangara plain with highly accurate fire. As the Marines' official history of the Central Solomons campaign noted rather drily: "Experience at Munda [proved] that when spotter planes adjusted fires, the 155mm guns' effectiveness was greatly increased."

From left to right, Captains Bill Box, Norm Pozinsky and Hank Reichner at Piru Plantation, late summer 1943. (Courtesy of Col. (Ret'd) Henry H. Reichner Jr.)

To thwart Japanese gunners attempting to down the observation planes and dive bombers hitting Kolombangara, the 155mm Group learned to coordinate its fire missions before the Dauntlesses and Avengers struck. It soon was apparent that each preliminary bombardment only tipped off the Japanese that an air strike was imminent. Whenever the shells began to fall, the enemy AA gunners would hide; whenever the shells stopped falling, the same flak crews raced back to their weapons, and nine Navy bombers were lost over the course of several days as a result. In response, Major Hiatt's gunners tried a new tactic. The Long Toms would fire a preliminary barrage, ostensibly warning the enemy that an air raid was imminent. "Three minutes later, after their opponents had time to man their guns, the 155's again would pour it on, catching the Japanese in their open emplacements. Then, upon completion of this second bombardment, the planes would attack." This new ploy worked well enough, and the Navy's aircraft losses to enemy AA fire ceased to be a problem.

Japanese fire from Kolombangara towards Piru continued sporadically from mid-August until early October. Knowing that the Japanese were fully prepared to make the seizure of Kolombangara a bloodbath, Admiral Halsey cleverly implemented an "island-hopping strategy." Halsey bypassed Kolombangara to land his forces on Vella Lavella, the next island in the Central Solomons chain, on August 15. This move shrewdly cut off Japanese reinforcements to Kolombangara, made the seizure of Bougainville, the next island on Halsey's agenda, a bit easier to achieve and made the taking of Kolombangara superfluous. Faced with a cut-off garrison, the Japanese withdrew what was left of their men from Kolombangara around October 3. XIV Corps's commander, General Griswold, had already declared success in the New Georgia area on September 23, and he now issued orders decreeing Operation TOENAILS to be an American victory.

There was, however, still no shortage of enemy targets for several weeks after "victory" had been pronounced by General Griswold. Because its defenders hid in their bunkers during daylight hours, the only Japanese soldier usually seen on Kolombangara during daylight was a motorcycle courier. He was spotted on his rounds at various times on successive mornings by a reconnaissance plane or by the crew in the OP treehouse. With the courier's apparent route across Kolombangara's open areas established after several days of such observations, Major Hiatt decided that this intrepid courier would be the Group's next target of opportunity. Henceforth, every morning during his usual departure time, all eight 155s opened fire all along his suspected routes. Somehow, with all the luck of Washing Machine Charlie, the courier miraculously escaped death by these bombardments, although it was reported that, after being blown off his motorcycle near a small bridge by a barrage of 155mm shells, he quickly dusted himself off, retrieved his motorcycle, and resumed his rounds otherwise unscathed. Bob Landon, another Battery B gunner, remembered: "We always said that the courier had a lot of courage, and we all bet that this was one Jap that was never constipated."

On October 3, while spotting over Kolombangara in his Avenger, a newly-commissioned Lieutenant Don Sandager observed large Japanese forces evacuating Vila, its main harbor: he was, in fact, watching the withdrawal of all Japanese forces off the island, amounting to 12,400 troops. This evacuation was completed by October 7, which effectively marked the end of combat in the New Georgia area.

As the Long Toms' targets disappeared from Kolombangara, Jack and Battery B were moved—yet again—from Piru Plantation to Roviana Island, southeast of Munda Point and due south of Zanana Beach, to again resume the old seacoast defense mission. These moves was accompanied by more administrative changes: Bill Box once more took charge of Battery B, while Walter Wells took over as CO of the 155mm Group's H&S Battery. At the same time, Battery A also moved from Piru Plantation to Nusalavata Island, to perform similar tasks. Colonel Scheyer, who had been with the Ninth through its toughest days to date, was relieved as CO on November 3 by Colonel O'Neil, who, in turn, was replaced by Major Hiatt.

Before leaving for his new job with I MAC headquarters, Colonel Scheyer saluted the effectiveness of the Long Toms in routing the Japanese:

> For the first time in this war the enemy had been driven from his base by bombing and artillery fire. At Kiska [in the Aleutians] it was bombing and ship's gunfire. At Kolumbangara [*sic*] it was bombing, Army artillery fire and the 9th Defense Battalion Seacoast that turned the tide. I am proud of the job that you did.
>
> Years from now you can look in the mirror and say, "I was there and I did my job—WELL."

General Griswold, XIV Corps's commander, issued a letter of commendation to the Ninth, crediting (if in something of the usual understatement of military bureaucracies everywhere) the Battalion's "effective antiaircraft protection" and "essential counter battery fire" as having been vital to the success of the New Georgia campaign. What was more, Lightnin' Joe Collins of the 25th Division, in appreciation for the 9th Defense's work, saw to it that the Battalion was awarded the Army Distinguished Unit Citation. Moreover, General Collins personally thanked the battered veterans of the Tank Platoon and Captain Blake for the tankers' share in making victory possible on the Munda Trail. To cap off the praise, the former CO of their old outfit on Guadalcanal, A.A. Vandegrift, now a three-star general and I MAC commander, passed on his personal thanks to Colonel Scheyer: "Please tell your officers and men how proud I am to belong to the same outfit they do." Given that General Vandegrift had fought so hard against the formation of the Defense Battalions and other special Marine units—plus the fact that he was regarded as being a marine's Marine—the General's compliment was high praise, indeed. It was Vandegrift himself who reputedly first referred to the Battalion as the "Fighting Ninth" after Guadalcanal; again, quite an honor from one originally so opposed to the Defense Battalion concept.

For many years, the fighting on and around Rendova, New Georgia and Kolombangara has remained a largely forgotten chapter of the American war in the Pacific. While much less well known than Guadalcanal and the Marines' bloody fights at Tarawa, Peleliu and Iwo Jima, for instance, Operation TOENAILS was a bitterly fought campaign, with well over three U.S. divisions and sizeable naval and air forces being engaged for more than two months to occupy an island group that were supposed to have been taken in less than half the time by a substantially smaller force. Jack and many of his fellow veterans would have bridled at Professor Eric Bergerud's assessment that the campaign was a "tactical victory for the United States, but a strategic failure" on the grounds that, even though it had cleared the Central Solomons of the Japanese, it had cost the American forces dearly: almost 1,000 dead and another 13,000 casualties from wounds or disease of out a force of 30,000. Of the dead, 811 Army troops were killed in action, followed by 132 Navy and 48 Marines of the 9th Defense and the 4th Marine Raiders. Sickness and casualties also plagued the Ninth, which coped with the evacuation of 142 of its men—some ten percent of its effective strength—during the month of July alone.

Also, by requiring Admiral Halsey to commit the strategic reserve for the Bougainville operation, TOENAILS had the effect of delaying the latter campaign. The campaign's veterans would doubtless, however, have agreed with Professor Bergerud that the New Georgia area was "one of the worst pieces of real estate in the South Pacific." Still, without the ultimate occupation of New Georgia, it is questionable whether the Bougainville operation would have succeeded. If nothing else, New Georgia and its environs were a valuable testing ground for new tactics that succeeded admirably on Bougainville and future operations, so in that sense, Operation TOENAILS did provide a "pattern for victory" in the Pacific, as the coastwatcher D.C. Horton entitled his history of the campaign. Or, as another student of the battle for the Central Solomons has written: "The importance of the New Georgia campaign's central event—the land drive to capture the Munda air base from its Japanese builders and defenders—resides not so much in a feat of American arms at a trying time but rather in the age-old and enduring lessons encountered in turning merely trained soldiers into veteran warriors." By the campaign's end, Jack and the Leathernecks of the 9th Defense definitely regarded themselves as "veteran warriors."

As the fighting moved away from New Georgia, a new and welcome piece of scuttlebutt ran through the ranks of the Ninth: the Battalion had served in combat areas, without interruption, since landing on Guadalcanal in late November 1942, sixteen months after leaving the States for Cuba. Wasn't it about time for a hard-charging unit like the Fighting Ninth to get some "R & R"? The unit's quartermasters began circulating uniform requisition sheets, including—it could not help but be noticed—orders for winter-weight green uniforms.

Could leave and a break in Australia or New Zealand be far away now? It seemed so close, and the uniform-resupply orders seemed to confirm that such were the likeliest places where the Ninth was now bound. To add to the evidence, XIV Corps headquarters had promised that the winners of the Corps's round-robin softball tournament would be granted leave in New Zealand, and after winning eight of ten games, the 9th Defense captured the Island Softball League's pennant, though not without a rocky start:

> Opening day arrived. By luck-of-the-draw, the Ninth's team, the only Marines among twelve teams, was to play the first game. By luck of the coin toss, the Ninth was at bat at the first pitch. The Polack [*a.k.a.* Stanislaus Pacholski, the team's pitcher and self-appointed manager] stood respectfully at the plate as Major General Wing of a National Guard division stepped up to make the first ceremonial pitch.
>
> The General, a figure more suited to smoke-filled back rooms than to war, delivered. The ball left his hand in a weak arc; it slapped down about halfway to the plate and dribbled erratically toward home. The first-base coach, a hard-bitten gunner, stared. The batter stood rigid. The umpire shouted, "Strike One!"
>
> The Polack went mad. "'*Strike One,' my ass!*", he yelled, ceremony or no ceremony, General or no General. He hated being behind in the count. The General and his aides retired in good order to his car and left the game to the enlisted men. The Polack went on to win.

It seemed like an eternity had passed since Jack and his buddies had seen anything resembling civilization. Most figured that they hadn't seen "civilization" since leaving Norfolk in February 1942. With no women or nurses in the combat zones around Guadalcanal and New Georgia—apart from a few Red Cross girls on the Canal later in 1943 and some air-evacuation nurses occasionally flying into Munda—the lack of female companionship was pretty well apparent to all. Christmas was spent around Munda Field, which had now sprouted semi-permanent tents, shacks and corrugated-metal Quonset huts. There was no turkey or trimmings for the holidays. Still, the chow, such as it was—"10-in-1 rations" of dehydrated eggs, potatoes and potted ham—was at least plentiful and edible, and occasionally, beer and Coca-Cola was now available. (For the lucky ones, these drinks might be chilled by a pilot thoughtfully flying up to 10,000 feet—for a price, of course.) Meanwhile, in some rear area, LCIs and transports were being mustered to ship the Battalion out to its next station. Jack had the pleasure of seeing old pals like Chadwick, Downs and Kruse, whose sections had been detailed to other parts of Rendova and New Georgia during the last few months. It began to feel like the "old gang" was together once again. Occasionally, he would get permission to visit with his hometown pal Reams Osborne in the Seabees' camp near Munda Point.

Jack and his pals remembered New Year's Day 1944 as being ushered in by the Ninth in spectacular fashion: it seemed like every Special Weapons' gunner had found a machine gun and loaded it with a belt of tracer bullets. The midnight sky around New Georgia was brightly lit by cascading flares and tracers. Everyone else not occupied in this impromptu "fireworks show" took cover from falling debris and spent bullets and cursed the boys in Special Weapons for all they were worth.

Would the New Year bring an even bigger present from Uncle Sam, a chance for romance and some highjinks in the lands of the kangaroo, the "Diggers" and "Cobbers?" In late December 1943, all the indications—the new uniform orders; the shipping schedules; XIV Corps's promise to the New Georgia Pennant winners—seemed that such would be the case.

Guess again, friend.

5

"R & R": Brief Interlude in the Russells

In January '44, we were told that, after our 14 months in the combat zone, we had certainly earned some rest and recreation. We filled out requisitions for winter weight uniforms, and we all felt sure that we were headed for either Australia or New Zealand. Wrong, it was the Russell Islands, about half-way between Guadalcanal and New Georgia. More drills and training, but with a twice a week ration of beer and cokes.

Jack H. McCall, Sr.

"Somewhere In the Pacific"

Somewhere in the Pacific
Where the Sun is like a curse,
And every day is followed
By another slightly worse;
Where the coral dust blows thicker
Than the shifting desert sand
And the white man dreams and curses
And prays for a better land.

Somewhere in the Pacific
Where a girl is never seen,
Where the skies are never cloudy
And the grass is ever green;
Where the flying foxes' chatter
Robs a man of blessed sleep;
And there's not a drop of whisky
And for beer the briny deep.

Somewhere in the Pacific
Where the nights are made for love,
Where the moon is like a searchlight
And the Southern Cross above
Sparkles like a diamond necklace
In the beautiful tropic night;
'Tis a shameless waste of beauty
I cannot hold you tight.

Somewhere in the Pacific
Where the mail is always late,
And a Christmas card in April
Is considered up-to-date;
Where we never have a payday,

And we never get a cent,
But we never miss the money
'Cause we never get it spent.

Somewhere in the Pacific
Where the ants and lizards play,
And a thousand fresh mosquitoes
Replace the ones you slay;
Take me back to dear Massachusetts,
And let me roam that dell,
For this God-forsaken outpost
Is a substitute for Hell.

Anonymous

Imagine the fury, disgust and disappointment of Jack and the men of the Fighting Ninth when, after New Year, they learned the "poop" that they were not heading for Australia or New Zealand, but instead to the Russell Islands! "What a raw deal," Jack recalled thinking at the time. His buddies would probably have been much more vocal and graphic in their responses to this unpleasant news—particularly had they learned that some of their own officers secretly favored this choice. Biggie Slater, a radioman and communications specialist, learned this tidbit by overhearing several of the Battalion's officers:

> The *real* reason we didn't go to New Zealand or Australia was the upper echelon's perception that the battalion would go berserk once it arrived; witness its predilection for places of ill-repute and boozing *a la* Caimanera. Thus, the decision was that, in order to keep this crowd of unpredictable liberty hounds together as a fighting unit, it would be best to keep

> them away from "civilization." So, 3rd Amphib [*i.e.*, III Amphibious Corps, formerly named I MAC] was cooperative.

The differences between the choices of "R & R" venue were so stark that they were scarcely worth comparison. The Russells were a small group of islands in the Solomons, sandwiched in between Guadalcanal (from which it was only 60 miles) and the New Georgia group. Other than the fact that the islands were in a very quiet sector far away from the current combat zones on Bougainville and Cape Gloucester, there was little to set the Russells apart geographically or climatically from any other part of the Solomons. Like those islands, the Russells had similar stands of coconut trees, monsoon seasons and the much hated, glutinous mud on every road and track; mosquitoes and outbreaks of malaria; and centipedes, land crabs, rotting jungle vegetation and the other local flora and fauna of the Solomons. Due to a shortage of transport prohibiting the movement of the entire unit all at once, from mid-January 13 to early February 1944, the Battalion sailed by batteries from New Georgia to Banika. This was one of the two largest islands in the Russells (the other, neighboring Pavuvu, was the R&R venue for the 1st Marine Division after its fight on Cape Gloucester). The anonymous poem "Somewhere In the Pacific" pretty effectively summed up the attitude of many of the Ninth's leathernecks, Jack included, when they landed on the Russells and surveyed their new "home." At least, it was something of a break, the first real stand-down in well over a year.

The voyage to the Russells provided its own share of adventures for some, as a Hooligan's Navy was impressed to move the Ninth in everything from LSTs and LCIs to patrol boats. Jim Kruse, for instance, found himself aboard the APC-50, "a small craft that took a couple of us from Roviana Island to the Russell Islands. We had to travel slowly as we were leading an LST that had its compass shot out. Why was I on this craft? Mine is not to reason why, mine is but to do or—hell, we made it."

When the Ninth first landed on Banika, the unit was ordered to bivouac next to a swamp and an aviation fuel supply dump. The camp's existence was literally threatened by the fact that fuel had leached into the soil through the water table. This fact became abundantly plain when Gunnery Sergeant Smith (*nee* Schmidt), one of Biggie Slater's senior NCOs, got the bright idea that all that was needed to dry up the marshy soil of their new campsite was to dribble some kerosene on the ground where each tent would be planted, light a match, and burn the ground dry. Seconds after the "Gunny" dropped his match, the surrounding ground exploded in flame as if it had been torched by a flamethrower, and a large pyramid tent nearby went up in flames, in Biggie Slater's words, "like a hot-air balloon." Further, with so many men already suffering from the residual effects of malaria and dengue fever, the presence of a large swamp next to the campsite sent Colonel O'Neil "over the top." O'Neil demanded permission from the island's garrison commander to relocate to a higher and drier area. His request to move the Battalion was finally granted, though not before quite a few more of his men came down with fevers and chills.

"*Don't you think I know what a swamp is, boy*?" Confirmation of Jack McCall's protestations to the author that the Ninth was originally encamped on Banika in a swamp. (Photo by Harry Jones, courtesy of David Slater)

The Russell Islanders, who could be seen from time to time, were much like the natives of Guadalcanal and New Georgia, being Melanesian rather than Polynesian in extraction. Despite the unwanted intrusion of the war into their lives, they were friendly and appeared to tolerate the Americans' presence on their islands. The mail, supply and hot chow situations were much improved; the supply of pogy bait, PX goodies and Coca-Colas were not exactly endless but were more reliable than on Guadalcanal and New Georgia. The Battalion also received several official, if limited, beer rations during its sojourn on Banika. Unofficial beer "requisitions" were, on the other hand, a different matter and provided good bartering opportunities. Biggie Slater recalled his section's escapades:

> There was a ration policy and each subordinate unit (battery and platoon) could send out transportation to the PX and a chit covering the unit allotment.

> Perhaps some groups were less enterprising than others; for example, 90 H&S. . .was off by itself on a spit of land and artfully forged chits for much more that our legitimate allotment and wound up with a large pile of beer. I counted 400 bottles stacked around our tent pole one day—"Red" Lenihan, "Bummy" Seifried, Pat Malloy, "Ruddy Ray" Sommer and myself. A few hundred yards offshore lay various supply vessels, including a refrigerator ship. We had salvaged a sort of clunky scowlike "boat" capable of holding 5 guys in a pinch. A couple of guys took several cases of beer out to the 'reefer' and traded them for a case of cured hams and a barrel of ice. For several days after that, we rarely left our tent area, having ham sandwiches, beer and coffee for chow.

There were the occasional Army and Navy nurses and a traveling USO show (with Ray Milland and several dancers and actresses, including a young, not-yet-famous Rita Moreno) to spice up life. Also, while there was still hard work to be done, drills and fatigue and guard duties, as always, the facilities were much less primitive than on the Ninth's earlier Pacific locations: when there was time off on the Russells, there were at least places to go, movies to see, and homemade baseball diamonds to enjoy. Still, when once asked what his R&R was like on Banika, Jack responded with one word: "Tedious." He and others found themselves engaged on a weekly basis in moving rotten coconut husks, which festooned the ground around the Ninth's campsites and which, when rotten, emitted a pungent stink, as well as being frequently turned into stevedores to move supplies at a nearby Marine logistics depot.

Although there was a small chapel with organized services on Banika Island where the Ninth was now posted, church religion, though, did not play a high role in those days for many of the Battalion's personnel. Happy as they may have been to have and use their personal Bibles when times were rough on Guadalcanal, Rendova and New Georgia (and Jack admitted thumbing through a "bulletproof" Bible that his parents had given him on quite a few occasions and saying the Lord's Prayer to himself when the time seemed right), organized religion and attending the "God Box" were not primary leisure-time activities for most young Marines. The 9th Defense's men were no exceptions; one frustrated Navy chaplain suggested that not mere chaplains, but heathen-converting missionaries, were what the Ninth really needed!.

The average Marine's generally cynical attitude towards religion may have partially resulted from the DIs' attitudes manifested at Parris Island. Frank Chadwick's experiences seem to be fairly typical. Boot Camp started every morning at 4:00 a.m. and generally ended at 9:00 p.m., except on Sundays. On the first Sunday of Boot Camp, church call for Chadwick's platoon was scheduled for 9:00 a.m.:

> The DI always said, "For God, country and Corps," but then said he could not make us go to church or believe in God. About forty of us went to church [out of a platoon of 64 men]. Upon returning about 10:30, the DI gave us permission to sit on the tent floor boards with our feet on the ground (no sand was allowed in the tents), but the other twenty or so Marines were nowhere to be found. They returned to the tent area just before noon chow. They were dirty and disheveled and all had toothbrushes, which they had used to clean the heads and garbage cans. From that day on, we were the most God-fearing, religious Marines you ever met.

But, in combat, whether or not they admitted it to their buddies, many otherwise religiously lackadaisical and worldly

Marines might well find themselves clutching rosary beads or, like Jack frequently admitted doing prior to the landings on Guadalcanal and Rendova, reciting to himself the 23rd Psalm or the Lord's Prayer. Others took to singing hymns, with Battery A's Sergeant "Smiley" Burnette particularly noted for organizing frequent gospel sessions. Hank Reichner recalled a few of his men's sing-songs on Guadalcanal:

> Our chief recreation at night was to sit around the gun pits singing a few Baptist hymns, such as "When the Roll Is Called Up Yonder" while watching the battalion searchlights pick up Japanese planes so our fighters could shoot them down. The hymns testified to the fact that "there are no atheists in foxholes" and also to the religious upbringing of many of the Marines.

After a few sessions like this, Smiley Burnette helped organize an *a capella* "barbershop quartet," which acquired a fairly sizeable following, including men from other batteries and nearby units. Smiley's little choir sang all the old Protestant favorites, full of longing for God, family and home, for a time of rest and peace, and for the simplicity of "that old-time religion." Their favorites included "*Amazing Grace*" and the poignant "*The Old Rugged Cross*." As Jack's H&S Battery pal, Jim Kruse, later reminded Pogiebait, it was not just the rarity of gatherings like these that made the 155mm Group's musical quartet special: "They were good, too. I found it amazing that these guys could sing so well together with no musical accompaniment."

However, Captain Reichner also remembered that aside from the hymns, "we also sang lustily other ditties." One of the most popular of these earthier numbers, sung to the tune of "*Bless Them All*," could often be heard as Jack and his buddies set off and returned from work details or as they sat around in camp commiserating as to their lot in life over some beer or homemade hooch. The song lambasted everything from the low promotion odds of the Christmas Tree Marines to the Leathernecks' favorite nemesis, "Dugout Doug." One can bet that, upon reaching their "vacation hideaway" in the Russells and finding that it was hardly New Zealand or Australia, this song was roared out with a new-found appreciation:

F—k them all, f—k them all,
The long and the short and the tall.
There'll be no promotion, this side of the ocean
So cheer up my lads, f—k them all.

They sent for MacArthur to come to Tulagi
But Douglas MacArthur said no.
He gave as his reason, it wasn't the season,
Besides, there was no USO!

F—k them all, f—k them all,
As off to our foxholes we crawl.
There'll be no promotion, this side of the ocean
So cheer up my lads, f—k them all.

While Jack and the men of the Ninth stand down in the Russells, let us explore several other facets of their life and times. In addition to reviewing their good and bad times on their Russell Islands break from combat, this chapter will explore other aspects of their life both in and out of combat. These aspects of Jack's wartime life in the Ninth include morale and entertainment in the harsh environment of the Pacific; the experiences of combat; attitudes towards women and sex; attitudes towards their enemy and their fellow servicemen; and life and death in the Pacific.

Horseplay, "Skylarking" and Morale

The Marines of the 9th Defense seldom suffered from a lack of diversions in their rare free time. Softball and baseball were always popular pastimes, with the Ninth winning the Island Softball League tournament on New Georgia. Card games—poker, red dog, acey-deucey—and crap-shooting were always popular as well. Given the relatively few legitimate outlets to spend one's newfound cash, the winner of each game could do little with his earnings except buy cigarettes, candy or PX supplies; trade it for Japanese loot (a trade certainly encouraged by Jack's grenade-deactivation business) or liquor; send some home for safe-keeping; or go for broke in another game of chance. As noted already, buying and trading Japanese gear was always a fruitful source of amusement and sometimes cash (particularly if the buyer was a fresh and gullible Army or Navy victim), as did the clandestine manufacture of "Japanese flags" on Guadalcanal until banned by General Patch and Colonel Nimmer.

The Ninth also had its share of fishermen, several of who developed novel ways of catching fish. Off Rendova and New Georgia, impromptu fishing parties would take advantage of the amphibious Alligators to wade into deeper waters and cast their lines. Sometimes, more active measures were taken. Some of the fishermen less patient with the traditional methods of the sport would shoot fish with their rifles, and some true daredevils, including Jack's Battery A pal, "Tojo" Whalen, went "TNT-fishing." The equipment of choice for this novel aquatic sport required 1/4 pound TNT blocks (used for demolitions, with two or three blocks strapped together usually being required to fell a palm or coconut tree), hand grenades, or small-caliber Japanese shells jury-rigged to explode underwater. TNT-fishing could be almost as deadly to the fishermen as it was to the fish, but it produced a large haul of dead and stunned marine life that floated to the surface. Unfortunately for one 9th Defense trooper who carried his love of grenade-fishing to the Russells, he had forgotten that Banika was hardly a combat zone and any large explosion there could likely trigger an alert. His efforts at grenade-fishing one afternoon started an island-wide panic, with trigger-happy soldiers and Marines suspecting a Japanese ship or submarine was attacking. For his pains, the hapless fisherman was almost court-martialed. TNT-fishing, however, amply supplemented the sparse and bland diet borne by the Ninth's Marines. This was especially so on Guadalcanal, as Captain Box's section of Battery B had learned to its benefit on Gavutu.

Another Marine who frequently indulged in this dangerous pastime was Gunnery Sergeant Smith of 90mm H&S. As David Slater remembered, he did so not without injury to himself and to a bystander after one TNT-fishing trip:

> Well, the Gunny, who lived in my tent and was usually drunk, came back from such an expedition in the possession of two blasting caps (used to detonate TNT blocks). These were wrapped in paper, which the Gunny absent-mindedly threw into the trash can (a topless 5-gallon tin that originally had held coffee). Then, after a last drag on his cigarette, he threw that, too, into the trash.
>
> Nearby, as I sat on my cot, engrossed in writing a letter, I heard two pistol shots (or so I thought). I immediately hit the deck and looked around. There was the Gunny, with a stunned look and a bloody foot next to the shredded can. I suddenly felt stinging all along my left side, from armpit to ankle (I was wearing only shorts and shoes). Looking, there were bloody spots galore. I had been peppered by tin

> shreds. Our nearby comrades then hustled us off to Battalion sick bay, where the Gunny was repaired, and the corpsman gleefully tweezered numerous splinters out of my hide.

While beer was now somewhat more frequently available in the Russells, black-market alcohol—sometimes filched from Navy or Army Air Forces officers' supplies; sometimes flown in from Australia and New Zealand by AAF crews; sometimes navy "grog" saved up by an Aussie or New Zealand sailor—was also available, if sold at exorbitant prices (often $30 or $35 per pint) and watered down to extend the supply. Other frustrated entrepreneurs took to brewing their own "hooch." This appears to have been a popular hobby wherever G.I.s were stationed, and the 9th Defense was no exception. Even Battery A's skipper, Hank Reichner, admitted sheeplishly to a certain pride in his unit's distilling efforts:

> On the lighter side, some of our people teamed up with a great CB [i.e., Seabee] outfit and managed to build a portable still. I guess we probably turned out the best corn whiskey in Guadalcanal until the troops got in the mash one night and got rather ill.

One highly potent blend was known as "torpedo juice." This earned its name as it was often made by mixing alcohol found in the propellant tanks of aerial torpedoes (or when available, pure grain medical alcohol, 190-proof) with whatever fruit juice happened to be handy, but which was most often grapefruit juice. The resulting concoction was also called "jungle juice." "Lord knows how many aerial torpedoes dropped from TBFs didn't travel five feet," David Slater wistfully recalled. John Hall, an enterprising Baltimorean in Battery E, was proud of his batch of "raisin jack," a highly popular form of hooch distilled from fermented raisins and sugar. As will be seen in a later chapter, however, the consequences of consuming wood alcohol or other non-potable fluids could be grim, indeed, a fact which seldom seemed to deter the Battalion's truly dedicated alcoholics and party animals.

One didn't have to be an alcoholic to find hooch to be a solace, however, and while the unit was out of the line, many of the Ninth's officers turned a blind eye to their men's occasional drinking. Hank Reichner recalled his tent mate and Battery A "exec," George "Doc" Teller, as an excellent junior officer and sidekick who somehow salvaged whatever hooch was necessary whenever the situation called for a good drink on the Canal:

> We were often visited by our friends from the infantry and managed to help them relax with our small supply of booze allocated to us from the battalion coffins. This supply dwindled and Doc saved the day, drawing on his experience as a medical student. At that time, he had learned how to make "noodle soup," a mixture of medical alcohol and lemon extract—a deadly combination. One drink was enough!

As was the case with units of all branches of service, nicknames were common. Nicknames were awarded due to some personal foible or goof-up (like Jack's well-known penchant for candy bars), physical appearance, overall attitude, or any similar distinguishing characteristic. (When left with no other alternative, "Mac" would always suffice, as in "Watch it, Mac!," "Up yours, Mac!" or "Semper Fi, Mac!") Jack was, of course, known throughout the Battalion as "Pogiebait." One of his pals, a bantamweight boxer named John Whalen, was nicknamed "Tojo" due to his small stature, and he was the butt of many jokes about his just passing the minimum height requirements to be a Marine, and Al Downs was called "Rosie," which was his hometown sweetheart's name. An ardent and unreconstructed Kentuckian, Bill Galloway, was labeled "Rebel;" John W.D. Morgan was "Mabel" (apparently either his girlfriend's name or due to his penchant, for which he was kidded as being effeminate, of sometimes wearing a sailor's hat he had filched from a hapless Navy "swab"); Charles D. Jones was "Zombie;" Robert Hausen was "Hercules" or "Herc", for short; David Slater of the Battalion's H&S Battery was "Biggie;" his pal and tormentor Jimmy Lynn was "Weasel;" William Seifried, a former Brooklyn cop, was "Bummie;" and the Battalion's baseball star Stanislaus Pacholski was "Ski" or, less flatteringly, "Polack." A beardless kid like Bill Sorensen or Chadwick, both being underaged Marines, was often called "Chick" or "Chicken," short for "spring chicken." In contrast, any married Marine or anyone older than 25 was likely to be called "Pop" or "Pappy." This was, after all, largely a young man's war.

Regardless of their efficiency or bravery, even the Ninth's staunchest officers and NCOs (and some less staunch ones, as well) had nicknames, too—sometimes used to their faces, usually not, depending upon the particular officer and his disposition on any given day. Any commanding officer was, in a pinch, the "Old Man," although he was never called this to his face. Captain (later Major) Walter Wells, Bill Box's successor as Battery B commander and later the Exec and CO of the 155mm Group, was known to all as "Waldo" and (sometimes by his friend Hank Reichner) "Waldo the Beast." A real straight-shooter, Wells would accept being referred to by his nickname by his enlisted Marines, although most of them knew their limits and when not to take liberties with this privilege. A few, however, unwisely crossed the line or incurred Waldo's wrath, much to their regret. As Chadwick recalled of Captain Wells, he was not a man who summoned up ambivalent feelings in anyone:

> Wells was a good Marine officer: he was a man you either loved or hated, no middle ground, but most loved him. He was respected and no one crossed him, no matter which Group you belonged to.

Wells's perspective was, in many ways, similar to that of General Patton inasmuch as, like Patton, he believed that to get his men to remember, he had to give it to them dirty and loud, for maximum effect. The general attitude of Battery B's Marines towards Wells as their new CO can best be described as being on a spectrum ranging from grudging respect and admiration to intense fear. For his part, Jack apparently got along well enough with Captain Wells or, at least, never got on his bad side, without having to engage him in the obnoxious rites of "earbanging," the currying of favor with a superior officer. In his own way, Jack respected Captain Wells but, secretly, he feared the Captain a little as well.

The overall attitude of Battery B towards its new CO, Wells, compared with his predecessor, Bill Box, was a study in contrasts. Depending on his daily disposition, Captain Box was "Sweet William" when in a good mood, or "Wild Bill" when in a bad mood and "on the warpath." Most of the men, however, recalled Captain Box as generally being of an engaging and sunny disposition, sincere without being perceived as overly familiar or in any way as weak. Battery A's leathernecks expressed similar feelings of pride and loyalty towards their Old Man. Captain Henry Reichner was known on Gitmo by his subordinates as "The Little General" or later as "Hammering Hank, the Horrible Hessian."

The balding and ruddy-complexioned Bob Hiatt was called "Turret Top" and "The Lobster" (when enraged over the latest snafu). For some reason, Lieutenant Wismer, one of the heroes of the Zanana Beach fight, was "Pinky." One pudgy lieutenant in Battery B, who joined the battery in the Russells and who somehow maintained his weight, even in the Pacific's strenuous climate, was called "Jelly Belly;" Jack was chronically amazed how he could find the food or the time to gain any weight. Green second lieutenants were "shavetails;" Gunnery Sergeants were universally known as "Gunnies;" any lesser degree of sergeant was, naturally enough, "Sarge;" and corporals (possibly due to their contemptuous attitudes as DIs at Parris Island) were "little colonels." While the enlisted men's ability to get away with calling some of the officers by their nicknames to their faces was certainly not common for all Marine or other military units, in a real sense, it reflected the high degree of camaraderie that existed between all ranks in a unit like the Ninth and the "no chickenshit" kind of attitude that permeated it from the top down.

The personality and geographical mix in the Ninth was highly varied, as well. As boots, the young Marines were fairly gullible and, although they may have fancied themselves to be young "men of the world," the DIs usually quickly proved them otherwise. In a society where newspapers, radios and movies had neither permeated society yet in a homogenized way nor created a mass culture such as that of today's United States, regional differences still abounded and were often highly noticeable. Many of the Ninth's enlisted men were from the North and Northeast, although there was a large contingent of Southerners—Jack being just one of several native Tennesseans in the Battalion. Some of the Northerners had been shaken up by their experiences with the DIs, who for some reason, tended either to be Southerners or to adopt a Southern-accented cadence. Having lived in Atlanta, Charlotte, Murray, Lynchburg and Birmingham prior to settling down in Franklin, Jack had traveled more frequently and earlier in life than many of his counterparts, who may had exclusively lived in the same town, city or farm until shipped off to P.I. The shared rigors of Boot Camp had helped break down most (if not necessarily all) of the regional and ethnic differences, and Jack found some of his closest buddies to be guys not from the deep South, but from places like Indiana (Kruse), Iowa (Hausen), New York (Chadwick and Whalen) and Pittsburgh (Downs). Still, whether Catholic, Protestant, Jewish or Greek Orthodox, they made up what seemed at times to be a big, raucous, disjointed and sometimes dysfunctional family called the 9th Defense; as Chadwick told Bergerud.

> The Marine Corps was like a brotherhood, you looked out for each other. It's hard to describe. You'd be playing cards; you'd get into an argument, get up, slug each other, and then get down and start playing cards again.

Of course, neither the Ninth nor each of its subordinate groups, batteries and platoons was truly a family. As surrogate fathers and big-brother figures, most of the battery commanders were roughly the same age as their enlisted men and were younger—often, ten or more years younger—than many of their platoon sergeants and battery gunnery sergeants. There were no maternal elements to this existence, and few fathers are ever forced to recognize that they may have to order their sons to die—and not just to die, but potentially to watch them die miserably. Too much sentimentality was a liability from a leader's perspective. Most of the Ninth's officers, however, somehow negotiated successfully the fine line between deeply caring for their men and their welfare, yet requiring them to make the maximum sacrifice when required.

The Ninth's Leathernecks were, in the main, a high-spirited

crew, despite their lack of real leave time and the tough conditions they had faced. Practical jokes and goof-ups ran rampant, including some that truly backfired. Frank Chadwick recalled one stunt that he and his tentmates played on one gullible Battery B Marine.

The man in question was utterly convinced that he was experiencing a nervous breakdown. For several weeks, every time he went to take a shower and emerged from the shower, his uniform and towel were nowhere to be found. He would sprint back to his tent, stark naked, only to find his dungarees, underwear and boondockers neatly laid out on his cot. The Marine would mumble, perplexedly, "How in the hell did my stuff get here?" "Aw, come on! Don't you remember walking out of here just like that?," his tentmates and neighbors would retort, grinning and winking stealthily at one another. After weeks of this bizarre, recurring behavior, the leatherneck finally got a referral from Doc Krepela to see a Navy psychiatrist. It was with both amazement and disgust that the practical jokesters soon found their prank had rebounded on them: the psychiatrist was in total agreement with their tentmate's opinion as to his failing sanity—and prescribed, as a cure, immediate departure from the combat area for a long course of treatment elsewhere.

A field-grade officer of the Battalion, whom we will call Lt. Colonel Baker and who served as one of the Group COs, was regarded as an odd but humorless martinet by the Battalion's enlisted men. His own junior officers were hardly any fonder of him, secretly referring to him in their personal code as "TORSOB"—"The Original Revolving Son of a Bitch." He was noted particularly for four things: his habit of frequently scratching himself, no doubt from an acute case of jungle rot (earning him yet another nickname, "Scratchy Ass"); his habitual wearing of khaki uniforms in lieu of the more usual olive-green dungarees, even in a combat environment like Guadalcanal; his penchant for collecting "girlie" magazines and pictures of nude women (which would have hardly been noteworthy if he had been an enlisted man but, in a time before *Playboy* and other such magazines were common, even the lowest enlisted men took notice when a field-grade officer indulged in this kind of behavior);[10] and his dog, which he had "promoted" to sergeant and which he took with him on his morning strolls down the beach, during which he would expect military courtesy to be rendered not just to himself, but to his dog as well. This colonel would, however, be burned in the end—quite literally.

While on Guadalcanal and the other islands in the Solomons group, because the water table lay so near the surface, trench latrines could not be dug in the usual manner. Instead, open-air latrines were made by cutting fuel drums in half and covering them with wooden planks to serve as benches. To destroy the detritus, each morning a work detail took leftover silk bags of gunpowder from the 155s, emptied the bags into the latrine drums, and lit the powder. The small amount of gunpowder used was fit for this function because it burned quickly and cleanly, without flame or explosion. On one morning latrine detail, however, a 155mm Group Marine realized he had no gunpowder left to complete the burn-off process. Instead, he emptied a jerry can of the only flammable substance reasonably handy, gasoline, directly into the cut-off drum. In his haste to get to the job, the man realized he also had forgotten to bring matches to light the mess. He headed back to the campsite to find a box of matches.

As he and the other members of the latrine-cleaning detail departed, they briskly saluted Colonel Baker *en route* to the latrines on his morning constitutional, cigarette well-lit in his mouth, but warning him as they passed that they had just finished cleaning the latrine in the usual manner. It was with horror that, seconds later, the detail heard a loud explosion and an agonized scream following the colonel's abandonment of the still smoking cigarette in the latrine then occupied by him—the very one that the detail had supposedly cleaned. With backside, genitals and khaki trousers roasted and with all shreds of dignity lost, the furious colonel painfully lurched to the 155mm Group's CP. After being treated for his burns, he demanded to see the duty logs to find out who had been on the latrine detail. For some "strange" reason, all the other duty rosters were present and complete—all, that is, except the roster for the latrine detail. Colonel Baker never learned the identity of the members of the latrine team that had elevated him so spectacularly.

There were ample opportunities to observe Colonel Baker's bizarre performances at close range on the Canal, where he was the 155mm Group's CO for a time. Several veterans recalled watching him parking his jeep near the Koli Point beach. Once there, he would stride off the beach to the water's edge and enter the surf up to his neck, casually smoking a cigarette and gazing at the horizon unperturbedly, as if he were anywhere but in a war zone. The only problem with this picture of bliss and contemplation was that the TORSOB was still fully dressed in boots, khaki shirt and trousers as he meandered in and out of the surf. On another occasion, his dog apparently refused to obey his orders to catch a fleeing rat. "Go get him, boy! Get him!" the Colonel roared, to no avail. The next day, Colonel Baker called a formation of all available hands from Group headquarters to witness a masthead ceremony called to discipline his obstinate pet—who was formally "reduced" in rank, in front of the baffled formation, from sergeant to a corporal.

On another occasion, Joe Pratl recalled that Colonel Baker was scheduled to conduct a full inspection of the Group's subordinate batteries. Battery A labored mightily to spruce up their tents and housekeeping arrangements, and the men cleaned and laundered their footwear and khaki "suntan" uniforms as best they could. On the day of the "big show," the Colonel's inspection of Pratl's platoon was short, indeed.

As the men nervously snapped to attention on the Colonel's entrance, Baker's gimlet eyes fixated almost immediately on a popular pin-up photo of Betty Grable. A weird smirk creased his lips, and the men suspected he was about to ream them out royally for their unauthorized artwork. Instead, with no further to-do, the Colonel briskly strode up to Pratl's platoon leader and platoon sergeant and barked out: "Great job!" In a flurry of salutes, the TORSOB hastened on to the next cluster of tents, leaving behind a relieved but utterly dumbfounded tentful of Leathernecks.

If his command style alone was not erratic enough, Colonel Baker's vehicular skills were also eccentric. Bill Galloway recalled some 155mm Group enlisted men who decided to test his driving in a peculiar way. Placing an orange crate in the spot where he usually parked his jeep next to Group Headquarters, the men watched amazedly as the TORSOB roared up to his usual parking space and, without pausing, flattened the crate and all its contents. He leapt out of the jeep, jaws set in his usual grim expression, without a word. The onlookers decided to repeat the experiment the next day, with similar results ensuing. Some six days and six pulverized crates later, the men gleefully exulted as, by order of the Battalion CO, Colonel Baker lost his driving privileges.

Already in his late 40s by the time the war had begun, Colonel Baker was, generally speaking, regarded by most members of the Ninth—officers as well as the EMs—as being "a real fruitcake," to quote Pogiebait. One of Baker's junior officers, Captain Reichner, recalled the Colonel as once taking a small boat and a case of grenades out to sea ostensibly to drop them, much like mini-depth charges, on submerged Japanese submarines supposedly lurking nearby! His patience sorely tried by his superior's stunts, Captain Reichner was discussing the TORSOB with Battery B's skipper Tom Stafford on a field telephone one day. When Major Stafford made a comment about Colonel Baker, "Hammerin' Hank"

Reichner spluttered without a second thought: "Him—that old bastard!" Unknown to both officers, however, "that old bastard" had tapped into their conversation from the 155mm Group's switchboard. This became immediately apparent when a new voice interjected: "*Reissh-ner*, I may be a bastard, but I am not old! *Come down to my tent*!" And so, Reichner dutifully trooped down to Colonel Baker's tent to accept his reaming-out.

Hearing rumors that Colonel Baker's sanity was being questioned, Colonel Scheyer, Baker's nominal superior on the Canal as Battalion Exec, put the question bluntly to Captain Reichner. Faced with a direct question, Reichner mustered an equally direct answer: "Sir, I believe that Colonel Baker has lost his mind." Colonel Scheyer naturally reported this to Colonel Nimmer, who confronted Colonel Baker with the reports he had received. Incensed, Baker somehow explained his way around his weird follies but he naturally wanted to know the sources of these opinions. Also, quite naturally, Colonel Nimmer told him, identifying Baker's subordinate Reichner as one of the sources—thus, once more proving the truth of the old military adage that *merde* rolls downhill. By now, Colonel Nimmer, too, was angry with Reichner, who somehow evaded his wrath: "He was furious, as he felt that my remarks about [Baker] were disloyal. Only by some divine intervention was I not relieved of my command. I suspect Lt. Colonel Scheyer was my guardian angel. As I did not initiate my remarks, but rather responded to questioning from a superior officer, I felt that I was blind-sided."

Reichner figured that with these slip-ups, he had given Colonel Baker all the ammunition he needed to court-martial him or, at the least, wreck his budding career with an unfavorable efficiency report. With a creeping sense of dread, Reichner took a call in Battery A's CP several weeks later from Colonel Baker, who dryly said over the field phone, "Come down to my CP, *Reissh-ner*. I want to show you your efficiency report." To Reichner's amazement, however, Baker had given him all "Excellent" ratings with one exception: a "Fair" for "Loyalty." "I guess he figured there must have been some truth to what I had said, after all," Reichner surmised. Unfortunately and with a regrettable sense of timing, Hank Reichner also chose to point this aspect out to Colonel Baker at the end of reviewing his "report card:"

> "Get the hell out of here," said he, and I fled back to my tent for a couple of "noodle soups" with the realization that any further promotion for me was a questionable bet. With all this, though, he and I stayed on pretty good terms.

"I guess he thought I was as crazy as he was," Hank Reichner ultimately concluded.

Doc Krepela's Antics

Besides being a gifted combat surgeon, Lt. Commander Miles Krepela, the unit's Navy doctor, was widely regarded as being one of the Battalion's leading comedians and a fair judge of separating the truly sick from the malingerers. On one occasion near the end of the Guadalcanal campaign, he was visited by an especially wan-looking Marine. "O.K., son, what's the problem here?" Doc Krepela asked with his best bedside manner. "Oh, Doc, I just think I'm cracking up. I don't think I can take it any more," the Marine sighed. "Well, what do you think will make you feel better?" Dr. Krepela asked skeptically. "If I could get a pass to New Zealand, I think I'd feel a lot better; but, you know," the Marine said, visibly perking up at the thought, "if I could only get leave to get shipped back over the water, stateside, I'm sure they could cure me there."

Without a word, Dr. Krepela stood up, unbuttoned his fly, and prepared to "take a leak" on the dirt floor of the pyramid tent serving as his office. "What are you doing, sir?" the incredulous Marine exclaimed. "Well, if that's all that it takes to get you back to the States, I'm going there with you!" Doc Krepela responded. "Forget it, sir; you're crazier than I am!" the newly cured Marine yelled as he ran out of Krepela's sickbay at a healthy trot.

On the other hand, Frank Chadwick recalled contracting a severe case of jaundice on New Georgia and being ordered to see Doc Krepela, who promptly had Chadwick deliver a urine sample. The glass vial was soon filled with a ghastly-smelling, yellowish-brownish liquid, which Doc Krepela held up admiringly to the light. "Oh, my! Look at that beautiful color!" the Doctor exclaimed in awe, as he turned the vial around in the light like a prism or kaleidoscope. "Have you ever seen such a perfect color? I've never seen anything like this in my life! This is just beautiful!" "Oh, Lord, what are you talking about, Doc?" Chadwick uttered in fevered amazement. The Doc turned around at Chadwick and winked: "Aw, quit your squawking; I'm sending you straight to the hospital. That's what you wanted to hear anyway, right?"

While often fondly remembered for his antics, however, no veteran of the Ninth ever apparently questioned the dedication, competence or bravery of Doc Krepela, his deputy Lieutenant Nate Gershon and their staff. The medical team's collective performance on Rendova—particularly in dodging exploding fuel and ammo supplies on Suicide Point to rescue wounded and dying Marines and Seabees after the July 2 air raid—was almost unanimously regarded as heroic. Despite having the chance to move the Suicide Point dispensary to a higher and safer ground, Krepela successfully argued to keep it in its position because such a move would not only make transportation of the wounded more difficult over the muddy trails, but because the dispensary's location would make it that much easier to move wounded onto the evacuation boats. Because of the dispensary's proximity to ripe targets for Japanese airmen, in the Black Friday air raid, one of Krepela's pharmacist's mates was felled by flying shrapnel. Although many of the Ninth's men recalled the fact that their Navy dentist, Lt. Jake Goodwin, was forced to ply his trade with a foot-operated drill, others also recalled his superhuman efforts at lifesaving after the Suicide Point raid as the dentist was pressed into service as a first-aid man and battlefield surgeon.

Doc Krepela was widely regarded as being something of a miracle worker among his charges for his creative responses to several other life-threatening incidents. On one occasion on New Georgia, he gingerly removed a live Japanese 57mm high explosive shell with a hair-trigger fuse that was imbedded in a Marine's thigh. In another incident on New Georgia, another Marine, Battery B's Ned Williams, was brained by the recoil of a 155mm gun, which as Frank Chadwick described, would "make you feel like you had been hit by a ten-ton truck at 60 miles an hour." The impact shattered Williams' cranium and threw a large fragment of skull loose, exposing his brain. Retrieving and cleaning the skull fragment with alcohol, and using a paste made out of flour, Doc Krepela repaired Williams' skull in his primitive field aid station and had him evacuated stateside for treatment. Amazingly, apart from chronic headaches, Williams apparently suffered no permanent side effects from this injury.

The huge number of men who survived deadly attacks of malaria and dengue fever is proof alone of the miracles that Miles Krepela, Nate Gershon, Jake Goodwin and their largely unsung Navy corpsmen worked in the jungles of the Pacific. As one of Krepela's corpsmen said to Sergeant Samuel Stavisky, the Ninth's assigned combat correspondent on Rendova: "When a Marine goes down, a corpsman goes up."

Camp Life in the Boondocks; "Scrounging"

> *Life in the Corps, according to one joke of the period:*
> "*Question*: What's the difference between the Marines
> and the Boy Scouts?"
> "*Answer*: The Boy Scouts have adult supervision."

Even in the rear areas of New Georgia and Banika, the more refined campsites of the Ninth lacked most of the basic creature comforts.The ever-present tropical humidity tended to rot the canvas tents, and a coating of mold and mildew would frequently blossom if left uncleaned for any length of time. The Marines' clothes, leather and canvas equipment and boots would likewise deteriorate rapidly; in some cases, men's underpants and trousers literally rotted off their bodies. As a result of the damp tropical climate, so many men in the Solomons suffered from trench foot, athlete's foot and other fungal rashes infesting their crotches and underarms—the "creeping crud." This was usually treated only by various tinctures, liberally swabbed on the victim by a bored and disgusted corpsman. The campsites themselves were studded with sandbag-revetted foxholes and trenches (often half-filled with rainwater) that served as bomb shelters from Pistol Pete's and Washing Machine Charlie's depredations. The roads and trails were more frequently than not mucky quagmires, and quite a few jeeps and trucks that entered the Ninth's campsites under their own horsepower left under "Marine power" at the end of a tow rope during the rainy seasons.

To conjure up a reasonably accurate depiction of the Ninth's campsites around Munda Field, one can picture a scene generally reminiscent of a tropical version of the 4077 M.A.S.H.'s campsite:

A collection of faded olive-drab tents are seemingly ensconced in a field of mud and beaten-down elephant grass. The entire area is surrounded by lush green foliage—giant banyan trees and coconut palms—but is covered overall with a tropical miasma, and a heavy afternoon rain has done little to cool down the atmosphere; in fact, if anything, it now more closely resembles a continual steambath. A one-lane, more or less circular trail meanders around the circumference of the tents and awnings. One knows that this is the Headquarters, 9th Defense Battalion because a circular sign proudly proclaims the fact to the world at the entrance to the campsite, along with another sign noting it as the home of Duke Radio, "Duke" being the Battalion's call sign.

The ubiquitous 55-gallon steel drum is everywhere in evidence and is put to every conceivable use: as supports for vehicle and generator revetments and Biggie Slater's half-underground, corrugated metal radio shack; as garbage and mess hall slop cans; modified as grills, burners and stoves; and cut in half as latrines; and, occasionally, for their intended use, filled with diesel or gasoline, for topping off the Ninth's vehicles. Elsewhere, five-gallon tin cans, originally filled with coffee grounds—the Corps's true lifeblood, preferably never consumed in any way other than jet-black and scaldingly hot—are as omnipresent and omnifunctional as the large steel drums, serving similar uses but on a more intimate scale. A few of Pogiebait McCall's Lister bags full of purified water, each looking just like "a huge cow's udder," as Captain Reichner described them, hang from tripods and tree limbs.

Palms and colossal banyan trees stud the hills and rises overlooking the camp. In places, the tumid smell of mud is overpowered by riper odors: slop from the

Battalion's mess hall and half-empty marmite cans of half-warmed, leftover Spam; the stink of the latrines, not yet burned off by the day's unused powder bags from the Long Toms; the pungent carcasses of hundreds of crushed land crabs and other New Georgia fauna;and, not far from the mess hall, the sinister reek of human death: the smells of decomposition from corpses and skeletons of Munda's dead Japanese defenders in a bulldozed cemetery—many of them killed in fact by the Ninth's bombardments—and whose outraged skulls, bones and limbs jut upwards from the overturned earth towards the damp tropical skies. A few radio antennas and field-telephone lines vie with the trees for altitude.

And—if the observer looks more closely—scattered among the tents, trees and bushes and hidden in the tall grass, one might notice various pieces of non-Marine issue equipment. Several jeeps on the edges of the perimeter, away from the CO's tents, seem to bear traces of fresh Marine-issue forest green paint, but in places barely covering a lighter and browner coat of original Army-issue olive drab camouflage.

The Ninth's scroungers have been hard at work.

The Ninth's Battalion Headquarters area on New Georgia, near Munda Field. (Photo by Harry Jones, courtesy of David Slater)

Although the Ninth had an excellent reputation for its combat discipline and efficiency, it had also earned quite a reputation for "scrounging" from the Army and Navy and for its off-duty life. As has been seen, the often doubtful logistics situation on Guadalcanal helped to encourage this kind of activity. This wilder, seamier side of the Ninth's existence continued into the Central Solomons campaign, despite the Battalion's augmentations and supplies of new equipment at the end of the fight for Guadalcanal.

As a result of their depredations on one Navy medical supply dump, in which the Marines used their five-finger discount method to help themselves to a supply of alcohol, the 155mm Group's officers and Army MPs conducted a fruitless shakedown at dawn for leftover hooch. Battery A had hidden its stash in a hole under a tent's main tentpole (and, as we have seen, later secreted it in a Long Tom's barrel). Battery B wrapped its leftovers in a blanket and hung it in the battery's head. Frustrated by its failure to nab the offenders, Island Command forced the Battalion to break camp one week early and live in beachside pup tents until boarding for Operation TOENAILS commenced. Orders were posted that any member of the 9th Defense found outside this impromptu "quarantine zone" would be subjected to a court-martial. After the Central Solomons campaign, with the Ninth scheduled to leave New Georgia but well recalling its prior marauding activities on Guadalcanal, that island's Army commander flatly refused to let the Battalion be stationed there ever again, with one apparent consequence being that it was sent instead to virgin territory in the Russells at the end of Operation TOENAILS.

Similar troubles arose on New Georgia at campaign's end. With a colorful band of characters as VMF-214's "Black Sheep" stationed nearby, it was inevitable that brawls and thefts would occur between these two units. One confrontation between a group of gunners and the Black Sheep over stolen hooch almost resulted in a shoot-out. Several Army units nearby began to lose large amounts of their gear, including several jeeps. David Slater recalled: "Legend has it that we had guys who could change an Army jeep into a Marine Corps jeep in an hour. A fast repaint and stenciling of U.S.M.C. ID did it." The culprits were identified, however, when an Army MP unit recaptured one of the jeeps with a Marine nestled behind the wheel. The Battalion now incurred the wrath of New Georgia's island commander, again an Army general, who had a new guardhouse in which he jailed the arrested Marine and on which a sign was posted, decreeing it to be "A Brig for Marines (9th)." As Chadwick recalled:

> The island commander swore he would fill it with Marines from the Ninth. He soon had more Marines in the brig. We felt lucky because we finally received our shipping for the Russells, or our whole battalion would have been his guests.

Their arrival in the Russells did little to dampen the Ninth's light-fingered miscreants. After having been ordered to pitch camp on Banika next to the fuel-filled swamp, Colonel Archie O'Neil, finally convinced the island's Army commander to authorize a move to better ground. It took about a month to build the new bivouac area and complete the relocation. Afterwards, with little to do but clean equipment and brush up on training, someone in the chain of command decided that the 155mm Group had an ample share of potential stevedores, and work parties were assigned to help unload ships and move cargo. The stevedoring detail lasted for several weeks until a supply officer noticed that too much of the cargo was vanishing. In one instance, a truckload of potatoes and salted mutton disappeared without a trace while being "unloaded" by a squad from the 155mm Group. While on another work party, Jack and Chadwick spied several forlorn-looking wooden crates labeled "Planter's Peanuts." Needless to say, several crates did not reach the new supply depot.

Back at the Ninth's base camp, Jack, Chadwick and their Battery B buddies eagerly broke open the crates to find not peanuts, but an even more welcome and tradeable treat—Chelsea cigarettes in the peanut tins, dispensed in increments of 50 ("tin fifties") or 100 to a can: "We had enough cigarettes to last the whole Battalion a hundred years." Best of all, the cans were perfect form fillers for the standard Marine-issue horseshoe backpack; as David Slater reminisced, "Heavy smokers would have more cigarettes than gear in their packs." This was a age when cigarettes were very popular, with teenagers furtively smoking at very young ages and remembering the illicit pleasure of their "first smoke" almost as keenly as their first kiss or first sexual experience. With so many young men already hooked on the habit, the U.S. military distributed them liberally as much as anything as a morale booster and as a substitute for alcohol as a soother of nerves. Accordingly, cigarettes were supplied in huge quantities and quite often for free. Where food in the Pacific lacked taste or otherwise was in short supply, the spicy taste of tobacco substituted for food and helped curb the appetite. Cigarettes were another ever-present feature of the Marines' landscape, both in and out of action, and it was a rare Marine who did not smoke after a few months of service. Jack had already picked up cigarette smoking before the war, but the war hooked him for good. Pogiebait McCall may have had only a few vices, but this one would get him in the end.

Why did the Battalion's penchant for scavenging go on to these extremes? It invariably seemed to the average Marine that not only did the Army and Navy have superior logistical systems, but the quality, quantity and diversity of things in these services' supply systems were vastly better than what was available in the Corps's logistics base. Part of this may have been due to a "strictly-business" attitude on the part of the Corps's logisticians. As opposed to the Army and Navy, which generally took more care to supply their respective troops with creature comforts, most Marines (until 1943) had volunteered for this and,as such, were likely expected by their commanders to tolerate a higher level of personal discomfort. Also, in much of Marine planning, the Corps's logistical structure was geared very directly towards combat and combat support items—strictly beans and bullets, at the general expense of beds, beer and "baloney." The infusion of the crusty and rambunctious "old breed" 5th Defense Polar Bears into the Battalion on Cuba may also have affected the younger Marines' attitudes at an early date:

We *learned* from the contingent of "Polar Bears" [David Slater recalled] that came down to Gitmo on the *Merak*. This was a rough crew: quite a few old Corps types, flotsam and jetsam of the Depression. On our arrival at Cuba, Nimmer had us take up a formation on the parade ground—I still see it in my mind's eye as though it were yesterday—and proceeded to ream us out as the scum of the earth hardly worthy of his command (and here quite a few of us were innocent young boots). He had perused the record books of the Polar Bears the night before and discovered that they were a rather tarnished bunch. However, he magnanimously announced, he would expunge their derelictions and allow them a new leaf in the 9th. (Fat chance!)

David ("Biggie") Slater exiting one of the Battalion's communications sheds near Munda Field. (Photo by Harry Jones, courtesy of David Slater)

As far as the Ninth's enlisted men could tell, the Battalion and Group commanders officially took a dim view of their troops' acquisitions made outside the standard channels of supply, and the Ninth's COs, from Colonel Nimmer through Scheyer and O'Neil, would periodically remind their subordinates of the consequences of theft and the need to maintain good supply discipline. Nevertheless, knowing full well the unit's unfulfilled requisitions and dire needs for larger pieces of equipment—trucks, jeeps, LVTs, etc.—not found on an authorized table of organization, the COs themselves actively sought to scrounge or borrow such equipment. We have already seen how Colonel Scheyer, with a little creativity of his own, rejiggered the unit-of-fire authorizations to get more ammunition before the Rendova landings than the Ninth would normally have received, and how he traded the Battalion's old artillery pieces with Army units for newer equipment. Before the New Georgia campaign, the Colonel and the Battalion's supply officer also signed temporary hand receipts to borrow nine additional LVTs and extra machine guns from the 3rd Marine Division. Given the sometimes shaky supply situation, then, it is hardly surprising that the battery and group commanders, at least, would turn a blind eye or drop subtle hints to their NCOs and junior enlisted when the latter took to their own alternative sources to beef up the unit's supplies and gear.

In May 1944, as the Ninth packed its gear and marched to its pre-invasion quarantine area, the Russells Island Command's quartermasters would have been amazed to find the quantity and variety of gear left behind in the Battalion's bivouac area. As Chadwick remembered:

> When we broke camp and started our walk (about four miles) to the pier, we looked back at the site and saw many jeeps, 1/2-ton trucks, unopened crates,

> wooden planks and many other odd items that were picked up in the Ninth's midnight requisitions. It was a sight to behold, and the Army recovered much of its missing property.

With good reason, Colonel Scheyer, on his departure as Battalion CO, was reputed to have said that if he ever faced combat again, he hoped it would be with a unit as great as the Ninth, but he also hoped he would never, ever have to command an outfit like the Ninth in a rear area again!

Attitudes Towards Women and Sex

If a poll were taken of the Ninth's young men as to what was most noticeably lacking in the Pacific, it would have been female companionship. There were few native women (except for the brief sojourn on New Caledonia, some of the inhabitants of Guadalcanal and New Georgia—who generally were not viewed as objects of romantic interest but frequently were hired through bartering goods or food by some members of the Ninth to help with laundry or menial chores—and later on Guam) to open up any opportunities for romance or sexual release. With the general absence of women in this sector of the South Pacific and the high testosterone levels of a bunch of young Marines, it was hardly surprising that things would get out of hand almost any time an attractive young woman appeared in the area.

During the Ninth's stay in the Russells, the unit had its first USO show of the entire war. The unit's carpenters had built a stage and amphitheater for showing movies, and a traveling USO Camp Show featuring Ray Milland and three beautiful starlets staged a two-hour show to the lusty roars, catcalls and applause of the sex-starved Leathernecks. After the show, the USO troupe was invited to the Battalion's officers' club for drinks and some banter. Unfortunately, there was an interval when the lights went out; one of the actresses felt herself being groped, and she began to scream loudly. As the lights came back on moments later, still screaming, the irate and tearful actress slapped the officer nearest her—who happened to be none other than Lt. Colonel O'Neil. Upon hearing her accusation, the red-faced (for more reasons than one) CO apologized to her for his officers' conduct and promptly closed down the party. An officers' call was held the next morning, in which the Colonel angrily demanded to know who had fondled the actress. Not surprisingly, the guilty party did not reveal himself. The enlisted Marines never found out precisely what the Colonel did to his officers in response to this misbehavior, but for several days afterwards, the Battalion's officers were noticeably close-mouthed and downcast.

In April 1944, not long before the Battalion's departure from the Russells, a similar incident occurred but on a larger and more serious scale. The Seabees had completed a hospital on Banika, Mobile Hospital 10 or "MOB 10," and Navy nurses were now being assigned to the island to staff it. The day after the nurses' arrival, a group of Navy medical officers took some of them for a jeep tour of Banika. Unfortunately, the day they had chosen for their tour was Sunday, when many of the Ninth's personnel usually took their semi-weekly showers. The Ninth's bivouacs were on a road leading to the hospital, the piers and the airfield. Since no females other than the indigenous Russell Islanders were generally found on Banika, the Battalion had never had cause to enclose the open-air showers. In the Russells' tropical heat, with uniform requirements being relaxed at best, "our crew was practically a nudist colony," David Slater recalled. It was well after Reveille, and many of the Marines were showering or doing their laundry in nothing more than their skivvies, when a cry of "*Women*!" arose from the far end of the road. That one-word yell, at full-throated volume, was all it took to provoke a stampede.

Within seconds, a large pack of semi-naked Marines ran down to the road, wolf-whistling and yelling. The Leathernecks in the open showers turned around to give the nurses and their escorts some unanticipated full-frontal nudity, some of them fondling themselves while hollering crude comments at the highly embarrassed MOB 10 nurses, who desperately tried to hide their faces and turn their heads. Whether out of apparent solidarity with the others or pure perversity, some of the otherwise semi-dressed Marines themselves dropped their trousers and skivvies, joining in the chaos by "flashing" the flustered nurses and doctors. In a cloud of dust and with an angry honking of horns at the catcalling and jeering mob, the jeep convoy rapidly left the area for the hospital.

In a matter of minutes, some of the Battalion's officers and NCOs descended on the group, "raising hell." By day's end, cheesecloth screens or tarpaulins enclosed the showers and latrines. An order was then posted to the effect that, because they had abused the lax dress privileges of the Russells, the 9th Defense's Marines would now be required to be in full dungarees at all times. The reports of the enlisted men's lewd behavior towards the nurses, plus longstanding allegations of their piracy of supplies, undoubtedly helped hasten the decision to expedite shipping schedules to get the Battalion redeployed from the Russells as soon as possible. Still, to the more warped minds and wits of the 9th Defense, the incident with MOB 10's nurses was a cause for some humor.

Although absent from the Ninth's postings in the Pacific, the mere existence of women Marines was an additional source of grousing and gossip, often obscene, among "the old salts," Jack included, who occasionally griped in later years: "I joined the Corps before there were women or dogs!" Despite their service to country and Corps, the members of the

Marine Corps Women's Reserve who served during the war were the recipients of much harassment from many of their male counterparts. (The female Marines, however, gave back as good as they got and came up with their own profane and colorful nicknames for their male colleagues.) Some apparently viewed the presence of women in the Corps as a diminishment of their manhood, while others argued that it would lead to a corruption of the Corps's traditions and fighting spirit. Despite his grousing, Jack would change his views somewhat on this subject later in the war.

In spite of the near-constant loneliness and the lack of female companionship, which was alleviated to some degree on Banika by contacts with a few American teachers, Red Cross girls and missionaries (but precious few dates), there were apparently few incidents of homosexual activity. This may have been attributable to the attitudes and feelings of the majority of the Ninth's Marines themselves, but it may have been curbed by the savage treatment meted out to those few caught engaging in such activities. In 1944, which was still several years before the issuance of the Kinsey Report and later psychological studies, homosexuality was not regarded merely as a behavioral proclivity or a preexisting psychological condition. It was deemed to be a form of mental sickness, and a particularly vile one at that. In civilian life, the prescribed medical treatments for homosexuals were grim enough; in the military of the 1940s, they were ruthless.

Years after the war, Jack, who was noticeably prudish about discussing sexual matters of any kind, recalled to his wife Pat the fate of the two men caught *in flagrante delicto* late one night aboard the *Hunter Liggett* before the Ninth's landing on Guadalcanal. They were hauled out in their skivvies and left on deck in an open cage or fenced-in area. They were fed only bread and water, and they were left to sit there, all day long in the sun, as an object lesson of sorts, for everyone to look at and laugh at. Some people threw things at them; others spat at or cursed them as perverts. "They were treated just like animals," Jack recalled to Pat. Of this same incident, Captain Reichner remembered the following line as he censored one of his battery member's postcards home afterwards: "They caught your artist friend eating meat at midnight, and he is now in the brig."

Once ashore on Guadalcanal, the 155mm Group's commanding officer, Lt. Colonel Baker, devised a grim dry-land punishment for these two. As Frank Chadwick recalled:

> He had them pitch their shelter halves in a small barbed wire area. They were given a canteen of water per day, one meal and were not allowed to wash. [Colonel Baker] placed signs over each tent [obscenely stating their respective roles in the offense.] They were dirty and beginning to smell very bad [by the time that the] chaplain heard about it and came over for a visit. He informed the C.O. [*i.e.*,Colonel Baker] that this was crude and disgusting and gave him one day to either court-martial them or put them back on duty. The chaplain came back the next day and found nothing had been done. He informed him that he was not going to bother the Battalion C.O. but send a wire directly to Admiral Halsey, who he knew personally, and let him deal with the problem. Needless to say, the two Marines left the Canal the next day for New Caledonia. No one ever heard what happened to them but the Battalion C.O. kept close reins on [Colonel Baker] thereafter.

Sex was a frequent subject of discussion, whether telling dirty jokes, bragging about one's own female conquests, or commiserating with the recipient of the dreaded "Dear John" letter. Skinny-dipping, communal showers, the traditional silliness of Equator-crossing rituals and playing "grabass" were all deemed permissible, too, and few seemed to think there was anything prurient or objectionable about such activities. In some respects, it was a much more naive time, and teenage and college-aged boys could do such things without fear of being labeled as being out of the ordinary. Homosexual behavior, however, was one social taboo that even wartime did little to break down, and the treatment to be expected from one's peers if caught experimenting in that fashion would have undoubtedly been even more vicious, in many cases, than the "semi-official" treatment inflicted by Lt. Colonel Baker. Not that the official punishments themselves were any more tolerable. There was certainly no "don't ask, don't tell" policy in effect in the military in those days. Anyone caught engaging in such acts would risk, at best, a court martial and dishonorable discharge, with the stigma attached thereto and a lifelong impediment against many jobs in the civilian work force, and, at worst, incarceration—either in a military prison or in a mental ward.

Regardless of how one felt about the offense in question, Jack later admitted to his wife that he thought the punishment administered was "a hell of a way to go."

The Haunted Finger: Attitudes Towards the Enemy

While it might be unpleasant to consider, one cannot disguise the overall deep and abiding hatred shared by most Marines towards their adversary. To a very real degree, the feelings of Pacific veterans towards the Japanese differed both qualitatively and quantitatively from the feelings of many European Theater G.I.s towards the Germans and Italians. This difference animated many aspects of the Pacific war and helped create an even more savage war than existed, in many respects, in the Allied campaigns against the Axis powers in Western Europe and North Africa.

To be fair, this is only a generalization: certainly, many

American troops and sailors despised the Germans. On a more personal level, many of Jack's fellow Franklin High friends certainly came to do so, for a variety of reasons. One met and married a young German refugee from the Holocaust, whose family fled Germany before the Nazis' war on the Jews reached its most murderous proportions. Several of his schoolmates helped liberate the Dachau and Buchenwald concentration camps in the spring 1945, and they would bear witness to the horrors they saw there for the rest of their lives. Jack himself would have added personal cause to hate the Nazis: one of Jack's closest schooltime friends, David Gentry, an Army Signal Corps lineman, was shot and killed by a German sniper in Italy as he strung telephone lines. By and large, however, feelings of anger towards the Germans tended to be directed either at individuals like Hitler and Goering or, more amorphously, to organizations like the Nazi Party, the Gestapo and the SS.

This was manifestly not the case in the Pacific: again, as a generalization, the enemy was defined as being all of the Japanese people. There were undoubtedly deeply racial overtones on *both* sides. For the Japanese, this involved resentment of the Americans dating as far back as Commodore Perry's 1853 forcible opening of Japan to foreign trade, one of the first episodes of "gunboat diplomacy," bolstered by the anti-Oriental immigrant hysteria of the late 1800s and the 1920s, and in certain circles, a contempt for Americans as racist, ill-disciplined and avaricious materialists. For Americans, jingoistic newspapers and magazines had deprecated the "Orientals" since before the turn of the century. There were also reports of Japanese brutality during the 1930s, which may have influenced some of the Marines in their prewar teenage years. These included reports, not necessarily exaggerated, of the "Rape of Nanking" in 1937; the sinking of the U.S. gunboat *Panay* by Japanese aircraft in the Yangtze River that same year; reports of Japanese gas attacks on Chinese civilians; and, hitting much closer to home, the first reports in 1943 of the brutal "Bataan Death March," in which thousands of U.S. and Filipino POWs—including several Middle Tennesseans—would suffer and perish en route to prison camps. These views were strongly reinforced by the Marines' training and by wartime propaganda—"The only good Jap is a dead Jap"—by an almost constant use of the epithets "Jap" and "Nip" in daily speech and in writings of all kinds. Added to this was the popular press's own contributions, in newspapers, magazines, movies and animated cartoons—many of which did not blossom until well after the Christmas Tree Marines had been inducted and en route to the front. Even so, some of this propaganda was available at a very early date in the war.

The local evening newspaper, the *Nashville Banner*, printed a poem of the utmost savagery on its front page on the day after Pearl Harbor. Placed next to a photograph of FDR asking Congress to declare war and under the headline "CONGRESS DECLARES WAR: 3,000 CASUALTIES AT HAWAII," the free-verse poem, composed by the *Banner*'s editor-in-chief, may have typified much of what appeared elsewhere in the popular press in the days and weeks to come, all of which helped set the tone and which reflected the anger and desire for revenge felt by many Americans after Pearl Harbor. This piece of doggerel also reflects some remarkably prescient comments about the nastiness of the war that was about to come to the Pacific:

At last we're at war.
At war with Japan.
We didn't want it.
We tried to avoid it.
We sought peace.
At the very moment
When Jap bombers swooped low

To murder Americans
On duty
On our ships,
Our air fields,
Our foreign stations.

We stood by too long.
We were too patient.
We trusted the dastardly Orientals too far.
We were just a bunch of saps.
So the Japs pounced down,
But they'll bounce back.

This isn't going to be child's play.
We're in for some tough fighting.
But not a circumstance compared
With what is coming
To the Sons of the Rising Sun.
No! Sir! They've asked for it.
Now let 'em have it.
Total war.
All-out war.
No quarter.

Let's make it what they started.
Let's track them to their holes.
Let's sink their fleet
If it takes our last ship,
Our last sailor,
Our last shot.
Let's blockade their population into starvation.
Let's bomb their cities to shambles.
Let's give them what they asked for.
Let's blast
And shoot

And bomb
And burn.
Let's put the dirty yellow beasts
Where they belong.

* * *

Japan is doomed.
Let's make that doom sudden,
Absolute.
Let's hasten the day
When the sun will set
On the land of the Rising Sun.
To Hell with the slant-eyed Son of Heaven.
To Hell with his seventy million little yellow devils.
That's my ticket.
I hope you like it.
Let's get going!

The *Banner*'s hymn of hate was, of course, hardly alone in expressing these sentiments. Jack recalled that, after Pearl Harbor, it seemed that every time he heard the words "treacherous," "deceitful," "yellow," "cowardly," "dastardly," "back-stabbing" or "sneaky," one word was almost certain to follow: "*Jap*" or "*Nip*." How much of an effect the *Banner*'s headlines and Stahlman's poem had at the time on Jack's decision to join up, I cannot say, but Jack preserved the headlines and the entire front section of the December 8, 1941 *Banner* in his scrapbook for years.

Still, it was not necessarily a question of "pure" racism, blindly applied to all Asian peoples. Many Marines, Jack included, harbored no grudges against Asians in general, and many harbored sentiments in favor of the Chinese, surely as oppressed a group of humans as existed in the 1930s and 1940s. More than a few American churches had sponsored missionaries to the Orient; Pearl Buck's novels of Asia were best sellers in the inter-war period; and, after the massive 1923 Tokyo earthquake, American churches, humanitarian groups and relief agencies contributed tons of supplies to the Japanese. Many young Marines like Jack, who were fairly naive and who had never traveled far from home until their departures for Boot Camp, probably could not have distinguished between a Japanese, a Chinese, a Korean or a Filipino unless somebody had pointed out the differences. For many, the feelings of anger toward their enemy were not preexisting but were acquired. It also must not be forgotten that hard kernels of truth supported many accusations made against the Japanese military, the newly-minted propaganda notwithstanding.

One piece of evidence occasionally cited by Jack and some of the Ninth's Marines that many claims of Japanese barbarity were not necessarily just "war stories" occurred after the Battalion's arrival on Guadalcanal, where some heard of the so-called "Goettge massacre." In the fall of 1942, the 1st Marine Division's chief intelligence officer, Lt. Colonel Frank Goettge, led a patrol to investigate a beachside area where a number of Japanese wounded had allegedly been abandoned by their forces. This patrol was ambushed and surrounded; the sole survivor, who feigned death and escaped at high tide, claimed that he had seen Japanese officers and men killing the prisoners and wounded of the Goettge patrol. Generalized talk about the Goettge massacre was just another stimulus for the very hard feelings directed towards the enemy. The overall attitude about the Goettge patrol's fate can be summed up by Frank Chadwick: "We all talked about it some, sure, but we all figured Goettge was just a do-gooder. We figured we wouldn't make the same mistake he did."

The scuttlebutt passed around that a Marine must never let himself be taken prisoner by the Japanese. The Marines' pride in neither surrendering nor ever leaving a dead or wounded Marine behind on the battlefield assumed a new, darker meaning, as it was widely suspected that the Japanese would torture and kill any POWs or mutilate the dead. The general expectation was that no Japanese soldier would, likewise, let himself be taken prisoner and would fight to the death. In time, tales would also circulate on Guadalcanal that the Japanese, because they were starving, would resort to cannibalism—a "tale" which, in some dire circumstances, was later proved to be true in certain instances on New Guinea and in the Bonin Islands. The grim fate of Wantuck and Rothschild, in the Ninth's own experience with a all-out Japanese assault, hardened these attitudes and imbued almost all members of the unit with a fanatical hatred of the enemy.

The Tank Platoon's discovery on the Munda Trail of the remains of a pair of Army medics, apparently shot down as they rescued a wounded machine gun crew, hardened the hearts of Captain Blake and his tankers who, only moments before, had pitied a mangled and dying Japanese antitank gunner whom they had shot. That even a literate and educated man like Robert Blake (an erstwhile reporter for the *Cleveland Plain Dealer*) could be moved to such bitter fury was representative of what the hatred and violence of the Pacific war was doing to men's minds:

> In a glance the story tells itself. These two medics had heard the wounded scream and crawled out to bring them in. They got as far as this, when the Jap machine guns caught them and they too lay and bled and begged for help, until death came for them at last. . . .
>
> The full impact of the crime the Japanese committed strikes me. . . . How I wish that I had shot that wounded Jap, hollowed out his skull point blank with my forty-five, or better, ripped him open with my

> pocket knife! I grit my teeth. I will kill them, kill them, kill them, a thousand lives for every one of ours! And if compassion ever tempts me, I will think of that field of blackened American corpses, of the dead gunner and his mate, of the riddled stretcher bearers, and of the wounded who lay and bled, and knew no help could come, and died in agony, forsaken, and alone.

Jack admitted: "We couldn't understand the Nips. It was like they were crazy people. They were fanatics, and the only way you could stop them was to kill them. Life just didn't have the same meaning to them as it did to us." The concepts that the Emperor was the living embodiment of the sun goddess Amaterasu and that Japanese soldiers who died bravely in combat would essentially be deified were religious principles so unlike the Judeo-Christian ethics of the average American as to be very difficult for the typical Marine, G.I. or sailor to comprehend in any way other than by simply deciding that the enemy was, in essence, "crazy."

The environment and climate of this kind of war itself contributed to the hatreds on all sides. In Europe, while many of the ordinary American creature comforts were lacking, the cities, towns and villages (those that were intact) roughly approximated what one might expect of American urban and rural life in the 1930s and 1940s. There, a G.I. had a reasonable chance of possibly finding such comforts and maybe even inhabitants with whom he could relate. This was scarcely the case in the South Pacific: the climate and terrain was far removed from anything that Jack and his counterparts had ever experienced; tropical diseases were rampant; and the natives frequently were in hiding and, when seen, were often regarded as childlike and backward by the majority of both the Americans and Japanese. The overall environment tended to reinforce a "backs to the wall" sense of isolation and deprivation—in the words of the poem, "*For this God-forsaken outpost/Is a substitute for Hell.*" This attitude could just as easily be applied to the average Japanese soldier as well as to the average Marine.

Both sides' pre-combat military training and indoctrination, of course, amplified the hatred to be expressed towards the enemy. While the Marines undoubtedly had ample cause to despise Boot Camp, the brutal training and abuse meted out to Japanese conscripts in all branches of that nation's military made many of P.I.'s worst rigors seem pale by comparison. Robert Edgerton writes:

> Derisively called "less than a penny" (the price of their draft-notice postcard), [Japanese] soldiers and sailors were hazed, sworn at, slapped, beaten and forced to complete degrading tasks. They had no privacy, and any form of protest was a capital crime. An officer or NCO who lost his temper might actually beat a recruit to death.

In consequence, few prisoners were taken by either side in the Pacific war. Perhaps more so than in Europe, flame weapons were extensively used: flamethrowers, both backpack-carried and tank-mounted, became a staple of island fighting, and their first usage by American troops was against the Japanese extensively on New Georgia. Despite home-front criticisms of their barbarousness, they continued to be extensively used in the Pacific. Although these were not a part of the Fighting Ninth's arsenal, making it just about the only kind of conventional weapon the unit lacked, flamethrowers were touted as the most effective way to clear Japanese caves and bunkers with minimal American casualties. Likewise, napalm bombs were also first used against the Japanese. There may be some grim irony in tracing the increasing use of flame-generating weapons, from the flamethrower roasting of Japanese troops in bunkers and caves in 1943 to the firebombing of Tokyo and the nuclear incinerations of Hiroshima and Nagasaki in 1945, as a literal embodiment of the American press' exhortations in 1941 to "send the Japs to Hell" and to make their doom, in the *Banner*'s words, "sudden" and "absolute."

Even the dead on both sides were often savaged. There were tales of mutilations of dead Americans by the Japanese, but such atrocities were not limited to the Japanese. Jack and others recalled seeing American ghouls who collected Japanese body parts and pried gold fillings out of the mouths of the dead. Some Navy personnel on the Canal decorated a boat landing on Guadalcanal with a row of skulls hung on a rope. Enemy graveyards, such as one near the Ninth's headquarters adjacent to Munda Field, were sometimes desecrated. At least one 9th Defense Marine carried around a skull he scavenged from this graveyard after its bulldozering on command of a Ninth Defense major, until he was finally forced by another officer to dispose of it. With a few exceptions, this type of ghoulish behavior was more common among new or rear-area troops who had not seen combat than among seasoned front-line troops who had gotten a bellyful of death and its residues. This behavior, too, may not have been an illogical extension of the war of unremitting savagery being waged between the two nations in the swamps, jungles and coral atolls of the Pacific. Somewhat appropriately, the unit's distinctive insignia carried by many of the Ninth's vehicles and on the turrets of the Tank Platoon was the number "9," fashioned into a death's-head with crossed cannon barrels behind the skull instead of crossbones.

Taken by a 9th Defense Marine from a Japanese cemetery on New Georgia, this skull was carried around as a souvenir until an officer forced him to bury it. Grisly souvenirs like this were not altogether uncommon sights among Marines and G.I.s in the Pacific. (Photo by Harry Jones, courtesy of David Slater)

While hate, in all its forms, was a significant aspect of the Marines' attitude towards their enemy, many Leathernecks—Jack included—had to admit to a grudging respect for the Japanese soldier's toughness, courage and resourcefulness.

Plenty of hard evidence of these traits could be found in the actions of the submarine commander off Koli Point; the tenacity of the Japanese aircrews in their raids over Guadalcanal and Rendova; the lonely stubbornness of the motorcycle courier on Kolombangara; in the desperate charge at Zanana Beach; and in the human-bomb attacks on Captain Blake's tanks. The ability of the average Japanese soldier to survive on little or no food, for weeks at a time, was impressive to the Marines, as was his ability to improvise bunkers and equipment from various means available. Admittedly, it was also easier to hate an enemy who was seldom seen when alive, who (at least for artillerymen like most of the Ninth, if not for its tankers) was never directly seen when being targeted for destruction. Such an enemy usually came into notice only in a gunsight or when found as a corpse. In time, though, several experiences on Guam would add some doses of compassion to Jack's and some of his comrades' views towards the Japanese as human beings and not merely as a faceless and monstrous enemy.

Still, some of what Jack may had seen in practice or heard discussed on Guadalcanal, Rendova and New Georgia resurfaced about 25 years later in the form of a fairly sick practical joke he played on his family. One Halloween, he called his two small children into the family kitchen. When the entire family was assembled there, he eagerly announced, "Hey, I've got a war souvenir I've never shown you before. You want to take a look?" In one hand, he cupped a small, cotton-lined white cardboard box, its lid partly ajar. As he took off the lid, he solemnly pronounced; "It's a finger I cut off a dead Jap on Guadalcanal—and look, there's some dried blood on the cotton. Hey, wait a minute: *it's still moving*!"

As his two very young children screamed wildly in fear,

the haunted "Jap finger" began wiggling around on its bed of cotton. As we ran to hide, tears rolling down our eyes, tears rolled down *his* eyes, too—of laughter. Our mother berated him, and Jack quickly and sheepishly admitted to his two distraught children that he had painted his own index finger with yellowish iodine and had cut a hole in the bottom of the box to fake his souvenir. "See? It's all okay, honey. It's not real!"

As far as Jack's practical jokes went, the "haunted finger" was definitely one that was hard to ever forget. As the war in the Pacific went, however, there were undoubtedly quite a few soldiers and sailors for whom such "souvenirs" were very real, indeed.

Gyrenes, Dogfaces, Seabees and Swabbies: Attitudes Towards the Corps's Sister Services

The Marines were long noted for their rivalries with the Army and Navy. The "swabbies" of the Navy were often the butt of the Marines' hazing for their "luxurious" life on board ship, with three good meals a day, frequent treats of milk and ice cream, and reasonably comfortable conditions compared with the rigors of field duty. The treatment meted out to the sailors paled, however, in comparison to that directed at the Army, which most often took the Leathernecks' worst abuse.

From Boot Camp days onwards, the Marines were taught that they were something special, volunteers who fought because they had the guts to do so, as opposed to mere draftees who went into the Army because they had to[11/] or National Guardsmen who had (it was claimed) joined before the war just to dress up and show off for their neighbors. The Marines, fairly or not, often blamed the Army for their logistical shortfalls, instead of the Navy, which, as we have seen, actually exercised the power of the purse over Marine logistics. Most, if not all, Marines also disliked General Douglas MacArthur, "Dugout Doug," whom they personally blamed for the abandonment of the 4th Marines on the Bataan Peninsula and the 1st Division's isolation and starvation on Guadalcanal.[12] Likewise, the Ninth's Marines harbored feelings of contempt towards several of the Army units they were assigned to work with, regarding them as rank amateurs at best or, at worst, dangerous to be around. These feelings of distaste were usually reciprocated.

The Army's 43rd Infantry Division garnered a good deal of disrespect from the Leathernecks. A National Guard division, the 43rd was originally assigned to pull garrison duty in Hawaii and had landed unopposed on the Russell Islands. Picked for the Central Solomons fight, its lack of basic combat skills shocked many of the Ninth's Marines, who found the average soldier in the 43rd to be much older than the average 19 or 20-year old Marine and who viewed the unit as less well-trained and well-led than themselves. (The landing of the Barracudas at the wrong place and time and the refusal of the 43rd's engineer battalion to land on the first day at Rendova has already been noted.) The Ninth's dislike of this particular division, however, predated Operation TOENAILS. As Captain Reichner remembered of his battery's encounters with the 43rd on the Canal: "We referred to this division as 'Hester's Happy Hustling Housewives.' We had also developed a custom of barking like dogs whenever a convoy of soldiers passed by or on other appropriate occasions. Of course, they referred to us as 'Bellhops.' " Around the end of February 1943, however, there were fewer opportunities for jeering and brawls between the "Housewives" and the "bellhops," as large elements of the 43rd left Koli Point on Operation CLEANSLATE to capture the Russell Islands in advance of the New Georgia campaign.

The hellholes of Rendova and New Georgia only deepened the mutual antipathy. Frank Chadwick recalled:

> The division set up tents and mess halls and did

> not bother with fox holes or other protection. They acted as if they were in a rear area and often suffered needless casualties before seeing actual combat. This unit would lose a large percentage of its soldiers due to combat fatigue after a few days of combat. Its leaders were relieved of command, and two additional divisions were called upon for the campaign—about 35,000 soldiers to wipe out 8,000 Japanese.

In all fairness to both the 43rd and its sister division of National Guard origins on New Georgia, the 37th Infantry, both were sent into combat half-trained and largely unprepared for the environment to be faced on New Georgia. Professor Eric Bergerud, a noted expert on the South Pacific fighting, writes: "Halsey gave the 43rd Division an extremely hard objective on one of the worst pieces of real estate in the South Pacific. It was one of the last places on earth to send a unit for initiation into the World War II charnel house. After reconstruction and leave, the 43rd and 37th returned to action in the Pacific [and when sent] back into action they served very well." Elements of the 43rd had also been severely retarded in their training and preparation for combat by the loss of much of their equipment in the December 1942 sinking of one of the division's transports while the division was en route to Guadalcanal.

This distrust was not necessarily directed at *all* Army soldiers or units equally. The Ninth's Marines generally doubted the capabilities of many of the units originating from the National Guard that they encountered, such as the 37th and 43rd Divisions, as they considered their leadership and training to be weak and ineffectual and their combat discipline to be lax. Of course, an element of snobbishness was also involved, shown in the demeanor of the cocky all-volunteer Marines towards the "civilians-in-peace/soldiers-in-war" men of the National Guard. Although these divisions ultimately learned their trade, their initial losses were high, their morale suffered, and the first impressions they made died hard with the Marines. For other Army divisions with a Regular Army core or the more experienced and better-led National Guard units—*e.g.*, "Lightnin' Joe" Collins' 25th Infantry or the 77th Infantry Division—the Marines developed a grudging respect. The Ninth's encounters with the 25th Division on both Guadalcanal and New Georgia were more favorable because its Leathernecks considered the 25th to be a much more professional outfit—and one that, being around, would be less likely to get you killed from inexperience or sloppiness. Despite the unforgiving terrain of New Georgia and its environs, the "Tropic Lightning" division evidenced "a combat edge" (in Professor Bergerud's words) "far superior to other Army units" in that sector. In the Guam campaign, the Marines of the III Amphibious Corps would be so impressed with the performance of Maj. General Andrew Bruce's 77th Division that many Marines would nickname the New York-based Organized Reserve division—in the highest token of respect a Marine could award to an outfit of G.I. dogfaces—the "77th Marine Division."

In contrast to many Army units they encountered and many of the ship-borne elements of the Navy, Jack and many of the Ninth's Marines had a deep, abiding appreciation for the Seabees, particularly the older members of such units. The Seabees were, of course, instrumental in helping the Battalion disembark at Rendova and, when let down by the Army engineers' refusal to come ashore, helped its artillery groups build positions and lug their guns into place. The average Seabee appeared to be much older than the average late-teen Marine, and a lot of good-natured teasing took place between the Ninth's Marines and the Seabees they met to that effect. One frequent joke was that the Ninth's young leathernecks ought to always be nice to the older Seabees, since—after all—most of the Seabees were probably some Marines' fathers!

The same warm feelings, however, were not necessarily applied by the Marines towards the younger Seabees, and Jack and many of his pals often viewed those Seabees closer in age to themselves with some suspicion. Pogiebait often wondered if such men had volunteered for the Seabees with the expectation that Seabee life would be an escape from the rigors of combat. Events like the Suicide Point air raid of July 2, 1943, however, proved that service in the Seabees was not immune to all the dangers of modern war.

On the other hand, the Seabees so frequently contributed to the assistance and comfort of the Ninth that it was tough for even the crustiest and most cynical Marine not to be appreciative. Before the 155mm Group's departure from Banika, it broke camp and was essentially placed in quarantine near the island's pier areas in flimsy pup tents. A passing Seabee officer remarked to several Battery B Marines that he was looking at a lot of Marines who would be going on board the nearby ships and not returning. When informed that they were part of those Marines, that their camp was torn down and mess equipment stowed, the Seabee officer ordered his mess hall to feed the waiting Leathernecks. Besides feeding a battalion-sized contingent of its own personnel, the Seabees' mess hall now also supplied several hundred Marines with chow three times a day for several days:

> They went out of their way to see we were taken care of [Chadwick recalled]. It was the best food we ever had in the Pacific, and we always thanked God for the Seabees. They were older than we were, and most probably did not have to be in the service at that time and they treated us as family members. We will forever be grateful to this group of men.

The Experience of Combat and Attitudes About Combat, Casualties and Death

Leaving aside combat with the enemy in all forms—naval bombardment, aerial bombings and infantry assaults—the Battalion's preparations for combat were often in themselves a war against time and the elements. Just getting a unit the size of the 9th Defense off-loaded from its transports and landing craft and to its battle stations was a massive undertaking in itself.

As already noted, the movement and positioning alone of the Seacoast & Field Artillery Group's 155mm guns required substantial labors. Designed for the static warfare of the Great War, with heavy cast-metal wheels sometimes fitted with wooden cleats (ostensibly to provide better traction in mud), the Group's original, World War I-vintage GPFs needed exhaustive manhandling simply to drag them in and out of their positions. The GPFs were most effectively positioned for seacoast defense when used with Panama mounts. The preparation of these gun mounts required even more labor in making and pouring concrete and—when ready to depart—in blasting or cracking the guns loose from their concreted turntables. The introduction of the M-1 model was a vast improvement, both in terms of maintenance and mobility when one had decent roads or trails. The Rendova landings were accompanied by intermittent but torrential rains and glutinous mud. Hence, whatever advantage was gained in off-road mobility was canceled out on Rendova by the need to lug this even heavier model of 155mm gun around by teams of men and bulldozers. It was not enough, of course, for the Ninth's battalion commander to worry about merely positioning his unit's 155s. Besides the eight Long Toms, he also had to contend with the siting and emplacement of eight tanks, twelve 90mm, sixteen 40mm , 28 20mm and 35 .50 caliber AA guns, as well as many smaller machine guns, radars, water purification gear (and, of course, Jack), sound detectors, searchlights, and listening posts. Organized for area protection, the 9th Defense occupied a much wider piece of terrain than the typical twelve-gun Army field artillery battalion of the lighter and more mobile, but less powerful, 105mm howitzers. This dispersal over a broad area led to another difficulty for the Ninth's commanders.

In military terms, this problem is referred to as "command, control and communications" or "C3" for short. Reduced to its essence, the C3 problem is one of being able to oversee and direct the daily operations and combat performance of a particular unit. In the case of a unit as large as the Ninth, whose positions were spread out over an area as large as thirty square miles, this simple-sounding concept encountered a high degree of complexity in practice. How can the Battalion CO ensure that his AA groups provide maximum coverage without leaving corridors through which enemy planes can penetrate? Further, how can the CO achieve this seamless web of defense without risking friendly fire casualties to U.S. aircraft landing during an air raid or to friendly ground troops if duds fail to explode or shell fragments fall onto their positions? How will the junior commanders set up their defensive perimeters to prevent infiltrators if batteries are in positions separated by several miles from one another? How will neighboring units get the word if enemy intruders are spotted? Each question like this absorbed massive amounts of time and planning, both before and after the unit's deployment. In the early days of the Battalion's existence, the unit had few radios—although it had early-model TBY "walkie-talkie" radios, these proved to be low-powered and unreliable—and had to rely extensively on field telephones and couriers to get messages to and from its various subordinate headquarters. Radios were used sparingly and only in an emergency, so as to compromise communications security as little as possible.

To a large degree, each Group was already semi-autonomous and partly self-sufficient, operating in the field much like a mini-battalion. This mode of operation permitted a certain amount of flexibility and tolerated ingenuity. Before Operation TOENAILS, for instance, Lt. Colonel Wright Taylor, the Special Weapons Group's new CO, had taken the initiative of forming his entire group into "gun teams," blended from the Group's various individual batteries and armed with a mission-specific mix of 20mm, 40mm and .50 caliber guns. These gun teams functioned more like miniature task forces instead of batteries or platoons as officially organized.

If C3 problems occupied much of the time of the battalion, group and battery officers, similar problems arose in the ranks. Spread out as the battalion was in a combat environment, holding a unit formation to pass on orders and information would be disruptive and perilous. The prime source of information for Jack and his pals seemed at times to be scuttlebutt, and that, usually, of a questionable nature. These difficulties were magnified at nighttime. As noted earlier, the tropical darkness had an utter stillness and a quality of pitch darkness unlike anything Jack or his peers had experienced. Terrified as one may have been of the dark, getting out of a tent or foxhole to seek out a buddy or pass on information was not a likely action: witness the fate of Battery A's sergeant who died during the first night on Rendova. At best, in a viny landscape covered with razor-sharp kunai grass, foxholes, ditches and latrines, a stumble in the dark under such conditions might lead to breaking or spraining a leg or ending up covered in stinking mire. At worst, one could get his head shot off. To help provide early warning of intruders, the Leathernecks fell back on an old World War I doughboys' trick of filling empty ration cans with pebbles and tying them to strands of wire, so that any movement through the wire would set the cans to rattling.

A pressing fear that sometimes bordered on panic among some troops in jungle combat was the threat of snipers and enemy infiltrators—"one of the great bugaboos of the

Guadalcanal campaign," in one historian's words. It was not for nothing that Colonel Scheyer's orders to the 9th Defense Battalion before it embarked on Operation TOENAILS stressed "a few words of caution" about this particular matter:

> Every unit, including the 9th Defense, when it landed on Guadalcanal, imagined it heard Japs and a good battle started in which our own men were shot. Bear in mind, always, that nighttime is the time for knife-fighting. Do no promiscuous shooting at any time, save your bullets for the Japs. It may be possible that one or two Jap snipers will fire at us from coconut trees, [but] that doesn't mean that every tree has a Jap in it.

In light of the coming campaign in the New Georgia area—witness the various "friendly fire" casualties—these proved to be wise and prophetic words. In the pitch blackness of the jungle at night, there tended to be a shoot first—ask questions later mentality, which needed to be curbed immediately. This was necessary both to thwart friendly fire and to prevent such firing from giving away one's own position if, in fact, there were Japanese patrols or snipers actually nearby.

The mere fear of snipers and infiltrators also tended to have a terribly demoralizing—in some units' cases, it is not too much to say paralyzing—effect. On New Georgia, the Army's 43rd Division suffered heavy casualties resulting from friendly troops' shooting one another over supposed "snipers." Episodes of chaotic behavior known as "jitterbugging" (so-called after the frenzied 1930s' dance craze) or the "jungle jitters," often involving nighttime friendly-fire shootouts, were widely reported throughout elements of that division. Speaking of one jitterbugging incident affecting an especially blighted regiment of the 43rd, the 169th Infantry, the Army's official historian of the New Georgia campaign writes:

> Some men knifed each other. Men threw grenades blindly in the dark. Some of the grenades hit trees, bounced back, and exploded among the Americans. Some soldiers fired round after round to little avail. In the morning no trace remained of Japanese dead or wounded. But there were American casualties: some had been stabbed to death, some wounded by knives. Many suffered grenade fragment wounds, and 50 percent of these were caused by fragments from American grenades. . . . The regiment was to suffer seven hundred [casualties] by July 31.

As Lieutenant Chris Donner wrote after the war: "We were amazed by the number of psycho cases being evacuated from the 169th Regiment. They told wild tales, accompanied by fearful gestures, of Japs who came after them at night with long metal pincers to pull them out of their foxholes." This frantic behavior only strengthened the aversion that many of the Ninth's Marines felt about that particular Army division.

In fact, the first clinical diagnoses of war neurosis, later labeled as "combat fatigue" (for which Lt. General George Patton would become infamous in the notorious "face-slapping" incidents in Sicily only a few months later), were identified on New Georgia, with 360 soldiers from the 43rd being evacuated for psychological treatment less than two weeks after the initial landings. The only immediate answers for such unit-wide instances of "jitterbugging" available at the time were training and adjustment, and the relief of the officers responsible for the men involved in such behavior. In particular, it was found that training to combat the *perception* that the Japanese were "supermen"—something wisely identified, very early-on, by Colonel Scheyer and addressed by him and his staff accordingly before the campaign began—helped make a difference in curbing the onset of such "mass nocturnal delusions and their natural consequence, panicky nocturnal fratricide;" but, after the rash of incidents during the first two weeks of the fighting on New Georgia, incidents of "jitterbugging" ceased to plague the 43rd as mysteriously as they had started.

In certain respects, at least, the Marines' pre-combat training and combat leadership appear to have been head-and-shoulders superior to that of certain Army units and helped keep the Ninth's casualties relatively low. This does not mean, however, that even proportionately better-trained Marines were immune from the fears and stresses generated by combat, as reported to Eric Bergerud:

> Air attacks, bombardments, and most combat is over very quickly. . . .Most guys weren't scared before things took place. We were awfully young, you know. During the chaos, you're so damn busy you don't really think. The training takes over. You're conditioned to act in a certain way. It's the thing to do to save yourself too. Afterwards, everyone starts to shake. You break out those cigarettes. You kind of lose it, really.

As far as fears of death went, the classic view of youth—"*It can't happen to me; I'm too young to die*"—was just about the best psychological defense available. Frank Chadwick recalled:

> We didn't know any better. We were so young. Most of us felt it will never happen to me. You knew people were killed and wounded all the time, but deep down you thought it would happen to some other guy. So we worried more about our buddies. You made

> yourself believe that nothing could happen to you, that you had to worry about your friends. It wasn't logical, but it would have been a lot harder to go on brooding about it.

Another defense against worrying about death was the very unreality of the situation, perhaps best captured by a sentence frequently used by many of the Ninth's veterans as to certain memories or vignettes of combat: "It was just like watching a movie" or, in David Slater's alternative phrasing, "I thought I was in a movie."

"*Just like a movie.*" War in the Pacific was, of course, nothing at all like a movie, and no Hollywood production could adequately depict war and its horrors—particularly, its smells. Still, Jack, Chadwick, Lieutenant Donner, Slater and Yemma, among others, recalled watching incidents that had a certain movie-like quality to them. There were instances that—at the time and not merely in hindsight—frequently gave one the sense that he was watching a gigantic panorama being played out in front of one's own eyes, instead of something happening in the here-and-now, in real time. For young men in their late teens and early to mid-twenties, these sights and sounds bore no resemblance to anything they had ever witnessed before. In so many respects, certain situations did have an air of unreality that helped place some mental distance and the appearance of safety (whether false or not) between the onlooker and the stark danger that was actually happening.

One of the best examples of this phenomenon, and one witnessed by such a large number of men simultaneously, is the July 4th bombing raid. Years later, this air raid and its aftermath were described by so many of the Ninth's veterans as being "just like a movie" or "better than a movie"—the words often used by Jack, Frank Chadwick and Frank Yemma, among others—and the onlookers had "ringside seats" or "front-row seats," to borrow other words used contemporaneously. None of the onlookers had ever seen—and likely never would again—anything like the awesome destruction of the Japanese bomber squadron in about three minutes, complete with pyrotechnics and sound effects. It was natural that young men raised in the 1920s and 1930s, America's first generation of children raised with Saturday movie matinees, mentally equated these sights into a spectacle worthy of Cecil B. DeMille. Like miniature comets, the Japanese bombers were smashed to fragments and cartwheeled to earth in pieces—wings, fuselages, and bloody scraps of people. Unlike most of its sisters, however, which simply disintegrated when hit, one particular bomber "[tumbled] to earth end over end, like a model that was built wrong."

Wreckage of a Mitsubishi "Betty" bomber near Munda Field. (Official U.S. Marine Corps photo, courtesy of Joseph Pratl)

The Japanese bombers' fatal and fiery end resulted in "[w]a-hoos, fist shakings and screams of delight," as Jack recalled, and "cheers . . .heard all over Rendova 'like a "Babe" homer in Yankee stadium.'" No matter that the bombers' occupants had met truly gruesome ends—ripped open, disemboweled and bleeding from shards of metal and glass and exploding ammunition belts; roasted alive by aviation fuel; or disintegrated as their planes' remains plummeted into Rendova Bay or the surrounding islands. Japanese aircrew did not normally carry parachutes, so their chances of escape were practically nil. With an enemy as depersonalized as were the Japanese, however, and so soon after so many of the Ninth's own personnel and Seabees had met such violent and gory deaths as they had on July 2, the deaths of the enemy airmen hardly mattered—except that killing more of the enemy might improve one's own chances of coming home alive. Hence, the sight of the enemy's aircraft being reduced to so much fluttering, falling and smoking scrap metal was seen by many of the Leathernecks as only improving their own chances of getting through the war alive. Of course, as also noted previously, it was much easier to kill the enemy without remorse if he was viewed as something impersonal—like an airplane, bereft of humanity—or was not seen at all. In some respects, the sights they witnessed on July 4 did not, at the time, seem so much like death to the Ninth's onlookers as like a giant, ghastly, yet enjoyable, fireworks show.

Death was a constant on the Pacific's battlefields. It lurked everywhere on Guadalcanal: in a medical tent, as David Slater lay next to a 155mm group gunner who died of malignant tertian malaria; in the Japanese bones, skulls and teeth pocketed by rear-area scavengers; and under the roots of a tree where a Marine had buried his buddy with the words of the Book of John carved in its bark: "*For God so loved the world. . . .*" Death was omnipresent at Suicide Point and on New Georgia as the Tank Platoon assaulted Japanese bunkers in support of the drive to take Munda Field. Often, the casualties were American troops. Captain Blake recounted the lonely death of one soldier on New Georgia, ambushed and separated from the rest of his unit on the Munda trail just as the fight for Munda came to a bloody end:

> Late that night, from far ahead came an anguished cry for help and a splattering burst of machine-gun fire. The cry faded out. All who heard it knew what it was. But no one will ever know the horror of the death that man died, lost, alone and forsaken in the jungle darkness.
>
> The next day we found him on the trail, face down in front of an abandoned machine-gun position. The campaign was over. He had been the last man to die. And he came so close to coming through alive. I cannot get him out of my mind.

When it came, death in the tropics was seldom clean and was never as prettily choreographed as Hollywood depicted it. The fates of many of those killed in the July 2 air raid on Suicide Point were quick, spectacular and grisly in the extreme, as Japanese bullets and bombs detonated a huge cache of Seabee explosives, the explosion of which left body parts and guts strewn in every direction. Many fatally wounded in combat, however, seldom had the luxury of dying as quickly from their wounds; certainly, Captain Blake's nameless dogface who fell on the Munda Trail died a lingering death, alone and abandoned until it was too late to save him. Death from malaria was, relatively speaking, cleaner than death in combat, but the process was almost as traumatic for those watching the feverish gibberings and screams, lasting for hours, of a man dying from malignant tertian fever as it was to see a buddy take a bullet in the head, chest or bowels. Decomposition set in rapidly in the tropics, as did flies and maggots, and the stench of rotting flesh quickly pinpointed the presence of the dead, overpowering the otherwise omnipresent stink of naturally rotting jungle vegetation.

The smell of death, in a most literal sense, wafted around Munda Field for weeks after the battle. The putrid odors emanated from the bloated corpses of its defenders, several of whom bodies lay unburied for days near Jack's position, and in the helmet Jack had found with portions of its owner's head still reeking inside. Jack recalled, "You could sense when death was near"—even if it was not necessarily your own death that was imminent. This frequent proximity to death throughout the Guadalcanal and TOENAILS campaigns hardened the Ninth's Marines in countless ways, even permeating their casual conversations and sense of humor with a grim edge.

By the time they had reached New Georgia, many of the Ninth's Marines could casually eat their chow, like Biggie Slater and his pals, and discuss whether a decomposing leg sticking out of a hillside pile of churned-up earth was Marine or Japanese in origin:

> The leg, showing halfway to the knee, was highlighted by [the] sky and seemed to be kicking against it. Down below, the men explored their rations and discussed the leg.
>
> "Hell, it's a marine—the shoe is G.I."
>
> "Yeah, sure looks like it; are there leggings?"[13]
>
> Bummie, a Brooklyn cop before the war, deadly aggressive under the influence of liquor or adrenaline, was sentimental and concerned about the man—if there was one—attached to the leg.
>
> "Let's put up a marker for Graves Registration."

> Two sticks were tied together and the men climbed to the crest of the ridge, Bummie carrying the cross. They gathered around the leg, examining the shoe. The color wasn't right. Doggie brushed dirt from the leg; it was wrapped in puttees.
>
> "Goddam Jap," said Bummie as he threw down the sticks.

Similarly, Jack recounted to his brother Al after the war that the remains of a leg was thrust out of the ground next to Munda Field, in the abandoned and bulldozed Japanese graveyard adjacent to the Battalion HQ's mess hall and some of Jack's Lister bags. A notice was tacked to its decaying foot: "HERE LIES A MAN WHO ATE AT THE 9TH DEFENSE'S MESS HALL!"

Humor acquired its own peculiar and pungent flavor in such an environment, where the relationship between life and death was often starkly visible in even the most mundane activities.

The terrors of a Japanese artillery bombardment have already been noted; the impact of Japanese air raids was similar. While Washing Machine Charlie and Louie the Louse were usually more of a nuisance than a real menace, these nighttime raiders occasionally dropped "daisy cutters," small but deadly anti-personnel bombs that scattered shrapnel low to the ground. Taking cover under a truck or vehicle did not offer much protection from a daisy cutter blast, since their shrapnel whizzed along at knee level or lower and could still hit a man cowering under a vehicle. Japanese bombs also made a distinctive sound as they fell. As Biggie Slater remembered,

"Quite often their casings had riveted parts, and the protrusions disturbed the air in ways that (at least as I heard it) caused a sort of warbling, whooshing sound."

No matter how much one wanted to ignore Charlie's noisy motors and go back to sleep, the Ninth's Marines could never be fully sure whether Charlie might only drop only empty *sake* bottles tonight, flares or the dreaded daisy cutters. Frequently, the Marines faced multiple air alerts in one night, sometimes as many as six or seven per night, spaced as little as an hour apart. *0100*; *0300*; *0445*—each time the call of "Condition Red" went forth, off to the bomb shelters or foxholes they would dash, or to the AA, radar or searchlight position if in crewing the 90mm or Special Weapons guns. Thus, another night's precious few hours of sleep would be lost in the process. Rest—*real* sleep, as opposed to a permanent semiconsciousness state—was, under the best of circumstances, a rarity. In the South Pacific war zone, what passed for sleep was, in David Slater's words, best described as an "axe-edged delicate balance between life-restoring unconsciousness and life-preserving alertness."

The major air raids on the Canal and in the Central Solomons campaign were on a magnitude far above Charlie's and Louie's nocturnal incursions. Chadwick fell prey to the same Japanese Zeroes that bombed Jack's LST in the Suicide Point raid. He was floored by a blast not far from Jack (only a few yards away, with Chadwick going down as he was running to get more 40mm shells from the ship's ammo locker). Jack was flattened by the same concussion that downed Chadwick but, apart from bruises and a ringing in his ears, Jack was otherwise unhurt. Chadwick, too, escaped that raid uninjured, but in a follow-on Japanese air strike later that day, he was wounded:

> They got me with a bomb. I heard this terrific noise, and felt an intense heat. The concussion

> bounced me around and I could hear the shrapnel flying all over. And then I was sitting there thinking, "What the hell happened?" You don't think very clearly after a bomb goes off, and I didn't really understand what was going on. I started getting this pain in my leg, reached down to rub it and my hand was all red. I think, "Christ, I've been hit." A numbing effect sets in. You start to get the shakes fast unless a wound is very serious. At that moment the second bomb landed and knocked me silly. It blew out a tooth and injured my mouth. The first thing I knew I was spitting out four or five teeth. I looked down and saw my wrist bone sticking through the skin. But it didn't hurt. . . .The doc [doubtless, the intrepid Commander Krepela or his staff] set my wrist bone, snapped it back into place, and put a splint on it. Then it hurt like hell. It was strange though. Lying there and being treated seemed like it took forever.

Just seeing combat and getting wounded was not enough, though, to guarantee a 9th Defense leatherneck a medal. In comparison to its sister services, the Marine Corps was notoriously stingy in awarding medals. For instance, only 68 Purple Hearts were awarded for the Ninth's combat casualties, while the Battalion had suffered many more casualties that this number of awards indicated. If the victims had been in an Army unit, they would doubtless have been awarded this medal. Despite his wounding on Rendova, Chadwick was not among the unit's Purple Heart recipients. Likewise, despite taking steel fragments from the 155mm explosion at Piru, Bill Galloway similarly received nothing, a situation that was rectified only many years after war's end. When each asked whether or not he was entitled to that medal, he was essentially told that, unless the nature of his wound was clearly documented in his medical records, no Purple Heart was authorized. As Chadwick reminisced:

> While all other services, especially the Army, awarded medals very easily, the Corps awarded very little and many so deserving received no decorations. The philosophy was that all Marines were volunteers, and you were expected to do your duty. Therefore, any award issued by the Corps at that time was well earned and deserved.

Jack himself believed that, for his length of service and clean record, he was entitled to the Good Conduct Medal, as was, in fact, to be reflected in his discharge papers. All his postwar inquiries, however, as to his eligibility for this medal resulted in denials. In his later years, Jack would semi-humorously grunt, when faced with his Army lieutenant son, who had already received several medals and ribbons in three years of peacetime: "What a jellybean! A peacetime Army shavetail, earning more medals than a combat Marine! It just figures." Even those making the ultimate sacrifice might be short-changed, in the eyes of many of their surviving buddies: after all, Wantuck and Rothschild only received Navy Crosses, not the Medal of Honor, for their deeds. Although, as noted before, there were likely certain valid reasons why these two were deemed ineligible (*e.g.*, lack of eyewitnesses), many of the more jaded Leathernecks just chalked it up to the way the Corps typically conducted its business.

The lack of promotions and delays in those that were granted were a similar cause for dissatisfaction, especially—or, so it seemed—for the Christmas Tree Marines: Jack was promoted from PFC to Corporal late in 1943 and, despite his record of good conduct, he held that rank until he left the Corps in fall 1945. The lack of timely promotions, and its effect on morale, was duly noted by the Ninth's officers, who were themselves often disappointed by the lack of credit their troops received for their efforts. "One of the most galling things to me," Battery A skipper Hank Reichner noted, "was the lack of promotions among the Christmas Tree recruits. It was even more so when new arrivals with less service were Corporals, etc. We were forgotten."

Despite whatever fears or secret terrors they may have harbored, few of the Ninth's Marines "broke down" or resorted to self-inflicted injuries as a way out of the war. This means of escape was less uncommon in some other units or taken by many engaged in the worst aspects of the European theater. Nevertheless, the Ninth's personnel were certainly not immune to wartime psychological stresses, and the unit had its victims: recall the Marine who leapt overboard from Lieutenant Donner's LST en route to Rendova. In another incident, Biggie Slater watched a 90mm gunner "crack" on Rendova three days after the landings:

> A young guy stood up from his hole (or ditch) and shoved a .45 into his mouth. He hesitated long enough for a bunch of us to swarm over him and take the pistol away. He was surveyed out [*i.e.*, evacuated]—as I recall, he was only about 17 and probably a field music (they carried side arms).

Still, the *esprit de corps*, the "gung-ho" attitude instilled in them, partly helped to keep the Ninth's Marines together as a team. There were other possible reasons, though, as to why this cohesiveness was the rule for this unit and others like it in the Pacific fighting. As noted previously, in the jungle and unlike France or Italy, escape in the Pacific was far less convenient: there was nowhere safe to run and hide. "You never wanted to let your buddies down," Jack recalled. This sentiment was cultivated not just from loyalty's sake or out of self-respect. It was also, frankly, due to a certain amount of self-preservation. Frank Chadwick elaborates why this was partly so:

> We had a saying that "it takes more guts to get up in the front line and run than it does to stay there." [This was because] you're afraid if you let them down that every one of your buddies is going to be right there on your ass.

Preparing for the Next Offensive: Into the Central Pacific

After five months on Banika, the Ninth got word in May that it was to be redeployed for a new offensive, not in the South Pacific or Solomons but in the Central Pacific. For Jack and the Ninth, it would be an entirely new sector of the Pacific and an entirely new kind of war. MacArthur's and Halsey's forces had been bludgeoning their way through New Guinea and the Solomons, respectively. While those campaigns were being waged, the Central Pacific theater in 1943, under the primary control of Admiral Chester Nimitz, had been the scene of additional "island-hopping" battles. Besides using the Central Pacific campaign as another stepping-stone to Japan, it was intended to draw the Japanese into areas where the U.S. Navy would be on its chosen field of action. Seizure of the Gilbert Islands, then the Marshalls and, then, the Marianas would provide the Allies with other options as well, from which they could mount the recapture of the Philippines or strike into Formosa and China. Following the occupation of the Gilberts in November 1943, including the bitter fight for Tarawa, Nimitz' turned next to seize the Marshalls in early 1944. The wide and deep lagoons of its coral atolls would make excellent air bases and fleet anchorages for Admiral Nimitz's next goal—the Mariana Islands.

After occupying the Marshalls in February 1944, the attentions of Admiral Nimitz and his staff focused on the

Marianas. This island group, including Saipan, Rota, Tinian and Guam, made up the first element of Japan's inner defensive ring. They dominated the west-central Pacific, sitting athwart the lines of communications from Japan and the Ryukyu Islands in the north to New Guinea in the south and the Philippines and Formosa in the southwest. While the 20th Air Force—the U.S. air force tasked primarily with the bombing of Japan—had already deployed its new B-29 Superfortresses to Chinese bases, Japanese counteroffensives there threatened those bases' security. The occupation of the Marianas would provide an excellent location for Admiral Nimitz's fleet against Japan's home islands, as well as providing another springboard for the liberation of the Philippines.

The Marianas would also provide a more secure and more easily supported base for the 20th Air Force's B-29 armada, the 21st Bomber Command, than did their existing Chinese airfields. From the Marshalls, the B-29s could accommodate the 3,000-mile round trip to the Japanese main islands and back with a full bomb load. Admiral Nimitz and his superior, Admiral Ernest King, had long pushed for taking the Marianas over the opposition of General MacArthur and other Army leaders. Now, the introduction of the B-29 gave them an unlikely ally in the Army Air Forces commander, General Henry "Hap" Arnold, earlier a longtime critic of the Navy's operational plans. Hap Arnold's support cinched the deal, and I MAC (renamed III Amphibious Corps in April 1944) and an Army division were tapped to conduct the recapture of the Marshalls.

For many older Marines, there was additional personal significance to the retaking of Guam. A U.S. possession since 1899, many of the "old breed" Marines had been stationed there, and there was a deep and abiding affection between them and the island's inhabitants, the Chamorros. Tactical exercises concerning Guam had been a Marine officers' training problem in their classes at Quantico since 1936, and those officers familiar with Guam's terrain knew its potential to be a tough nut to crack. There were also underlying matters of national pride and humanitarianism at work, which, while secondary, preyed on the minds of some of the planners. As the first U.S. territorial possession to have been seized by the Japanese, Guam's recapture would have immense symbolic value, not just to the American people but also to those in other Japanese-occupied countries that their own liberation day would soon be coming. Furthermore, while not generally known to most of the rank-and-file participants in the upcoming landing, the conditions of Guam's largely pro-U.S. citizenry were becoming increasingly desperate.

Despite receiving relatively benign treatment at first (at least by the standards of conduct in other occupied territories in the "Greater East Asia Co-Prosperity Sphere"), by late 1943, the island's populace became subject to increasingly savage treatment by the Japanese occupants. Guam's schools were closed; Christian religious services were forbidden; and one priest, who was especially vocal in protesting the Japanese authorities' treatment of his flock, was tortured and beheaded. Several mass murders of civilians were perpetrated for no apparent reason other than for terror and intimidation. Many thousand Chamorros were relocated by the *Kempetai*, the Japanese secret police, to forced labor camps, where they worked under brutal conditions. Others were shipped to labor camps in Japan, where their treatment was, if anything, quite possibly worse than those of the miserable Chamorros left encamped on Guam.

The fate of the Guamanian people after the Japanese invasion was shared by one family connected with Jack's hometown: the Johnstons, whose father, William, was a Franklin-born boy who had settled in Guam after being posted there as a Marine in 1909. Before the war, Bill Johnston served as Guam's Commissioner of Public Works, and his Guamanian-born wife, Agueldo, was principal of Agana High. All this changed after the Japanese landings: he was arrested, the Japanese closed down the school system and also confiscated a small movie theater the Johnston family owned. In June 1944, Bill Johnston was seized by the *Kempetai*; Agueldo and the seven children were herded into a concentration camp and were barely surviving. Unknown to them in their captivity, the Johnstons' home in Agana had been leveled by pre-invasion bomb strikes.

As the mighty Liberators soared overhead on their pre-invasion bombing runs in mid-summer 1944, the Johnstons and the other inmates of the six concentration camps studding Guam were heartened that their liberation would be coming soon. The historian and wartime Marine William Manchester recounted the song the Guamanians composed as they waited for their liberation:

Oh, Uncle Saum,
Oh, Uncle Saum,
Won't you please come back to Guam?

All this, of course, was unknown to Jack and his buddies, who had not yet been briefed on the precise nature of their next mission, although the increased tempo of their activities assured them all that something big was imminent.

In their Russell Islands backwaters, the pace of training and personnel reshufflings began to pick up as Pogiebait and the Ninth's men readied for their next operation. The Battalion bade farewell both to Captain Blake and his intrepid tankers, who were transferred to form a III Amphib Corps tank battalion, and to the first contingent of its Marines to be shipped home. Under the so-called "5% Plan," for those Marine units that had been in the Pacific Theater for at least 24 months, five percent of its personnel who had been overseas for such period were subject to rotation stateside. As a result, orders were cut for the return home of two captains (one of the two being the much-admired Captain Box), a warrant officer and 65 enlisted men. One of those lucky enough to get his rotation orders was Jack's buddy Al Downs. Their friendship went back to Boot Camp days, when Al was one of the witnesses to Pogiebait McCall's "christening." While Jack was delighted that a good man like Al was going to get home to his beloved Rosie and thus might survive the war after all, it was still a let-down and a loss of a good friend to have around.

Before Al's and the other short-timers' scheduled departure in mid-March 1944, Jack and Al played a farewell game of poker with their buddies. Whether from a parting lucky streak or an unbeatable poker face, Al's luck held, and he netted $70 from the pot. With half of his winnings, Downs bought a watch. With the other $35, he tracked down and bought a fifth of Australian rum, but he and Jack and Al were only able to rummage up one lukewarm bottle of cola. In a flashback to their "good old days" on Cuba, where the beer and rum flowed more freely, the two buddies split their rum-and-cola and exchanged wisecracks and tales about what they had been through together. They drank some last toasts to salute Al's great, good luck in making it through the war to that point and to the hope that all the rest would be able to get stateside and home again, in one piece.

As had occurred on the Canal before the beginning of Operation TOENAILS, the Battalion began receiving new pieces of equipment—notably, new-model radars, the first of their kind to be received by any American unit in the South Pacific—and the training schedule began to pick up tempo again in preparation for the next offensive. The 155mm batteries were put to work test-firing their renovated Long Toms at towed sea targets; the AA gunners fired at airplane-towed targets; and radar crews plotted intercepts and calibrated their new sets. By April 1, Colonel O'Neil declared the Ninth to be fully combat-ready. Then came the order to break down the Battalion's camps and move beachside into pre-invasion quarantine. "Here we go again!," the old salts grumbled.

As much as many of them dreaded going back into action, nobody was exactly heartbroken to be leaving Banika. Mimi Canu, a veteran of the Ninth's Headquarters Battery, summed up the feelings of many:

> [The Russells] were a pain, always the same kind of working party to pick up coconuts, getting our gear repaired, waiting to go to New Zealand for a rest, even was told when [we would go there], but the army never showed up to relieve us . . .

But, as the editor of the Fighting Ninth's newsletter philosophized, some fifty years later, about the Battalion's sojourn on Banika: "What the H___, you can't winnem all."

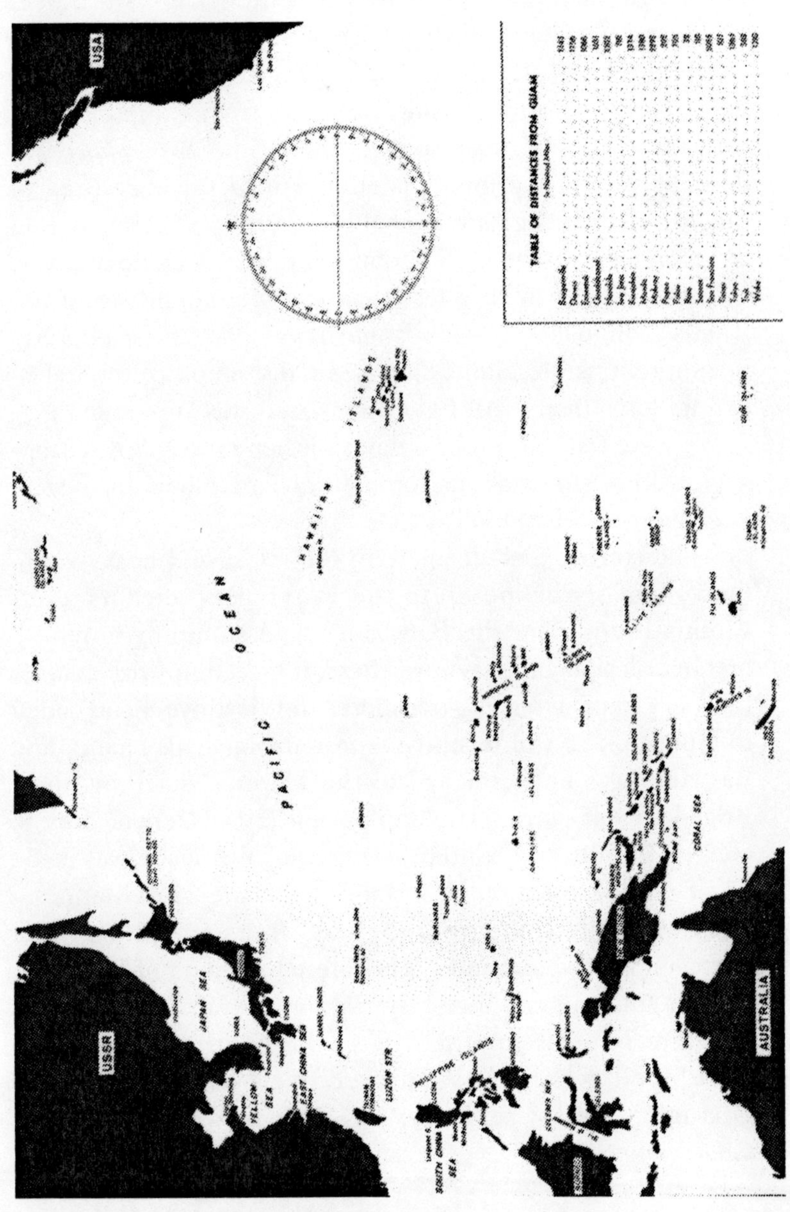
USA
USSR
AUSTRALIA
PACIFIC
OCEAN
HAWAIIAN
ISLANDS
JAPAN SEA
YELLOW SEA
EAST CHINA SEA
LUZON STR
SOUTH CHINA SEA
PHILIPPINE ISLANDS
CAROLINE ISLANDS
CORAL SEA
TABLE OF DISTANCES FROM GUAM

After staying beachside in quarantine for days, beginning on May 10, the Ninth was moved by batteries to a small fleet of waiting transports and LSTs. Jack found himself bunking aboard the U.S.A.T. *Sea Fiddler*, a grimy Army transport. Conditions on this wretched ship were scarcely an improvement over those on the dreary old *Kenmore.* The *Sea Fiddler* was described by Harry Jones, a fellow 9th Defense denizen of the vessel, as being "a remarkably dirty ship with some kind of green algae growing in various corners" and skippered by a Dutch captain with a less-than -perfect command of the English language: "As his English was poor, he was pretty incomprehensible and, being generally ignored, tended to extend his remarks. All I ever translated was 'You men . . .' . . . We were fed only twice a day and then mostly Spam sandwiches from stores *we* had brought aboard. Chow lines were very short on that ship!"

The convoy first steamed, in the midst of a heavy storm (and more seasickness), to the Purvis Bay anchorage off Florida Island near the Battalion's "old stomping grounds" on Guadalcanal and Gavutu. There, it linked up with a larger fleet of Green Dragons, transports and destroyers and sailed to Eniwetok in the recently captured Marshalls chain. The Battalion was now attached to the Marines' 1st Provisional Brigade, itself part of III Amphib under Lt. General Roy S. Geiger. Besides the Ninth, the Provisional Brigade was made up of the reconstituted 4th Marines and the 22nd Marines.

The sight that greeted Jack and company as the Battalion's transports and LSTs entered the atoll of Eniwetok was an amazing and awe-inspiring one, which left radically different impressions from those the Ninth's Marines had developed when they entered New Caledonia's and Guadalcanal's waters in 1942. In the words of Frank Chadwick:

> As we dropped anchor, there were more ships than we had ever seen. In the latter stages of the Canal, the Navy had only one carrier, the "Big E" [the aircraft carrier *Enterprise*], and here in less than 1 1/2 years we saw 80 carriers at one time (both fleet and baby flattops) in the lagoon.[14/] There was no doubt in our minds as to who would win this war; the question was when and whether we would be around to see it.

Although primarily assigned to serve as an occupation force once Guam was recaptured, the Battalion would also support the landings and seize various key objectives on Guam. It was also part of an on-call, floating reserve for the first landings in the Marianas on Saipan—which was defended by a large, well-armed and fanatical detachment of Japanese troops. Given those missions, the issue of "whether we would be around to see it" was a considerable question.

Jack, too, wondered how much longer this war was going to last, and whether he, himself, would be around to see the end. From what he had seen, though, one other thing was clear in his mind, though: whenever and however it arrived, the end would be messy, indeed.

6

Operation FORAGER: The Invasion and Occupation of Guam

> The [Guamanian] prisoners' morale soared. Their confidence in the United States was intact. In fact, it had never waned. During the first two weeks of the war they had expected the Marines back by Christmas. Chagrined then, they nevertheless continued to follow grapevine reports of struggles on other islands with high hopes. A surviving testament to their loyalty is a crude U.S. flag, sewn in Yono concentration camp. There are but twelve stars and nine stripes—the seamstress had no more cloth—but it is all the more stirring for that.
>
> *William Manchester*
> *Goodbye, Darkness*

A Voyage "From Tedium to Apathy" and Back

From Eniwetok, the fleet for the Marianas invasion, Operation FORAGER, steamed for the southern Marianas, about 1,000 miles away. The initial goal of this task force was to seize Saipan, the headquarters and logistical hub of the Japanese war effort in the Central Pacific. As it was located north of Guam, Rota and Tinian, the capture of Saipan would theoretically make the seizure of those islands simpler. Saipan's occupation, however, was anything but simple: its capture became a bloodbath for both sides.

The 1st Provisional Brigade and the 9th Defense were designated as "floating reserves" for the Saipan landings. As part of deception operations for the invasion, in order to dupe the defenders as to the place of the actual invasion, the 4th Marines were to simulate a landing on the eastern side of the island; when the mock landings came under fire, the 4th's landing craft and LVTs turned tail and returned to the main body of the fleet. With many of the Japanese forces now redeployed facing east, the genuine landings took place on Saipan's southern beaches the next day, June 15, yet these were still bitterly contested. The Ninth's ships and LSTs lay at anchor off Saipan for several more days, and Colonel O'Neil was informed by III Amphib's staff that, in the event the 2nd Marine Division had any major difficulty breaking out of its beachhead, the 9th Defense would land to reinforce the breakout attempt. The 2nd Marine Division's breakout off the beaches succeeded; the Army's 27th Infantry Division then came ashore. (Later, both divisions would encounter *banzai* charges and massed suicides of Japanese soldiers and civilians once they moved inland.) Accordingly, the 1st Provisional Brigade's floating reserves, including the 9th Defense, were released. The Provisional Brigade's miniature armada now steamed back across the 1,000-odd miles it had already traveled to the Marshalls. To the disgust of the Ninth's Marines, however, they learned that all the Navy personnel, including the crews of the troopships and LSTs they were aboard, had been authorized to add a "battle star" to their decorations for their "participation" in the Saipan landings—even if they had not fired a single shot or been fired at themselves—while the Marines of the Provisional Brigade and the

Ninth received no battle credits. The Leathernecks were informed that, as far as the Corps was concerned, if they had not landed on the beach, they were not actively engaged in the battle for Saipan and were, therefore, not entitled to any award notable of the event.

Jack and his pals were overjoyed to see the blue waters of Eniwetok's lagoon again after being cooped up on board the hot, poorly ventilated transports and LSTs for weeks. Water and space had been as scarce onboard the "tubs" as on the old *Kenmore*, and so the battery commanders authorized their men to string up tents and tarpaulins on deck in an effort to provide some kind of shade. The itchy, sunburned Marines figured that, even though they had missed getting a battle star for Saipan, their luck was looking up and they just might get a break. A coral atoll surrounded by deep-blue water, Eniwetok was beautiful in a tropical-island way that the Canal, Rendova or the Russells had never been, and it promised to be a real break in itself just to get ashore after days afloat.

Once more, however, this was another hoped-for blessing that failed to materialize, much to the disgust of Jack and his compadres. With the exception of work details sent ashore to draw fresh rations and other supplies and engaging in some landing exercises and drills on its local beaches, the men of the Ninth did not set foot on Eniwetok during their offshore sojourn. The bulk of the 9th Defense's Marines remained on their cramped, stinking transports and Green Dragons. Incredibly, III Amphib's Chief of Staff, General Silverthorn, claimed that despite their lengthy confinement shipboard, the Marines "suffered no debilitating effects from such long captivity." This statement flies in the face of Jack's experience and those of most veterans of the Ninth. The heat was oppressive, and the tropical sun beating down on the steel hulls and sides turned the transports and LSTs into floating pressure cookers for many of their hapless inhabitants. The

Battalion's history noted the "intolerable heat and scant opportunity for bathing," summing up the health effects: "All of the men had prickly heat rashes and various types of skin disease." These ailments, however, had to remain largely unalleviated because of the lack of fresh water for showers or even saltwater baths. Soon enough, however, another massive convoy formed up near the lagoon, with orders to join Task Force 53 and to commence operations to recapture Guam. After ten days in Eniwetok's waters, the flotilla (minus the third echelon contingent, who remained at Eniwetok) set sail again, back the way they had come, 1,000-odd miles to the southern beaches of Guam. Finally, on July 20, 1944, the first echelon of the task force sighted the coast of Guam, and Pogiebait sensed that, for the first time in over two months, he was finally about to be back on dry land.

In all, Jack and much of the 9th Defense had spent nine weeks aboard their grimy little fleet. During this nautical odyssey, most of the Ninth's Marines never set foot on dry land, and, for those that did so, only briefly at best. The bone-wearying boredom of the Battalion's voyage resembled that depicted that of the U.S.S. *Reluctant*, a fictitious Navy supply ship operating in the Central Pacific, depicted in Thomas Heggen's postwar novel and play *Mister Roberts*, as it sailed "on its regular run from Tedium to Apathy and back" with "an occasional trip to Monotony," and a one-time voyage "all the way to Ennui, a distance of two thousand miles from Tedium."

Ironically, when the poop circulated that they would be landing with the Provisional Brigade on the southwestern beaches of Guam to support the 3rd Marine Division's drive against 18,500 Japanese defenders, many of the Ninth's Marines were not as sobered by the news as they normally might have been. Indeed, many of them were ecstatic. More than one yelled to his buddies or nobody in particular, in an outburst of pure joy: "Hot damn! *Finally*, we're gonna get off of these goddam stinking tubs and back on dry land where we belong!" Soon, their days of being "web-footed Marines" would be over! As Chadwick satirically recalled of their oceanic roamings through the Central Pacific, "We now had more time at sea than most sailors."

"W-Day": The Ninth's Landings on Bangi Point

The 9th Defense's assigned missions on Guam, in support of the 1st Provisional Brigade, were similar to its prior duties on Rendova and New Georgia, but this time it included beach security, removal and demolition of Japanese booby traps, obstacles and mines, and the grim but necessary duty of graves registration. The Battalion was divided into three echelons for the invasion: the first, an advance party under Colonel O'Neil, made up of much of the Battalion H&S Battery and the Special Weapons Group; the second and largest, under Lt. Colonel Taylor, was comprised of the rest of H&S and both the 155mm and 90mm Groups. A small rear echelon remained for the time being at Eniwetok. The Battalion was scheduled to land on the southern beachhead in the area of Bangi Point and would then move due north towards the coastal village of Agat.

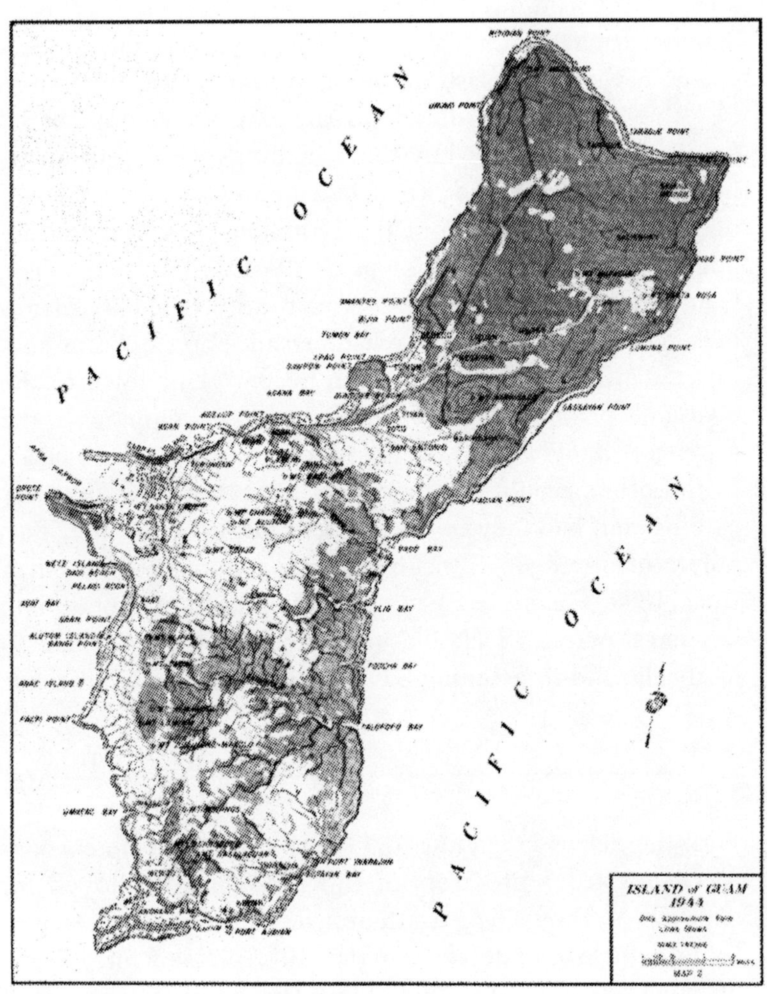
PACIFIC OCEAN
PACIFIC OCEAN
ISLAND of GUAM
1944
MAP 2

While not as bad a "snafu" as were the initial Rendova landings, the Ninth's landing had its share of problems. First, the unit was scheduled to land its first echelon at 9:00 a.m., Despite thirteen days of air and sea bombardment by Rear Admiral Richard L. ("Close-in") Conolly's task force—after 28,761 naval shells blasted the island in what was reputed to be "the best bombardment of the war"—the Provisional Brigade's and the 3rd Division's landings were held up by much stiffer resistance than had been expected. Consequently, disembarkation of the Battalion's first echelon did not commence until 10:30 a.m on "W-Day," July 21, 1944. Coming ashore several hours after the initial combat landings, the Ninth's first echelon had to wade approximately one-quarter mile before "hitting the beach." Unknown to the invasion's planners, sharp coral reefs and outcroppings in the waters off Bangi Point, extending from one side of the beach to the other, would have ripped the bottoms out of many landing craft had they continued their run-in at low tide. This failure of intelligence was even more surprising given that, since 1899, Guam had been an American protectorate and key naval outpost. Jack and his buddies would soon face directly the life-threatening consequences of this intelligence gap.

With the delays in landing, the Ninth's first echelon encountered low tides precisely at the time they deployed for landing. As they slogged ashore, they passed landing craft, LVTs, vehicles and debris from the initial invasion force, many of which were still burning. They also passed a number of corpses, both American and Japanese. The loss of many landing craft, especially the prized amphibious LVTs, in the first wave of the Guam invasion hindered the Battalion's and other units' ability to get assembled and on shore rapidly. All the while, Japanese snipers continued a desultory fire at the Ninth's Marines as they waded ashore laden with personal gear, weapons and ammo.

For Jack and his buddies, the basic landing drill was much like what they had faced on Rendova: a hearty and traditional early-morning ("o-dark-thirty") pre-landing breakfast of coffee, steak, eggs and fried potatoes, then assembling by squads, platoons and batteries for the landing and, for those on board the transports, down the treacherous rope cargo nets into the pitching and rolling landing craft or LVTs. As they waited and watched the 4th and 22nd Marines' landings during the early morning, many of the Ninth's Marines

> scanned self-made maps and sketches and followed the progress of the battle by radio reports and field glasses [according to Marine correspondent Sergeant William Allen, who was assigned to follow the landings alongside the Ninth's headquarters element]. This was the first taste of battle for many of the men, yet none of them showed the slightest outward tremor of fear or excitement.

As several blood-covered Marine infantry casualties from the earlier landings were hauled on board the transports for aid by Dr. Krepela's staff around noontime, however, Sergeant Allen noticed a change in the disposition of many of the onlookers:

> For the first time during the day some of the Marines hardened. They had crowded around to watch the wounded brought aboard and what they had seen was not pleasant. They quietly walked away.

For the "new boys," and the old, of the Ninth, it was

quite a sobering experience. They now knew that they would become participants in something that many of them dreaded, after hearing the tales of the bloody invasion of Tarawa the previous year and of Saipan only days before: an assault landing under direct enemy observation and fire.

In his personal effects, he carried a pocket-sized Bible, its cover encased in a sheet of brass inscribed "*May This Keep You Safe From Harm*," which his parents had sent him as a Christmas present in 1943. While his part of the Battalion prepared for landings on Bangi Beach, and as he watched from the *Sea Fiddler*'s railing the landing craft bringing back the first casualties, Jack undoubtedly pulled out of his pocket the "bulletproof" Bible his parents had given him and said a few prayers to himself.

At least on Guadalcanal and Rendova, the landing craft and LVTs had more or less gotten everybody directly onto the beach. Off Gaan Point and Bangi Point, the unforeseen jagged coral reefs forced the landing craft to disgorge their loads of men far from shore. These coral barriers required the troops to wade in from the edge of the reefs, well within rifle or machine-gun range of any defenders who had not yet been killed or scattered. Because it lacked knowledge of the reef's existence and scope, Close-In Conolly's bombardment force had accordingly done little to blast holes through the reefs for the landing craft to pass through safely to the beachline. Worse, due to the damage already inflicted on the first waves, the resulting lack of sufficient LVTs required many of the men to stagger ashore through the surf in full battle gear. The amphibious model of the ubiquitous 2 1/2-ton cargo truck, the DUKW or "Duck," was rendered impotent as the trucks' rubber tires were slashed to ribbons on the sharp edges of the reef. Even with the benefit of prior experience—or maybe, because of it, as the old salts now knew what to expect—the Guam landings were, therefore, a much more terrifying experience than on the Canal or even Rendova.

Laden with 70-odd pounds of gear, ammunition, and weapons (M-1 Garands or the smaller and lighter M-1 carbines for most; for others, BARs, machine guns and pistols for the machine gunners), anyone falling down in the surf had to fight hard just to get back on his feet and keep from drowning. The sharp coral of the reef sliced and bruised the hands and knees of anyone who fell. Everyone trudged cautiously through the waist-high waters to avoid stepping on underwater mines or obstructions or into a deep shell hole or tidal pool. Even though three combat regiments (the 4th and 22nd Marines and the Army's 305th Infantry) had already landed, the small geysers of water sporadically plinking upwards—even if at a reasonably safe distance—reminded everyone (as if any reminder was necessary) that this was definitely a "hot" beachhead. Since much of the sniper fire seemed to come from two small islands just off Bangi Point, Lt. Colonel O'Neil called for a detachment to wade out to the islands (the landing craft still being blocked by low tides and the reef) and deal with the snipers. As the detachment neared the first island, the Leathernecks—both in the surf and further ashore on the beach—craned their necks at the sound of a fast approaching motorboat. The boat roared out of a cove on the second small island and made at full speed for the Orote peninsula, about two miles to the north. As the fully loaded little boat sped across the bay, the startled Marines opened fire. Despite hundreds of rounds being fired, there was no apparent effect on its Japanese occupants, who were seen landing the boat and running pell-mell onto the rocky shore of the peninsula. While the Marines' enthusiasm was excellent, their marksmanship was lousy: each of them would have earned the embarrassment of the hated "Maggie's Drawers" flag had they been back at P.I. "There was a lot of kidding, short lived, about sending everyone back to the rifle range," Frank Chadwick ruefully recalled.

During the initial landings and for most of their stay on Guam, the Leathernecks were delighted to encounter almost no Japanese aircraft, a fact which lessened the primary duties of the 90mm and Special Weapons Groups considerably. In mid-June, as the Saipan invasion began, the naval forces encountered what would be the last major direct engagement between the air arms of the U.S. and Japanese fleets. In the Battle of the Philippine Sea, the U.S. Navy inflicted a crushing defeat on the Japanese Combined Fleet and naval air forces, sinking three carriers and, depending on who's counting, destroying between 270 and 475 aircraft in the process for a loss of only 29 American planes. This lopsided victory, the "Great Marianas Turkey Shoot," effectively eliminated Japanese air power in the Central Pacific and the Philippines.

The absence of Japanese air power over Guam was, at least, one great blessing for which Pogiebait and his pals were deeply thankful. Unlike Rendova, however, the beach was still taking some shelling from enemy mortars and small field guns. For the moment, the area held by the Ninth on Bangi Point was certainly much smaller than the area it held down on Guadalcanal or Rendova, but that was of little comfort: with more of the Battalion massed in one place, it just made a better target for the Japanese. During that first night on Guam, the area near the Battalion's perimeter was hit by a brief but massive counterattack, as flares exploded overhead to illuminate the area and as huge shells—this time, U.S. naval ones—fell, some as close as 200 yards from the men in the Ninth's frontline foxholes. Fortunately for them, the brunt of this attack by the Japanese fell on the 4th and 22nd Marines and not on the Ninth.

Next morning, the larger, second echelon landed, with Jack joining in as a participant. Except for the fact that fewer Japanese shells and bullets were pinging around them, little had changed since the preceding day to make this echelon's landing any less treacherous. The formidable coral reef barriers remained intact and continued to prevent the LCMs and LCTs from taking their occupants closer in to the beach. Like the earlier waves, Pogiebait and the Marines of his echelon had to step off their landing craft at the reef's edge. Unlike the first waves, however, since there were no available LVTs waiting to ferry them the rest of the way, this group had to wade through about 1,200 yards of surf and water to reach the beach. Jack recalled sloshing through the chest-high surf as American shells rocketed overhead, "sounding like a freight train," to explode several miles away onto Japanese targets. As the high tide rolled in during his slog to the beach, Jack plunged into a tidal pool over his head: encumbered by 70-odd pounds of equipment, he had visions of drowning. The same panicky feeling erupted that he had felt on Rendova when he was trapped under the LST's door, but he somehow clambered out of the deep pool and staggered to dry land.

The scenes on the beach offered little respite or comfort from the terrors of the surf: one day after W-Day, the Bangi Point beach was still a wreck. Despite efforts at clearing the beach, battered American equipment and stinking dead bodies littered its shore or floated in the tide. With most of its men now ashore, the Battalion began the laborious process of moving in Special Weapons' light AA guns. Jack and his battery mates cursed and groaned as they strung barbed wire, dug foxholes and uneasily manned the Ninth's outer defensive perimeter in the Guamanian summer heat. The 90mms and 155mms remained on board the ships lying off Eniwetok, at least for the moment, as did the Battalion's last echelon.

The scene on the beaches near Bangi Point encountered by the Ninth's men. (Official U.S. Marine Corps photo)

With many of the Japanese beach defenders now stranded on the Orote peninsula north of Agat, the Provisional Brigade was ordered to turn north on July 23. The 22nd Marines were told to lead the way, followed by the 4th Marines, with the Army's 77th Division to hold the areas previously occupied by those regiments. This move was intended to cut off the Orote peninsula and seize the major Japanese airfield on the peninsula. As Army units moved in, including an AAA battalion, the 9th Defense was tasked with defending a much smaller perimeter than it first had. The new perimeter stretched from Agat to Bangi Point, the latter being a small peninsula jutting out about 1,000 yards south of Gaan Point. To protect this area, however, the Ninth would have to run infantry-style patrols and help drive Japanese stragglers north towards the 9th Marines (an infantry regiment of the 3rd Division, not to be confused with the Ninth) and the 77th Division. Fortunately, firefights were few, as most groups of Japanese encountered were small and fled rapidly. Amazingly, many of these stragglers did not seem to be equipped with weapons, which was explained later by the fact that many were later discovered to be Navy service troops or Korean forced laborers from the Japanese navy yard at Piti. Although these live-to-fight-another-day tactics annoyed the Ninth's officers, few of the enlisted Leathernecks were troubled. "We were not dismayed that they did not stand and fight but fled. As combat goes, this was a relief, as we would rather chase them than stand there and get shot up," Frank Chadwick recalled.

At least, the Ninth was spared from the desperate charges launched against the 21st and 9th Marines and from the fighting in the ridges and hills around Guam's capital, Agana. This fighting included relatively rare attacks by Japanese tank units. Wild rumors abounded that many of the Japanese defenders who had launched some particularly frenzied *banzai* charges on the 22nd Marines and 77th Division's dogfaces were blind, staggering, out-of-their-minds drunk. These rumors soon were confirmed as having been correct. Supply stashes around Orote contained huge stockpiles of booze—beer, sake and scotch—"enough alcohol in its godowns to intoxicate an entire army," as 1st Provisional Brigade member William Manchester recalled. To the disgust of Jack and many of the Fighting Ninth's parched mouths, however (and doubtless to the relief of Colonel O'Neil and his staff!), most of the contents of these hooch depots fell into the marauding and appreciative hands of the no-less-drymouthed infantrymen of the Provisional Brigade and 3rd Division.

By the end of July, with the Japanese flushed out of the areas around Gaan Point, Bangi Point and Agat, those elements of the Battalion not providing security or manning foxholes were clearing the beach of obstacles, debris and mines.

The Bangi Point beach had been strewn with mines of various types, including a peculiar kind of hemispherical anti-ship mine, but oddly, many of the mines' fuses were not activated. The reason may be found in the fact that the Japanese had impressed local Guamanians, or Chamorros, into forced labor on the beach defenses. Many mines had been emplaced by the reluctant local draftees, and this Japanese use of slave labor had backfired, as the Chamorros frequently planted mines without removing the fuses' safety pins.[15/] With their Long Toms not yet ashore, both batteries of the 155mm Group were put to work blasting holes, removing mines, wrecked vehicles and occasionally dead bodies. After a week or more of lying unburied, the corpses were in an advanced state of decomposition and stank to high heaven in the Guamanian heat and humidity.

From Agat to Agana

Orders to move out again reached the 9th Defense. Provisional Brigade headquarters directed Colonel O'Neil to march the Battalion from its area around Agat to assume the defense of the island's largest airfield near Agana, Guam's capital. This next slog required a 20-mile road march from Agat to Agana, on a very dusty and narrow winding road about the width of a single truck. Moving in two columns down the side of the road, with jeeps and other Battalion vehicles taking up the middle of the road, the Ninth began this march around dawn on or about August 3.

For Jack and the majority of the rank-and-file, slogging along the edge of the road, this latest march was "just miserable." Clouds of dust churned up by the unit's trucks and jeeps soon coated the faces, mouths, exposed arms and nostrils of the sweaty, tired Leathernecks, and flies and mosquitoes alighted on the men's bare skin. En route, the Battalion passed the northern sector landing area of the 3rd Marine

Division, an area studded with high cliffs and well-emplaced Japanese gun positions. The western beaches had not yet been fully cleared of the detritus of battle, and Jack and his buddies marveled that *anyone* could have made a landing there and survived. It took the Ninth about ten hours to complete its march to Agana in 100-degree heat. The Battalion reached the city's outskirts around dusk, and Jack and his buddies immediately began digging in. A few Japanese patrols and stragglers were driven off with rifle fire during the night.

Agana was a wretched sight. The capital of Guam and the home of over half of the island's prewar population of some 19,000 people, most of its one and two-story buildings and homes had been pounded to piles of shapeless rubble, in large part from the U.S. pre-invasion bombing and shelling and also by the 3rd Division's recent push through the city. Agana Cathedral, the Church of San Antonio, the Bishop's Palace (the Guamanians were largely Catholic), government buildings and the central plaza and heart of Agana, the once beautiful Plaza Espana, were all battered or leveled outright. The fighting had left hundreds of Chamorros homeless, and the Japanese themselves had concentrated many more in camps in the southern and eastern corners of the island. One U.S.-run refugee camp near Agat alone would accommodate and feed over 12,100 civilians. One such refugee was a teenager, Vincente T. Blaz, who would later act as a local guide for several of the 9th Defense's patrols. Later in life, "Bennie" Blaz would become a Marine Corps brigadier general and a U.S. Congressman for the Territory of Guam.

The dusty march to Agana. (Official U.S. Marine Corps photo)

Biggie Slater recounts an incongruous moment in the rubble of Agana, as well as one ego boost for the capital city's liberators:

> Guam was American. Biggie and his comrades knew it with certainty when they saw the smashed soda fountain in the rubble of Agana's main street. The counter marble had burst from a shattered building: syrup pumps and seltzer taps drew cheers from the files of men moving past.
>
> [Despite the destruction, the] Guamanians seemed happy to greet the new conquerors, even though twenty thousand Japanese still remained,

> hemmed in on the northern part of the island. They showed their joy in homey, hospitable ways. Within a few days of the initial assaults, a Chamorro impresario organized a troupe for entertainment of the troops. The revue had a smash hit finale: "Mr. Sam, Sam, dear old Uncle Sam, won't you come back, please, to Gu-a-a-m."

The finale song, of course, was the plaintive tune composed by the Chamorros as they had languished in the *Kempetai*'s concentration camps and dreamed of their day of liberation. Jack and the men of the 155mm Group, however, spent little time in the debris of Agana and basking in the happiness of its now-freed citizens. Battery A was next assigned to clear an area of cliffs to the northwest of Agana, and Battery B was ordered to "mop up" a nearby airfield on its northeastern outskirts, while the rest of the Battalion was tasked to engage in a "sweep" of the central part of Agana.

"*Mopping-up.*" "*Sweeping.*" The words made the difficult and relentless work of patrolling and hunting down the enemy sound so easy and hygienic, as if they were the commonest of kitchen chores. Jack and his brethren came to detest these euphemisms, for they cloaked the harsh reality of the situation. In the case of Battery B, this mopping-up would become substantial and bloody work, as Major Wells and Captain George ("Doc") Teller, Bill Box's successor in April 1944 as Battery B's commander (and Hank Reichner's "noodle soup" provider), received intelligence reports that the Marines of the 155mm Group might be up against a much larger force of 1,500 or more Japanese. Granted, the enemy was starving and low on materiel, but so had been the Japanese on nearby Saipan, who had claimed 16,525 American casualties in less than one month's time under very similar circumstances. It was with some trepidation, then, that Batteries A and B began their grim work of patrolling, as the timing and circumstances were ripe for a desperate *banzai* attack.

The day after the Battalion arrived on Agana's outskirts and before the Ninth again moved out, the 3rd Marines swept through the Agana airfield area with little resistance. Battery B moved into the airfield area later that evening, setting up a base camp, digging foxholes and stringing up a barbed-wire perimeter. Time was of the essence: the Seabees were waiting for the airfield to be cleared of Japanese stragglers before they could begin grading and improving it to provide the 8,000-foot finished runway needed to accommodate each of the huge B-29s. Wells, Teller and their battery officers were bluntly told by Colonel O'Neil that only two days could be spared for the mopping-up operations. At least, that was the plan.

In actuality, it would take Pogiebait and his buddies over twice that long to clear the area.

Patrolling Around Agana

The perimeter of Agana airfield was thickly wooded and entangled with vines, providing excellent cover for its defenders. The airfield itself was a wreck: smashed aircraft, fuel stores and huts littered the runways and adjoining landscape. Although the majority of the Japanese (approximately 10,000 of them) were hemmed up in the island's north, around Finegayan, Barrigada and Mt. Santa Rosa, substantial numbers of them remained outside the better-defined northern pockets of resistance, eking out a meager existence by raiding U.S. units' supplies. On its first patrols, Battery B began encountering some of these small groups of Japanese, which varied in numbers from four to 20 men. Unlike the splintered groups encountered near Agat, these bodies of the defenders were somewhat more organized and fully armed. Again, however, most of these small groups chose not to open fire with their weapons, instead scattering when challenged and taking cover in the dense thickets all around. From the various reports flowing into the battery and 155mm Group CPs, the initial estimate was that Battery B was up against some 1,200 Japanese. It was soon apparent, however, that the actual enemy forces were somewhat less, since many of the defenders were moving from one sector of the airfield to another and were being double-counted. Fortunately as well, when firefights broke out, their infantry tactics were uncoordinated.

The Battalion's work in this respect was tough and nasty: in the first few weeks of its patrols, which would last for months, several hundred Japanese were killed in brief but rapid firefights, often at close range in the jungle and underbrush. Still, the mop-up action was far from complete and was two full days behind schedule when Lt. Colonel O'Neil arrived at the airfield to give his subordinate commanders in the 155mm Group a dressing-down for the delays. The Colonel was "not about to go hat in hand" to the 1st Provisional Brigade's hard-pressed CO, Brigadier General Lemuel C. Sheperd, and ask him for help. The pressure was on to increase the Group's patrols, by day and by night. After two more days of running patrols, the surviving Japanese defenders withdrew to the northeast and out of the Ninth's sector, into an area between the two U.S. divisions in the campaign.

The Seabees finally arrived by mid-August, with all their heavy equipment, to begin the reconstruction and expansion of the airfield to accommodate the colossal B-29s that soon would be based there. The Ninth did not move from the area, however, since the lightly armed construction engineers still required its presence for perimeter and AA defense. Battery B's patrols continued, although fewer and fewer Japanese were found around the airfield as the days passed. After several more days, a 900-man Army MP battalion arrived to provide rear-area security for the airfield and to relieve the 140-

odd weary Leathernecks of Battery B from their patrolling duties.

Jack and his peers thought they had earned a respite from the hard work that Battery B had been carrying out since the opening days of the campaign. They soon found out how sadly mistaken they again were to expect a break.

Patrolling brought hazards of various sorts. On the third day of Battery B's patrols around Agana airfield, shortly after dawn, a host of weary Marines were standing in line at the base camp for hot chow served from marmite cans. Near the end of the breakfast line, Jack and Frank Chadwick heard a commotion behind them and turned to look. Four figures stood at the end of the line, in uniforms that looked like the faded olive-drab herringbone fatigues of the Marines, but their footwear was radically different from anything American: black, split-toed rubber shoes, called *tabi*, which looked more like goats' hooves rather than anything like boots. They were unarmed, but they were clearly Japanese infiltrators. Jack, Frank and several others quickly leapt out of line and pulled the intruding Japanese out of the chow line. It was clear from their emaciated condition that the prisoners were starving and that, in desperation, they had crept into the chow line, hoping to get some food and pass themselves off as Marines in their captured uniforms.

As they wrestled with the starving prisoners, a green "shavetail" lieutenant, who had joined the Battalion in the Russells as a Battery B platoon leader and whom Jack habitually referred to as "Jelly Belly," ran over to see what was happening. He was already heartily disliked by the men of his platoon and tended to bring out the worst in them. When confronted with the POWs, Jelly Belly whined about how handling this situation would spoil his breakfast. The lieutenant had violated two of the cardinal rules of military leadership: a good officer eats last, and no matter how difficult a situation he is faced with, a good officer keeps his composure in front of his peers and subordinates. More damnable in the eyes of his Marines was his apparent concern about his personal welfare, and not the more serious concern that they obviously had that these—and undoubtedly other—Japanese infiltrators were roaming freely around the base camp. This "Lt." had lost the respect of his subordinates, and now they smelled blood. When the shavetail, in considerable agitation, asked, "Well, what the hell are we going to do with them?" he received an answer from one exasperated Marine: "No problem, *sir*. We'll just take 'em over there, over to the bushes, and shoot 'em. Then, *sir*, we can all have a quiet meal."

Despite the shocking bloodthirstiness of this answer, the lieutenant's Marines had no intention of following through on the threat, as they were fully aware of the consequences, both legal and practical. Rather, it was delivered as a test of Jelly Belly's backbone, an effort to "pull his chain" and gauge how he would respond. He had been found lacking:

> We knew we couldn't do this [Frank Chadwick recalled], as Maj. Wells would have a fit and we would all pay for it (Wells was about 6' 2", weight about 200 pounds, and an all-American heavyweight wrestling champion in college and taught judo. He never court-martialed anyone but was prone to taking someone to the boondocks and settle it there; he was no man to mess with). The more the Lt. got excited, the harder we pushed the issue . . . until we reached the point [that] he was screaming at us and was going to run up to find the Major. We knew we had pushed him to the limits and we didn't want to face the wrath of the Major. We calmed him down, got Wells, called the MPs and intelligence to pick up the prisoners. From that

> day on, the lieutenant was always nervous and a little scared as to what the men under his command would do . . . . [16/]

As will be seen, this particular lieutenant still had good reason to be afraid of his men.

While patrolling around Agana, the Ninth began encountering more of the native Chamorro people, who, with the Japanese withdrawing, came out of hiding to barter with the Marines for food, clothing and fuel. The Marines soon found that the Chamorros had one item well worth any bartered rations or blankets: potent concoctions called "tuba" or "aggie."

Tuba was a wine made from fermented hearts-of-palm sap. Aggie began as a thin, milky fluid, which was extracted from the shoots at the top of coconut trees. This juice was allowed to ferment for four to six days, during which time it congealed in thickness and acquired a reasonably high alcohol content. Although it could be drunk in this form (as tuba), it was often further distilled into a near 180-proof, clear drink, which could be turned into an especially nasty variety of torpedo juice. As Chadwick remembered:

> We'd pour this in our aluminum canteens, add lemon powder to kill the taste. The alcohol reacted with the aluminum, and the canteen got so hot you could not hold the canteen in your hand. One or two sips of this and you didn't know which end was up. We realized we couldn't handle this and continue our patrols, so most everyone dumped the contents. I had two drinks, lost all sense of reality, and then dumped everything.

Not all the alcoholic liquids on Guam were even as drinkable as these wretched concoctions, however, and the consequences of drinking some of them were far worse than what Chadwick and others faced in their experiments with tuba and aggie. In one effort to keep a particularly obnoxious party going after all the usual varieties of hooch and "jungle juice" were consumed, a sergeant of the Ninth and four others were poisoned by drinking denatured alcohol salvaged from Japanese stores. As a result, the five died in considerable agony, as David Slater recalled:

> They roistered until the homemade liquor was exhausted. The farmhouse stood a few hundred yards from the edge of a demolished airstrip which was strewn with dismembered planes, scattered fuel drums, and the debris of disrupted war. One of Willie's pals, a self-proclaimed expert on alcohol (he had run some moonshine in Tennessee) led an expedition to replenish their supply.
>
> The group went to the strip, where a treasury of torpedo fuel—almost pure alcohol—might be found, or perhaps a tin or two of medical stuff. They discovered an untouched drum of clear liquid and poured a sample. Then they lit it, and it burned with a pale blue flame. The "expert" pronounced the contents fit for consumption; it had passed the tests of appearance, odor, flame, and, finally, taste.
>
> At first they retched. It was more than a drunken emptying. A frightened [Guamanian] woman ran to the encampment and brought back ambulances. The heavier drinkers were already blind. The drum had contained coolant for Zero engines. Willie and four

of his partying companions convulsed and died, Willie cursing off the Chaplain's comforts.

The sweeps of northern Guam were conducted by the 1st Provisional Brigade up the western coast, the 3rd Marine Division through the island's center and the 77th Division along the east coast, while the Ninth continued to run patrols and improve its AA gun positions around Agana. On August 10, it was announced that "all organized Japanese resistance" on Guam had ceased and that the island was secured; Guam was, officially, American territory again. Even before this announcement, in a ceremony fraught with symbolism on July 29, the U.S. flag was raised up the flagpole of the U.S. Marine Barracks, which had been captured by the Japanese in December 1941. By the end of this stage of the campaign, American casualties were 1,350 dead and 6,450 wounded, a cheap victory compared with bloody Saipan. Of these, the Ninth had suffered—despite its active role—one killed in action, five other deaths, and six severely wounded, but again with several hundred others evacuated for lesser injuries, malaria and dengue.

In mid-August, the 1st Provisional Brigade had withdrawn to Guadalcanal for R & R and to form the 6th Marine Division. The 77th Infantry Division withdrew in preparation for its eventual redeployment to the Philippines. The 3rd Marine Division remained in base camp on Guam until February 1945 as it readied for its bloody but triumphant campaign on Iwo Jima. Of the other original units that participated in the landings on W-Day, only the Ninth, the 14th Defense Battalion and a few other units were left to garrison Guam—but, by no means did it mean that Japanese resistance was eradicated. Large pockets of Japanese forces remained yet to be dealt with: by mid-August, the Americans controlled only 75%

of the island, and as some 7,500 of the original 18,500-odd Japanese defenders had not yet been killed or captured, there was still much fighting and killing—and patrolling—to be done.

Until this time, the Battalion's big guns had not been brought ashore. On August 20, the final elements of the Ninth, which had been left in reserve at Eniwetok, disembarked at the former Japanese Navy docks at Piti Point. The arrival of this last echelon included the heavy artillery, as well as the 90mm Group, which joined the Special Weapons' gunners in constructing AA positions around the Agana airfield. For Pogiebait and the men of the 155mm Group, who had come ashore without their Long Toms some 45 days earlier, there was no rest for the weary. With the possibility of Japanese naval raids being very remote and with no suitable field artillery missions for the Long Toms, they remained the 9th Defense's own "infantry" component. For weeks, their artillery pieces sat in a gun park at Piti, while both Batteries A and B were "chopped" from the rest of the Battalion to provide infantry, recon and patrolling support to the 3rd Division. The infantry skills they had learned years ago at Guantanamo would get more of a workout in the next four months than at any earlier time in their war.

The Navy Beats a Hasty Retreat

Shortly after the arrival of Admiral Nimitz and his staff on the island in early August, the Ninth began to encounter more Navy officers, sometimes in fairly improbable circumstances. Jack, Chadwick and a small group from Battery B were on patrol one day along the side of a fairly steep ridgeline. A group of Japanese defenders were clearly dug in at the top of the ridge, and the 3rd Marines, part of the 3rd Marine Division, were supposed to be somewhere nearby on the patrol's flank. The Ninth's patrol had strict orders to proceed no further from its general vicinity until it had linked up with the

3rd Marines. As the patrol edged along cautiously, a jeep came bouncing along a dirt trail, with two cocky but junior navy officers, immaculate in fresh khaki uniforms and "saucer" caps.

Jack and his buddies scurried over to them, cautiously so as not to draw more attention to the scene than the officers already had, and challenged the officers in a chorus of dry-lipped, croaking voices: "Hey, you can't come through here!" "This is a restricted area!" "Get the hell out of here! You wanna get us killed or something?" The Navy officers bluntly responded that, as members of Admiral Nimitz's staff, they were entitled to greater respect than they were getting from this ragtag bunch of enlisted Marines, and they noted in passing, less than subtly, that they were out hunting for a few good souvenirs.

Still squatting down low to the ground, the patrol's members scratched their stubbly chins and gazed around thoughtfully, wondering what would be a suitable response to the rubber-necking officers without earning themselves a court-martial in the bargain. Finally, one of them said, pointing with his rifle barrel up the hill: "I know where you can find some really good souvenirs, sirs. Just keep on this trail, and go up to the top of that ridge. You'll find *all* the souvenirs you'll want." In a few minutes, after the officers gunned the jeep up the steeply-angled slope of the hill, small arms fire crackled: the two Navy men had not counted on their souvenirs being attached to some very live and hostile Japanese soldiers, and the jeep quickly swerved around in reverse. The Navy officers were livid as they pulled up next to the patrol and, with suitable profanity, demanded to see the patrol's CO. The patrol members told them how to find the 155mm Group CP, where a newly promoted Major Wells, now serving as the Group XO, H&S Battery CO and Major Hiatt's future successor as the 155mm Group's CO, was monitoring the progress of his subordinate batteries' various patrols.

Soon after, the two naval officers found the Major at the CP. Having gotten their side of the story, and with much more important problems (for instance, coordinating the linkup with the 3rd Marines) to worry him than assigning Marines to shepherd wayward Navy staff officers, an irritated Waldo Wells mastered his anger and remained calm. Slowly but firmly, he said: "Get your asses out of my area, *now*, or I'll give you both rifles, and you can go out on patrol with us. Do I make myself clear?" In a flurry of salutes, the Navy officers beat a hasty retreat from the Ninth's area of operations, albeit without their "souvenirs." As one of the members of the patrol recalled, "We all had a good laugh over the incident [at the time]. This was our sense of humor, but now as we look back, we could have gotten these Navy combat sailors killed."

After that incident, there were fewer unwanted or unplanned intrusions by the Navy.

Jack's Close Encounter With the Nisei

With more than 9,000 Japanese troops still on Guam in the late summer and early autumn of 1944, because it was the largest U.S. battalion on the island, and with a negligible likelihood of Japanese air and naval counterstrikes, the Ninth's Marines were dispatched frequently on infantry patrols to flush out holdouts. In a few cases, there were success stories in which Japanese troops would surrender with token resistance. Sometimes, however, the defenders would fight, and fight hard, with the result that Army and Marine teams would resort to grenades, four-pound demolition charges and flamethrowers to seal up the Japanese in their caves and bunkers. In some cases, bunkers would be occupied by entire squads of Japanese who had died gruesomely but speedily, via suicide by hand grenade. Thankfully, unlike earlier on nearby Saipan, there were no massed *banzai* charges on Guam. In the hopes of talking more Japanese into surrendering and learning from them useful intelligence, Guam's Island Command began sending out psychological warfare and intelligence teams with the Army and Marine patrols. These groups were often equipped with propaganda leaflets, megaphones and loudspeakers, and they included Japanese-speaking linguists as interpreters. These "psy-war" teams were tasked with talking the island's derelict defenders into giving up.

On one of their patrols, Jack and other members of his Battery B platoon were combing the boondocks of Guam for Japanese holdouts. The ravines and hills of Guam were not quite as heavily jungled as Guadalcanal, Rendova or New Georgia, but the foliage was very dense nevertheless. As he looked around on this patrol, Jack saw a figure moving in an area where he did not expect to see any Marines or Army troops. He crouched low, striving to identify the figure. As the man drew closer, Jack could see that he was wearing a G.I. helmet and fatigues and carried a rifle—but the face was certainly not Caucasian or Chamorro. There was but one logical explanation: a Japanese soldier had found an American uniform and was trying to infiltrate or escape their positions! Jack stood, scuttled behind a tree, and chambered a bullet into his rifle. The sounds of the rifle cartridge being loaded and the click of the bolt were loud enough so that his buddies could hear it, which also meant that the Japanese soldier, who was only a few feet away by now, probably could hear it, too.

Jack was sweating profusely, and not just from the Guamanian heat and humidity: Guadalcanal included, it was the closest he had ever gotten to a live, armed, hostile, Japanese soldier. He had never killed anyone in combat, face-to-face, although he felt fairly certain that he'd helped kill people from a distance by serving part-time on the 155mm crews. The soldier was moving away; *good*, thought Jack, *he hasn't heard me loading the rifle*. Jack knew he needed to act, and act fast. He pulled the butt of his M-1 carbine—most of the Ninth's men now had these smaller guns, in lieu of Garands or

Springfields—in tight against his shoulder, drew a bead on the man through the carbine's sights, ensured the safety catch was off, and prepared to squeeze the trigger. A muffled command hissed from behind stopped him cold:

"*Don't shoot*! *He's a 'Nissy*!'"

"What? What the hell you mean, 'don't shoot'?" Jack cocked his head slightly and softly croaked out the words. "He's a Nip, ain't he? And what the hell's a 'Nissy?' "

A hand deftly grabbed the barrel of his carbine and pulled it downwards. "He's no Jap, goddammit! He's one of ours! O.K.?" Jack now learned, first-hand, one of the better-guarded American secrets of the Pacific war.

As part of American psy-war and intelligence operations, Marine and Army teams had begun in 1943, late in the Guadalcanal campaign, to use Japanese-speaking *Nisei* soldiers and officers in the field to help negotiate the surrender of Japanese troops and act as combat interpreters. Despite their internment (and the ongoing internment of their families and friends until 1944), the *Nisei* wanted a chance to prove that they were as American as any boys from New York, Tennessee, Indiana or California. Despite the shoddy treatment meted out to them and their families, the *Nisei* were truly the "Yankee samurai": their language skills were invaluable, and their courage was first-rate. Four teams of *Nisei* interpreters were deployed on Guam: two with the 3rd Marine Division, one with the Provisional Brigade, and the last divided among the infantry regiments of the 77th Infantry Division. One of these individuals assigned to the 1st Provisional Brigade's section had earlier suffered the ignominy of having been "captured" by Marines on Bougainville; despite his protests in fluent English, he had been displayed to the actor Gary Cooper, there with a USO show, as the first Japanese POW captured on that island! Jack had unwittingly just drawn a bead on one of these highly dedicated interpreters and intelligence workers, but he fortunately had been stopped in the nick of time. "That was the closest I ever came to shooting a Japanese soldier. Good thing I learned he was a Japanese-*American* soldier, just in time!," Jack recalled.

All of this, however, apparently remained unknown to the interpreter who had so nearly been shot by Jack:

> When the [Guam] campaign was over the [*Nisei*] team reassembled in a rest area, drinking their first beer since leaving Hawaii. It made them slightly high, and some. . . broke into Japanese song. Years later, at a reunion of survivors, they wondered "how we never got shot!"

Oh, had the interpreters only known how close at least one of their number had come to that fate! "Friendly fire" casualties were prevalent enough among U.S. forces in World War II—witness, for instance, the sinking of the *McCawley*, the shooting-down of the Marine Corsair pilot off Rendova harbor, and the deadly effects of the nighttime "jitterbugging" incidents on New Georgia—and it is an open question how many of these courageous U.S. citizen-soldiers were injured or killed by their own side's guns. To Jack's and the *Nisei* soldier's mutual good fortune, however, each man emerged unscathed this day on Guam.

Battery B's Move to Pago Bay; Encounters With a Desperate Enemy

Finally, after weeks of infantry-type work, the order came to the 155mm Group to deploy its guns: Battery A to the Adelup Point area near one of the W-Day beachheads, and Battery B to the Pago Bay area on the eastern coast of Guam near the village of Yona. Batteries A's and B's missions were twofold: each battery was to "mop up" its assigned area and to set up a clifftop fire base for its four long-idle Long Toms.

The Group's move was accomplished around August 31, 1944, though not without an incident typical of the fighting "after the fighting was over" on Guam. As the Battalion's history records of Battery B's move:

> As fire control officer, Don Sandager set out to find a battery position which had been selected from air photographs. His recon with a rifle squad of the 3d Marines found there "were still many snipers and the terrain was extremely rocky and wooded." When he and Walter Wells reported back that it was not feasible to move 155mm guns into the area, they were told to go anyway. After some negotiation a compromise position was reached near the point and a road built to reach it. [Shortly after] the position was occupied a group of Japanese stragglers came down a footpath into the camp.

While Captain (soon to be Major) Reichner's Battery A was en route to Adelup Point, Major Wells, Captain Teller, 155mm Group headquarters and Battery B were ordered to move to the Pago Bay area to emplace their Long Toms for the seacoast defense of Guam's eastern approaches.

The building of the Pago Bay trail and base camp was, for Chadwick, Landon and Battery B's other old salts who had survived Gavutu's Hill 181, eerily reminiscent of those earlier labors. First, a trail had to be hacked by hand through the dense jungle to the cliffs where the Long Toms would be dug in. Battery B's Leathernecks left their old camp near the airfield and marched to Pago Bay, their gear stowed in accompanying trucks and joined by a bulldozer. En route, the Marines marveled at the large number of Japanese bunkers, OPs and gun emplacements on the high ground around the bay and thanked their lucky stars that the defenses were now abandoned. As Frank Chadwick recalled:

> It was very evident that whoever had planned the beach defenses was a real professional. The defenses were defenses-in-depth and [the] interlocking firing from all points on the beach was something that they could be very proud of. The only drawback was that the Japs manning the lower beach defenses had no method of withdrawing. Knowing the Japs, this was a problem by design as it meant that every man had to stay in his position until anyone making the landings were driven off or the defender was killed.

The "old-fashioned" artillerymen of Battery B also had their first taste of a new mode of modern warfare: rocket bombardment. Two Navy rocket ships—likely converted LCI(G) landing craft—sailed past the marching Marines and, on reaching the northernmost point off Pago Bay's beach, began launching salvoes of ground bombardment rockets. The rockets' flash and roar were an awe-inspiring sight, but when patrolling the target area a few days later, these same Marines were disappointed to find that the practical results of these barrages were less impressive. The rocket bombardment had cleared away much of the underbrush (which undoubtedly aided patrolling), left several large craters and knocked down some trees, but several dud rockets were also found. Chadwick remembered:

> We found that any enemy in caves, fortifications or below ground would be safe unless a direct hit had been achieved and if this had occurred on the fortification, they would have been shaken but still able to continue to fight. This was a great disappointment but, watching the firing that morning, we took this as a black omen to the upcoming operation.

Under Major Wells's and Captain Teller's scrutiny, Battery B began building its newest base camp. Telephone lines were laid back to the Battalion's CP, and a barbed wire perimeter was strung. The bulldozer was used to widen the trail to the width of a truck; unfortunately, the trail itself remained little more than sand, coral and soil, which would quickly turn into a glutinous mess with the addition of any rain. Most of the trees were left in place around the base camp to aid in camouflage and to afford some additional cover from the elements, but the vines, scrubby bushes and tough grass covering the ground had to hand-hacked by machete, the bulldozer failing to make a significant dent in such foliage. "Home" for Jack and his Battery B buddies, at this point, was little more than their foxholes, covered with shelter halves or rubberized ponchos. These jerry-rigged coverings did little to keep the rain out, and the foxholes filled rapidly whenever it rained, a frequent occurrence in the Guamanian summer. While Captain Teller put half of the battery's 80-odd gunners to work in setting up camp and gun positions over the next few days, the other half ran patrols around the campsite. From their observations on earlier patrols, the Marines had learned the Japanese were starving and would take any opportunity to raid foodstuffs or garbage dumps for anything edible.

With the nearest American positions to the battery's Pago Bay location being some seven miles away, it was left to its own devices in matters of self-defense. The base camp was surrounded by double rows of barbed wire. The wire was intermittently festooned, as usual, with pebble-filled tin cans to provide early warning of movements against the barrier. Several tripod-mounted machine guns were emplaced at each side of the trail near the entrance into the camp. Interlocking fields of fire were cleared for the machine guns, and sandbagged strongpoints placed at intervals along the wire. Still, knowing that only a few miles away, Guam was being turned into a vast supply dump with many of the "creature comforts" available in the rear areas was an immensely frustrating fact to Jack and his buddies. Reduced to eating cold "10-in-1" rations and with only a 500-gallon tanker of water delivered to provide three days of sustenance for about eighty men, "it just didn't seem fair," as Chadwick moaned.

Pogiebait (on the left) and several of his buddies at Battery B's Pago Bay camp near Yona, late summer 1944. (Author's collection)

Patrolling was very much a cat-and-mouse game, and when on patrol, Pogiebait, Chadwick, Bob Landon, Zombie Jones, Leo McDonald and their brethren were ever fearful of stepping onto a hidden mine or booby trap, never mind the risk of being "pegged" by a sniper.

> Half of the time, you saw no enemy but only areas he used for bivouac, foot prints on a trail, left-overs of a fire or broken branches to indicate the enemy were still in our area. Frustrating, scary and living like cavemen, dirty and stinking to high heavens in this hot, humid climate and no bathing, we were a pretty rancid, stinking bunch of Marines.

With the average temperatures on Guam and the other Marianas that summer ranging between 77 and 88 degrees but with near-80% humidity, and an average summer rainfall of six to nine inches, Pogiebait and his buddies sweltered and stank in another tropical steambath.

After about ten days in these conditions, more house-keeping gear was brought into the base camp. Eight-man pyramid tents were erected; patrols were cut by two-thirds, and the barbed wire fencing and gun positions were improved. A hole was scooped outside the camp perimeter to serve as a garbage dump, which, in time, would become a lure for more starving Japanese desperate for anything resembling food. A field kitchen and four showers made from converted 55-gallon drums were also set up. "We were really living high on the hog, or so we thought," Chadwick recalled.

By August 10, however, intelligence reports determined that the roving cliques of Japanese in the battery's area had grown from mere two or three-man clusters to groups of 10 to 20, and then platoon-sized elements of 30 to 40. The Marines sensed they were likely to face greater trouble when, while attempting to flush a squad of Japanese out of the brush surrounding the base camp, a patrol came upon a second trail—one tramped out by the Japanese, tracing a rough circle around the base camp's entire perimeter and up to the cliffside heights overlooking the camp. Full patrols were quickly resumed. One day, Chadwick found himself assigned by himself in an isolated position outside the perimeter along the main trail. When he placed Chadwick there, his sergeant ordered him to fire as many rounds as possible if he spotted any enemy patrols, both to put the camp on alert as well as to kill as many infiltrators as possible. Meanwhile, now beginning to suffer from dengue ("breakbone") fever, Jack was put on a work detail in the base camp during the daylight hours and was assigned to man a machine gun position on the perimeter during the evening.

Several days after getting the first reports of the larger concentrations of Japanese soldiers in the area and finding the enemy-made trail, the base camp was attacked by about 100 Japanese soldiers, which began a running firefight of about two hours.[17/] The next morning, the Marines found 18 dead Japanese and nearby, fresh shallow graves for perhaps twenty more, with numerous blood trails leading back into the brushes. With about 50 to 60 Marines manning the base camp at this time (the rest being on patrol or ill with malaria and dengue fever, both of which were recurring with a vengeance), the odds were slightly against Battery B if more attacks of the kind continued. Twenty-four-hour patrolling soon resumed, with particular care being given several hours before dawn for all Marines not on patrol to "stand to" and man the perimeter until well after sunrise.

The night of the attack, although still feeling brittle and feverish from the effects of dengue, Jack was on guard duty, helping man a .30 caliber machine gun in a perimeter foxhole. To his right was another team armed with a machine gun, rifles and grenades. Towards dawn, he was awakened from his torpor by the sound of rapid machine-gun fire, followed by several rifle shots, then by the blast of a grenade. Pogiebait fingered the trigger of his machine gun and hunkered down lower in his foxhole, desperately looking all around in his front to discover whether he was the next to be attacked. He was particularly edgy because he was less than familiar with how to operate his machine gun. After a few minutes, there was only the silence of the Guamanian jungle.

Later that morning, following the dawn stand-to before breakfast, Jack and one small patrol headed out of camp near the trail's entrance to see what had happened and to make sure that the survivors of the attack had not set up an ambush. One of the foxholes beside the trail's entrance had been in the direct line of march of a large patrol of Japanese stragglers who were apparently trying to infiltrate the base camp. When he had heard the enemy patrol approach, Leo McDonald and several of the guards challenged the group with a hoarse yell of "*Halt!*" and a whisper for the password. When no response was forthcoming, the Marines fired the machine gun, which jammed after several rounds; Leo then grabbed his rifle, which also jammed; and then he threw a hand grenade. It was all over in a matter of seconds, but now the bodies of 18 Japanese lay near the trail. While their uniforms were ragged, several had carried captured U.S. field equipment as well as perfectly serviceable M-1 Garands in place of their country's Arisaka rifles.

Jack looked at the dead Japanese: though many of the corpses were mangled and bloody, they seemed so young, and all looked half-starved. Then, someone said, "Hey; look what this Jap has in his mess tin!" In the mess tin, still clutched tightly in the soldier's hand, was a battered sliver of chocolate cake—apparently, some nearby American unit's dessert (but definitely not the Marines' dessert—no such luxuries for them) from the night before. Pieces of cake were in several other mess tins carried by the other dead Japanese. Some of them had obviously already gotten inside somebody else's mess area or garbage pit undetected, had gotten their food and gotten out, but had encountered the perimeter defenses of the base camp where they were mowed down.

"They died for *cake*," Jack thought. He thought of their ages, and how small they looked, and how they were obviously starving to death. Then he thought to himself: "*The poor little bastards.*"

Only somewhat later did Jack realize that it was the first time he had allowed himself a sympathetic thought towards the Japanese—*any* Japanese—in years.

Sometime after this incident, a patrol set out by jeep and was moving slowly down the trail when someone noticed a pile of freshly turned-up dirt. The obvious conclusion was that someone had recently planted a land mine. Swerving to avoid the patch of fresh earth, the driver pulled off the road and around it, and seconds later, he halted the vehicle to examine the pile of dirt. Indeed, a Japanese patrol had recently planted a yardstick-type landmine in the trail. The clumsy placement of the mine seemed too obvious and smacked of a set-up, so the patrol spread out cautiously, certain from the footprints and tracks nearby that there was a large body of Japanese waiting in ambush nearby. As they moved back hurriedly to the vehicle, they found the driver had stopped inches away from another landmine just off the edge of the road, perfectly placed so that—had he not stopped the jeep as quickly as he did—he would have rolled over this second mine.

Another Battery B patrol set up an ambush late one evening near a known watering hole. As dawn broke, the patrol spotted a solitary Japanese soldier with ten or more canteens hung on a pole slung over his shoulder. The patrol bided its time as the "water boy" filled each canteen, debating all the while whether they should they try and capture him, wait to see if others would join him, or just "let him have it" after he completed his mission. Even when trying to be as quiet as possible, Marine patrols sometimes had a way of letting the enemy know of their presence. Frank Chadwick recounted the Japanese water-bearer's insouciant response, as he soon became aware that he was being watched: "When he filled all his canteens, the Jap looked directly at us, gave us the finger and fled. We got to laughing so much over his grin and fingering us, no one got off a shot." Chadwick also recalled another unexpected episode:

> On another patrol, we flushed out six Japs and they surrendered, and we later found out they were from a medical unit. We made them strip down [to search for hidden weapons and grenades] and, to our amazement, one was a woman (apparently a nurse). This was the only time I felt sorry for a Jap. She was filthy, skinny, you could count her ribs, her breasts looked like leather pancakes, and she had burrdocks in the hair of her head . . . . We couldn't help feeling sorry for her.

Although their food situation was hardly great, Jack and the Marines of Battery B were faring exceedingly well in comparison to the starving Japanese. The journal entries of a Japanese medic, killed in November by a Marine patrol, reveals their desperate state:

> *12 August*—Fled into a palm grove feeling very hungry and thirsty. Drank milk from five coconuts and ate the meat of three.

> *15 August*—Tried eating palm tree tips but suffered from severe vomiting in the evening.

> *23 August*—Along my way I found some taro plants

> and ate them. All around me are enemies only. It takes a brave man, indeed, to go in search of food.
>
> *10 September*—This morning I went out hunting. Found a dog and killed it. Compared with pork or beef it is not very good.
>
> *19 September*—Our taro is running short and we can't afford to eat today.
>
> *2 October*—These days I am eating only bread fruit. Went out in search of some food today but it is very dangerous.
>
> *15 October*—No food.

Under these circumstances, it is little wonder that the members of a Japanese patrol would have risked their lives for anything edible—even moldy, discarded chocolate cake—or fight with such desperation whenever trapped.

Since the POW incident in the chow line near Agana Field, "Jelly Belly," the new lieutenant, had not garnered much confidence in his abilities from his subordinates. With large concentrations of Japanese stragglers being reported almost daily around Pago Bay, "Doc" Teller and Waldo Wells assigned him to lead a reconnaissance patrol. Instead of taking the point position or another position near the head of the patrol, the lieutenant placed himself in a position of relative safety in the middle of the patrol, a fact not lost on his patrol members. To compound things, instead of placing the BAR towards the middle of the patrol, he placed this—the patrol's most valuable weapon—at the "point" position, much to the dissatisfaction of the BAR's two-man crew. This was because the BAR's gunner (who carried and fired the automatic rifle) and his assistant gunner (who did little more than carry extra ammunition and help find targets for the gunner) were prime targets for enemy snipers. These would often ignore everyone else in a Marine patrol to first try to kill the automatic weapons crewmen, since they carried the patrol's heaviest firepower.

As the patrol neared a cleared field, the lieutenant ordered the entire group to make a headlong dash across the field, instead of using local vegetation and cover to work their way around its edge. It seemed an idiotic order and, in the ever-possible presence of Japanese defenders, quite likely a suicidal one as well. Lugging the BAR and its ammo, Chadwick and his co-gunner Carl Diterando chose instead to traverse around the edge of the field. By the time the BAR team had navigated around the field, the rest of the patrol was out of sight. Separated from the patrol, Chadwick and Diterando opted to "pack it in" and moved as quickly as possible back to Battery B's base camp. On their arrival back in camp, the two were met by the full fury of Waldo Wells's wrath:

> Wells was upset with us even after we explained and really chewed us out. When the patrol returned, Wells chewed out [Jelly Belly], told him to get his gear, get in the jeep and get his ass out of camp. He then got on the field phone, called the Colonel and told him what happened. He told the Colonel that if he [Colonel O'Neil] sent him back, he (Wells) would shoot him on sight. We never knew where he was reassigned to, but he never rejoined us.

Most of the Battalion's patrols did not end up in firefights, but when these did break out, such skirmishes usually lasted only five to ten minutes before the Japanese would fade back into the brush. Their uniforms were often tattered, but they were relatively well armed. Besides standard-issue Arisaka rifles, some of the dead found at the scene of such encounters had Garands or English-made Enfield rifles (the latter likely having been captured from British stocks in Burma, Hong Kong or Malaya) and American field gear. Occasionally, the Japanese dead would be found wearing U.S.-issue fatigues, most likely looted from a supply depot. Another patrol of the Ninth shot two Japanese: one had American gold coins and change apparently seized in the Philippines, along with English-script Japanese occupation currency, and the other was found with a Marine Corps ring, also apparently taken from a member of the star-crossed "old breed" 4th Marines in the Philippines. Nevertheless, despite the heterogeneous collection of uniforms, arms and gear and their own sorry logistical situation, the Japanese evaders encountered by the 155mm Group's patrols were still very resourceful, stealthy and tenacious.

Battery B's last major firefight occurred on a patrol Chadwick accompanied as a BAR gunner. The group spotted and flushed a Japanese fugitive out of the brush not far from the base camp. As he jumped out of the brush with hands over his head, somebody in the patrol shot him, without any apparent effort being made to take him alive as a POW:

> It was then we discovered [Chadwick recalled] it was an ambush, and he was the bait. He had been shot before, and gangrene had set in. We pushed around the bushes and flushed out 10 more Japs who headed

> back into the jungle. The Jap we killed had gold U.S. coins plus other American coins he apparently picked up in the Philippines.

One thing seems apparent from this account: little effort, if any, was made to take this wounded Japanese soldier prisoner. The *ex post facto* justification for this one killing, however, emerges after the dead man is searched and is found to have American coins on his person—therefore, it could be assumed that he must have been a veteran of the savage battle for the Philippines, could have been a veteran of the barbarous Bataan Death March and had probably inflicted abuse on U.S. prisoners in similar conditions. Hence, his death was arguably justifiable—"an eye for an eye"—to his potential captors.

Although this was the 155mm Group's last shootout with a Japanese patrol, it was hardly the last firefight for the rest of the Battalion. Moving frequently, hoarding their food and equipment in caves and ransacking garbage dumps, camps and Chamorro homes for food, small bands of Japanese soldiers roamed the northernmost reaches of Guam's jungles and mountains after the "end of hostilities" were declared in mid-August 1944. The last large groups of these stragglers were targeted in late October 1944 by the 3rd Marine Division. Accompanied by elements of the 9th (now renamed the 9th AAA Battalion), this drive to the north of Guam killed some 100 Japanese. The Ninth's last combat casualty was killed in a firefight during this operation.

These elements of the 9th, however, pointedly did not include the 155mm Group: Major Wells had a run-in with Colonel O'Neil, who had ordered Batteries A and B to take part in this "sweep." With the men of both batteries having seen 90-odd unbroken days of patrolling in the "boondocks," and with each of them soon due for rotation stateside, Walter Wells refused to comply with the order. Colonel O'Neil and

Major Wells already had developed a mutual dislike for one another, and O'Neil apparently viewed Wells's refusal as rank insubordination. Yet, "Waldo" prevailed in the end, and the 155mm Group ultimately did not go on this mission, much to the relief of its men:

> This order was particularly agitating to him [as Chadwick recalled] because all of the original members of the 9th had already left and we were awaiting our turn. Wells was told he would be relieved of his command, but he stood his ground. Thank God we didn't have to go, but the Marines from the 9th H&S Group replaced us.

Small, diehard groups of Japanese defenders still lingered in the boondocks for months—years, in fact—to come. Several MPs were killed as late as December 1945, some four months after the formal end of hostilities, in a firefight with stragglers who refused to surrender. The final holdouts would linger tenaciously for several decades: two more were captured in 1960, and Sgt. Shoichi Yokoi, one of the last two Japanese soldiers to surrender, did so on Guam in early 1972 at the age of 58, 27 years after war's end.

While patrolling and "mopping-up" operations continued to occupy a significant portion of the 155mm Group's time, the second mission for its two batteries—building 155mm firing positions—was also of paramount importance. Jack's time with Battery B in the Pago Bay base camp resulted in another life-threatening incident involving high explosives arising from this second mission.

Ever since his departure from the Russells and his official assignment to Battery B, Jack had been removed from his water purification duties and served just like any other 155mm Group artilleryman. On Guam, of course, these gunners were all serving more like Marine riflemen. His high school knowledge of chemistry, however, had not been forgotten by the powers-that-be, and he had acquired a new, informal specialty: powder monkey. With new gun positions to be carved out of the hard coral of Pago Bay, with no jackhammers to do it and only steel bits of different lengths and sledge hammers, dynamite was deemed to be the answer. Several boxes of surplus dynamite were obtained from a Seabee unit, and the demolition team got to work, with the "spring chicken" Chadwick, "Zombie" Jones, Leo McDonald and Jack among its members.

First, the work detail pounded away at the coral with the steel bits and sledgehammers to bore roughly a six-foot-deep hole. Next, Jack would pack each hole with dynamite, seal the hole tightly with coral chips and water to form a kind of coral-based cement, and set off the blast by means of a detonator. The explosives he was using, however, were old Navy-issue dynamite, noticeably wet to the touch. Anyone experienced with explosives would have likely suspected that such dynamite was especially dangerous in this state: the wetness leaching from the sticks was nitroglycerin, the highly unstable key explosive component of dynamite. Since Jack and most of his pals had never used dynamite before, apart from a few with limited experience in "bunker-busting" during the past year's clearance of Kindu Point, and had never received much official training in how to use explosives properly, they knew no better and thought little of it.

As he had already done several times before, Jack moved over to a freshly completed hole. He packed several sticks of the soggy dynamite into the hole and inserted a blasting cap as the fuse into one of the sticks; the blasting cap was already connected by a thin electrical wire back to the detonator box. Before the hole could be packed down, however, a massive explosion erupted, throwing Jack head-over-heels backwards. He disappeared in a cloud of dust and debris. Jagged coral chips sailed in all directions, and everyone else nearby had their "bells rung" from the concussion.

Chadwick, Jones and McDonald were fully convinced that their old buddy Jack was dead, and they ran through the haze of coral dust expecting to find Jack's body either inert or in pieces. To their amazement, a dazed Pogiebait coughed and slowly pulled himself to his feet. Jack was covered from head to toe with dust and coral fragments; his ears were ringing, and he was bruised all over, but he was otherwise unscathed. The mission still had to be completed, however, and yet all they had to use were the tools and dynamite supply with which they had started. Slowly and more cautiously and after Pogiebait was patched up, the team resumed blasting, but with no more premature explosions.

A War Without End

Of all the stories my father of his service in the Marines, the greater number concerned life on Guadalcanal, the Central Solomons and Banika, or his service after his return stateside in early 1945. Significantly, very few of his tales *ever* concerned Guam. This was a realization which did not occur to me until many years later. Why was this the case? Essentially, this must be because Jack's war on Guam was replete with terrors he had never encountered on the other islands. From conversations with my father and his friends, it became apparent that while the Ninth had some good times on Guam, later on in the campaign, the good times usually were fewer and farther between there than there had been in its earlier campaigns. Although they were nominally reorganized as an AAA battalion, augmented by the 155mm Group for seacoast defense, the tales of many of the Ninth's troops on Guam sound more like tales one would expect of an infantry unit.

Indeed, with all the emphasis on patrolling and mopping-up for its first four months on Guam, much of the Ninth—in particular, the 155mm Group—was largely functioning as a *de facto* "leg infantry" outfit.

Many of the veterans' reminiscences paint a picture of near-constant stress: a nagging suspicion that enemy stragglers lay in ambush behind every bush or trail, and a conviction that, if the "mopping-up" patrols did not end soon, a Japanese bullet, landmine or malaria would eventually finish off the last remainders of the 9th Defense's war in the Pacific. When they actually succeeded on rare occasions to capture Japanese troops, by then any sense of exultation was about the last emotion the Ninth's leathernecks felt. The more common feelings, particularly for the Battalion's "old-timers," officers as well as EMs alike, seem to have been more basic: "*Hell, how many more of the bastards can be left? How much longer is this goddam frigging war going to last*?" And, of course, like a marathon runner nearly out of energy, "*Am I going to make it to the end*?" A bitter rhyme began making the rounds about this time: "*Golden Gate in '48; bread line in '49.*"

Even the terminology used by many veterans of the 9th Defense's Guam campaign to describe their time there has, in the light of more recent American history, an eerily familiar ring to it. *Ambushes*; *base camps*; *patrols*; *infiltrators*; *napalm*; *mopping-up*; *sweeps*; *psy-war*; *body counts*. Viewed from over fifty years, the Battalion's and other units' activities on that island seem to prefigure so many of the terms, tactics and concepts of guerrilla warfare. Hard lessons that may have been learned at great cost on Guam would need to be re-learned, twenty years later, in the jungles and highlands of another Asian country, Vietnam.

After months of hard campaigning with little respite, the bitter fighting on Guam and the stresses caused by the 90-odd days of daily patrolling around Pago Bay also caused some of the Ninth's Marines to question whatever had become of their youth and idealism and caused them to take on a more fatalistic attitude. As one of the Battalion's "old timers," Frank Chadwick, recalled, Battery B's struggles now truly felt like a war without end:

> It all seemed to be lost as our youth had been spent; things seemed to be done by rote, with no relief or even hope of relief. You had no idea what day it was, even sometimes what month it was, and the time of day did not matter, as the sun rose and set and time went on. Talk about zombies or robots: we were in that classification. The old timers knew it and felt it. Despair was a good word for it.

Despite the absence of combat casualties in the fall of 1944, there were still several hundred victims of the Ninth's old nemesis, disease. Jack himself was incapacitated for several weeks on Guam by dengue fever. It was not without good reason why dengue was also called "breakbone fever": he felt as if he had aged forty or fifty years overnight, his joints and cartilage ached, and every movement resulted in massive onrushes of pain throughout his body. For many other old salts of the Ninth, who in days past had suffered heavily from tropical diseases, it was the end of the road: many were surveyed-out from malaria and dengue, including Dave Slater and John Dobkowski.

As Biggie Slater lay on his stretcher in the 3rd Marine Division's hospital outside Agana, awaiting treatment for a massive case of malaria, even in his feverish state, he felt something odd, like someone was stroking his arm. This time, he was not delirious: he looked up through feverish eyes to see his gunnery sergeant, himself awaiting evacuation but almost out of his own mind from fever and from the effects of long-term alcoholism. Not a word was spoken, but as Biggie looked up at old Gunny Smith, he could see that he was mur-

muring something unintelligibly to himself, with tears in his eyes. "The Gunny took care of his own. I guess he felt like it was the only way he could say goodbye to one of his boys," Slater remembered.

For the older members of the Battalion, perhaps the saddest thing was not that their buddies had left—after all, even if they were sick, at least they might have another chance at life—but so frequently, many of those who were well (or, at least, those less obviously sick) and on patrol or off-site would come back to camp to find their sick friends long gone, without a trace and without a chance to say goodbye, thanks or good luck by using the Marines' shorthand expression for almost any sentiment or situation, "Semper Fi, chum." One of these was John Dobkowski, evacuated while his buddies since Cuba, Chadwick and Pogiebait, were out (Chadwick being on patrol and Jack himself being laid up in a medical tent with dengue fever) and not around to say even a hasty farewell.[18/]

All told, Jack simply did not like to talk very much—and to this date, his peers still have little to say—about the Ninth's time on Guam. From what we have learned, it may be easy to see why he, and they, felt that way. Of all the stories he told about it, however, the ones he most frequently recounted to his family were his recollections of nearly drowning as he came ashore; of finding the dead members of the Japanese patrol at Pago Bay, their mess kits filled with American cake; and of how he almost shot the *Nisei* interpreter. The impressions made on him by these incidents were indelible.

One of the more unusual series of pictures Jack kept in his postwar photo album and scrapbooks was a grouping of about a dozen snapshots, apparently taken in fall 1944 around Yona, Guam with a old-fashioned Brownie camera someone had acquired. This sequence of photos depict him and other Leatherneck buddies playing what can only be described as a game of "Marines and Japanese." In some pictures, Jack is wearing his old campaign hat and is drawing a bead with an M-1 carbine on the back of a bare-chested Marine wearing Jack's Japanese sailor's cap. In other pictures, the roles are reversed. Someone else—often, Mabel Morgan, Leo McDonald or Zombie Jones—is wearing the campaign hat and clutching the carbine, and Jack is the shirtless "POW." In these pictures, Jack is either sitting unperturbedly while a "crack Marine sharpshooter" draws a bead on him, face flushed with triumph—*I got the rat*!—or, with hands held high, is cringing servilely, his face contorted with mock panic as he is taken prisoner. "Hey, Nick, did you ever see the picture of my Jap prisoner?" my father teased me when he first showed me some of the pictures in which he was shown "capturing" a fellow Marine. I once asked him, "What were you all doing here?" "Aw, son, we were just goofing off!" One of the ideas at the time was that, with these pictures, everyone in the battery could have a photo that he could send home to his family or girlfriend and that would make him look like the conquering hero.

"Heroes" and "prisoners," Yona, Guam, fall 1944. (Author's collection)

To me, now, it is a little amazing that, after everything they had endured, these prematurely aged youngsters still could muster the humor and energy to reenact a favorite childhood game, playing "cowboys and Indians"—only, in this case, using real weapons and in a much grimmer situation. A psychologist might analyze this as being a form of role-play that would help lessen their fears of the Japanese by casting the enemy in a ridiculous light and also by humanizing a still largely unseen foe. A simpler explanation, though, may be that, despite everything they had endured, Jack and his buddies simply were still overgrown boys with time on their hands for the first time in months, and they used this time to blow off steam in a juvenile, but creative, manner.

That Jack and his pals could do this, even at this late stage of the war, may have been one sign of hope that they would somehow survive and resume their old prewar lives and that the war would someday end.

The Culinary (and Other) Delights of Guam

Even with the rigors of base camp and patrolling, though, there were at least some opportunities for amusement on Guam. One patrol brought back the carcass of a cow they had killed, and a feast was planned for that evening's dinner. The meat was tough and chewy but, for Marines who were subsisting largely on C and K rations again and had not had beef since the invasion began, it was a change of pace, and it tasted pretty good. While the beef was being prepared, Colonel O'Neil arrived on a surprise visit to the base camp and, since rank has its privileges, was promptly served the choicest piece of steak. He ate it with evident enjoyment but, oddly enough, without comment. Regardless of the Colonel's strangely quiet behavior, everyone else present ate his beef with gusto.

When dinner was over, Colonel O'Neil asked to see the Group's officers in private. When they were all assembled, he said tersely, "Thank you for the excellent meal, gentlemen. Now, tell me, *why* aren't any of you familiar with our standing orders that we can't shoot domestic animals?"—and he then excoriated them roundly for sanctioning the killing of just such a domestic animal. Indeed, orders against the killing of Guamanian livestock had been posted since before the invasion. The Marines all listened attentively, but they also duly noted that nothing was said until after the Colonel had finished his meal.

Standing orders and O'Neil's wrath aside, little deterred the Ninth's hardier field gourmets from trying to cook up other local farm animals, or—when especially lucky—having a friendly Chamorro woman kill and roast a local pig for a hungry patrol and, for an added treat, serve up some highly potent "tuba" or "aggie" on the side. One Battery B patrol shot a pig and, as stealthily as they could manage it, smuggled it back to base camp. The returning leathernecks knew nothing about how to dress a hog, but one of their buddies back in camp had some farm-boy experience. He patiently explained to the patrol members how to dress a pig by gutting it and by scalding it, boiling off its hair in a tub of hot water. While several of the Marines began gutting the pig, others searched for a suitable boiler. Forgetting momentarily that they also needed to collect firewood, they scavenged half of a 55-gallon drum and filled it with water. Only then, they realized they had not prepared a fire, and off they meandered to gather the makings of one. Unfortunately, even in September on Guam, afternoon temperatures could soar to well over 100 degrees, and this day was no exception. Several hours had now passed between the pig's killing and the time that enough kindling and materials were available for a good-sized fire. By the time the squad's labors were complete and the water began to boil, the pig's gutted carcass was swarming with flies and stank to high heaven. Battery B's cook was called to give his professional judgment on the matter. With one look—and, more to the point, one quick smell—he assured the assembled group that if he cooked and served the pig, it would only kill them all. The dejected patrol members now served as the hog's funeral detail. "Five Marines worked all day over what we thought would be a good meal but only ended up working even harder to bury it," Chadwick lamented.

As the campaign wound down, several base hospitals were constructed on Guam and, where there were hospitals, there were nurses. Where there are personnel, there must be latrines; and, in the case of one hospital erected near Piti Point, the nurses' latrines were built along a narrow wooden pier reaching out into the sea. Like the Ninth's "seagoing heads" on Guadalcanal, the toilets opened directly, without benefit of plumbing, into the water lapping beneath them. The privacy screens around the latrines were modest at best, so protection from "Peeping Toms" was minimal.

As one nurse responded to the "call of nature" one day, she was startled to see something moving in the water directly under her latrine seat. She leaped up and realized that what she saw moving under the seagoing head was a man's face. The nurse's frantic screams drew the attention of some nearby MPs. Rushing down to the water's edge next to the latrines, they took aim and prepared to fire at what they assumed was a Japanese straggler, only to be greeted by plain English yells of "*Don't shoot*!" Stepping from the water under the latrine, hands held high, was a nearly naked Lt. Colonel Baker, the dreaded "TORSOB" and the bane of existence of many of the Battalion's men, clad only in his skivvies. For his punishment, although he was soon to be eligible for rotation Stateside, in lieu of a court-martial, the Colonel soon found himself being transferred—to a Marine artillery battalion preparing for thc Okinawa invasion, ironically enough in the chain-of-command of Brigadier General Nimmer, now III Amphib Corps's senior artillery officer.

Regrettably, however, this was not the only incident of sexual misconduct to occur among some members of the 9th Defense, however, as the unit's Guam campaign wound to a close. Former sergeant and now 1st Lieutenant Don Sandager, who had won a Silver Star for his actions on Rendova and New Georgia as one of Major Hiatt's airborne forward observers, was ordered to supervise a POW compound. The American forces had taken over the concentration camps in the south of Guam, originally built by the Japanese for their Chamorro prisoners and slave laborers, and converted them to impound their former keepers. Some of these POWs included Japanese civilian women and nurses, Korean "comfort women" forced into prostitution by the Japanese Army, and Guamanian female collaborators with the Japanese.

The POW camp assigned to Lieutenant Sandager and a detail from the 155mm Group was split into two compounds: one for male Japanese POWs and another for the female prisoners. After a few days on duty, word reached Sandager through official channels of claims that some of the women were having sexual relations with some of his Marine guards. He rejected this claim outright as being too fantastic to be believed because the female compound was surrounded by heavy concertina-wire fencing. Still, given the number of complaints reaching intelligence officers and interpreters from the female prisoners, the lieutenant decided he just had to see for himself and disprove the rumors, once and for all.

To his consternation, he found out that the claims were all true: Over the course of several evenings, Lieutenant Sandager observed as several Marine guards attempted to engage in sexual relations with the women through the barbed wire. Enraged and embarrassed after having vehemently denied to his superiors that this was happening, Sandager reported several of the guards for summary courts-martial and other punishments.

While these incidents were extreme, many of the men of the Ninth found more opportunities for sexual peccadilloes or, in a higher form, real romantic attachments on Guam than elsewhere among the Battalion's other Pacific outposts. As noted earlier, many Guamanians harbored a longtime affection for "their" Marines that preceded December 1941, so it should come as no surprise that once the shooting stopped, many of the Leathernecks fell for the Guamanian girls and *vice versa*, although sometimes with heartbreaking results. Besides the obvious cultural difficulties and the fact that "there [was] a war on," the long-standing institutional attitudes of the Corps, combined with strict anti-fraternization rules, had a way of thwarting wartime love affairs. This was best summed up by a longstanding gripe of the old-salt Marines: "If the Corps wanted you to have a wife, it would have issued you one."

In the case of one of Biggie Slater's and Harry Jones' Commo Section acquaintances, a telephoneman named Russell, the young Marine fell hard for a beautiful young Guamanian girl. He began surreptitiously dating her and soon was regarded as practically a member of her family. Russell, Jones and their pals would often visit her family's small village of partly-thatched huts, and Jones remembered her and her family as being "very poor but always neat and clean and very friendly," and as wearing the only readily available shoes on the island, the odd cleft-toed *tabi* sneakers of the Japanese soldiers. In time, however, Russell decided that his feelings for the young woman were deeper than merely a passing fancy, and despite his friends' entreaties not to do so, he decided to marry her. As Jones laconically noted: "He went to see the Chaplain about this and was immediately transferred to an unknown dimension and was seen no more."

Such harsh actions by the authorities may have deterred serious romantic relationships from forming between the majority of the Ninth's men and other Guamanian girls, although little could stop them from making friendships or other kinds of relationships.

Now the youngest man in the Ninth, the beardless Bill Sorensen of its radar detachment befriended the Murray family, the father of whom had been the island's Superintendent of Schools before the war. The family allowed Sorensen and a group of his buddies to pitch camp on their land near Agana, and they would occasionally prepare supper together and pool their own meager fare with "Chick" Sorensen's and his buddies' rations. In 1994, Sorensen and his wife flew to Guam for the fiftieth anniversary of its liberation; on landing, he was greeted by a pair of attractive women holding a sign, "*Where's Bill Sorensen?*" Bill's wife Evelyn coolly eyed her husband and asked, "Is there's something you hadn't told me yet, Bill?" The unexpected welcoming reception was provided by the granddaughters of old Mr. Murray, who had come to meet Bill at the airport at their family's behest.

On the less platonic level, Chris Donner recalled a guitar-playing Battery A gunner from California who "obviously possessed a romantic soul" to match his romantic lyrics:

> After we had established ourselves on Guam and were even granting "liberties" for visiting, [he] used to go forth quite frequently. But when he overstayed a couple of liberties, Townsend [who had received command of Battery A on Reichner's departure to become the 155mm Group's Exec] gave him special duty and restriction. On the next liberty day, the Californian said he was sick, but our corpsman declared he could find nothing meriting removal of the man to the hospital. [He] thereupon gained access to Townsend and told the latter he was the cause of many

> nightmares. Townsend was astounded and ordered [him] out, he then claimed his right to see the Chaplain, and was sent up to Bn. Hdqts. The "Padre" called us up later and said he was placing our man in sick bay although he could not see anything wrong with him. That was at 5 p.m. At 8 p.m. the Chaplain again phoned. "Townsend," he said indignantly, "I am putting your man on report. No one is going to hide behind the cloak of the Lord and get away with it so far as I'm concerned." "Where was he found?" "In an enlisted man's head, with a Guamanian girl!" (Rear echelon!)

In partial defense of the lovelorn Californian, perhaps Chris Donner could only have said as has so often been said: "All's fair in love and war."

An End and a Beginning

In September 1944, the 9th Defense Battalion was officially redesignated the 9th AAA Battalion, with the Seacoast & Field Artillery Group being administratively attached. A new CO, Lt. Colonel Frank Reinecke, who had already served as the Battalion XO on Guam, assumed command from Lt. Colonel O'Neil. In November, after several months of patrolling and manning its guns as well, the 155mm Group handed over its Long Toms and gun positions at Adelup Point and Pago Bay to a full-strength Army coast artillery battalion. By this time, Battery B had dropped from about 120 men at its peak strength, then to 80-odd men and finally bottoming out at about 45 able-bodied Leathernecks; malaria, dengue fever, other tropical diseases and miscellaneous wounds had claimed the rest. "Turret Top" Hiatt became Battalion Exec, having been replaced by Walter Wells as 155mm Group CO, and the entire Battalion was now generally a reintegrated outfit again for the first time since leaving Banika six months before, with its headquarters and billets near Agana.

The unit was now officially an AAA unit, and with most of its flak positions being clustered around Agana Field, Jack and his buddies could watch the gigantic B-29s of the 21st Bomber Command as they left for their missions to Japan and returned from the already finished air bases on nearby Tinian. One would occasionally land on the soon-to-be fully constructed Guamanian airfields. The enormous size and power of the "Superfortress" impressed Jack immensely. How mightily powerful—and how technical and impersonal, as personified by the B-29—this kind of war seemed! "You really felt kind of small around them all," Jack recalled. By late 1944, Jack and his pals was able to watch hundreds of B-29s and P-51 Mustang fighters en route to Japan from the Marianas. Their unpainted, bare-metal wings and bodies shimmered high above in the tropical sun as the Guam-based fighter squadrons linked up with their sister bomber wings from nearby Tinian and Saipan. The sight of this air armada helped erase the last lingering doubts he had as to *who* would win the war. Yet, the ever-present question remained: "Will I be around to see it?" Apart from stragglers (still a serious enough matter), the war on Guam was basically over and, with the fighting getting ever nearer Japan, the worst was doubtless yet to come. Jack knew his rotation stateside was close at hand, but how long would any time at home last before the war began again for him? Would there ever be peace again?

The 9th Defense Battalion received one Navy Unit Commendation for its actions on Guadalcanal, another Navy Unit Commendation for Rendova, and a third for Guam. The Ninth shared with the 1st Marine Division a Presidential Unit Citation for Guadalcanal and a fourth Navy Unit Commendation awarded to the 1st Marine Provisional Brigade for Guam, as well as an Army Unit Citation for New Georgia, plus numerous letters of commendation from the Army, Navy and Fleet Marine Force. Despite its foibles and occasional lapses, the Battalion had amassed quite a reputation as a unit that trained good staff officers. Of its eight battalion commanders, five left the Corps at general rank, including Colonels Nimmer (who commanded III Amphib's corps artillery as a Brigadier General during the savage fighting on Okinawa and retired as a two-star) and Scheyer (also retiring as a Major General) and O'Neil and Reinecke (retiring as Brigadier Generals) and Major Wallace Thompson, the original CO of the 9th Defense Training Detachment in February 1942 (retiring as a one-star general).

Certain qualities had made the Fighting Ninth a unique unit within the American military of World War II. First, few other U.S. ground units could claim that they had campaigned against *both* of the principal Axis enemies—the Germans (*U-94*, of course, and the other U-boat attacks) and the Japanese. Part of this uniqueness was undoubtedly also attributable to its peculiar role as one of a limited number of defense battalions. Still, other aspects of its makeup and service provided the Ninth's men with a higher degree of camaraderie than may have existed in more conventional and better-known military formations. To this day, its veterans often speak of the 9th Defense as being more like a family than a military unit; moreover, many of their wartime letters and papers (which could hardly be chalked up to postwar nostalgia) seem to elicit the same feelings. What contributed to this sentiment?

Certainly, the Battalion had taken relatively few serious casualties (apart from the large numbers of victims of tropical illnesses, there were only 77 combat-related casualties—eight combat deaths, one missing in action, and 68 wounded in action—during the entire war) during its existence and, while facing very difficult and dangerous conditions, had, with notable exceptions, not experienced the frontline rigors of Marine infantry units like those Marine regiments and battalions savaged at places like Tarawa, Saipan, Peleliu, Iwo Jima and Okinawa. Its casualty percentages and turnover of personnel could scarcely compare with that of some Army combat units in Europe, like the 28th Infantry Division, which experienced over a 175% statistical turnover rate in a nine-month period, during which the division saw 196 days of combat and had almost twice the number of battle casualties to non-battle casualties. By comparison, in one of its hardest fought battles, the Rendova/New Georgia campaign, the entire Ninth had a tiny number of serious casualties: 13 deaths (including non-combat deaths), one MIA and some 50 wounded in action. Even with several hundred men surveyed-out due to illness or wounds, the Ninth still had a relatively small turnover between February 1942 and March 1944, the time of its first rotations stateside. Consistently, the larger number of its casualties were non-battle casualties from malaria and dengue fever.

Yet, ironically, it may have been the Battalion's long-term exposure to hazardous duty, without suffering the high casualties of many other combat units, that gave it this unique quality of feeling like a giant extended (if wild-and-woolly) family. In combat units that have already experienced heavy losses, new troops are often shunned: hardly anyone wanted to get to know a green soldier fresh from a replacement depot, who is only likely to be killed or seriously wounded in a short period of time anyway, or who through his inexperience may well get one killed; especially when old buddies have long since become casualties. In units like the 9th Defense, though, there was more time to assimilate and train—both formally and informally—the "newbies," and relatively more time to break them into the customs and routine, even in combat areas, than in a unit constantly engaged in direct frontline combat. Unlike many combat units, too, that saw extremely bloody and violent action but usually faced it within a compressed time frame before being pulled out of the line for R&R, the 9th Defense faced chronic dangers, maybe less direct than storming trenches or bunkers in hand-to-hand combat but every bit as deadly. The unit's experiences were as likely to kill one just as dead as if one had been shot in a direct assault. Naval and air bombardments, Pistol Pete's shellings, and Japanese infiltrators and stragglers, extending over a proportionately longer period of time, were very hazardous.

Also, given the length of time in the Pacific that the Battalion had been deployed with very little break and with few wholesale infusions of new troops or departures until late 1944, there were some critics who believed that the entire unit had "gone Asiatic." This term, originally applied to Marine units that had been stationed for prolonged time periods in China, was hardly intended as a compliment. Like "gone native," the similar British army expression for regiments garrisoned in India for substantial time periods, it might connote certain negative traits and would likely be taken as a form of insult, since it implied a certain slackness and informality, of not going strictly "by the book." To the men of the Ninth, however, "going Asiatic" was something of which they were proud, since few units had seen the kind of unbroken, lengthy service in the Pacific that the Ninth had, and it, too, contributed to the unique character of the unit.

With an exceptionally high proportion of its original members serving with the unit from its formation in February 1944 up until its conversion to an AA battalion on Guam in late 1944—with something over 40% of the personnel who formed the original battalion being with it "for the duration"—there was at all times a core of experienced, long-serving members of the original unit to help train and break in new arrivals.

The infusion of the more experienced enlisted men and NCOs of the 5th Defense's Polar Bears on Cuba can only have helped to establish a sense of "belonging." The Ninth's initial makeup may also have helped contribute to this feeling, with such a high proportion of its original enlisted men coming in as the Christmas Tree Marines, straight out of Boot Camp. The leavening was provided by its cadre of senior NCOs and senior officers, who, in a unit as small as the prewar Corps had been, had either already served together or, at least, had an ample number of common experiences and connections to help tie them together. The shared hardships of the Ninth's campaigns and combat and (as its veterans even today frequently note) the dearth of leaves or rotations stateside further forged the bonds made in Cuba. Lastly, the "agony and the ecstasy" of July 2 and 4, 1943—from the horrors of the first raid, to the triumph of the second—also helped bond all of the Ninth's original men together. "I don't think we ever would have been as close as we were if it wasn't for those two days," Joe Pratl of Battery A reminisced.

Jack and his fellow "Pearl Harbor Avengers" and "Christmas Tree Marines" may have signed up in 1941 out of patriotism, a desire for revenge or simply to seek adventure and get away from home, but by war's end, something more tangible than ideals or military discipline held the men of the Ninth together. One Second World War G.I. tersely explained that tangible factor in this manner:

> Ask any dogface on the line. You're fighting for your skin on the line. When I enlisted I was as patriotic as all hell. There's no patriotism on the line. A boy up here 60 days . . . is in danger every minute. He ain't fighting for patriotism.

On the other hand, it wasn't merely a question of saving one's own skin. As another former Marine (there are no "ex-

Marines") of Jack's generation, the author William Manchester, put it:

> Those men on the line were my family, my home. They were closer to me than . . . my [civilian] friends had ever been or ever would be. They had never let me down, and I couldn't do it to them . . . . Men, I now know, do not fight for flag or country, for the Marine Corps or glory or any other abstraction. They fight for one another.

"I love you like a brother!" Jack would frequently exclaim to his fellow veterans of the Ninth whenever he talked with them years after the war's end. In fact, he would also note to his family that he often felt closer to them than he did to his own brothers. Jack had experienced trials and hardships (good times, too) with the Marines of the 9th Defense that he had never faced with his brothers: "You had to be able to trust them like brothers; it was the only way we'd ever get out of that war alive." The bonds and trust of Marines between themselves had been the keys to their survival, both collectively and individually.

Going Home

I'm only a private
In the 155's;
To me 'tis a wonder
That I am alive—
So I'm singing the blues,
For the rest of my cruise,
As a private in the 155's.

Ditty inscribed in Jack McCall's wartime photo album.

To the joy of all concerned, by October 1944, it was clear

that a large part of the Battalion's old salts, particularly the 155mm Group, would finally be rotated home from Guam. As an additional Christmas present—as if anything else was needed under the circumstances—Battalion issued promotion orders in early December, making Jack's promotion to corporal permanent. Had he been back at P.I., he would be a "little colonel," too, but Pogiebait's buddies took pains to ensure that the promotion did not go to his head. The Seacoast & Field Artillery Group's and Jack's departure from Guam was not, however, without some last harassments and petty indignities.

Shortly before the 155mm Group's departure, Major Wells provided one last gesture, which many of his Marines appreciated and for which he was remembered fondly. He unofficially spread the word that a shake-down inspection for contraband would be conducted before the Group's departure by Island Command's MPs. The MPs had orders to confiscate all diaries, personal papers and souvenirs. The Major casually hinted that his men might, that evening, want to hide in the brush surrounding their billets any of these articles they might have, since the inspection would probably occur the next morning, December 6. As Wells had hinted, the MPs held an inspection early the next morning but, to their surprise, they netted little contraband. After the puzzled MPs had left, the Marine artillerymen retrieved their carefully camouflaged goodies, broke camp, folded their tents and—for the first time in years—turned in their weapons and ammunition—the latter activity being a sure sign they were "going home" for good. After stacking their arms and boarding trucks for departure, they took a last look back at their campsite. Frank Chadwick recalled: "We looked back and couldn't believe that we just abandoned all those arms, ammo and supplies. We now believed this was how the Japs had so much of our equipment found during the mop-up campaign."

After arriving at Apra, Guam's now bustling major port,

the members of the 155mm Group was ordered to fall in, and a young Navy lieutenant attempted to take a roll call of the unit and complete a passengers' manifest for the troopship. It was a fruitless effort. Excited by the prospects that they were finally going home, Jack and his buddies laughed, joked, smoked and generally milled around in a throng, grabassing and congratulating each other on their good fortune. The lieutenant tried everything to get the mob of happy and jaded Marines into formation: he yelled, tried to begin the roll call, and barked out "*At ease*!" and "*Fall in*!" until he was hoarse. Totally frustrated with his inability to get them into order, the incensed Navy lieutenant blundered: he broke into a torrent of profanity, which earned him the wrath of one of the 155mm Group's crustier platoon sergeants. The "sarge" told the Navy shavetail to "watch his mouth," as he was dealing with a group of Marines who had been overseas for three years, had several campaigns under their belts, and were good and ready to go home. The irate platoon sergeant concluded with a warning: "And, *sir*, if you give these Marines any more shit, *sir*, they'll just throw your ass in the bay!" Muttering to himself that he'd had enough of this insubordination, the lieutenant stormed off.

In a few minutes, the lieutenant returned, accompanied by a Marine captain and two squads of Marine MPs. The MP captain drew himself up and announced, with tongue firmly in cheek, that it was either going to be the brig for everyone standing there or a boat to the waiting troopship. Jack and his buddies took the hint, and in due course, they were all aboard the *U.S.A.T. Sea Corporal* and en route for Hawaii.

This leg of Jack's trip homeward took twelve days and, by comparison, made all the Ninth's previous voyages seem like only a bad dream. The *Sea Corporal*, another Army transport much like the grimy old *Sea Fiddler*, arrived off Pearl City and Pearl Harbor on December 18, 1944. In Europe, the last Nazi offensive, the "Battle of the Bulge," was underway through the worst winter weather in decades. In Hawaii, the weather was unusually miserable: it was cool and rained frequently. As the returnees were clad only in their frayed and faded dungarees without field jackets and with many still feverish from the after-effects of malaria, the chill was even more noticeable. They moved into a temporary tent city that served as the FMF-Pacific Transient Center and ate Christmas dinner while they waited for the next ship to the mainland. The fare mainly involved leftovers from a Navy mess hall—some turkey, cold potatoes and stuffing, washed down with coffee—but, at least, it was the first true semblance of a holiday dinner that any of them had eaten since December 1941. A Christmas Eve service was held at the Transient Center's chapel and, grateful that he had survived to see this day, Jack attended. Many of them also saw Pearl Harbor's Battleship Row and the shattered, sunken remains of the battleship U.S.S. *Arizona*. For Jack, the events of December 1941 were now turning full circle, as he witnessed the once far-off place where "his" war had begun while he looked forward to his first trip home in three years.

On December 26, Jack and the 155mm Group (minus Jim Kruse, who somehow—possibly due to lingering malaria—had finagled a flying boat ride back to "Frisco") boarded ship again and set sail for the U.S. mainland on board the angelically-named U.S.S. *Evangeline*. The ship arrived off San Francisco near midnight on New Year's Day, Jack having been heartbroken by listening to the 25-0 loss of his beloved Tennessee Volunteers to Southern California in the Rose Bowl, a game broadcast over the *Evangeline*'s intercom. Knowing his often professed love for Tennessee football, his buddies ensured that Pogiebait got "the treatment" for Tennessee's debacle, and he was teased mightily by his pals.

As the ship entered San Francisco Bay, it was like a dream: the troopship sailed under the Golden Gate Bridge, and as the undimmed lights of "Frisco" shone over the bay's waters, ships' bells, horns and whistles ushered in the New Year, and a large illuminated sign near the harbor greeted the arriving ships: *"Welcome Home, Boys!"* The sign really touched everyone, as the men of the Ninth thronged the *Evangeline*'s rails and feasted on a sight many, if not all, once believed they might never see again. "I don't believe there was a dry eye on board," Chadwick recalled. Of all of his New Year's celebrations, that New Year's Day 1945 was the one that stayed in Jack's memory most fondly: he was home again, alive and in one piece. Since that was more than could be said for many of his friends, Jack was duly appreciative of this homecoming.

As the *Evangeline* docked at the San Francisco Navy Yard on January 2, a Navy band waited pierside. The Navy personnel were the first to disembark, and as they stepped off the gangway, the band struck up "Anchors Aweigh." The Marines had at least expected the band to play the Marine Corps Hymn when it came their turn, but the band had already left before they stepped off the ship. Never mind: the happy and emotion-filled group marched proudly down the gangplank to a ferryboat that took them across the bay to the nearby Treasure Island naval base. The first treat there was the food: a real breakfast, fresh meat and eggs, fresh milk and juice, and ice cream for the first time in 35 months. It was a place where Ration D bars, rice, canned or powdered food or Spam—or mutton or cans of orange marmalade—were nowhere to be seen. They gorged themselves until they all felt sick. "We'd forgotten such food existed," Jack recalled. "So this is how the rest of the services lived; what a change."

After two days of what seemed like paradise on Treasure Island—the base's name seemed so wholly appropriate—Jack and the other men of the Group boarded a train for the Marine Corps Recruit Depot at San Diego. There, they received new uniforms, their own dress greens and field scarves, not ones they'd have to turn in again as after graduation from

P.I.. With the new uniforms came campaign ribbons, and best of all, movement orders for the East Coast complete with leave papers—the first leave Jack and his buddies ever had. *Finally*, he'd be going back home to Franklin! And—for the moment, at least—they were "home alive in '45."

Despite the joy, there was still an air of sadness because it meant that the Seacoast & Field Artillery Group, 9th Defense and AAA Battalion, soon would no longer exist. Although many of the Group's leathernecks knew they would be reunited in other units after their furloughs were completed, the atmosphere was still infused with a sense of loss. Frank Chadwick recounted the scene:

> The Marines of the 155mm Group arrived [in San Diego] 36 to 37 months after their enlistment. This was a great and happy time to be back but it was a sad day in many ways. It was like breaking up a family that had been together so long, fought many campaigns and suffered so many hardships and disease. A bond was formed through these trials of wartime that has lasted a lifetime.

Then came Major Wells's last formation and his last orders to the weary remnants of the 155mm Group: "*Fall out*! Dismissed."

There was a lot of address-swapping going on before everyone boarded buses and trains for their furloughs, and several Marines bought souvenir booklets to record their chums' addresses. Although many of them suspected they might meet again, who knew for certain? While their war in the Pacific was at least temporarily over, nobody left the depot under any false illusions: there were many bloody months of fighting and killing left, and each of the Marines suspected that he might be drawn back into the war before too long, joining a unit possibly far different from the Fighting Ninth.

It would be a different group of Marines from the ones he'd lived, worked, drank, brawled and commiserated with for three years.

The war still went on; the killing still went on. Only the faces, and the lives, had changed.

7

"Home Alive in '45"

Was I glad we dropped [the atomic bomb]? You're damn right I was glad! It saved my life [and] it saved a lot of other peoples' lives . . . Let me tell you: it was the happiest day of my life because I knew I was going to make it.

Jack H. McCall, Sr.

In January 1945, Jack made it back to Franklin on a month's furlough. His train pulled into Union Station in Nashville—the very place from which he had left three years and three weeks before for Parris Island—and which was just a few blocks south of the Customs House where he had enlisted. His mother and father were waiting for him at the platform behind the station. His mother cried as the train steamed slowly into the passenger shed area. She was beside herself with happiness and, for that matter, so too was tough old A.G. McCall. It was a great family reunion for Jack, and it gave him his first chance to shed his uniform and be a Franklin boy again after three long years.

One of his mother's first questions was, "Son, what would you like to eat?" Jack had been mulling over his answer for this occasion for 36 months, and he had ample time to consider his choices. He didn't skip a beat in telling Ruth what he wanted: "Mama, you know those little cucumber-and cream-cheese sandwiches you make for your church tea parties; the ones with the crusts cut off of 'em?" A.G. squinted suspiciously at his son, wondering if the tropical sun and malaria had baked his boy's brain. "Are you *sure* that's what you want, son?" Ruth asked hesitantly. There was absolutely no doubt in Jack's mind: her finger sandwiches were exactly what he wanted for his first civilian meal. They were fresh, crunchy and creamy at the same time, a little "frilly" and decadent and, therefore, totally unmilitary. The sandwiches were like absolutely nothing he had eaten in years. And so, he spent his first day of leave at home with his folks, drinking glasses of cold milk, as if he had never tasted it before, and munching contentedly on his mother's finger sandwiches. He thought he might have to pinch himself to make sure it wasn't just a dream.

It was *so* good to be back home in Williamson County.

Jack's furlough passed quickly, and he spent every minute seeing friends and people he had not seen in years. Everything seemed so clean, organized and different from everything he had faced at P.I. and on Cuba and in the Pacific. He felt as though he was living in a different world, which indeed was the case. He learned that one of his old Franklin acquaintances had become an air hero. Claiborne Kinnard, whose family owned the Willow Plunge pool where Jack and his Franklin High friends had spent many a hot summer day, was an Army Air Force lieutenant colonel and fighter group commander in England. With 14 confirmed German kills to his credit, three of which fell prey in one action, "Claib" Kinnard would win the Distinguished Flying Cross and several Air Medals, among other decorations. Even more exotically, old Class of '40 pal and fellow Marine "Red" Caldwell was now a diplomatic courier, accompanying various official U.S. delegations to London, Paris and Moscow, and Jack eagerly read Red's occasional cards and letters from such destinations with fascination and maybe just a little envy.

While it was a very joyful time for him, Jack also learned the sad news about other Franklin friends who had gone off to war and would not be coming back or who would eventually come home suffering from their battlefield injuries. During his absence in the Pacific, Jack's family had debated about whether to write Jack about the deaths of several of his close friends while he himself was in peril. After much agonizing, and despite Bob's and Al's objections, his parents decided it would be best not to tell him until he returned home. "Our mom made a bad mistake in not telling him about his friends who had died while [he was] overseas," Al McCall noted years later. "She didn't tell him until he got home. Jack took it really hard."

The first piece of this bitter news was the worst: soon after arriving in Franklin, he asked his mother if she had heard any news about his best friend David Gentry. Ruth then was forced to reveal to Jack that David had been killed in Italy earlier in 1944, sadly telling her boy that she and A.G. had not told him for fear it would discourage or depress him in his own dire straits. "So, who else haven't you told me about?" Jack bitterly asked his parents through his tears.

Now, he learned the grim roll call of his dead friends and schoolmates: *Roy Alley*, a lieutenant in the 13th Air Force, killed in action in a B-25 Mitchell over Borneo; *Tommy Lyons*, missing in action after his B-24 disappeared over Italy; *Billy Lynch*, killed in action on June 6, 1944 on D-Day itself, dying "somewhere in France;" *Leroy Suggs*, after surviving a host of B-17 missions over Germany, killed in a mid-air collision while in training at Clovis Field, New Mexico; *Owen Sweeney*, killed on an airbase in China; *John Waldren*, another airman and a B-17 turret gunner, killed in action on a bombing mission in October 1944. The grim list went on and on: *Bobby Akin;*

Scoby Burchett; Vance Burke; Felix Hood; Reedy Sears; Cecil Sims—in all, 103 citizens of Williamson County would not come home alive from the war.

Another son of Franklin who would not survive the war was Bill Johnston. Arrested by the Japanese not long after their invasion of Guam, he was deported to Japan along with many other American-born residents and Marine and Navy defenders of the island, dying in miserable squalor in a forced-labor camp in Kobe in October 1943. He left behind his Guamanian-born wife Agueldo and seven children to fend for themselves in the ruins of Agana after its liberation. In a county as small as Williamson County was in 1945, it was virtually impossible to be a resident of the area and not know at least one family who had lost someone in the war.

Although it was an immediate shock to him to learn who had died, it took Jack a longer time to absorb these facts: many of his best hometown friends were dead, and he was alive—at least, he was for now. While Jack's furlough was enjoyable, while he was able to have a few dates with several old girlfriends, and while he was *very* glad to be home, the knowledge that he was alive and reasonably well—plus the culture shock of being in a civilization far removed from the horrors of the Pacific war—was unsettling to him. With so many of the young men his age away in service—or dead—Franklin seemed like a sort of ghost town to Jack during his furlough visit home. He found it difficult, if not impossible, to explain the vast gulf between his Pacific experiences and the relatively unchanged pace of life in Franklin to his family members, neighbors and civilian friends. Like so many of his peers, he found his experiences to be best understood and appreciated by someone who had faced similar experiences. Possibly as a result of these feelings, "he never talked much about the war to us," his brother Al recalled.

After a month's leave, Jack had to report to his next duty

station, the Norfolk Navy Yard at Portsmouth, Virginia, from which he and the Ninth had departed three years earlier for their war. He bade a tearful goodbye to his parents at Union Station. He spent the next several months at the Navy Yard and at other nearby stations, mainly serving as an MP in the 1st Guard Company guarding naval and Marine supplies and facilities. To his delight, Jack learned that a large contingent of his 9th Defense buddies, including Tojo Whalen, Ken ("Hargy") Gibbs, Zombie Jones, Bill Galloway and Herc Hausen, were also posted to the Navy Yard. He was at Norfolk when he heard the news of FDR's death; he felt it was a terrible tragedy to the nation and the world and, like many others, went to a memorial service on post. Jack also met a beautiful young female Marine, whom he dated for quite awhile. Although, like many of the "old salts," he once had his doubts and griped when women were admitted to the Corps, he now allowed that, on reflection, he may not have appreciated the female Marines and given them the credit they were due.

Despite serving as MPs in the Navy Yard's Guard Company, Pogiebait and his buddies were hardly prudes or models of decorum. Bill Galloway indulged his "need for speed" by buying a motorcycle, which landed him in a local jail near Portsmouth when caught speeding by a traffic cop. Low on cash and expecting to be there awhile, Galloway was amazed when the traffic court judge told him he was a free man: hearing the poop about Galloway's plight, Jack and several other pals raised enough cash to pay off Galloway's fine in full. Jack and another old 9th Defense pal, Tojo Whalen, "used to be the nemesis to the S.P.'s" of Portsmouth. Not that the SPs couldn't track down a pair of obnoxious Marines, however. As Jack sheepishly recalled one incident with the SPs: "They caught us one night about midnight strolling down the street with a case of beer on our shoulders." Dropping their case of beer, Pogiebait and Tojo took off running and eluded their pursuers.

Pogiebait and buddies off-duty at Norfolk. Left to right: Bob "Herc" Hausen, C.D. "Zombie" Jones, McCall and Lloyd Whisnant. (Author's collection)

It was spring 1945, and the war seemed far away again, yet it once more loomed ever closer. Despite Nazi Germany's surrender on May 7, the weapons, planes and ships continued to pour from America's arsenals: later that month, Jack served as a member of an honor guard at the launching of the mighty new aircraft carrier *U.S.S. Tarawa*, dedicated by several of the heroes of Tarawa, including Colonel David Shoup, that fellow survivor of "Black Friday" at Suicide Point. Thereafter, Jack and many of his 9th Defense buddies soon learned that many of them would all be sent to Camp Lejeune, North Carolina together for additional artillery training. Large numbers of Marines, some heavily decorated veterans of the Pacific war, were being gathered together from dispersed postings into Norfolk and Camp Lejeune for advanced training in preparation for the invasion of Japan. One such combat veteran, barely 17 years old, had been decorated several times with the Purple Heart and was billeted in Jack's barracks. Here, the "chick" was frequently and good-naturedly tormented by Jack and his buddies with, "Hey, kid! Ain't you a little young to be a Marine?" "When are you gonna see some action, kid?"

With their artillery training and on-the-job experience, the Corps still had a need for Jack and his pals, even though the Ninth's 155mm Group no longer existed. The U.S. military was experimenting with rocket artillery: rocket-launching landing craft had already seen service in the Pacific (as Jack had, of course, already witnessed on Guam) and during D-Day on the Normandy beaches. By early 1945, the U.S.M.C. was creating field artillery units, often sardonically dubbed the "Buck Rogers' Boys," so named after the extra-terrestrial rocket man of the comic strips and movies, using truck-mounted multiple rocket launchers. Each launcher, mounted on a one-ton truck chassis, could fire a salvo of 36 4.5-inch rockets within seconds at ranges of up to 4,600 yards, and—better yet for its crew—could displace rapidly—"shoot and scoot"—to a new firing location almost as quickly, thus helping the unit to avoid Japanese counter-battery fire. Jack learned that his new mission would be to train with such a unit, one of five Marine provisional rocket artillery detachments, in preparation for the invasion of Japan. He and his peers were told that their new unit could expect to be in the front of the next landings, scheduled for Japan's home islands in the fall of 1945.

The prospects filled him with enormous dread. On Guam, Jack and his buddies had heard of the suicides of hundreds of Japanese civilians and soldiers on nearby Saipan and of the *banzai* charges and last-ditch fights there, ending only after 14,000 Americans had been killed and wounded and with about 30,000 Japanese dead after 24 days of fighting. Of course, they had seen the desperation of many Japanese troops in their patrols on Guam. At Norfolk, Jack heard about the savage fighting on Iwo Jima in February 1945, and the poop was already making the rounds as to the horrors of the latest battles on Okinawa. If the war was almost over, the Japanese surely did not seem to know it yet, and at the time it seemed obvious to every Marine that the Japanese would fight fanatically for every piece of their home real estate.

By July 1945, assigned again to III Amphib, Jack was scheduled to go to Camp Pendleton outside San Diego, in preparation for the formation of the rocket artillery units. These would be lead the first waves of Operations CORONET and OLYMPIC, the planned invasions of the Japanese home islands of Kyushu and Honshu. Jack prayed that something would happen, that somehow the war would end before he found himself on a landing craft heading to another landing and another beachhead.

On August 6, 1945, Jack was aboard a troop train bound for Camp Pendleton *en route* from Camp Lejeune. He now knew that after his advanced training at Camp Pendleton, he would be heading once more to the central Pacific, where III Amphib was being reconstituted for the Japanese invasion. He steeled himself to his mission and prayed and knew that, with B-29s blasting Japan day and night and all those Allied troops freed from Europe preparing to come to the Pacific, the war had to end soon. Still, that nagging question lingered, gnawing at his thoughts: "*When the end comes, will I be around to see it?*"

Then came August 6 and 9, 1945, and two events that removed all doubt in Jack's mind that he would be a survivor and see Franklin again.

Jack's Thoughts on the A-Bombs

If there was one aspect of the war about which Jack was unequivocal, it was his approval of President Truman's decision to use the atomic bomb. On several occasions, when asked what he thought of the use of the A-bombs, Jack responded, "Was I glad we dropped it? You're damn right I was glad! It saved my life, it saved a lot of other peoples' lives, and, listen, if it hadn't been dropped, son, I wouldn't be here, and you and your sister probably wouldn't be here. Let me tell you: it was the happiest day of my life because I knew I was going to make it." Jack was absolutely convinced that, had an actual invasion of Japan taken place, he would have been killed—and let me be clear: not merely injured or even severely wounded, but *killed.* That the atomic bomb saved American lives, he was absolutely confident; that it may have also saved Japanese lives was nice. But, since he mainly viewed it as a question of personal survival and his buddies' survival, the argument that the use of the A-bomb saved other Japanese lives was, frankly, of much less consequence to him.

Jack's wartime buddy Robert "Hercules" Hausen was stationed on occupation duty in Japan not long after the end of the war, and he traveled to Nagasaki only a few months after the A-bomb strike of August 9, 1945. In 1975, Herc and his wife Maxine drove from Iowa to Franklin to visit Jack and the family, and Herc brought along a book of wartime and postwar photos he had taken, including pictures of the devastation of Nagasaki. From his first-hand, Ground Zero view of what the place looked like only a matter of weeks after the A-bomb had been dropped, Herc was, pretty frankly, horrified at the devastation the bomb had wrought, even though it had helped hasten the war's end. For his part, though, Jack accepted that the atomic bomb had changed the world in some pretty horrible and incalculable ways. Still, he never expressed feeling particularly sorry that it was used, and he thought that arguments that the United States should apologize for bombing Hiroshima and Nagasaki or that the *Enola Gay* (the B-29 that bombed Hiroshima and had flown on its mission from Guam's nearby sister Tinian) should be denied a place in the Smithsonian's Air and Space Museum were patently ridiculous. To quote Jack: "They started it, at a place called Pearl Harbor. We ended it, and a lot of good American kids died in the process." Or, as bluntly: "Son, if it hadn't been for that bomb, you and your sister wouldn't be here today." And, as far as Jack was concerned, that was the end of the discussion.

Many of us, living in the present at the end of the 20th century and with the hindsight of history, can—and undoubtedly will—disagree on whether the decision to use the atomic bomb was morally, legally or religiously justifiable, or whether by creating and using it, the United States helped set the Cold War in motion and opened a Pandora's box that threatened humanity's existence and someday still may yet end it. As an adolescent during one of the Cold War's scares, I vividly recall having a nightmare of mushroom clouds going up over Nashville and being able to see them in my dream from my home in Franklin. For Jack, however, as for many veterans of the Pacific War, the rigors of fighting the Japanese, and the absolute conviction that any continued war with them would mean fewer and fewer of them coming home intact or alive, outweighed any postwar niceties against the use of the A-bomb. While a grim view, it appeared wholly justified to those who had taken part in the Pacific fighting.

To Jack as well as his pals, it was purely a question of survival, both personally and for all the buddies made over the course of almost four long, arduous years. The accounts of fanatical Japanese resistance on Saipan, Iwo Jima and Okinawa and the horror stories of some survivors of the Bataan Death March who had escaped to Australia early in 1944 were daunting, combined with what Jack and his peers had already seen first-hand: witness the I-boat's foolhardy torpedo attack on the *Kenmore* off Koli Point; the near-suicidal strafing runs by the Zeroes over Rendova (prefiguring 1945's *kamikaze* attacks); the wild bayonet charge faced by the overwhelmed

Wantuck and Rothschild—where not even their machine guns could stop the attack—and it was only Lieutenant Wismer's AA guns, firing at almost point-blank range and maximum depression, that would do so; the human-bomb attacks on Captain Blake's tanks; the diehard refusals to surrender and the suicides in Guamanian caves—made life seem cheap and the life of a first-wave Marine artilleryman in a prospective invasion of Japan's mainland "not worth a plugged nickel." Also, when even many of the scientists and military planners who designed the atomic bomb apparently failed to conceive of their offspring as anything more than an enormous conventional bomb and rejected the first Japanese reports of radiation sickness among the survivors of Hiroshima and Nagasaki as mere propagandizing, the Pacific War's veterans might be forgiven their failure to recognize at the time that the A-bomb's long-term consequences would haunt their lives and those of their children and grandchildren in the years to come.

On Guam in summer 1945, now serving as a BAR gunner with the 1/21st Marines, 3rd Marine Division, Frankie Yemma learned that his infantry outfit was scheduled to hit Kyushu in the fall of 1945. After hearing that his battalion, already bloodied by Iwo Jima, was to spearhead the invasion of Japan, "I said, 'Oh my God!' I thought I was dead, no kidding,' Yemma grimly recalled. When the news of the A-bombs filtered down to Frankie and his peers, the response was ecstatic: "God bless Truman, he dropped the bomb and ended the war. . . .we were just tickled pink."

There ought to be little wonder, then, that the news of Hiroshima and Nagasaki, horrible as their consequences were, cheered Jack and many others like him as little else had for months: they now *knew*, beyond a doubt, that they had—and would—finally survive the war. On board his Camp Pendleton-bound troop train, the first news reports reaching Jack was little better than rumor—a bomb that could level an entire city? "We couldn't believe the damage the rumors had [reported]," Jack remembered. As the awesome truth dawned that, indeed, one bomb had wrought so much devastation, so did the realization that the end was now in sight.

While war's end brought a burst of spontaneous exuberance not seen in America in years, for Jack and many veterans, it brought something more sacred, special and humbling: silence, peace and quiet—and, when thinking about good friends lost, the silence was that of the grave. For some, the feeling was not unlike that of condemned prisoners who had now been granted not merely a stay of execution, but a pardon. The emotional release for many was, not surprisingly, tears, without shame and such as they had never shed before. As another veteran of the Pacific fighting remarked:

> When word got around that the bombs had forced the Japanese surrender, we knelt in the sand and cried. For all our manhood, we cried. We were going to live. We were going to grow up to adulthood after all.

In Jack's words, "I was just so damn glad it was all over."

For Jack, following the war's end, the last few months of his service was spent in camp in California, and the time passed quickly: more details, more MP duty, more of the usual police calls, drills and inspections, more of the usual "chickenshit." Nothing, however, could alter the fact that he would be going home, for keeps, very soon. During this interval, a Marine recruiting sergeant tried to convince Jack that a good, well-trained Marine Reserve corporal like him could make a decent career for himself in the peacetime Corps. Jack paid him no attention. Although he had enough memories of the good times with his buddies, he also had enough of the bad times to keep him from giving the proposal much thought. It was time to get out of the Corps and get on with his life. *To hell with it*, Jack thought. *It's time to get back to Franklin.*

Jack was discharged at Oceanside, California on October 2, 1945, about three months short of the fourth anniversary of his enlistment. In less than a week, he would be back home in Franklin, via the Atchison, Topeka & Santa Fe Railroad to Union Station—and, this time, he was coming home for good.

One thing that struck him as peculiar soon after his arrival home, much like he had felt during his furlough in early 1945, was the enormous oddity of it all. His homecoming to his small town of Franklin, which had visibly changed little—the sights, sounds and, possibly most of all, the smells were the same as he had left it in 1941—was full of incongruous moments. Perhaps most jarring of all to Jack and so many of his fellow veterans was the apparent but usually unvoiced expectation for them to "put it all behind and just forget it ever happened," as if nothing overly significant had occurred over the last four years and with no time-outs for transitions or introspection. They were joyously welcomed home, but after all the cheering and American Legion rallies stopped, it was back to a business-as-usual ethos.

For many, this made for a somewhat awkward initial return to civilian life, Jack included. The absence of their wartime buddies, who themselves were going back to school under the GI Bill or trying to make a living in the new postwar economy, was also subtly affecting. Instead of the expected emotions—of happiness to be coming home, to be reunited with families and sweethearts, and just to have survived—other sentiments often manifested themselves. These were a reflection of the loss of certain kinds of security: the loss of security of comradeship, of the dead schoolmates, of being surrounded with people who had played, suffered and fought together—the loss of the companionship of others, as

Justice Oliver Wendell Holmes eulogized of the veterans of an earlier war, whose hearts, in their youth, were "touched with fire." Benis Frank, a 1st Marine Division vet and contemporary of Jack, captured the pangs of these unexpected feelings of alienation and loss that were felt by so many after they were "demobed" and heading for home:

> I was discharged at Bainbridge Naval Base on 14 February 1946 and caught a B&O train for Newark, from which I had to take a ferry to New York to go to Grand Central Station to catch a train to Stamford, Connecticut. It was only a 48-minute trip from New York to Stamford, but it seemed longer than that. As I got closer to home and to my parents who were waiting at the train station, I wished that I could have turned around and returned to my old outfit and my buddies where and with whom I felt secure and comfortable. Of course, life had to go on, and so it did.

It took some time, really, to get reaccustomed to life in peacetime America. Despite the GI Bill's and Veterans Administration's best efforts, some vets, of course, never wholly bridged the gap, the yawning mental chasm, between the young men they had been before December 7, 1941 and the new, hardened men they had become. For even those reasonably well-adjusted veterans like Jack McCall—to be called "Pogiebait" no more—who made the transition back to civilian life fairly easily, the war never really left their psyches and memories.

But, then again, when the experience of war had changed so much, including men's souls, how could life ever be the same again?

Epilogue:

The Laughter and the Tears

I came out of the Marines like a wildcat.

Jack H. McCall, Sr., 1987

Years from now you can look in the mirror and say, "I was there and I did my job—WELL."

Lt. Colonel William J. Scheyer, 1943

The young man who does not cry is a savage, and the old man who does not laugh is a fool.

George Santayana, 1925

Jack McCall would occasionally say to family and friends, "Once a Marine, always a Marine." He was proud to have served as a Marine, but he knew from hard experience that a military career was not for him. The terrors of combat, the tedium and repetitive tasks of his stateside garrison duty, and the countless petty indignities he put up with as an enlisted man convinced him that the civilian life was just what he needed. In his own words, when he left the Marines, he came out "like a wildcat." So, apart from various business travels and his 1959 honeymoon with his "Georgia peach bride," Patricia Holmes, by his choice, my father spent the rest of his life in Franklin. I think he truly "lived a lifetime in four years," another expression he sometimes used when talking about his time in service during World War II. He had seen enough of other parts of the country and the world to convince him that home—Franklin—was where his heart was. It was the kind of town where, as the Southern saying goes, its residents "know when you're sick, and care about you when you die." To some degree, in time, that would change: there would come a time when Jack would go downtown and "not recognize a soul," but until the mid-1980s, Jack seldom walked Franklin's streets without seeing at least once person he knew and liked. To some veterans, surviving the war made them feel indestructible. For Jack, it had a mostly and markedly different effect, with him realizing how precious life is and how quickly it can vanish. By his and his friends' reckoning, there were at least six instances of which Jack was consciously aware that he had almost been killed during the war, and probably many more times of which he was unaware. Over time, Jack became a much more cautious man and, to use another pet expression, more of a "worrywart" regarding his family's and friends' safety.

As an old salesman himself and National Stores manager, A.G. lectured Jack, "Don't you *ever* get in the dry goods business, son!," but to no avail. In an effort to make his fondest pre-war dream become reality, Jack took his G.I. Bill benefits and started as a freshman at the University of Tennessee in the fall of 1946, but the time he spent in Knoxville as a 25-year-old "college kid" and Sigma Phi Epsilon fraternity pledge did little for him, and he left college after a year. Despite his father's advice to the contrary, Jack decided to become a traveling salesman in the dry-goods business. As a salesman, business manager and vice president for several clothing manufacturers, his business had its exciting moments, but what he liked best was the opportunity it afforded him to interact with people, to tell jokes and swap stories while making the sale. The war had given him an ample stock of stories that he would share with family and friends but in which he never made himself out to be a hero. He generally downplayed the hardships and terror, although in later years, he would gradually admit to more of those. It was not until 1993, though, that he finally admitted that the greatest fear he had ever known were the times when he had almost drowned at Rendova and Guam.

Jack was fearful of thunderstorms and tornado warnings. As a child, during a power outage as the whole family huddled in the blacked-out family den during a particularly fierce electrical storm, I recall him saying, "You know, that thunder reminds me a lot of a Jap bombardment." Distant heat lightning would also sometimes remind him of the long-distance naval shelling he had watched from afar on Rendova and New Georgia. Whether his reactions to storms predated or followed his time in the Pacific, I cannot say, but if he had always hated thunderstorms as a youth, the shellings he had experienced in the Solomons could only have amplified his feelings. Jack seldom seemed attracted to water sports, swimming pools and large bodies of water, and the family never made a trip to the beach. In retrospect, one wonders whether his life-or-death experiences on Rendova and Guam were so painfully seared into his psyche to afford Jack any real pleasure in lakeside or seashore amusements.

When I was in third grade, my parents gave me a geology kit for Christmas. This gift was a big hit until Jack realized that the kit included some fairly explosive chemicals for heating rocks and giving mineral samples an acid test. No more geology kit! Given how his own high-school chemistry experiences had landed him in some precarious situations, I now also wonder if he did not secretly breathe a sigh of relief when I decided, ultimately, to study history and political science or practice law after leaving the Army, instead of going into science or the clothing business.

Occasionally, anger would bubble up: while it was sometimes ordinary parental irritation at my or my sister's childish foibles, one could sense, at times, a deeper source of frustration. This may have stemmed partly from the subconscious realization that, after being a small part of a major event in his nation's and the world's history, many aspects of Jack's daily life seemed trivial by comparison, and everything that followed seemed eclipsed by his own participation in the events of 1941-1945. Few things in his subsequent life could either be the same, or as simple, as they were for Jack in the fall of 1941. The war had altered his and his family's life in incalculable ways, starting perhaps with his own outlook on daily life. It is also possible that, at times, Jack may have felt a dose of survivor's guilt for all those friends killed or crippled by the war.

When I once told him in eighth grade that I had gotten into a fight with some boys over their claims that the "real war" was in Europe and that "nothing happened" in the Pacific, his eyes flashed fire, and, although occasionally a profane man, his voice hardened even more noticeably. "Those little twerps and their dads weren't there," he growled to me, "so do you *really* think they know what the hell they're talking about?" His response to me needed no answer, but it definitely helped to set me on my own personal quest to learn more about his Pacific campaigns and what he had faced there. Without denying the perils of combat in Europe, my own research only confirmed for me what he had remarked often for years: some of the horrors of "his" war in the Pacific were unrivalled by some elements of the European campaign, and the outcome of that war was every bit as decisive to the fate of the nation and world as the battles that raged in the deserts of Tunisia and Morocco, in the hills of Italy, or on or above the fields of France and Germany.

Sometimes Jack's job provided its own unexpected brushes with the past. One day in the early 1980s, as he pitched a dry-goods sale to a man roughly his own age named Vandegrift, he stopped in the midst of his deal-making: "Pardon me, but I have to ask if you're related to a Marine general named Vandegrift. You see, he was my old commanding general on Guadalcanal." "Why, yes; he was my uncle!" the man replied. Jack was as pleased that he had met and talked with A.A. Vandegrift's nephew as if he had met the "Old Man" himself.

In short, much of Jack's postwar life seldom seemed as real, as tangible, and as immediate as what he had felt and seen during his four years of war. While he never went so far as to call his war years the "best years of his life," there was an immediacy and a sense of doing things that really mattered and made a difference in the here-and-now—being a part of a team, in the truest sense of the word—during the war that, I suspect, eluded Jack in many aspects of the remaining 50 years of his life. In the first ten-odd years after the war, he tried to recapture it—and, maybe, forget the bad memories of the war in the process—with fast cars and honky-tonk partying and a little hellraising.

One favorite new postwar stunt, often played out with Hoyt Doak, an old high school buddy, called for Jack to show up at a roadside inn. On his arrival, he would grandly throw open the door and loudly announce: "I'm looking for my father!" Hoyt, his obliging partner in crime who was already comfortably ensconced, would chime back: "You better watch out for those swinging doors. Who's your father, kid?" Jack would respond, "Luke McLuke." "*Luke McLuke*? *I'm* Luke McLuke!" "*Father*!" "*Son*!" This goofily-staged "family reunion" scene never failed to get an appreciative captive audience for Jack's pratfalls, plus occasionally a free drink or meal on the house. Several events, however, curbed his appetite for late-night honky-tonking.

The deaths of his parents—Ruth in the fall of 1952, A.G. in the summer of 1959—further lessened his fondness for the wild times. His father's death, just a few hours after he visited him in Williamson County Hospital, saddened Jack immensely, but his mother's death hit him especially hard. As her "baby," Ruth had often doted on Jack—after all, her cooking and sandwiches were one of the fondest memories he had of coming home after his absence in the Pacific—and she had provided the brothers with a sense of grounding, stability and unconditional love that they sometimes found wanting in their father. Her loss, and his efforts to help out his ailing father during A.G.'s last years, had required Jack to give up many of his dreams of going west like Bob or of setting off on a course of his own. Jack stepped back further onto the straight-and-narrow path after he met a beautiful and gentle, but savvy, Georgia girl, Pat Holmes, whom he married in 1959.

In 1950, when he was given an invitation to relive his Marine experiences in the flesh by joining a Marine Reserve unit in Nashville, plus getting a shot at making lieutenant and with better privileges that he had ever dreamed of as a corporal in the old-time Corps of 1941, Jack thought about it but declined. That decision may have saved his life: a large portion of the Nashville Marine Reserve unit (and several 9th Defense veterans, as well) fought and died with the 1st Marine Division in the frozen hell of North Korea's Chosin Reservoir later that year. Other 9th Defense veterans, including now-colonels Bill Tracy, Hank Reichner and Walter Wells (with the latter two commanding elements of the 11th Marines during some of the most bitter fighting in Korea), became two-war Marines in the process.

Jack's wartime experiences tended to give him an ability to grasp the wider essence of life and fostered a wholehearted aversion to those he called "pettifoggers," people obsessed with ridiculous or trivial details. His lifelong love of history, cultivated as a kid playing in Fort Granger and finding Minie balls in Franklin, was passed on to his children. When I was three years old, Jack took me to see the centennial celebration of the Battle of Franklin, complete with reenactors on the grounds of what had been the Willow Plunge pool, one of his old swimming holes. On fall and winter nights, he helped his old pal Fred "Brutus" Isaacs build a diorama of the battle to be placed in the Carter House museum. I watched, fascinated, sitting on the Isaacs's basement steps, as Fred and Jack painted and emplaced the miniature troops, horses and guns, and built from scratch the tiny models of the Carter House itself and its cotton gin, the locus of some of the bloodiest fighting in the battle.

He would also, on occasion, take his children with him to Franklin's Confederate Cemetery, where he would muse on life and death as he surveyed the 1,500 graves there. One grave, in particular, was a place that often made him stop and think: it was that of a young European-born Confederate named Hermann Bruner from Esslingen, Germany. The fact that this teenaged immigrant died at about the age Jack had been when he entered the Marines probably added to his curiosity as to the circumstances that had brought poor young Hermann Bruner to the United States, only to die in the Civil War.

Jack became quite a model hobbyist, and soon, his son's room was festooned—it still is—with the plastic planes, ships and tanks he made. The Corsairs, Lightnings and Zeroes, with Hellcats, Wildcats and B-17s, even a miniature Long Tom in Marine olive-green, all came to a landing on the shelves of my bookcase. (He also attempted to paint an oil self-portrait from a drawing made of him on Banika in 1944, but the result more resembled Barney Fife than it did Jack McCall.) This transplanted love of history led, in part, to my decision to try a military career, even if it was not in the Marine Corps but as an Army officer. "Everybody ought to spend some time in the service," Jack said as we drove to my pre-ROTC physical at Fort Campbell, Kentucky during my senior year of high school. "It gives you a better appreciation of things. It'll give you an education, son, and I don't just mean getting a college degree."

I did *not* fully appreciate what he meant at the time, but I began to get a inkling the next day, as a harried Army nurse jabbed my arm three or four times, searching for a vein to draw a blood sample, much to my onlooking father's stifled mirth. My high school years had been a tough time for me and my father, just as I suspect that Al's, Bob's and Jack's high-school years had tested their own relationships with A.G. McCall. Later, after I was commissioned as a lieutenant and as I gnashed my teeth in frustration over some bureaucratic hassle, he and I found that we could share a laugh together and swap stories of our own respective bouts with military snafus. Given that the Marines were frequently dispatched to all the "hot spots" of the 1980s—Lebanon, Grenada, Panama, etc.—I also suspect that my father was secretly relieved that I had received an Army, but not a Marine, ROTC shcolarship, thwarting my desire to become a Marine officer. If he felt this way, however, he would never admit it openly, and he kidded me often about becoming a mere Army "shavetail." Since Jack tended to be a worrywart about his family members' safety under the best of circumstances, the knowledge that his son was out on a recon patrol somewhere or en route to Haiti or Beirut would not have helped him sleep any easier at night.

Jack was a heartfelt patriot, a father who delighted in serving as a Cub Scout and Webelos troop leader and a man who flew the flag every Memorial Day and Fourth of July. He never glamorized war or its horrors, however, as he had seen the consequences of war first-hand. While the McCall clan emerged reasonably unscathed from World War II, he often recalled the hurt and pain the war had inflicted on many of his friends' families or, for instance, on the Solomons Islands natives or the poor Guamanian civilians who had lost all their worldly possessions in the ruins of Agana. He was disappointed that some Americans of later generations did not seem to understand and appreciate what freedom meant, or what others of his generation had endured to protect freedom. When I would ask him whether he thought the American people could ever pull together behind a cause such as they had done during the Second World War, he would take a puff on his cigarette, blow the smoke out pensively, and say quietly, "Son, sometimes, I just don't know." He was no xenophobic nationalist, though, and he was as irked by right-wing reactionaries, ostensibly acting in defense of freedom and democracy but hiding behind the U.S. flag, a uniform or a veneer of "patriotism" as he was by any left-wing agitators.

Jack tended to vote as a Democrat, just as his own father had. This provided a rich source for countless arguments with his brother Bob, who had been Chief of Staff to the Republican governor of Idaho in the 1950s and early 1960s and who later served as an active participant on educational issues in many annual Republican Governors' Conferences. Still, Jack firmly believed it was far more important to vote for the man and not the party, and proved it on several occasions by voting for Republican candidates, much to Bob's immense satisfaction. When brother Bob, a good party loyalist, once kidded Jack on his political views by saying, "Aw, come on, let's face it; you're just a mugwump: your mug's on one side of the fence, and your 'wump's on the other!" his younger brother just responded: "Yep, and I'm damn proud of it!" Despite the hard knocks that he and others of his generation had taken in the Great Depression and the war—or, maybe, because he had survived those crises—Jack retained his sense of humor, even if he was not always possessed of the greatest equanimity in times of stress. He believed in the principle "Character counts," long before any pundit had coined its use as a political catch phrase.

Jack McCall with his family in later years; from left to right, Jack, cousin Lucy Robinson, the author, wife Patricia, and daughter Holly. (Author's collection)

As he watched the decline of much of American industry, including his beloved clothing industry in the mid-1970s and 1980s, Jack sometimes felt very disappointed. He watched as each of his own old companies shut down their domestic plants and outsourced production overseas or closed down permanently. He was not so obsessed with the past, however, as not to own a practical car, even if it was Japanese-made. By 1983, he would be driving a Toyota Tercel. This led to some ribbing from several of his Marine pals, who nicknamed the car "Tojo's Revenge" and claimed Jack was "selling out" in his old age to the enemy of 1941. His pal Jim

Kruse needled him in a 1985 letter: "Sorry to hear you drive a Toyota, but I guess you are entitled to one mistake. Just WATCH IT!" With a sweet sense of irony, though, Jack proudly embellished his Tercel with a 1st Marine Division Association decal and a Marine Corps League sticker.

Still, while other Asia-Pacific Theater veterans may have harbored lifelong grudges against the Japanese, Jack reserved his anger for the wartime Japanese leaders, whom he blamed for most of the atrocities. As for the Japanese soldiers, he philosophized: "They were just poor soldiers, just like the rest of us. We had to fight and kill 'em then, and they had to do the same to us. They didn't have any choice." While others in the Ninth had killed the enemy at close range, Jack was adamant that, so far as he knew, he had never killed a man directly. It was undoubtedly easier for his conscience to know that whatever killing he was involved with was only as a part of a team, as an occasional member of a 155mm gun crew, and not as one who had watched a man die at arm's length as the direct result of one's own actions.

Jack remained similarly philosophical when he witnessed a videotaped chance reunion between his old wartime buddies Bill Box and Frank Chadwick and a retired Japanese businessman during their return to the Solomon Islands in 1988. His attitude was similar when Chadwick shared with Jack some of the off-camera details of this encounter between former enemies. The businessman, who had been stationed on the Canal, New Georgia and Bougainville and had been on the receiving end of the Ninth's bombardments, by coincidence was visiting his son who now resided on New Georgia:

> The old man [Chadwick recounted to Eric Bergerud] told us: "You chased me out of Guadalcanal, you chased me out of here, and then you chased me out of Bougainville." And he described their condi-

> tions. "You were sick and hungry and had one meal a day. But we would smell your food or see you eating. Sometimes we ate grass." He was bitter towards the fools running the Japanese Army. They would land troops with ammunition. But they only had three days' food supply each. The supporting stuff wasn't there. Medicine ran out. Our Marines had to put up with malaria, jungle rot, and dengue. The Japanese, he told us, faced the same thing, but their medics couldn't do anything to treat problems. It had to be horrible... .[After Guadalcanal he] was evacuated to Munda. The old man told us, "We were given some good food. Then an officer gave us a big speech about our great victories to come. I thought to myself, the son of a bitch is crazy. Most of my crew were killed on Munda by American artillery. It was asinine."

Toshihiro Oura, the malaria-plagued young officer near Munda Field whose unit was so battered by the Ninth's Long Toms, would likely have agreed with his compatriot's sentiments.

Other experiences and postwar accounts that he had read of the privations and suffering of the average Japanese soldiers and civilians had much reduced the level of animosity Jack had felt towards the Japanese people as a whole during the war years, and he would have undoubtedly agreed with the retired businessman's comment about the "fools running the Japanese Army." While he tended not to brood about such things, Jack would sometimes ruminate on the mysteries of life and death on such occasions. These were much like the sentiments he had expressed about Hermann Bruner, the dead German immigrant buried in the Confederate Cemetery, on the ironies and tragedies of life and how the "little man"—whether American, German or Japanese, whether white, black or Asian, and whether in 1861, 1914 or 1941—

seemed to have scant control over his own destiny. Unlike Chadwick, Bill Sorensen or Bill Box, however, Jack never expressed any desire to revisit the scenes of his former "glory days"; his once-in-a-lifetime sojourn in the Pacific was quite enough for him.

While he never was actively involved with veterans' groups like the VFW and American Legion except for a brief time during his first years as a civilian, Jack kept in close contact with many of his buddies from the Ninth. Every July 4th, the telephone would ring: "Is this Pogiebait's boy?" "Yessir." "I'm one of your dad's old Marine buddies. Can I talk to him?" Talk on such occasions, as it did at the Fighting Ninth's reunions, usually focused on the good times—"You have to talk about the good times, or else you'd never want to talk about it again," as Colonel Box, Chadwick and Bob Landon recalled on separate occasions. In fact, the closeness he felt towards men like Downs, Kruse, Chadwick, Galloway, Colonel Box, Herc Hausen and Tojo Whalen grew stronger in later years. Jack was saddened to hear of Tojo's and Herc's deaths as if they had been members of his own family. He was unable to attend a 1987 reunion at Parris Island when many of the surviving members dedicated a memorial in honor of the Battalion's 45th anniversary, but he placed a photo of the memorial on the wall next to his framed medals and campaign ribbons. Although diagnosed with emphysema in 1990, Jack was able to muster the energy to make it to one reunion of the Battalion in Nashville and to see some old faces he had not glimpsed in years. The feelings of brotherhood he felt towards his buddies of the Ninth were in large part—to borrow the words of one historian—"the centerpiece of his soul." When his children asked, "Were you a hero, Dad?" Jack's inevitable response was, "No, I'm no hero. I just did my job, like everyone else. We all had to pull together back then."

On Memorial Day weekend of 1997, Jack called as many of his surviving pals from the 9th Defense as he could find, as well as many of his old business colleagues, relatives and friends. His disease was very pronounced by this stage, confining him indoors for his last nine months of life; and, possibly unknown to all around him except himself, by May he also had contracted pneumonia and was very weak. Jack had a premonition that his end was close, even telling his wife that Saturday that he felt death was nearby—to be exact, that he perceived death as being closer than at any time since the war—but his sense of duty was such that he wanted to close the loop with each of his friends and loved ones, one last time, before he left us for good.

Jack McCall died one week later on a Saturday afternoon, 75 years and one month after he was born, surrounded by his wife and children as they recited the 23rd Psalm. For the most part, it was as peaceful an end as he could have wished. Despite his frail condition, he rallied enough towards the end to tell jokes and make wisecracks with his family and with the hospital staff. But, when it became apparent several days after he was admitted to the hospital that he would not be going home this time, he steeled himself with a remarkable fortitude and said his goodbyes to his wife and children with few tears but with a lot of love. "Take good care of your mom and sister," he told me, and then said, "Go on home, son; you've done all you can do for me here. I mean it, boy. *Go home.*" But, this time, I disobeyed him: I did not go, and I think my father knew that none of his family would leave him until the end came. In a coma before he died, however, the old fears reemerged: he began muttering, and while much of it was inarticulate, some of it came forth very loud and clear: "*Take cover! Get down! Tell the Old Man we need help down here!*" As my mother and sister listened helplessly, it was quite clear that he believed he was back in action again, and he was replaying, one last time, all the terror of that day on Guadalcanal when he was surrounded by the Japanese patrol and thought he was to die. Then, later, there was a merciful silence, and peace.

When he died, it was as if he had simply let himself go; it was as if he knew his time had come. All those years of war, life and struggle were gone, in an instant. He died less than a week after Veterans' Day 1997, a day of remembrance for wars and veterans gone by and a day which none of his surviving family will ever regard again in a casual and unthinking way as "just another holiday."

It's strange what one remembers thinking at times like that. The evening that Dad died, his family—wife Pat, daughter Holly, daughter-in-law Jennifer and I—took a long walk through downtown Franklin, several hours after he had passed away. It had rained for six or seven days, but that Saturday evening, as we crossed the Harpeth River bridge next to the ruins of old Fort Granger where Jack had played so often as a child, the clouds broke, and the sky was painted in bright pastel colors of blue and pink. Swallows and chimney swifts skimmed through the early evening air. I did not recall ever having seen a sky in those colors before. As we neared the square, the old granite statue stood, an eternal sentinel silently watching over Franklin as it had for almost one hundred years. The ebbing sun over the roofs of the town provided a fiery backdrop.

I thought to myself, *Dad, you know, you often had a tough life, but you also had a good life. You died the way everybody should: in your home town, surrounded by your loved ones, with no pain. But, boy, am I ever going to miss you.* And, many months later, I still do.

I have often since wondered what it was that gave my father the bravery and humor that he mustered in his last months and hours to hold on against a treacherous disease for as long as did—he survived a full three years longer than his own doctors had predicted when his illness was diagnosed. How strongly it seemed to me that he faced that last lonely challenge, from which he knew there could be no hope and no escape. I can only hope that I will be able to summon up a similarly rare fortitude within me when my own time comes, whenever that day may be.

A few weeks after Jack died, I looked among some of the artifacts he had kept and mentally tallied up something of what was left of him as tokens of proof of his existence on earth: a lock of his hair; several scrapbooks of faded newspaper and magazine clippings; his dress-green uniform, slightly moth-eaten but in remarkably good shape for a fifty-year-old suit of clothing; a battered Marine campaign hat with a large hole in its crown, nibbled away by a long-dead Cuban rat; a picture frame full of medals and campaign ribbons; a battered metal box for his water purification gear, with a brown, topless dancing girl painted on one side next to the words "Russell Islands;" photographs and drawings and a brass-sheathed Bible; and a black-and-white photograph of a young, toothy Marine, after long campaigning still looking much like he had just graduated from high school, taken over fifty years and a lifetime ago. Scrapbooks and photo albums full of faded clippings and pictures. A tombstone. A family and dear friends that miss him.

And memories of a fine man, a loving father, a good friend to have on one's side, and a proud Marine to the end.

"Semper Fi, Mac"

"Once a Marine, always a Marine."

Inscribed on the 9th Defense and AA Battalion Memorial, Parris Island, South Carolina

Among Marines of all ranks, one of the most common sayings—both for those in World War II and even for today's Marines—is the expression "Semper Fi." At its simplest, the phrase is a contraction of the Marines' official Latin motto, *Semper Fidelis*, "Always Faithful," and this motto is emblazoned on the Marine Corps's anchor-and-globe insignia, where it is inscribed on a scroll clenched in the beak of an American eagle sitting on top of the world. In everyday Marine usage, though, "Semper Fi" was more than just a mere motto: like the Hawaiian word "*Aloha*," it could mean either "hello" or "goodbye." Depending wholly on the context and the way it was uttered, the phrase was capable of having a wide range of sometimes contradictory meanings. As one wartime Marine officer noted, the meaning and usage of "Semper Fi" far surpassed its literal translation: "[I]t is commonly used by marines, as occasion demands, for 'Frig you, Mac—I got mine,' or 'Pull up the ladder, Mac—I'm aboard.' " As another Marine veteran put it:

> But you know, what [Semper Fi] really meant was, "Look, pal, you got to take care of yourself out here." You might ask another Marine for a cigarette and he'd tell you, "Semper Fi, Mac." Then the chances are he'll give you one, but what he means is for you to try and get your own the next time. It was no picnic in the Pacific and you had to take care of yourself.

At its essence, "Semper Fi" served as a shorthand recognition symbol, a code instantly identifiable by any Marine. To a Marine in trouble, the yell meant that help was on the way. To a Marine griping about his lot in life, the retort meant, "Quit your bitching, chum; you volunteered for this." To a Marine screwing up, the challenge meant that he had better get himself squared-away or he would have to face the consequences. To a Marine departing for another shore, the valediction meant that his buddies were thinking about him and, in their own subtle way, were saying goodbye. It can be used as a salutation and, as Taps are played over a solitary grave, it is uttered by Marines as they bid a last farewell to one of their own, as a kind of martial Kaddish. Sometimes, when they say it, some of them will let themselves cry. Most of the old veterans, however, remain as stoical as they can at these ceremonies of departure. This was a generation that grew up with incredible sadness, discipline and privation, and tears still do not come easily to those who were trained that more respect is shown to the departed by retaining one's composure than by letting it all go. "Not showing our emotions doesn't mean we love them any less," Dave Slater once remarked to me. "After all, they were our buddies through thick and thin. It's just what they'd want us to do, and what we'd want them to do for us when we go."

At each annual reunion of the Ninth, fewer of Jack's buddies gather due to the infirmities of age or the costs of travel, yet nobody wants to end these reunions and few wish to consolidate with other defense battalions' reunions. Such a move would imply more than the physical death of the unit's members, like cells in a living organism: it would imply a death of the Battalion, of the organism itself. "I guess we'll continue to hold a reunion until the last two of us meet in our wheelchairs in a phone booth somewhere," David Slater, secretary of the Ninth's "alumni" association, wistfully remarked to those gathered at the latest reunion. Sadly, that day may not be far off.

Of the twelve million who served in all the various branches of the American armed forces during World War II, in 1998, only approximately half were still surviving, and according to Department of Veterans Affairs estimates, these are dying at a rate of about 32,000 a month—in other words, over one thousand *daily*. As the old veterans of the Ninth and their brethren face the future, over fifty years after the end of their war, they find that they are saying "Semper Fi" more and more frequently as a last goodbye to their buddies. Will somebody be there to say it over their own graves? I, for one, fervently hope so.

It is also one of the last things I ever said to my father, as he lay on his deathbed. By the time I uttered them, he was unconscious and had only a few hours left to live, but as I whispered them to him, I could swear I saw his dark eyebrows flutter ever so briefly. I would like to think that those words gave him a last, pleasant memory of times and friends long gone. I whispered it again to myself, some two and a half months later, as a squad of young Marines fired a rifle salute over his and his brother Bob's grave and as the mournful sound of Taps rolled forth, as their family laid them to rest, side by side, just as brothers should be, on a cool September morning, in the soft, dark, Tennessee earth outside Franklin. Two of A.G. and Ruth McCall's boys were finally back home again.

Semper Fi, Mac. Semper Fi, Dad. Goodbye, old timer. I love you.

They shall not grow old as we that are left grow old.
Age shall not weary them, nor the years condemn.
At the going down of the sun and in the morning
We shall remember them.

Robert Laurence Binyon

ACKNOWLEDGMENTS

This could never have been prepared without the help, advice and incredible assistance (and patience) of various persons, all of which contributed to make this project a true team effort.

First and foremost, I would like to thank several of Jack's personal friends, Frank Chadwick, Al Downs, Bill Galloway, Jim Kruse and Frank Yemma, who have graciously spent much of their personal time and energy in helping provide me with their memories and details of their experiences that augmented what my father had told me or what he had recounted in his own letters, notes and papers. In a real sense, this story is their story as well, since it recounts many experiences they all shared together during four grueling years. In particular, Frank Chadwick has spent a considerable amount of time talking with me, providing me with correspondence and notes derived from his own and considerable research and recollections of the 9th Defense Battalion; in commenting on several drafts; and in sharing with me and my father several years ago a copy of a remarkable videotape, prepared by him and Bill Box, on a visit to Guadalcanal and Rendova-New Georgia in 1988, in which the two veterans revisited what must have been almost every piece of real estate on which the 155mm Group had been stationed from late 1942 to 1944. Frank is a veritable living history museum of the Marine Corps and in particular, one small part of it, the 9th Defense Battalion. I owe an immense debt of gratitude to Frank, as without his "labor of love," I sincerely doubt if this book could have advanced as quickly and as completely as it has.

I am equally indebted to David ("Biggie") Slater, who graciously spent the better part of a month reviewing and commenting on several early drafts of this book as well as sharing his own personal reminiscences of the Pacific war, *Jungle Vignettes*, portions of which are published here for the first time, and to Colonel Hank Reichner, Colonel Bill Box, Dr. Chris Donner, and Joe Pratl, each of whom also spent a considerable amount of time reviewing and commenting on early drafts of this book and who also generously shared their own accounts of the fighting with me.

I am deeply indebted to other members of the "Fighting Ninth," in particular, to Paul Berry; Horace ("Smiley") Burnette; Ray Carman; Cliff Cribbe; Milt Davis; Herb Dougherty; John Dobkowski; Willie Dufour; John Hall; Ted Hitchcock; John Henry Johnson; Colonel (Ret'd.) Bob Landon; Jerry Morris; Brother Andrew Sorensen (who also provided copies of his sketches drawn overseas); Bill Sorensen; Dr. George W. ("Doc") Teller; Nick Zingarelli; the late Amsa Bodine; and to the numerous other members at large of the 9th Defense and AAA Battalions Association for their contributions to the unit's alumni newsletters, *Poop!* and *Son of Poop*!, which provided me with scores of tidbits and insights I have been able to work into this narrative.

Acknowledgments are due to the following, as well: for his critiques of an early draft of this book and for sharing with me his own accounts of life as a 1st Marine Division leatherneck in World War II and Korea, former Chief Historian of the Marine Corps Benis M. Frank; the late Professor Charles Johnson, Director Emeritus of the University of Tennessee Center for the Study of War and Society, for encouraging me to take this from a 100-page manuscript to a full-fledged book; Louise Lynch, Chief Archivist of the Williamson County Archives, Franklin, Tennessee (where Jack's uniform and some of his other personal effects from the war are on display); Major (Retired) Charles Melson, the current Chief

Historian, U.S. Marine Corps, himself a noted expert on the Ninth and its sister defense battalions (and son of 155mm Group vet Bill Melson) and for graciously providing his time and the fruits of his own research on the Marine Defense Battalions; and, for his own comments and encouragement, Professor Eric Bergerud, author of *Touched with Fire: the Land War in the South Pacific*, who is currently at work on a sequel dealing with air and anti-aircraft operations in that theater.

Others to whom my thanks are fully due include my law colleagues John A. Lucas and Martin B. Bailey of Hunton & Williams (the latter who was instrumental in helping me tracking down the fate of *U-94*, the German sub whose crew was guarded by the Ninth); Donald F. Paine and Robert W. Ritchie, who reviewed several early drafts with me and provided me with their insightful criticisms; Jeffrey Bucheit of the Historical Electronics Museum in Baltimore, Maryland, for sharing with me his museum's extensive archives on the early development and usage of radar by the U.S. military; military historians and writers Mark F. Cancian, Jon T. Hoffman, and Dr. Frank N. Schubert; and for their general comments, observations and encouragement, former Marine combat correspondent Samuel E. Stavisky; Damon Gause; Captain (Retired) Wilbur Jones, U.S. Navy; Dr. Toni E. Lesowitz; Lisa R. Lee; Maj. General (Retired) William B. McGrath, U.S. Army; Edward T. Brading; Bennett Cox; Lyn Sullivan Pewitt; the late Wilson Herbert; Colonel (Retired) Joe G. Wheeler; John Doak; Hoyt Doak; Billy Inman; Major Joseph A. Sharbel, Headquarters, U.S. Marine Corps; Ernie Tracy of Tracy Photography, Knoxville, Tennessee; and Mr. Wade Davies.

My late debt of gratitude is overdue to several professors and teachers who cultivated my own love of history and literature over the years, namely Ron Pritchard; Dr. Tom Phelps; my father's old high school friends, Coach Jimmy Gentry and Fred and Julia Isaacs; and several Professors of History and

Political Science at Vanderbilt University, Charles Delzell, my faculty mentor Robert H. Birkby, William C. Havard and the late Professors Howard Boorman, Forrestt Miller and Captain Sidney Banks.

I also have to thank my mother, Patricia H. McCall, my sister Holly McCall Dolloff, and my uncle and aunt, Albert G. McCall, Jr. and Dorothy McCall (Mrs. Robert McCall) for their recollections and remembrances of my father, Bob McCall and other family members, which have been integrated in this account as well. I also thank my wife, Jennifer Ashley-McCall, and my daughter, Margaret, for their patience and love in allowing me to take considerable amounts of time and energy away from them in preparing this. I dedicate this account to Margaret, in the hopes that she and her generation never have to contend with anything as deadly and savage as the war in which my father participated, and that, if she must—God willing—she survive it with the same sense of humor and high spirits that helped her "Tete" to survive.

Last, I wish to thank my father, Jack H. McCall, Sr., for making this account—and me—possible in the first place, and for providing me with friendship, love, support, discipline and a hero through 36 years of my life. My only regret is that he was not able to tell this story himself, in his own words. I hope that he would be proud, nevertheless, of this accounting of his life during four momentous years and I hope I have done credit to the memory of a fine man, a great father, a good friend to have, and a true Marine.

I respectfully dedicate this account to his memory, and to the memory of another fine Marine and former Franklin boy, his brother Robert B. McCall (1916-1994), and Jack's friends and buddies of the 9th Defense Battalion, Fleet Marine Force, U.S. Marine Corps, 1942-44, and of Franklin High School's Classes of 1940 and 1941.

Jack H. McCall, Jr.
Knoxville, Tennessee

Appendix A

After the Colors Faded: A Selective History of What Happened to Them After the War

Lt. Colonel "Baker" (155mm Group CO): After the war, Colonel "Baker" apparently remained in the Corps for several more years. He was last seen by Hank Reichner—also (and undoubtedly to his former superior officer's amazement) a career Marine—running the Second Division Officers' Mess in Sasebo, Japan during the occupation of Japan, and married to a very attractive young woman. As many a man of the 155mm Group might have said of their temperamental and eccentric former group commander: "Go figure."

William T. Box (CO, Battery B; 155mm Group Staff): In a 1985 letter, Bill Box shared his life after the war with Jack McCall:

> Certainly, for us, WWII was the "Good War" and a period of time we fondly remember. You and I and the 9th were part of that. I lost a son in the "Bad War," Vietnam. He was in the Army. I had six children. My first wife died in 1956. I married a widow with three

> boys; we've been married 26 years [in 1985]. We got all our children through college. They're all good people and making their way in life.
>
> I've been fairly successful in business. I was President of a manufacturing company that made equipment for the oil industry. I'm now semi-retired. At the moment, we have four grandchildren, so we're not doing too good in that department.

Now retired from the oil business (and a retired Marine Corps Reserve colonel, as well), Bill Box lives in the San Francisco Bay area. He and Frank Chadwick revisited the scene of their "glory days" in fall 1988, traveling to Guadalcanal and the Central Solomons.

Horace (Smiley) Burnette (Battery A): After the war, Platoon Sergeant "Smiley" Burnette returned to the East Tennessee hills and became a dental technician in Sevierville, Tennessee. Only retired since 1997, he now lives with his family outside Charlotte, North Carolina. Undoubtedly one of the best-loved NCOs in the 155mm Group, Smiley never forgot his "boys," however: he and Colonel Hank Reichner were instrumental in pressing the Department of the Navy to award, some fifty years after the fact, a long-delayed Purple Heart to their battery mate, Bill Galloway, for the wounds Bill received in September 1943 when the defective 155mm shell destroyed Galloway's Long Tom at Piru Plantation, an incident that almost killed or maimed Jack McCall in the process.

Francis Chadwick (Battery B): After the breakup of the 155mm Group and a tour of duty stateside, Frank Chadwick reenlisted in the Corps for another two years on the promise of 30 days leave, promotion to Platoon Sergeant, and a choice of duty station on the Eastern Seaboard. After being stationed at Brooklyn Navy Yard for only two weeks after getting married, Frank was transferred to Bermuda for two years. He left the Corps in December 1947. Chadwick writes: "Upon my discharge from the Corps I decided I needed an education to support my wife and daughter. When I joined the Corps, I had an *eighth grade* education." He went back to prep school for a year, attended Tri-State University on the G.I. Bill and graduated in three years with a B.S. in chemical engineering. After several jobs, Chadwick began a lengthy career with IBM that led to more higher education—a M.S. in Engineering Management and later a Ph.D. in Engineering Economics. Dr. Chadwick retired as a Senior Engineer—Project Engineering (Chemical) from IBM at the age of 59. He now splits his time between his home in Florida and visiting with his family in his old home town of Binghampton, New York.

John J. Dobkowski (Battery B): After his discharge from the Corps, John Dobkowski became involved in the plastics and manufacturing industries and ultimately started a business in his hometown of Erie, Pennsylvania that specialized in the manufacture of various types of prototype products for various companies. This was quite a booming enterprise, and it stood John in good stead for many years. Now semi-retired and a widower for several years, he delights in traveling in his recreational vehicle throughout the United States and in enjoying the leisure time he seldom had for much of his life.

Christopher S. Donner (Battery A): Due to his lack of sufficient points for rotation stateside with the rest of the 155mm Group, Chris Donner was not among those who were present in San Francisco at the Group's formal disbanding. Instead, after Christmas liberty in Hawaii, Captain Donner was ordered to join the 1st Marine Division's artillery regiment, the 11th Marines, in time for service in the invasion of Okinawa on April 1, 1945. He was assigned as a forward observer and artillery coordinator to the 7th Marines, an infantry outfit. As an "FO," Chris participated in some of the most hellish fighting of that campaign alongside the 7th's infantrymen in the assaults on the village of Kakazu and Wana (Dragon Tooth)

Ridge. Finally "up" for rotation home, Donner was en route to Pearl Harbor aboard the carrier *Card* when word of the A-bombings reached him. A retired Marine major who (like several other veterans of the Ninth) was reactivated for the Korean War, former Penn State sociology professor and high school teacher and counselor, Donner returned to visit the Solomons in 1967, and he wrote of his experiences for the *Marine Corps Gazette*. An avid scuba diver and snorkeler, Chris Donner now lives in Florida.

Al E. Downs (9th Platoon, Parris Island; Battery B): After leaving the Ninth on Banika in 1944, Al Downs returned home to marry his beloved Rosie at Camp Lejeune, North Carolina, a marriage that has lasted over fifty years. He was stationed at Camp Lejeune and Jacksonville, Florida and, like so many other Marines, was awaiting orders for the invasion of Japan at war's end. He returned home to his native Pittsburgh and was a municipal bus driver for 25 years before retiring to his family's home of over 70 years just outside Pittsburgh, where he still lives, a proud father and grandpa.

William Galloway (Battery A; Norfolk Navy Yard and Camp Lejeune): Bill Galloway became a tugboat and barge boat skipper and operator after the war and lives with his wife Maril in Titusville, Florida. Bill finally received, some 45 years after the war, the Purple Heart he justly deserved for his wounds from the exploding Long Tom, thanks to the efforts of Colonel Reichner and the musically talented Sergeant Smiley Burnette (a retired dental technician now living in the Charlotte, North Carolina area).

Robert (Hercules) Hausen (Battery B; Norfolk Navy Yard and Camp Lejeune): An Iowa farm boy, "Herc" Hausen left the Marines in 1946 and moved back to Iowa to follow his long-time plans of working a family farm. Like many Midwestern farmers, however, he fell on hard times in the mid-1980s and finally sold his farm. He died in th late 1980s. Jack and Herc's

Marine friends chalked the cause of his death up to heartbreak, as much as to natural causes.

Otto Ites (Oberleutnant zur See, U-94, Kriegsmarine): Previously the destroyer of 14 Allied ships and holder of the *Ritterkreuz* ("Knight's Cross," roughly the Nazi equivalent of the U.S. Medal of Honor), Otto Ites—one of the first of many POWs taken by the Ninth—survived his wounds and life in a U.S. POW "cage" to become at first a dentist after the war. With the creation of the West German government and *Bundeswehr*, though, he next joined the Federal German Navy in 1956. Ironically enough, given his own experiences off Cuba in 1942, Ites served as the skipper an anti-submarine destroyer. He retired as a rear admiral in 1977. A wartime enemy turned postwar ally, Ites died three days before his 64th birthday in February 1982 in Norden/Ostfriesland, West Germany.

James V. Kruse (9th Platoon, Parris Island; H&S Battery, 155mm Group): After the war, Jim Kruse returned to his hometown of Elkhart, Indiana, where he served as a member of the Elkhart Police Department and for many years was a member of its scuba and rescue squad. He now lives in Florida.

Robert Landon (Battery B): After returning from the Pacific with the 155mm Group, Bob Landon did not leave the military for many years. After completing his active duty Marine service, he transferred to the Air Force, just in time to be sent to the Korean War. He became an Air Force commissioned officer and was responsible for the security of several Air Force nuclear missile units. These responsibilities were later shifted to the Army's Military Police Corps, so Bob then found himself becoming an Army officer, retiring as a full colonel in the MPs in 1973 after several command tours. After his retirement, Bob was the warden of the North Dakota State Penitentiary for several years and served in various capacities in Virginia's Department of Corrections, including service as that department's director. He retired in

1987 after spending several more years as an executive with the Corrections Corporation of America. Bob now lives outside Chattanooga, Tennessee with his wife, Yvonne.

Albert G. McCall, Jr.: Jack's oldest brother, Al spent the war years as a draftsman and aircraft designer for the Glenn Martin Aircraft Company (later to become Martin Marietta and now, Lockheed Martin) in Baltimore. At Martin, he was a member of the design teams for the B-26 Marauder medium bomber, the PBM Mariner and Mars flying boats, and other aircraft. He remained with Martin after the war and was actively involved in the design of other Martin aviation products, including the Air Force's MATADOR and MACE cruise missiles in the 1950s, the Project ORION anti-satellite missile program of the early 1960s (one of the precursors of the SDI/"Star Wars" missile defense programs), and the Air Force's DYNA-SOAR and lifting body projects in the mid-1960s, which were predecessors of today's Space Shuttle. After leaving Martin in 1969, Al began a second career with Teledyne Isotopes and designed components of the SNAP nuclear generators used to power various NASA satellites, including the 1976 VIKING Mars probe. Now 86, the proud father of two children and the grandfather of two, Al McCall resides in a Baltimore suburb.

Robert B. McCall (2d Defense Battalion): After leaving the Corps in 1945, like his older brother Al, Bob McCall never moved back to Franklin. He and his wife Dorothy moved from California back to Idaho, not far from his duty station at the naval depot in Pocatello, where he joined the Idaho State Police. Bob became locally famous as a radio celebrity with his own weekly public-service shows, *An Idaho Tragedy*, sponsored by the Idaho State Police. The popularity of this radio show and his own statewide contacts provided Bob with a springboard into state and national Republican politics. He served as the Chief of Staff to Idaho's Governor Bob Smiley. Afterwards, Bob moved to Denver and became the executive director of the Education Commission of the States, a non-governmental education agency, a consultant on state-level education and funding for education, and a frequent participant in the annual National Republican Governors' Conferences for many years. He and Dot later sold their small ranch in Idaho and condominium in Denver and moved to Fargo, North Dakota, the home of his daughter and only child and her family. Bob McCall preceded his little brother Jack into one last challenge—this time, into death—after waging his own brave and lengthy battle with cancer in February 1994.

Joseph Pratl (10th Defense Battalion; Battery A, 9th Defense): After the 155mm Group's breakup, Joe and his longtime sweetheart Barb were married in their hometown of Chicago on his 30-day furlough, but their wartime honeymoon was short. After serving at Camp Peary, Virginia and Camp Lejeune, Joe was preparing for reassignment in August 1945 to Camp Pendleton for advanced infantry training and, after that, the invasion of Japan. With war's end, Pratl was transferred to Washington to guard the Navy Department's headquarters and was discharged at Quantico in October 1945. Joe became a machinist, which had long been a dream of his. After working a series of machinist jobs, he ultimately worked for 20 years for the Chicago Transit Authority, retiring in 1986. Joe and Barb Pratl raised seven children, one of whom died as an infant. Still, Joe reports, "Life has been good to me here in Chicago."

Henry H. Reichner Jr. (CO, Battery A): Following the breakup of the 155mm Group, Hank Reichner served as Operations Officer of the 3/10th Marines on Saipan and in the occupation forces in Japan until 1946. Lt. Colonel Reichner served in Korea from 1952-53 as a staff officer and later as commander of the 4/11th Marines. Later, he taught at the Naval War College and served as Chief of Staff to the U.S. Naval Mission to Haiti; CO of the 10th Marines; Deputy

Chief, Far East Plans, to the Joint Chiefs of Staff; and Assistant G-3 (Plans), Military Assistance Command-Vietnam. Retiring from the Marines in 1968 as a full colonel, he embarked on a varied second career in the business and civic affairs of his hometown, Philadelphia. He still serves as a securities arbitrator for the New York Stock Exchange, the National Association of Securities Dealers and the Municipal Bond Securities Board, as well as being a director of the Philadelphia Belt Line Railroad and Independence Blue Cross. As Hank Reichner says: "In short, my civilian career of 30-plus years has three years on my service with my beloved Marines."

Maier Rothschild (Battery I): Severely wounded in the Zanana Beach fight by a sword-wielding Japanese officer, Maier Rothschild also faced the ordeal of watching his buddy John Wantuck die gruesomely in the savage nighttime attack. Awarded the Navy Cross in lieu of the Medal of Honor, Rothschild soon distanced himself from his peers after his recuperation. Unlike some other Marine Corps heroes, though, he seemed reluctant to take advantage of his potential celebrity as a Navy Cross winner, when he could possibly have done so honorably to return stateside for War Bond, recruiting or USO tours. After the war, Rothschild broke off contact with his fellow 9th Defense veterans after apparently returning to his native New York City, but disappearing into anonymity and has not apparently been heard from again. Like his buddy Wantuck, Rothschild, too, was another casualty of the hellish New Georgia campaign.

David Slater (H&S Battery, 9th Defense; Battery E): Discharged in 1946, David Slater used his GI Bill benefits to obtain a Masters degree in electrical engineering from New York University. He was employed by NYU's Engineering Research Division from 1951 to 1970, becoming a Senior Research Scientist and Project Director. An offshoot of his last project became the Palisades Institute for Research Services, Inc., of which "Biggie" Slater served as President and Chairman. From 1954 to 1973, he was an NYU adjunct professor. From 1961 to 1994, he was also a director, treasurer and consultant of Tensor Corporation, which ultimately became SoftNet, Inc. After 25 years as its secretary, Dave had become the Secretary Emeritus of the Advisory Group on Electron Devices, an activity of the Undersecretary of Defense for Research and Engineering. He is still an active NYU alumnus and a former member of its Board of Trustees. One of "Biggie" Slater's proudest accomplishments and participations, however, has been his role as a director and former President of the 9th Defense & AAA Battalion Association.

Jack (Brother Andrew) Sorensen (10th Defense Battalion; Battery A): After returning to civilian life, Jack Sorensen, the Battalion's prize illustrator and a beloved member of Battery A, took orders and became a Catholic brother. He now resides at a monastery in Nebraska and makes an annual "pilgrimage" of sorts to attend the Ninth's annual reunion every fall.

William Sorensen (Battery E): Bill ("Chick") Sorensen now lives in Connecticut, after working in the aviation business. He maintains quite a collection of Marine Corps memorabilia and, despite suffering a stroke, remains active. He is the current President of the 9th Defense & AAA Battalion Association.

Samuel E. Stavisky (Marine Combat Correspondent, 9th Defense): After his time with the Ninth on New Georgia, Staff Sergeant Sam Stavisky reported on the fighting on Bougainville later in 1943, ultimately spending a total of 34 months as a Marine combat correspondent. At war's end, he resumed his pre-war employment with the *Washington Post* as a reporter, staff writer and editor until 1954. He also wrote for various magazines, including *The Saturday Evening Post*, *Look*, *Life* and *Collier's*. In 1954, Sam Stavisky started his own public relations and lobbying firm with offices in Washington, D.C., New York, and several other cities internationally. Stavisky and his wife Bernice divide their time between Washington, D.C. and Singer Island, Florida; the couple has two daughters and a grandson. His autobiography of his days as a Marine combat correspondent was published in 1999.

George W. ("Doc") Teller (Batteries A and B): After the war, "Doc" Teller returned to his first love, medicine. After many years of medical practice, he is now a retired physician in Eugene, Oregon. One wonders if he still recalls his recipe for the "noodle soups" so prized as a tonic by by Hank Reichner and Battery A's officers.

William Tracy (CO, Battery E): Following his retirement as a "bird colonel" from the Corps, Bill Tracy became an active participant in the civic life of his home town, Meriden, Connecticut, serving in various local political roles, including service for several years as its mayor. The former Battery E commander and one of the heroes of the "Glorious Fourth" of July in 1943, Colonel Tracy now divides his time between Meriden and a home in rural New Hampshire.

Frank Yemma (Battery B): After being evacuated with malaria from the Russell Islands, "Frankie" Yemma was posted to Camp Lejeune in mid-1944 for advanced artillery training. There he experienced a surprise: "They're putting us through all this schooling, how to fire a 155mm rifle. They're showing combat films, and they're pictures of us! I told the instructor, 'For God's sakes, that's us on Rendova!' And he laughed and said, 'Yeah, that's the way it goes.'" By early 1945, Yemma was transferred to Camp Pendleton for infantry training and in April 1945 was shipped to Guam to join the 1/21st Marines, 3rd Marine Division, in preparation for the invasion of Kyushu. After briefly working for the Carrier Corporation after war's end, he served for 20 years as a professional firefighter for the City of Syracuse, New York. After retiring from that career at age 49, Frankie went back to work for the U.S. Postal Service as a mail carrier in Vero

Beach, Florida for another 8 1/2 years. Following his retirement from the USPS, Frank now lives in Florida, where he is active with the local chapter of the Marine Corps League and the Italian-American War Veterans, volunteering frequently at the local Veterans Administration clinic.

Walter (Waldo) Wells (CO, Battery B; Exec, 155mm Group): Like his friend and erstwhile rival Reichner, Columbia-educated Walter Wells made the Marine Corps a career, retiring as a full colonel after some thirty years of service, including Korea and during the Vietnam War. Although in his eighties, he is still living an active life in California, maintaining a physical training regimen that would tax many men much younger than himself. Colonel Wells has stated to the author that, although he met many Marines during his lengthy career, "the men of the Ninth Defense BN, on average, were superior when compared to those I knew later in my career." Quite a tribute, indeed, from the long-serving, tough and fearless "Waldo!"

John (Tojo) Whalen (Battery A): Already known among his wartime Marine buddies as being pugnacious and scrappy (not least of which may have been because of the nickname he was saddled with), the short but wiry "Tojo" Whalen became a semi-professional boxer for several years after war's end but hung up his gloves to resume his main prewar occupation as a barber in the Catskills' resort of Ballston Spa, New York. He died in the early 1990s.

Appendix B

Abbreviated Organizational Chart, 9th Defense Battalion (Mid-1943)

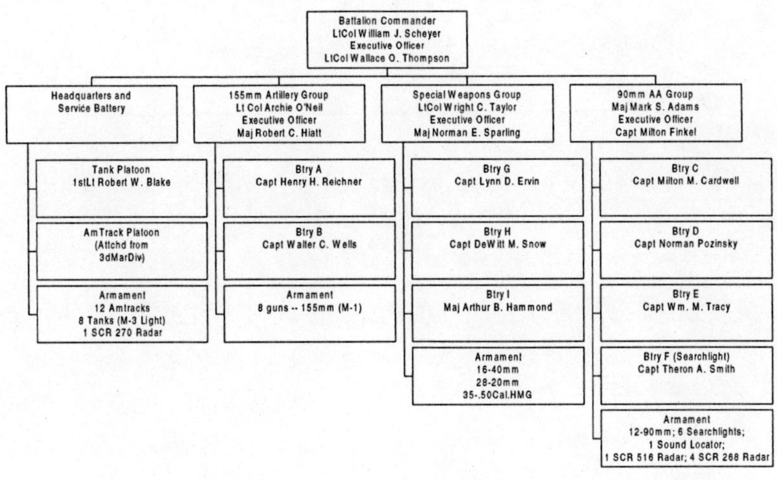

Appendix C

Navy Unit Commendation for the 9th Defense Battalion

The Secretary of the Navy takes pleasure in commending the

NINTH MARINE DEFENSE BATTALION

for service as follows:

"For outstanding heroism in action against enemy Japanese forces in Guadalcanal, November 30, 1942 to May 20, 1943; Rendova-New Georgia Area, June 30 to November 7, 1943; and at Guam, Marianas, July 21 to August 20, 1944. One of the first units of its kind to operate in the South Pacific Area, the NINTH Defense Battalion established strong seacoast and beach positions which destroyed 12 hostile planes attempting to bomb Guadalcanal and further engaged in extensive patrolling activities. In a 21-day-and-night training period prior to the Rendova-New Georgia assault, this group calibrated and learned to handle

> new weapons and readily effected the conversion from a seacoast unit to a unit capable of executing field artillery missions. Joining Army Artillery units, special groups of this battalion aided in launching an attack which drove the enemy from the beaches, downed 13 of a 16-bomber plane formation during the first night ashore and denied the use of the Munda airfield to the Japanese. The NINTH Defense Battalion aided in spearheading the attack of the Army Corps operating on New Georgia and, despite heavy losses, remained in action until the enemy was routed from the island. Elements of the Battalion landed at Guam under intense fire, established beach defenses, installed antiaircraft guns and later, contributed to the rescue of civilians and to the capture or the destruction of thousands of Japanese. By their skill, courage and aggressive fighting spirit, the officers and men of the NINTH Defense Battalion upheld the highest traditions of the United States Naval Service."

All personnel attached to and serving with the NINTH Defense Battalion during the above-mentioned periods are authorized to wear the NAVY UNIT COMMENDATION Ribbon.

/s/ JOHN L. SULLIVAN,
Secretary of the Navy

Sources

I. Published books and monographs on the 9th Defense and its battles and campaigns:

Joseph H. Alexander, *Storm Landings: Epic Amphibious Battles in the Central Pacific*. Annapolis, Md.: Naval Institute Press, 1997.

Eric Bergerud, *Touched With Fire: The Land War in the South Pacific*. New York: Viking, 1996.

Richard B. Frank, *Guadalcanal: The Definitive Account of the Landmark Battle*. New York: Random House, 1990.

Harry A. Gailey, *The Liberation of Guam*. San Francisco: Presidio Press, 1988).

Eric Hammel, *Munda Trail* (New York: Orion Books, 1989.

D.C. Horton, *New Georgia: Pattern for Victory* (New York: Ballantine Books, 1971).

Edwin P. Hoyt, *The Glory of the Solomons*. New York: Stein & Day, 1983. Graeme Kent, *Guadalcanal: Island Ordeal*. New York: Ballantine Books, 1971.

Maj. O.R. Lodge, *The Recapture of Guam*. Washington, D.C.: Historical Branch, G-3 Division, Headquarters, U.S. Marine Corps/Govt. Printing Office, 1954.

Maj. Charles D. Melson, *Condition Red: Marine Defense Battalions in World War II: Marines in World War II Commemorative Series_*. Washington, D.C.: History & Museums Division, Headquarters, U.S. Marine Corps, 1996.

Maj. Charles D. Melson & Francis E. Chadwick, *The Ninth Marine Defense and AAA Battalions*. Paducah, KY: Turner Publishing, 1990.

Maj. Charles D. Melson, *Up the Slot: Marines in the Central Solomons: Marines in World War II Commemorative Series.* Washington, D.C.: History & Museums Division, Headquarters, U.S. Marine Corps, 1993.

John J. Miller Jr., *Cartwheel: The Reduction of Rabaul.* Washington, D.C.: Department of the Army, Office of Chief of Military History, 1959.

John J. Miller Jr., *Guadalcanal: The First Offensive.* Washington, D.C.: Department of the Army, Office of Chief of Military History, 1949.

Cyril J. O'Brien, *Liberation: Marines in the Recapture of Guam: Marines in World War II Commemorative Series* . Washington, D.C.: History & Museums Division, Headquarters, U.S. Marine Corps, 1994.

John N. Rentz, *Marines in the Central Solomons.* Washington, D.C.: Headquarters, U.S. Marine Corps/Govt. Printing Office, 1952.

Henry I. Shaw, Jr., *First Offensive: The Marine Campaign for Guadalcanal: Marines in World War II Commemorative Series.* Washington, D.C.: History & Museums Division, Headquarters, U.S. Marine Corps, 1992.

Henry I. Shaw, Jr. *The United States Marines in the Guadalcanal Campaign.* Washington, D.C.: Headquarters, U.S. Marine Corps/Govt. Printing Office, 1962.

Henry I. Shaw, Jr. & Douglas T. Kane, *The Isolation of Rabaul.* Washington, D.C.: Historical Branch, G-3 Division, Headquarters, U.S. Marine Corps/Govt. Printing Office, 1963.

Samuel E. Stavisky, *Marine Combat Correspondent: World War II in the Pacific.* New York: Ivy Books, 1999.

Charles L. Updegraph, Jr., *Special Marine Corps Units of World War II.* Washington, D.C.: History & Museums Division, Headquarters, U.S. Marine Corps, 1972.

Maj. John L. Zimmerman, *The Guadalcanal Campaign.* Washington, D.C.: Headquarters, U.S. Marine Corps/Govt. Printing Office, 1949.

II. General sources on World War II, the Marines and the Pacific Theater:

Various authors, *Reporting World War II.* New York: The Library of America, 1995 (2 volumes).

Captain Henry H. Adams, *1942: The Year that Doomed the Axis.* New York: Warner Paperback Library, 1973.

Stephen E. Ambrose, *Americans at War.* New York: Berkley Books, 1998.

Stephen E. Ambrose, *Citizen Soldiers.* New York: Simon & Schuster, 1997.

Colonel Joseph H. Alexander, *A Fellowship of Valor: The Battle History of the United States Marines.* New York: HarperCollins, 1996.

Enzo Angelucci & Paolo Matricardi, *World War II Airplanes* (2 vols.) Chicago: Rand McNally & Company, 1977.

Robert D. Ballard (with Rick Archbold), *The Lost Ships of Guadalcanal.* New York: Warner/Madison Press Books, 1993.

Carl Berger, *B-29: The Superfortress.* New York: Ballantine Books, 1970.

Eric Bergerud, *Fire in the Sky: The Air War in the South Pacific.* Boulder, Colorado: Westview Press, 1999.

Henry Berry, *Semper Fi, Mac: Living Memories of the U.S. Marines in World War II.* New York: Quill/William Morrow, 1996.

John H. Bradley, Jack W. Dice & Thomas E. Griess, *The West Point Military History Series—The Second World War: Asia and the Pacific.* Wayne, N.J.: Avery Publishing Group, 1989.

Tom Brokaw, *The Greatest Generation.* New York: Random House, 1998.

Martin Caidin, *The Ragged, Rugged Warriors.* New York: Ballantine Books, 1973.

Peter Calvocoressi & Guy Wint, *Total War.* New York: Ballantine Books, 1973.

William G. Dooly, Jr., *Great Weapons of World War I*. New York: Bonanza Books, 1969.

John W. Dower, *War Without Mercy: Race and Power in the Pacific War*. New York: Pantheon Books, 1986.

Paul Dull, A Battle History of the Imperial Japanese Navy. Annapolis, Maryland: Naval Institute Press, 1978.

Robert B. Edgerton, *Warriors of the Rising Sun: A History of the Japanese Military*. New York; W.W. Norton & Company, 1997.

George Feifer, *Tennozan: The Battle of Okinawa and the Atomic Bomb*. New York: Ticknor & Fields, 1992.

George Forty, *U.S. Army Handbook 1939-1945*. London, England: Ian Allan, 1979.

Paul Fussell, *Wartime: Understanding and Behavior in the Second World War*. New York: Oxford University Press, 1989.

Bruce Gamble, *The Black Sheep: The Definitive Account of Marine Fighting Squadron 214 in World War II*. Novato, California: Presidio Press, 1998.

Meirion & Susie Harries, *Soldiers of the Sun: The Rise and Fall of the Imperial Japanese Army*. New York: Random House, 1991.

Joseph D. Harrington, *Yankee Samurai*. Detroit, Michigan: Pettigrew Enterprises, Inc., 1979.

John Hersey, *Into the Valley: A Skirmish of the Marines*. New York: Schocken Books, 1989.

Ian V. Hogg, *The Encyclopedia of Infantry Weapons of World War II*. London: Bison Books, 1977.

Ian V. Hogg, *Barrage: The Guns in Action*. New York: Ballantine Books, 1970.

Saburo Ienaga, *The Pacific War, 1931-1945*. New York: Pantheon Books, 1978.

Edward Jablonski, *Airwar* (2 vols.). Garden City, New York: Doubleday & Company, Inc., 1971.

Captain (Ret'd.) Wilbur D. Jones, Jr., *Gyrene: The World War II*

*United States Marine.*Shippensburg, Pennsylvania: White Mane Books, 1998.

John Kirk & Robert Young, *Great Weapons of World War II.* New York: Bonanza Books, 1961.

Robert Leckie, *Strong Men Armed: The United States Marines vs. Japan.* New York: DaCapo Press, Inc., 1997.

William Manchester, *Goodbye, Darkness: A Memoir of the Pacific War.* Boston: Little, Brown, 1979.

John C. McManus, *The Deadly Brotherhood: The American Combat Soldier in World War II.* Novato, California: Presidio Press, 1998.

James M. McPherson, *For Cause and Comrades.* New York: Oxford University Press, 1997.

Office of the Surgeon General, U.S. Army, *Neuropsychiatry in World War II, Volume II: Overseas Theaters.* Washington, D.C.: Gov't. Printing Office, 1973.

Zenji Orita (with Joseph D. Harrington), *I-Boat Captain.* Canoga Park, California: Major Books, 1976.

Gordon Rottman & Mike Chappell (Lee Johnson, ed.), *Fighting Elite—US Marine Corps 1941-45.* London: Osprey Military/Reed International, 1998.

Saburo Sakai (with Martin Caidin), *Samurai!.* New York: Nelson Doubleday, 1977.

S.E. Smith, *The United States Marine Corps in World War II.* New York: Random House, 1969.

Ronald H. Spector, *Eagle Against the Sun: The American War With Japan.* New York: Vintage Books, 1985.

U.S. War Dep't, *Handbook on Japanese Military Forces.* London: Greenhill Books, 1991 (reprint of U.S. War Department Technical Manual TM-E 30-480, Oct. 1, 1944).

Gerhard Weinberg, *A World At Arms: A Global History of World War II.* New York: Cambridge University Press, 1994.

Peter Wyden, *Day One: Before Hiroshima and After.* New York: Warner Books, Inc., 1985.

III. Periodicals

Thomas B. Allen & Norman Polmar, *Gassing Japan*, *Military History Quarterly*, Autumn 1997, pp. 38-43.

James A. Crutchfield, *World War Heroes Were Williamson Countians*, *The Tennessean* (Nashville, Tenn.), Nov. 7, 1996, at p. 3F.

Edward J. Drea, *Previews of Hell*, *Military History Quarterly*, Spring 1995, pp. 74-81.

Stanley L. Falk, *"A Nation Reduced to Ashes"*, *Military History Quarterly*, Spring 1995, pp. 54-63.

Richard Goldstein, *Col. Robert S. Scott Dies at 85; Won Medal of Honor in 1944*, *N.Y. Times*, Feb. 12, 1998, at A22.

Peter Maslowski, *Truman, The Bomb, and The Numbers Game*, *Military History Quarterly*, Spring 1995, pp. 103-107.

Lt. Col. H.B. Meek, *Marines Had Radar Too*, *Marine Corps Gazette*, Oct. 1945, pp. 16-19.

Sgt. Bill Miller, *Ack Ack Etc.*, The Leatherneck, Pacific Edition, Sept. 15, 1944, pp. 3-5.

Williamson Murray, *Armageddon Revisited*, *Military History Quarterly*, Spring 1995, pp. 6-11.

Rod Paschall, *Tactical Exercises: Olympic Miscalculations*, *Military History Quarterly*, Spring 1995, pp. 62 & 63.

Ron Suciu, *Christmas Tree Marines*, *Leatherneck*, Jan. 1993, pp.48-50.

Nashville Banner (Nashville, Tenn.), Dec. 8, 1941, at p. 1.

The Review-Appeal (Franklin, Tenn.)(various years and issues).

IV. Official Documents

9th Defense Battalion. Historical Section, Division of Public Information, Headquarters, U.S. Marine Corps, File No. AG-1265/HPH, Dec. 17, 1947.

Extracts, Ship's Log, United States Ship *William P. Biddle*, for period February 12, 1942 to February 20, 1942, pages 99-115.

Headquarters, U.S. Department of the Army, Technical

Manual TM 9-3305, *Principles of Artillery Weapons*, May 1981.

Headquarters, U.S. Marine Corps, *Standing Operating Procedure for Radar Air and Surface Warning and Radar Fire Control in the Marine Corps*, May 15, 1943.

Headquarters, Ninth Defense Battalion, Fleet Marine Force, In the Field, "Chronological Record of Operations of Ninth Defnse Battalion for period 29 JUne to 31 July, 1943, inclusive."

History of the First Antiaircraft Artillery Battalion, Redesignated Second 90-mm Antiaircraft Artillery Gun Battalion, Battalion Bulletin No. 5-47, File No. 1990-50-20, Mar. 17, 1947.

The Initial Use of Radar by the U.S. Marine Corps, Maj. John A. Kelly for Maj. D.F. Bittner, Independent Studies in Military History, Marine Corps Command & Staff College, Quantico, Virginia, May 1977.

Language Section, G-2 (Intelligence Section), 37th Infantry Division, translation of captured Japanese war diary of Probationary Officer Toshihiro Oura, *Record of the Decisive Battle Against Aircraft* (T/3 Dye Ogata and T/3 Frank Sanwo, translators; undated).

Military Personnel Records Files of Corporal Jack H. McCall, U.S. Marine Corps Reserve, National Personnel Records Center, St. Louis, Missouri.

V. Films, Unpublished Works and Miscellaneous Sources

Videotape, Colonel (Ret'd.) William T. Box & Francis E. Chadwick, *Return to the Solomon Islands*, autumn 1988 (author's collection).

The 9th Defense & AAA Battalion Association, *Poop! A Newsletter* and *Son of Poop!* (various years and issues, author's collection).

Letter, Jeffrey P. Bucheit, Assistant Director, Historical Electronics Museum, to Charles D. Melson (Feb. 16, 1993).

Virginia M. Bowman, *Historic Williamson County*. Nashville, Tennessee: Blue & Gray Press, 1971.

Ambrose W. "Red" Caldwell, *Secrets of a Diplomatic Courier-World War II*. Nashville, Tennessee: privately published, 1992.

James A. Crutchfield, *The Harpeth River: A Biography*. Nashville, Tennessee: Blue & Gray Press, 1972.

James A. Crutchfield, *Williamson County: A Pictorial History*. Virginia Beach, Virginia: The Donning Company, 1980.

Thomas Heggen, *Mister Roberts*. New York: Houghton Mifflin Co., 1946.

Louise G. Lynch, *Our Valiant Men*. Privately published, 1976.

Joseph Frank Marshall (Christopher S. Donner, ed.), *The "Fighting Ninth"—9th Defense Battalion* (unpublished, undated manuscript).

James Lee McDonough & Thomas L. Connelly, *Five Tragic Hours: The Battle of Franklin*. Knoxville, Tenn.: University of Tennessee Press, 1983.

Colonel (Ret'd.) Henry H. Reichner Jr., *Battery A* (unpublished manuscript dated 1999).

Lt. Col. John Sayen, "Marine Heavy Artillery and the Defense Battalions," *The Old Breed News* (Newsletter, 1st Marine Division Association, June 2000), at 24.

David Slater, *Jungle Vignettes* (unpublished, undated manuscript).

Lyn Sullivan, *Back Home In Williamson County*. Nashville, Tennessee: Williams Printing Co., 1986.

Wiley Sword, *Embrace an Angry Wind: The Confederacy's Last Hurrah: Spring Hill, Franklin and Nashville*. HarperCollins Publishers, 1992.

U-Boat Net, Internet home page, available at <http://uboat.net/boats/u94.htm>.

Leon Uris, *Battle Cry*. New York: G.P. Putnam's Sons, 1953.

Sam R. Watkins, *Co. Aytch: A Side Show of the Big Show*. New York: Collier Books, 1962.

VI. Interviews, Photographs and Correspondence

Amsa Bodine +
Colonel (Ret'd.) William T. Box
Horace Burnette
Ray Carman
Francis E. Chadwick
Clifford Cribbe
Milton Davis
Alfred R. Downs
John Dobkowski
Dr. Christopher S. Donner
Herb Dougherty
Willie Dufour
Benis M. Frank
William Galloway
John Hall
Wilson Herbert +
Theodore T. Hitchcock
John Henry Johnson
James V. Kruse
Colonel (Ret'd.) Robert Landon
Albert G. McCall, Jr.
Jack H. McCall, Sr. +
Patricia H. McCall
Major (Ret'd.) Charles Melson
Jerry Morris
Joseph J. Pratl
Colonel (Ret'd.) Henry H. Reichner Jr.
David Slater
Brother Andrew Sorensen
William Sorensen
Colonel (Ret'd.) William E. Tracy
Colonel (Ret'd.) Walter Wells
Frank Yemma

+ Deceased.

Glossary

AA Antiaircraft (also sometimes called "ack-ack").

AAA Antiaircraft artillery (also sometimes called "triple-A").

AAF U.S. Army Air Forces (the predecessor of today's U.S. Air Force).

APC Aspirin with caffeine tablets (widely used as both an analgesic and a stimulant).

Aggie A homemade Guamanian alcoholic beverage, distilled from fermented heart of coconut palm sap. See also entry for "Tuba."

Alligator LVT-1 amphibious, fully-tracked tractor and cargo carrying vehicle. Also called "amphtracks" or "amtracs," LVT stood for "Landing Vehicle, Tracked." The LVT-1s issued to the 9th Defense for the New Georgia campaign were unarmored, light-steel vehicles, with no landing ramps or built-in armament. Later models of LVT were armed with. 50 caliber machine guns (several models being equipped with tank turrets), were partly armor-plated and had rear-mounted landing ramps for greater safety in disembarking troops and supplies from the LVT when under fire.

Arisaka Japanese 6.5mm and 7.7mm bolt-action rifles.

Arundel Island located off the westernmost tip of New Georgia, due south of Kolombangara.

Atabrine Anti-malarial drug issued to U.S. forces in the South Pacific as a substitute for quinine.

Avenger See entry for "TBF."

AWOL Absent without leave. The Marines' terminology for this offense was "unauthorized absence."

B-24 See entry for "Liberator."

B-25 Douglas twin-engined medium bomber, known as the "Mitchell," which was one of the most common U.S. Army Air Force bombers (and was also the plane used by General James Doolittle's raiders in their raid on Japan in spring 1942). Roughly the shape of the Nell—both had a twin-rudder tail configuration—the two bombers were occasionally mistaken by AA gunners for one another. Several Marine medium bomber squadrons also used the Mitchell, called "PBJ" by the Marines and Navy.

B-29 Large, four-engined Boeing heavy bomber, officially nicknamed the "Superfortress," used by U.S. Army Air Forces for long-range bombing of Japan in 1944 and 1945. The B-29s *Enola Gay* and *Bock's Car*, stationed on the island of Tinian, not far from Guam, dropped the atomic bombs on Hiroshima and Nagasaki on August 6 and August 9, 1945, respectively.

Baanga Small island off the tip of Munda Point, New Georgia, on which the Japanese stationed the New Georgia versions of Pistol Pete.

Banika Island in the Russell Islands where the 9th Defense was posted in early 1944.

BAR .30 caliber Browning Automatic Rifle. Really a light machine gun, the 19.5-pound, 48-inch-long BAR resembled a large rifle mounted on a folding bipod, which was attached to the front of the barrel, and fired a 20-round clip.

Battery Artillery unit equivalent of a company; usually commanded by a captain.

Betty Allied codename for Mitsubishi G4M2 (Type 1) two-engined Japanese medium bomber.

Black Sheep Nickname of the members of Marine Fighter Squadron VMF-214, commanded by the famous Maj. Gregory ("Pappy") Boyington and based in mid-1943 at Munda Field on New Georgia.

Bofors The name of the Swedish designer and manufacturer of the 40mm M1 light, automatic antiaircraft gun often used by U.S. and Allied forces. Capable of firing a nearly two-pound shell at the rate of 120 rounds per minute to a range for four miles, the clip-fed Bofors gun could be used against ground targets and tanks as well as aircraft and was credited with 50% of the enemy aircraft downed by U.S. AA fire between 1944 and 1945.

Boondocks Marine slang for rough terrain, particularly if woody or jungled, and derived from a Filipino word for mountain or hill.

Boondockers Marine Corps-issue field boots.

Boot Marine nickname for a new recruit undergoing basic training at "Boot Camp." See also entry under "P.I."

Breakbone fever Dengue fever.

Brig Navy and Marine term for a jail.

Bucket issue Initial issue various sundry items to boots at Parris Island, known as a "bucket issue" because they were placed in a metal wash bucket.

Butts Pits at the Parris Island rifle range from which the paper targets were raised and lowered.

C Ration "Ration C" featured a cardboard box containing two cans: one filled with crackers, powdered coffee or tea, candy, toilet paper, various condiments, and four cigarettes, and the other filled with food to be warmed—among other "menu items," hash, stew, chicken and noodles, and (more frequently than not) the ubiquitous Spam. Less often encountered in the Pacific theater.

C3 Command, control and communications.

CB Official abbreviation for a Naval Construction Battalion. See "Seabee."

CO Commanding officer (the "old man;" an endearment never expressed to his face, however).

CP Command post.

Caimanera Village on the outskirts of Guantanamo Bay, Cuba, noted for its bars, black markets and brothels; nicknamed "Caimanooch" by the Ninth's Marines.

Caliber See entry for "mm (or MM)."

Campaign hat Old-style Marine hat, with wide, round brim and a pointed conical top, now worn only by Marine DIs, resembling the "Smokey the Bear" hat.

Canal, The Nickname for Guadalcanal.

Carney Field American airfield built in the Koli Point area of Guadalcanal and used mainly by B-24 bombers of the 13th Air Force.

CARTWHEEL Allied codename for a series of operations (including mid-1943's Operation TOENAILS and later landings on Bougainville in November 1943) intended to outflank the major Japanese air and naval bases on New Britain island, including Rabaul.

Cat fever Catarrhal fever.

Catalina Consolidated PBY twin-engined seaplane, used by the U.S. Navy. A version called the "Black Cat" was used for night operations.

Central Solomons The portion of the Solomon Islands encompassing New Georgia, Rendova, Kolombangara, Vella Lavella and their environs.

Cerveza Spanish word for beer.

Chamorro A native of Guam; "Guamanian" is now the preferred term for citizens of Guam.

Chick Marine nickname for any especially young or beardless Marine (derived from "spring chicken").

Chop Detachment and reattachment of a military unit from its normal controlling headquarters (short for "*ch*ange of *op*erational control").

Chow Marine slang for food.

Christmas Trees Nickname given to Marine recruits who volunteered between Pearl Harbor and New Year's Day 1942. Also sometimes called the "Pearl Harbor Avengers."

Cobber Nickname for a New Zealander, derived from New Zealand slang for a buddy or friend (and adopted as such especially by the men of the 1st Marine Division, who were sent to New Zealand for R&R after Guadalcanal).

Commo Contraction for communications.

ComSoPac Commander, South Pacific Area; from late 1942, this position was held by Navy Vice Admiral William ("Bill" or "Bull") Halsey.

Condition Black Highest stage of non-AA alert: Enemy landing imminent.

Condition Green "All clear."

Condition Red Highest degree of air alert: air raid imminent or ongoing.

Condition Yellow Air raid expected. In practice, once unidentified aircraft ("bogies") were picked up by radar and were on a bearing for the unit, "Condition Yellow" was announced. Once the bogies passed a certain point and remained on the same bearing, the alert status was upgraded to "Condition Red" (see above).

Corpsman Navy medical technician, assigned to serve as a medic in a Marine unit, and most often called simply "Doc."

Corsair Vought F4U single-engined fighter; readily identified by its gull-shaped wings and long nose, the Corsair was a mainstay of U.S. Marine and Navy fighter units beginning in February 1943. Called "Whispering Death" by the Japanese, due to the (relative) quietness of its engine.

D Ration A hard, vitamin-reinforced chocolate bar.

Dauntless Douglas SBD single-engined dive bomber, with a two-man crew, used by U.S. Marine and Navy bomber squadrons.

Diamond Narrows Channel of water between the Munda and Kindu Point areas of New Georgia and Kolombangara.

Digger Nickname for an Australian soldier (ostensibly originating from the Australian troops' expertise at trench-digging during their Gallipoli campaign in Turkey during World War I).

DI Marine drill instructor.

Doc Nickname for any Navy surgeon, doctor or corpsman. (Also used as the personal nickname for Battery A's Exec, who later served as Battery B's CO, George Teller.)

Dogface Nickname, usually applied to Army infantrymen, but also applied to other troops in other combat services; thought to derive from the stubbly-bearded and haggard appearance of soldiers after several days or weeks in combat.

Dugout Doug Sarcastic Marine nickname for General of the Army Douglas MacArthur, the Allies' Southwest Pacific Area commander.

Duke Radio call sign for the 9th Defense Battalion's headquarters element.

Ear-banging Attempting to curry favor with a superior ("brown-nosing").

EM Enlisted man.

Exec Executive officer (second-in-command). Also later called the "XO."

4-F Lowest Selective Service draft rating: unqualified or physically unfit to serve in the military.

.45 Colt .45 caliber M1911A1 automatic pistol.

.50 Browning M2 heavy machine gun. Often fitted on a portable tripod for ground usage (in the M2-HB—"heavy-barrel"—model) or on an M2 pedestal with water-cooled jacket for AA use or on vehicular mounts, the .50 caliber machine gun was often used for AA defense but was originally designed in 1919 as an antitank weapon.

F4U See entry for "Corsair."

FA Field artillery.

FCO Fire control officer.

Feather merchant Marine slang for a short or lightweight person.

Field Music Marine term for a unit's bugler or other musician.

Field scarf Marine Corps-issue khaki necktie.

Fleet Marine Force The administrative and command designation used for the Marine Corps "in the field"; that portion of the Corps made up of all deployed field units, from Corps and Division level downwards to the ship detachments on board U.S. Navy vessels. The Fleet Marine Force ("FMF," for short) was further subdivided into theater-level components (e.g., Fleet Marine Force-Pacific), which might loosely be viewed as being the U.S.M.C.'s equivalent of an Army/Army Group command.

FMF See entry for "Fleet Marine Force."

FMF-PAC Fleet Marine Force-Pacific.

FO Forward observer.

FORAGER U.S. code name for the operation involving the recapture of the southern Mariana Islands group, including Saipan, Tinian, Rota and Guam.

Garand .30 caliber M1 semiautomatic rifle.

Gavutu Small island just to the north of Guadalcanal, due south of Florida Island.

G.I. Nickname for Army troops (derived from the Army abbreviation for "government issue").

Gitmo Marine nickname for Guantanamo Bay, Cuba.

Gizmos Nickname applied to Jack and his fellow water purification experts in the Ninth and, more generically, to any technicians whose jobs required working with anything mechanical, electrical or hydraulic in nature.

Goettge Massacre Incident involving the isolation and shooting of members of a small Marine reconnaissance patrol on Guadalcanal, led by Lt. Colonel Frank Goettge, the 1st Marine Division's G-2 (chief intelligence officer).

Goldbrick A slacker or lazy person.

GPF Another name for the old model (M1918) 155mm gun, originally used by the 9th Defense's Seacoast Group. Commonly thought to stand for "Great Power French," GPF was a French abbreviation for "Grande puissance Filloux" (Filloux being the French designer's name).

Grabass Marine slang for horseplay or a bull session.

Green Dragon See entry for "LST."

Gunner Marine Corps rank equivalent to that of an Army warrant officer.

Gunny Marine nickname for a Gunnery Sergeant (Marine NCO rank comparable to an Army Sergeant First Class or E-7).

Gung Ho Chinese expression meaning "Work together," popularized by the Marine Raider Battalion Colonel Evans Carlson, and later coming to mean anyone exhibiting a can-do, aggressive or positive attitude.

Gyrene Term of abuse used by Army and Navy against Marines (possibly originating as a contraction of "G.I. Marine").

H&S Headquarters and Service.

Head Marine and Navy slang for a toilet or latrine (so-called because these facilities were usually located at the "head" of a sailing ship).

Henderson Field Major U.S. airfield on Guadalcanal.

Hester's Happy Hustling Housewives Term of abuse used by members of the 9th Defense for the Army's 43rd Division, commanded by Maj. General Hester.

Hooch Slang for alcohol.

I MAC First Marine Amphibious Corps (later renamed III Amphib Corps in spring 1944).

Ironbottom Sound The part of The Slot bounding Guadalcanal, Savo, Florida and Gavutu Islands.

Jellybean Slang expression, popular in the 1920s and 1930s, for a dandy or a nattily dressed man.

Jitterbugging Also called the "jungle jitters," this was the nickname given to outbreaks of combat neurosis and panicky nighttime shootings that occurred in several American units during the New Georgia campaign; so-called after a popular dance craze of the late 1930s and early 1940s.

Jungle juice Alcoholic drink made by mixing whatever kind of fruit juice was handy with any kind of drinkable alcohol or "torpedo juice."

K Ration More frequently encountered in the Pacific theater than the C ration, this was provided in three forms, "B," "L," and "D" (the initials should be self-explanatory), Ration K's boxes contained ham-and-eggs (the usual breakfast entree), canned cheese (the usual lunch selection) or Spam, corned beef hash or other meat selections, crackers, instant coffee, candy, cigarettes, toilet paper and gum.

KP Kitchen police (kitchen or mess-hall preparation and cleanup duty, generally regarded as one of the grubbiest duties and epitomized by wartime cartoons of troops peeling piles of potatoes). More usually called "mess duty" by the Marines and Navy.

Ka-Bar Marine Corps-issue knife used for various field chores and self-defense.

Kamikaze Japanese suicide plane or its pilot. Means "divine wind," in honor of a medieval typhoon that destroyed an invading Chinese fleet and saved Japan from foreign occupation.

Kempetai Japanese military secret police.

Knee mortar Japanese 50mm grenade launcher, with a curved base plate that led Allied troops to think it was supposed to be braced on the fire's leg. It definitely was *not* intended for such purpose, as attested to by the broken legs of numerous Allied soldiers who tried firing the mortar off their legs and knees.

Kokorana Small island off the northernmost tip of Rendova.

Koli Point Small cape located on the central northern coast of Guadalcanal, where most of the 9th Defense Battalion was stationed from late 1942 to June 1943.

Kolombangara Island in the Central Solomons adjacent to (northwest of) New Georgia and southeast of Vella Lavella.

Kunai A type of tropical grass commonly found in the Solomons and New Guinea, noted for its sharply-edged leaves and often growing four to five feet tall.

LCI Landing Craft, Infantry. Dubbed the "Elsie-Eye," by 1944, some LCIs were converted to light gunboats ((LCI(G)s) or rocket-launching platforms for 3.5-inch bombardment rockets, several of which were used to support the landings on Guam.

LCM Landing Craft, Medium (also called a Higgins boat, after its inventor).

LCP Landing Craft, Personnel (early-model Navy landing craft, without a bow ramp for unloading troops).

LCT Landing Craft, Tank.

LST Landing Ship, Tank. Because these vessels were often heavily camouflaged in green paint during the 1943 Solomons campaigns, they were nicknamed "Green Dragons." Due to their bulkiness, the abbreviation for these vessels was also said to stand for "*L*ong, *S*low *T*arget."

Lt. Lieutenant.

Lt. Colonel Lieutenant colonel.

LVT Landing Vehicle, Tracked. See entry for "Alligator."

Leatherneck Nickname for U.S. Marines; derived from a heavy leather collar often worn by early U.S. Marines in the late 1700s and early 1800s to help ward off saber blows to the neck.

Leggings Marines' term for their distinctive, light khaki-colored canvas field spats or gaiters.

Liberator Consolidated B-24 four-engined heavy bomber, used by both the Army Air Forces and the Navy (called the PB4Y in Navy service).

Lightning Lockheed P-38 twin-engined fighter-bomber, used by U.S. Army Air Forces.

Lister bag A kind of sanitized rubberized canvas bag, similar in size to a duffel bag and fitted with small faucets, used for storing and dispensing drinking water.

Long Tom Common nickname for 155mm guns of both models (GPFs and Mls).

Louie the Louse See entry for "Washing Machine Charlie."

mm (or MM) Millimeters. "Millimeter" and "caliber" refer to the diameter of a gun's bore, measured at the mouth of the barrel, caliber being this measurement in inches or fractions of inches (i.e., .30 caliber being equal to .30 of an inch in diameter). U.S. weapons were gauged in millimeters, calibers and inches (the latter mainly for naval ordnance), with caliber usually being used for small arms (i.e., machine guns, rifles and pistols), and millimeters for larger guns (20mm and up). Note, by way of example, that .50 caliber is equal to 12.7mm.

M1 Depending on the context, this refers to either the .30 caliber Garand rifle (see entry for "Garand") or the smaller, .30 semiautomatic carbine. Also the official model number for the newer model 155mm heavy gun issued to the 9th Defense after Guadalcanal (see entry for "Long Tom").

M-3 U.S. light tank, armed mainly with a 37mm gun and several .30 caliber machine guns. Officially nicknamed the "Stuart" tank, for the Civil War cavalry general Jeb Stuart.

MIA Missing in action.

MP Military police.

Maggie's Drawers Nickname for a red flag used to identify the score of a boot who completely failed to hit a target during rifle range training at Boot Camp. (The racy implication behind the nickname was that "Maggie's drawers," or her panties, were stained red from menstrual blood, as her lover had "fired a blank" in making love to her.)

Magnetic mine Japanese oval, grenade-type explosive, with several large industrial-strength magnets attached, often used as an antitank bomb. Because the "mine" was not intended to be buried but had to be attached by hand to the hull of an enemy tank, it was virtually a suicide weapon.

Marianas Chain of volcanic islands in the western, central Pacific, the largest islands in the group being Guam, Tinian, Rota and Saipan.

Marmite can A kind of insulated container used for storing and serving food.

Marshalls Chain of coral atolls in the central Pacific, approximately 1,000 miles south of the Marianas, comprised of Kwajalein, Bikini and Eniwetok among other islands, and located approximately 2,500 miles west of the Hawaiian Islands.

Masthead Marine and Navy term for a non-court-martial disciplinary proceeding.

Meatball Red "Rising Sun" insignia painted on Japanese aircraft and many ground vehicles.

Mitchell See entry for "B-25."

Munda Point Prominent spit of land located at the southwestern tip of New Georgia and the location of the Munda Field airbase, the prime U.S. objective of the Rendova-New Georgia campaign.

90mm Principal U.S. medium anti-aircraft gun of World War II, the M1A1 was originally issued to Army AA units and began being issued to Marine Defense Battalions in the summer of 1942, the Ninth having 12 of these guns. It had a horizontal range of 18,890 yards and a vertical range of 11,273 yards. The 90mm fired a 23.4 pound shell and required a full crew of 10 men, who, if well trained, could fire 28 rounds per minute. The gun had a distinctive, honeycomb-patterned firing stand, and for firing, the bogey wheels were dismounted. 9th Defense 90mms of Battery E destroyed 12 Japanese high-altitude bombers and one fighter with 88 shells on Rendova on July 4, 1943, setting a world record.

NCO Noncommissioned officer (*i.e.*, corporals and all grades of sergeant).

Nalimbiu Central river on the northern coast of Guadalcanal, located near the Koli Point area.

Nambu 6.5mm automatic pistol, often carried by Japanese officers and externally resembling the German Luger pistol. Also applied to several models of 6.5mm or 7.7mm Japanese light machine guns, both pistol and machine guns having been designed by a Colonel Nambu of the Japanese army.

Nell Allied codename for Mitsubishi G3M2, or Type 96, two-engined Japanese medium bomber.

New Georgia Island located in the central Solomon Islands.

Nisei Japanese-American citizens. (Technically, the term is applicable only to second-generation Japanese-Americans, the first generation being known as *Issei.)*

Nissen hut Prefabricated, corrugated-metal building.

Noodle soup Personal codename used by Battery A's Captain Hank Reichner and his Exec, Lieutenant George

("Doc") Teller, for Doc's favorite cocktail, a lethal mix of 190-proof medical alcohol and lemon extract.

Nusalavata Small island off the northern tip of Rendova.

1-A Highest qualification rating for eligibility for the draft issued by the U.S. Selective Service Board. The polar opposite rating was "4-F."

OD Officer of the day (staff duty officer) or officer of the deck (watch officer on board ship).

OP Observation post.

Oerlikon The name of the Swiss designer and manufacturer of the 20mm light, automatic AA gun often used by U.S. and Allied forces. Capable of firing 450 rounds a minute with a 4,800-yard range, the 20mm Oerlikon was roughly similar to a large machine gun and, by mid-1943, were often issued to Marine Defense Battalions in pairs mounted on four-wheeled, automatically operating gun carriages and called "Twin Twenties."

Old Man, The Generic nickname for a commanding officer (although never used to his face).

Old salt A veteran sailor or Marine.

P-38 See entry for "Lightning."

PBY See entry for "Catalina."

PFC Private, first class.

P.I. Parris Island, South Carolina, home of the Marines' recruit depot and Boot Camp.

POW Prisoner of war.

PT **Physical training.**

PT Boat Lightly armored, 78-foot plywood-hulled motor boat used by the U.S. Navy as a fast torpedo and attack boat ("PT"="Patrol Torpedo"). Usually equipped with two torpedo tubes and an assortment of .50 caliber machine guns and 20mm Oerlikon guns and occasionally a 40mm Bofors gun. The most famous example may be John F. Kennedy's *PT-109*, which was part of a PT squadron based on Rendova.

P.X. Post exchange.

Panama Mounts Semi-permanent concrete pedestal mounts with turntables often used for 155mm guns in a seacoast-defense role; the name was derived from similar mounts first emplaced for coast defense guns stationed around the Panama Canal.

Pappy Marine nickname for any older Marine; also the personal nickname of Major Gregory Boyington, CO of VMF-214 (the "Black Sheep" squadron).

Paramarines Marine parachute troops (not their preferred nickname) of the 1st Parachute Battalion and similar units.

Pearl Harbor Avengers Another nickname for the Christmas Tree Marines.

Pistol Pete Nickname for Japanese gun or guns that sporadically shelled New Georgia, particularly Munda Point, from Kolombangara; derived from a gunfighter character in a Walt Disney cartoon of the time. (Another Pistol Pete was active on Guadalcanal in 1942 in shelling Henderson Field.)

Pogey bait Marine and Navy slang for candy, snacks or sweets. While also commonly spelled as "pogy bait," Jack McCall chronically spelled it as "pogiebait" when using it as his nickname.

Polar Bears Nickname given to Marines from the 5th Defense Battalion, so called because of their assignment to Iceland in late 1941/early 1942. While stationed there, these Marines wore, as a gesture of solidarity, the shoulder patch of a British division that was the principal British garrison of Iceland, the 49th (West Riding) Division, which was a polar bear standing on an ice floe.

Pollywog Anyone who has not been initiated during a crossing of the Equator.

Poop Navy and Marine slang for information or news (probably derived from the maritime term "poopdeck," from which a ship's master would often issue orders to the crew). See also entry for "scuttlebutt."

Poop sheet Marine slang for a newsletter, newspaper or orders.

Psy-war Psychological warfare.

Q-ship Term used for a surface raider or "auxiliary cruiser" disguised to resemble a civilian steamship, often by use of neutral flags.

R&R Variously, either "refitting and recuperation" or "rest and recreation."

Rabaul Large village and anchorage on the island of New Britain, off the northeast coast of New Guinea, which was the headquarters for large Japanese air and naval units in the South Pacific.

Recon Contraction of "reconnaissance."

Reising .45 caliber submachine gun, only issued to Marines (usually, to personnel of Marine Raider and parachute units) but supplied to several hundred of the 9th Defense's personnel on Guadalcanal. The Reising was supplied in two models: one with a fixed wooden stock, and one with a folding metal stock.

Rendova Island in the Central Solomons adjacent to (due south of) New Georgia.

Rikusentai Japanese for "special naval landing force," *i.e.*, Japanese naval infantry. These were naval infantry units, often used in a garrison capacity on occupied islands or in roles roughly similar to that of U.S. Marine defense battalions. While sometimes described as the "Japanese Marine Corps," this is not entirely correct, as it implies a separate organization and higher level of training than was often the case for SNLF units. Still, in many cases—Tarawa, for instance—*rikusentai* troops proved to be ingenious and fanatical fighters.

Roviana Small island adjacent to Rendova and New Georgia.

Russells Island group in the south-central Solomon Islands, roughly midway between Guadalcanal and New Georgia.

SBD See entry for "Dauntless."

SCR-268 Early-model U.S. fire control radar, used for direction of AA searchlights and guns. The 9th Defense Battalion had five of these, beginning from mid-1942 ("SCR" was an Army abbreviation standing for "Signal Corps Radio").

SCR-270 Early-model U.S. long-range surveillance radar, with a range of 200 miles. The 9th Defense Battalion had one of these, beginning from mid-1942.

SCR-516 Early-model U.S. height/elevation-determination radar, with a range of 50 miles.

SNLF "Special Naval Landing Force" (in Japanese, *rikusentai),* or Japanese naval infantry; a rough Japanese equivalent of the U.S. Marine Corps, comprised of sailors and naval officers given light infantry training and usually intended for beach landings or garrison duty. Frequently encountered by U.S. forces in the Solomons area.

SP Shore Patrol (the Navy equivalent of military police).

Scuttlebutt Navy and Marine slang for gossip or rumors (derived from an old maritime word for the ship's drinking water bucket, which is where rumors often were naturally circulated on-board ship). Related to "poop."

Seabag Marine and Navy term for a duffel bag.

Seabees Members of a U.S. Navy Construction Battalion ("CB").

Seagoing heads Open-air latrines built on a ramp or pier extended out over the waterline of a bay or beach.

Secure the butts Marine expression, originally meaning to close down a rifle range ("butts" being the rifle-range pits from which the bullseye targets were raised and lowered), but extended through common usage to mean the cessation of any kind of activity.

Semper Fi Marine abbreviation and popular saying, derived from the Marines' motto, *Semper Fidelis* ("Always Faithful"), whose all-purpose meaning at any given time—whether as a greeting, a farewell, a jeer, a threat or a grouse—depended entirely upon the context.

Sgt. Sergeant.

Shavetail Sardonic nickname, popular among enlisted Marines, for any second lieutenant.

Shellback Anyone who has been initiated during a crossing of the Equator.

Skipper Another popular Marine and Navy nickname for a CO.

Skivvies Marine slang for underwear.

Skylarking Marine slang for horseplay or "goofing off."

Slop chute Marine slang for a bar or tap room that served mainly beer and snacks, but often widely used for any bar or watering hole.

Slot, The Officially named Sealark Channel, the channel of water running between the Central Solomons and Guadalcanal.

Snafu Acronym for "Situation normal: all f—cked up."

Snapping-in A form of exercise done with rifles and involving moving quickly into various rifle-shooting positions. The "snap" is the click of the hammer as the rifle's trigger is squeezed.

Solomons Chain of South Pacific islands generally to the east of New Guinea and to the north and northeast of Australia; location of Guadalcanal, New Georgia, Rendova, Kolombangara and Bougainville and the Russell Islands.

Southern Cross Constellation of stars, only visible from the Southern Hemisphere

Springfield M1903 .30 caliber bolt-action rifle. Also called the "03" for short.

Stuart See entry for "M-3."

Superfortress See entry for "B-29."

Surveyed out Marine term for being medically evacuated.

Swab (also Swabby or Swab Jockey) Term of abuse used by Army and Marines towards sailors (from their regular daily chores of mopping and scrubbing their ships' decks).

.30 Caliber of bullet used for the BAR, Springfield and Garand rifles and also for the M1917 and M1919 light machine guns. A smaller .30 caliber round was used by the M1 carbine.

III Amphib Third Amphibious Corps (the successor to I MAC from spring 1944).

TBF Grumman Avenger single-engined Navy torpedo and attack bomber. Also extensively made by Eastern Aircraft, a subsidiary of General Motors, whose variant was called the TBM, Navy Avengers were used by 9th Defense FOs for scouting and reconnaissance missions on New Georgia and Kolombangara.

TD-9 Caterpillar-made tractor, similar to a bulldozer but without the shovel blade, used as a prime mover for the Ninth's 155mm and 90mm guns. A larger model was known as the TD-18.

Tabi Split-toed, rubber shoes frequently worn by Japanese soldiers.

Tanambogo Small island connected to Gavutu by a 300-foot causeway.

Ten-in-one rations Rations intended to feed ether one man for ten days or ten men for one day, usually featuring a much wider selection of entrees than were found in C rations and K rations.

TOENAILS U.S. codename for the Rendova/New Georgia campaign.

Tokyo Express American nickname for Japanese naval convoys to and from Guadalcanal, often commanded by Rear Admiral Raizo ("Torpedo") Tanaka.

Tokyo Rose Japanese radio personality who often directed her broadcasts to American forces in the Pacific. Over twenty women broadcast radio commentary and music programs as "Tokyo Rose" from Radio Tokyo, in a generally fruitless effort to lower U.S. troops' morale.

Tombusolo Small island adjacent to Rendova and New Georgia.

Torpedo juice A highly potent alcoholic drink devised by Marines and sailors in the Pacific, usually mixed with lemonade or fruit juice.

TORSOB Abbreviation for "The Original Revolving Son of a Bitch": sobriquet applied to "Lt. Colonel Baker," one of the Ninth's senior field grade officers.

Trashcan Charlie See entry for "Washing Machine Charlie."

Trench knife A particularly vicious-looking U.S. military knife designed during World War I, whose hilt (handle) included a set of brass knuckle-dusters, and which was once popular with many Marines.

Tropic Lightning Nickname for the U.S. Army's 25th Infantry Division, partly derived from its shoulder patch, which featured a lightning bolt on a taro leaf. Commanded by Maj. General J. Lawton ("Lightning Joe") Collins, the 25th served alongside Marine units on Guadalcanal and New Georgia.

Tuba A homemade alcoholic drink made on Guam from hearts of palm sap, fermented for several days into a form of wine.

Tulagi Small island and anchorage just to the north of Guadalcanal, due south of Florida Island and due west of Gavutu.

Twin Twenties See entry for "Oerlikon."

Washing Machine Charlie One of the Marine nicknames for Japanese reconnaissance bombers that made solo nighttime raids over Guadalcanal and New Georgia and drop bombs and flares (and sometimes empty bottles) for nuisance value. Also called "Louie the Louse" or "Trashcan Charlie," among other variations.

U-boat German submarine (from *unterseeboot*, or "undersea boat").

U.S.A.T. United States Army Transport.

U.S.M.C. United States Marine Corps.

U.S.S. United States Ship, the designation for all official Navy (as opposed to Army or Merchant Marine) vessels, both combat and non-combat.

V-mail "Victory mail": miniaturized U.S. military forces mail delivered from the combat areas to the United States. To reduce shipping sizes and bulk quantities, Marines and G.I.s would write a letter home on specially prepared paper; the letter would then be put on microfilm, reconstituted and printed out in the United States, and mailed, so that parents, friends and loved ones would receive a miniature letter as the final product.

Val Allied codename for Aichi D3A1 (Type 99) single engined Japanese dive bomber.

Vella Lavella Island in the Central Solomons northwest of Kolombangara and the New Georgia group.

W-Day "D-day," or first day of the invasion, on Guam, July 21, 1944.

WAAC Women's Auxiliary Army Corps (later shortened to Women's Army Corps, or "WAC.")

Wildcat Grumman F4F single-engined fighter. The Navy's principal fighter aircraft in the early stages of World War II, the Wildcat was largely superseded by 1943 by the F6F Hellcat.

Zero Allied codename for Mitsubishi A6M-series single engined Japanese fighter.

Zoot suits Marine nickname for camouflaged uniforms issued in the Pacific, derived from a popular style of baggily-cut men's civilian suits of the 1941-42 period.

ENDNOTES

1/ This was a bit of an understatement: this letter was written during one period of monsoon-like rains, which swamped the 9th's entire area and completely flooded out all of the radar and 90mm gun positions.

2/ He is referring here to Reams Osborne, the son of his Franklin next-door neighbors Nathan and Elona Osborne, who had enlisted in the Navy and would end up in the Seabees. In a few months, Jack would meet up with Reams under some fairly improbable circumstances.

3/ Jack is probably referring here to the draft rating "4-B," which meant that his father had an extremely low chance of *ever* being drafted! The lowest rating was "4-F;" Jack, at the other end of the spectrum, had been picked as "1-A."

4/ To reduce shipping space during the war years, Marines and GIs would write letters home from overseas on specially provided and lined paper; the letter would then be put on a microfilm-like paper and would then be printed out and mailed, so that parents, friends and loved ones would receive a miniaturized copy of the original letter as the final product. This final product was known as "V-mail." Most surviving pieces of V-mail also bear another hallmark of the war years:

a military censor's stamp. Each unit had one officer with a designated additional duty of reviewing all mail before it was sent, both to prevent disclosures of military secrets ("Loose lips sink ships") and to gauge the unit's overall morale.

5/ Access to Tokyo Rose's broadcasts was more readily available to radiomen like David Slater than to the average radio-less Marine. As he recalled:

> As a radioman, I had access to receivers, although my CO, Major "Sparky" Adams, at one time reamed me for wearing down the batteries. On the 'Canal, her broadcasts began with the *Stars and Stripes Forever* and her greeting [was] to "the soldiers, sailors and Marines beyond the horizon." By New Georgia, [her morning greeting] had become "*on* the horizon."

6/ Contrary to many depictions, coconut trees were not all that common on many South and Central Pacific islands, although they were indeed plentiful in many parts of the Solomon Islands. Between the wars, Lever Brothers had built numerous plantations on New Georgia and the surrounding islands for the cultivation of coconut palms. The Japanese used their tough, fibrous trunks to reinforce many of their bunkers and defensive positions on New Georgia, Rendova and Kolombangara.

7/ It was from this same anchorage, one day later, that *PT-109*, under the command of Navy Lt. (j.g.) John F. Kennedy, began its fateful mission in which it was rammed by the Japanese destroyer *Amagiri*, with Kennedy helping to save the lives of his surviving crewmen.

8/ Some 45 years after the war, the wreckage of the

"Pistol Petes" were found still in place on Baanga Island by Bill Box and Frank Chadwick in the fall of 1988.

9/ It took 46 years for Bill Galloway to be awarded a long-overdue Purple Heart for this wartime injury, finally getting it on June 29, 1989 after some heavy lobbying by Colonel (former Captain) Hank Reichner and Sgt. Horace "Smiley" Burnette of Battery A on Galloway's behalf.

10/ David Slater remembered serving as a communications man in the 90mm Group's CP on New Georgia when an air raid alert was called. "Upon Condition Red, here comes [Lt. Colonel Baker], cussing all the while, yelling, 'I just finished with Lana Turner and was starting upon [some other actress' pictures] when these yellow bastards got me up!' "

11/ Of course, by mid-1943, the Marine Corps itself was forced to accept draftees because of wartime expansion and shortage of volunteers. Several of the draftees first joined the 9th Defense, to the horror of the old salts, just in time for Rendova and New Georgia. "At first, a lot of them had lousy attitudes, but we broke them in, and they became pretty good Marines," Jack once recalled, winking: "But not as good as us volunteers."

12/ Ironically, the 9th Defense missed, by only the closest of margins, the opportunity to have directly served under MacArthur. Following the 1st Marine Division's action at Cape Gloucester and with all available Army units in the Southwest Pacific fully engaged, MacArthur requested that the Joint Chiefs of Staff provide him with additional Marine support for his upcoming operations on Emirau in the Admiralty Islands, but the Ninth's Marines were "saved" by Admiral Halsey:

> The pace of preparations for Emirau was so swift that it put a crimp in the [Joint Chiefs'] plans for employment of Marines released by the cancellation of the Kavieng operation [and on March 14, 1944] MacArthur received and passed on to Halsey for compliance, a JCS directive that the 3rd Marine Division, the 4th Marines, and the 9th and 14th Defense Battalions were to be released to [MacArthur's control] immediately. By the time the Admiral received this order, it was too late to replace the 4th Marines and still meet the Emirau D-Day of March 20....

As one crusty veteran of the Ninth sarcastically noted years later in the Battalion's newsletter: "Well, guys, it looks like we missed another great opportunity to live it up in one more tropical paradise and maybe have become Dugout Doug's personal Defense Battalion. Instead, we have the incredible good fortune to see Banika and Ray Milland with his USO beauties. What the H___, ya can't winnem all."

13/ A sartorial note: despite the olive-brown and greenish colors of their uniforms, Marines could be readily distinguished from the Japanese by their choice of legwear and footwear. Marines often wore light khaki-colored leggings, which were side-lacing spats that reached over the ankles. Japanese troops were frequently issued puttees, wrap-around woolen strips resembling an Ace bandage, which reached to mid-calf and which were worn with short boots or *tabi*, an odd-looking rubber sneaker with a cleft big toe separated from the other four toes.

14/ Here, Chadwick is mistaken in his count: this number is more truly representative of the overall number of major combatant ships that made up the air and bombardment support flotillas of the naval task force for Operation FORAGER.

Official records indicate that a total of 24 aircraft carriers of all types—still, hardly a trivial amount of airpower—plus eleven battleships, 24 cruisers and 152 destroyers comprised the U.S. Navy's mightiest battle group assembled to this point in the Pacific Theater. The total fleet allocated to the Guam portion of Operation FORAGER was 274 ships, landing and supporting 54,000 soldiers and Marines.

15/ This kind of sabotage was not unlike the results of Nazi slave labor efforts: some Army GIs in Europe recalled the frequent late-war ineffectiveness of many German artillery shells and shell fuses, a sizeable number of which had been sabotaged by slave laborers and concentration camp inmates forced to work in war production plants, much as described by the novelist Thomas Kennealy in *Schindler's List.*

16/ Other parts of the Battalion had similarly bizarre experiences. One evening, while the Battalion HQ staff were watching movies outdoors with some neighboring Seabees and Guamanian civilians, the projectionist and his assistant captured several Japanese infiltrators among the spectators. In another instance, a mess cook investigated someone rustling among the mess hall's crates and supplies, and he took a stick to drive away what he thought would be a scavenging Marine. Instead, he was faced with a starving, knife-wielding Japanese soldier, whom he bludgeoned to death.

17/ For his part, as one of the team assigned to daytime patrolling missions, Frank Chadwick was not on duty during the evening and was asleep in one of the eight-man tents when the shooting broke out:

> All I remember is that I was on my cot sleeping when

an estimated column of over 100 Japs came down the road and the attack was on. It had rained hard that evening. A pool of water covered the area inside the tent. I rolled off my cot on the wrong side into the water and could not find my rifle. It took me a few seconds to realize my predicament and take corrective action.

Wartime memories have a weird way of resurfacing in the present-days lives of veterans. Some 53 years after the Pago Bay firefight, a hot water heater burst and flooded the floor of Frank Chadwick's home with about a half inch of water. In the middle of the night, Chadwick rolled out of bed and into the water. Immediately, "I was frantically looking for my rifle and was scared to death when I couldn't find it. . . . This apparently triggered something in the back of my mind and it took over 3 months or more to forget it again. Believe it or not, it took me about 5 minutes to realize I was on my bedroom floor laying in the water, now about an inch deep, and finally pulled myself together and got the water turned off." "Sounds foolish," Chadwick noted ruefully. Many veterans, however, have recounted similar "flashbacks."

[18/] Only almost fifty years later, at a Ninth Defense reunion, would Chadwick see Dobkowski again and finally learn then what had happened to him.